IBN ABĪ ṬĀHIR ṬAYFŪR AND ARABIC WRITERLY CULTURE

In spite of the considerable attention devoted to the third/ninth century by scholars of Arabic literature, credit for the elaboration of the notion of *adab* in its wider meaning of writerly culture has been concentrated upon only a handful of writers. The disproportionate emphasis, within and outside the Arabic literary-historical and critical traditions, has been at the expense of certain crucial aspects of that tradition.

With a particular focus on a central but neglected figure, Ibn Abī Ṭāhir Ṭayfūr (d. 280/893), poet and prose writer, schoolmaster and copyist, "independent" scholar, member of important literary circles, and a significant anthologist and chronicler, this study re-evaluates the literary history and landscape of the third/ninth century. The author demonstrates and emphasises the significance of an important and irrevocable transformation, namely the one signalled by the transition from a predominantly oral-aural culture to an increasingly writerly-based and book one.

This transformation had a profound influence in the production of learned and literary culture; on the modes of transmission of learning; on the nature and types of literary production; on the nature of scholarly and professional occupations and alliances; and on the implications of such phenomena as patronage and plagiarism. This book will appeal, therefore, to anyone interested in deepening their understanding of classical and medieval Arabic literary culture and history, and also to those with an interest in books, writing and authorship.

Shawkat M. Toorawa is Assistant Professor of Arabic Literature in the department of Near Eastern Studies at Cornell University. He is the co-author of *Interpreting the Self: Autobiography in the Arabic Literary Tradition* (2001), translator of Adonis's *A Time Between Ashes and Roses* (2004) and co-editor of *Arabic Literary Culture, 500–925* (2005).

ROUTLEDGECURZON STUDIES IN ARABIC AND MIDDLE-EASTERN LITERATURES

Edited by James E. Montgomery, *University of Cambridge*,
Roger Allen, *University of Pennsylvania*, and
Philip F. Kennedy, *New York University*

RoutledgeCurzon Studies in Arabic and Middle-Eastern Literatures is a monograph series devoted to aspects of the literatures of the Near and Middle East and North Africa both modern and pre-modern. It is hoped that the provision of such a forum will lead to a greater emphasis on the comparative study of the literatures of this area, although studies devoted to one literary or linguistic region are warmly encouraged. It is the editors' objective to foster the comparative and multi-disciplinary investigation of the written and oral literary products of this area.

1. SHEHERAZADE THROUGH THE LOOKING GLASS
Eva Sallis

2. THE PALESTINIAN NOVEL
Ibrahim Taha

3. OF DISHES AND DISCOURSE
Geert Jan van Gelder

4. MEDIEVAL ARABIC PRAISE POETRY
Beatrice Gruendler

5. MAKING THE GREAT BOOK OF SONGS
Hilary Kilpatrick

6. THE NOVEL AND THE RURAL IMAGINARY IN EGYPT, 1880–1985
Samah Selim

7. IBN ABĪ ṬĀHIR ṬAYFŪR AND ARABIC WRITERLY CULTURE
A ninth-century bookman in Baghdad
Shawkat M. Toorawa

8. RELIGIOUS PERSPECTIVES IN MODERN MUSLIM AND JEWISH LITERATURES
Edited by Glenda Abramson and Hilary Kilpatrick

IBN ABĪ ṬĀHIR ṬAYFŪR AND ARABIC WRITERLY CULTURE

A ninth-century bookman in Baghdad

Shawkat M. Toorawa

RoutledgeCurzon
Taylor & Francis Group
LONDON AND NEW YORK

First published 2005
by RoutledgeCurzon
2 Park Square, Milton Park, Abingdon, Oxon OX14 4RN

Simultaneously published in the USA and Canada
by RoutledgeCurzon
270 Madison Ave, New York, NY 10016

RoutledgeCurzon is an imprint of the Taylor & Francis Group

Typeset in Baskerville by LaserScript Ltd, Mitcham, Surrey

Transferred to digital printing 2010

British Library Cataloguing in Publication Data
A catalogue record for this book is available from the British Library

Library of Congress Cataloging in Publication Data
A catalog record for this book has been requested

ISBN 978–0–415–29762–2 (hbk)
ISBN 978–0–415–59589–6 (pbk)

786

for
Zubeida Mahmood
Asiya Maryam
and
Parvine

Mens humilis, studium quaerendi, vita quieta,
Scrutinium tacitum, paupertas, terra aliena ...

Bernard of Chartres (d. *c.* 1130)

CONTENTS

Preface		viii
Acknowledgments		ix
Note on transliteration and dating		xi
Glossary		xii
Abbreviations		xiii
	Introduction: Ibn Abī Ṭāhir Ṭayfūr and Arabic writerly culture	1
1	From memory to written record	7
2	The presence and insistence of books	18
3	Reciting poetry, telling tales	35
4	Being a bookman	51
5	Navigating partisan shoals	71
6	Precedence and contest	87
7	The "Bad Boys" of Baghdad	102
	Envoi: Revisiting Arabic literary history of the third/ninth century	123
Notes		130
Bibliography		180
Index		208

PREFACE

The ninth century of the Common Era (third century Ḥijrah) was an active one indeed for the Arabic humanities, not least because of the far-reaching effects the appearance of paper and the proliferation of writing and books were to have on Arab-Islamic culture in general. I am certainly not first to signal the importance of the phenomena associated with the changes brought and wrought by writing. This study is, however, the first attempt to look at a practitioner of writerly culture for traces of those changes – what Brian Stock might style the *implications of literacy*, though I prefer to speak about *writerly culture* than to speak about *literacy*. Writerly culture is also one useful way (among many) of thinking about the meaning of a term that has long eluded precise translation (or comprehension), namely *adab*. Like Stock, I provide no palliatives for those in search of oversimplified pictures of literary history and historical growth; unlike Stock, mine is not a magisterial study of the implications of literacy, especially as they can be plumbed through close readings of cultural products and practices, but an attempt, rather, fruitfully to nuance the general understanding of Arabic literary history in a significant century. The illustrative practitioner of writerly culture on whom I focus is Ibn Abī Ṭāhir Ṭayfūr (d. 280/893), a bookman of Persian origin who lived in Baghdad.

Notwithstanding the French adage 'qui s'excuse, s'accuse,' I ought to point out that this study is neither a monograph on Ibn Abī Ṭāhir, nor a comprehensive study of what survives of his works, namely three volumes of the *Kitāb al-Manthūr wa-al-manẓūm* (Book of prose and poetry), one volume of *Kitāb Baghdād* (Book of Baghdad), scattered quotations from others of his works, and about four hundred verses of his poetry. Both – a monograph and an analysis of his works – are desiderata to be sure, but my focus here is on providing a general view of writerly culture in ninth-century Baghdad by using the example of Ibn Abī Ṭāhir (and his peers). What is more, this book is aimed not only at specialists of Arabic literature of the Abbasid period, but also in particular at all who are interested in classical or medieval writerly culture in general. Indeed, I have attempted to write with both specialists and non-specialists in mind.

ACKNOWLEDGMENTS

This is the revised version of a doctoral dissertation I completed at the University of Pennsylvania where I received tremendous moral, intellectual and financial support over the years from the Department of Oriental Studies, later Asian and Middle Eastern Studies. I began the dissertation under the sage and gentle guidance of the late George Makdisi, my debt to whom will be apparent. I completed it under the guidance of Everett Rowson, who supervised with expertise, care, and friendship a work he could have done far better himself; Roger Allen, my teacher and mentor for 25 years now, who provided advice, affection, and support; and Barbara von Schlegell, a wonderful source of encouragement and kindness. At Pennsylvania, I am grateful also to Edward Peters for having taught me much; and to Peggy Guinan and Diane Moderski for years of indulgence and affection.

My RRAALL colleagues – Kristen Brustad, Michael Cooperson, Jamal Elias, Nuha Khoury, Joe Lowry, Eve Troutt-Powell, Dwight Reynolds, Devin Stewart, and Nasser Rabbat – continue to provide rare intellectual and affectionate support. Over the years, Aisha and Ahmad Dewangree, Marc Ostfield and Michael Savino, Aditya Agarwal and Diana Kunze, Satti and Rita Khanna, Salim and Hoor and Ashraff, and especially Joe Lowry and Vanessa Albert opened their homes and hearts in ways I can never repay.

My thanks go also to: Anthony Appiah, Miriam Cooke and Bruce Lawrence, Skip Gates, William Hanaway, Michael Hopper, Sherman Jackson, Philip Kennedy, Ruqayya Khan, John Ledoux, Abdul Rashid Mahaboob, Iliass Patel, Ivonne Prieto, Yasin Safadi, Abdul Rashid Toorawa, Shabbir Ahmad Toorawa, Herb Wolfson, and Areff and Chotane Bahemia.

At Cornell, I am grateful to the wonderful staff of the department of Near Eastern Studies – Chris Capalongo, Denise Huff and Julie Graham – and my exceptional colleagues, in particular my chair, Ross Brann. I should also like to thank Iftikhar Dadi, Ed Gunn, Ellen Gainor, Ali Houissa, Shelly Marino, and Chris Minkowski.

I am deeply grateful to Wolfhart Heinrichs, Hilary Kilpatrick, James Montgomery, and Devin Stewart for reading an early draft of this book and for making countless suggestions many of which I have ignored at my own peril.

I thank James Montgomery also for his enthusiasm to include it in this RoutledgeCurzon series. And I thank Joe Lowry for constant and expert feedback, and for routinely and cheerfully doing much beyond the call of duty.

Portions of the Introduction and Envoi appear in 'Ibn Abi Tahir vs. al-Jahiz,' in *'Abbasid Studies. Occasional Papers of the School of 'Abbasid Studies. Cambridge, 6–10 July 2002*, ed. James Montgomery, Leuven: Peeters, 2004, and 'Defining *adab* by (re)defining the *adīb*: Ibn Abī Ṭāhir Ṭayfūr and Writerly Culture,' in *Defining Fiction and Adab in Medieval Arabic Literature*, ed. Philip Kennedy, Wiesbaden: Harrassowitz, 2005. I thank the editors and publishers for permission to reprise that material here.

At RoutledgeCurzon, Amritpal Bangard, Rachel Green, Dorothea Schaefter, Lucy Swainson and Joe Whiting have been exemplary and patient: in today's writerly culture, one cannot ask for anything more.

My greatest debts are to: *marḥūm* Baba Noormohammad Quadri, for taking on an unworthy *murīd*; to Fareena for her *iḥsān*; to my parents, Mahmood and Zubeida, who have made too many sacrifices to count; to my children, who deserve more time than I have given them; and to my wife and soulmate Parvine Bahemia, who has been spectacular considering she has had to share me with Ibn Abī Ṭāhir from the very day we met…

...وأصدّر كتابي هذا مستعينا بالله راغبا اليه

NOTE ON TRANSLITERATION AND DATING

I follow the Library of Congress Arabic transliteration system (with negligible modification), principally because I would like this book to be as user-friendly as possible to non-specialists. For the same reason: I omit diacritics from common words, from names that have currency, and from derivatives of Arabic (e.g. Abbasid, dinar, Hadith, Khurasanian, Shiite); I use English translations of Arabic titles after their first mention in Arabic; and I provide both Ḥijrī and Common Era dates (e.g. 204/819, third/ninth century). When I quote poetry by Ibn Abī Ṭāhir, I provide the Arabic and English in the main text; for all other poetry I provide only the English in the main text, typically in a rhyming (and sometimes loose) translation. Specialists may consult the Arabic directly.

GLOSSARY

adab Conduct; good manners; professional knowledge; general culture and refinement; belles-lettres; writerly culture

adīb (pl. **udabāʾ**) A person exhibiting or embodying *adab*; a practitioner of writerly culture; a cultured man (or woman: *adībah*) of letters

akhbār see *khabar*

badīʿ Novel expression; a new and manneristic style exhibited in poetry, especially in the third/ninth century

balīgh (pl. **bulaghāʾ**) Lit. eloquent; a prose stylist

dīwān The collected poetic works of a poet or tribe

Hadith A transmitted account of something the Prophet Muhammad said, did, or tacitly approved or disapproved, authenticated by an *isnād*

ḥalqah, ḥalaqah (pl. **ḥalaqāt**) Study circle

isnād A chain of authorities who transmit a report or account

kātib (pl. **kuttāb**) Copyist; scribe or secretary in government employment; writer

kitāb (pl. **kutub**) Book; letter; any piece of writing

khabar (pl. **akhbār**) A piece of transmitted information, usually historical or biographical; a report, account

kuttāb (pl. **katātīb**) A preparatory or elementary school, also called *maktab*

majlis (pl. **majālis**) Lit. a place of sitting; a social, scholarly or literary gathering, which could be formal or informal

maktab see *kuttāb*

mujūn Licentious poetry

rāwī (pl. **ruwāh**) Tranmsmitter, of poetry, accounts, and tradition

sariqah (pl. **sariqāt**) A borrowing, literary theft or plagiarism in poetry

udabāʾ see *adīb*

warrāq (pl. **warrāqūn**) Copyist; bookseller; bookman

ẓarf Elegance, refinement, sophistication; a social ideal of the third/ninth century

ẓarīf (pl. **ẓurafāʾ**) Someone exhibiting *ẓarf*

ABBREVIATIONS

Aghānī	Abū al-Faraj, *Kitāb al-Aghānī*, Dār al-Kutub edn
Kitāb Baghdād	Ibn Abī Ṭāhir, *Kitāb Baghdād*, ed. al-Kawtharī
Kitāb Baghdād, ed. Keller	Ibn Abī Ṭāhir, *Sechster Band des Kitâb Baġdâd*
Balāghāt al-nisā'	Ibn Abī Ṭāhir Ṭayfūr, *Balāghāt al-nisā'*, ed. al-Alfī
CHALABL	Ashtiany *et al.* (eds), *'Abbāsid Belles-Lettres*
CHALEUP	Beeston *et al.* (eds), *Arabic Literature to the End of the Umayyad Period*
Dispute Poems and Dialogues	Reinink and Vanstiphout (eds), *Dispute Poems and Dialogues*
DMBI	Āzarnūsh, *Dā'irat al-ma'ārif-i buzurg-i Islāmī*
EAL	*Encyclopedia of Arabic Literature*
EI	*Encyclopaedia of Islam*
EI2	*Encyclopaedia of Islam*, 2nd edn
Fihrist	Ibn al-Nadīm, *al-Fihrist*, ed. Tajaddod
GAL	Brockelmann, *Geschichte der arabischen Litteratur*
GAS	Sezgin, *Geschichte des arabischen schrifttums*
HIL	Rypka *et al.* (eds), *History of Iranian Literature*
Inbāh	al-Qifṭī, *Inbāh al-ruwāt*
Irshād	Yāqūt, *Irshād al-arīb*, ed. Rifā'ī
Lane	Lane, *Arabic-English Lexicon*
Manthūr C	Ibn Abī Ṭāhir, *al-Manthūr wa-al-manẓūm*, MS Cairo
Muḥāḍarāt al-udabā'	al-Rāghib al-Iṣfahānī, *Muḥāḍarāt al-udabā'*
Murūj	al-Mas'ūdī, *Murūj al-dhahab*, ed. Pellat
Qaṣā'id	Ibn Abī Ṭāhir, *al-Manthūr wa-al-Manẓūm: al-Qaṣā'id . . .*, ed. Ghayyāḍ
Rasā'il al-Jāḥiẓ	al-Jāḥiẓ, *Rasā'il al-Jāḥiẓ*, ed. Hārūn
SUNY	State University of New York
Ṭabaqāt al-shu'arā'	Ibn al-Mu'tazz, *Ṭabaqāt al-shu'arā' al-muḥdathīn*, ed. Farrāj
Ṭabarī	al-Ṭabarī, *Ta'rīkh al-rusul wa-al-mulūk*, ed. de Goeje
Ta'rīkh Baghdād	al-Khaṭīb al-Baghdādī, *Ta'rīkh Baghdād*
WKAS	Ullmann *et al.* (eds), *Wörterbuch der klassischen arabischen Sprache*

INTRODUCTION

Ibn Abī Ṭāhir Ṭayfūr and Arabic Writerly Culture

In spite of the considerable attention devoted to the third/ninth century by scholars of Arabic literature, credit for the elaboration of the notion of *adab*, in its wider meaning of literary culture, is given to and concentrated upon only a handful of writers. The disproportionate emphasis, both within and outside the Arabic literary-historical and literary-critical traditions, on such figures as Ibn al-Muqaffaʿ (d. after 139/757), al-Jāḥiẓ (d. 255/868) and Ibn Qutaybah (d. 276/889), has been at the expense of certain crucial aspects of those traditions. What is more, studies of the third/ninth century (a century described by Gérard Lecomte as "un des moins mal connus", one of the least badly understood),[1] have typically either focused (narrowly) on specific individuals (e.g. Ibn Qutaybah), on single works (e.g. al-Jāḥiẓ's *Kitāb al-Bukhalāʾ* [Book of misers]), or on specific institutions (e.g. the vizierate).[2] There have in fact been very few attempts to describe larger literary or cultural phenomena. This study represents an effort to re-evaluate the literary history and landscape of the third/ninth century by demonstrating and emphasizing the significance of an important – and irrevocable[3] – transformation witnessed that century, namely the transition from a predominantly oral and aural literary culture to an increasingly textual, book-based, writerly one. Because of the importance of books, textuality, and writing, I refer to this new situation as "writerly culture," a term that I suggest also in part conveys the meaning of *adab*. An *adīb* (pl. *udabāʾ*) can then usefully be thought of as someone who embodies and practices writerly culture.

Literacy, in its broad sense of the ability to read and write,[4] had existed since the time of the early grammarians' study of the Arabic language and its primary text, the Quran. Books were not new either. But the now widespread use of writing, occasioned especially by the needs of administration, did create a new market for books and, indeed, for ideas. Writing and books were no longer the privilege of a very narrow elite, but now the prerogative also of students, scholars, bookmen, autodidacts, and others, and included many works written specifically for autodidacts and those wishing to accomplish their learning in *adab* on their own.[5]

The new readership expanded to include landlords and landowners, merchants and entrepreneurs, judges and jurists, physicians, poets and littérateurs, teachers, and of course, other scholars.[6] This is clear if only from the fact that these individuals and groups or classes, among others, became the objects of writers' attention, praise, and satire. The needs of empire meant that civil servants and other government bureaucrats were also a significant readership. In order to better their writing and to sharpen their minds, they sought and solicited works that classified information and knowledge in an easily verifiable and convenient way. Books were handy because they were available twenty-four hours a day, were portable, and were reproducible. Knowledge was now accessible and verifiable in black and white.

My broad argument is that the arrival of the technologies of the word – notably paper and its principal consequence, books – had profound influences on the production of learned and literary culture, on the modes of transmission of learning, on the nature and types of literary production, and on the nature of scholarly and professional occupations and alliances. I show this by focusing on the figure of the Baghdadi bookman, Ibn Abī Ṭāhir Ṭayfūr (204–80/819–93). The professional activities, literary output, and personal networks of Ibn Abī Ṭāhir help to clarify the impact and importance of the transition to an environment where texts and writing, specifically books, played an increasingly important role.[7] My aim is not to provide a detailed analysis of the changes in mental and social structures occasioned by writing,[8] but rather to suggest ways in which Ibn Abī Ṭāhir is illustrative of that shift.

The transformation from the predominantly oral/aural to the increasingly book-based and writerly has, to be sure, not gone unnoticed. In 1983, for instance, A. F. L. Beeston – considering the impact of the introduction of paper *c.* 153/751,[9] and the related rise of an urbanized elite secretarial class, and of *adab* – wrote of "a change of attitude" and of a "radical shift" from which followed three significant interrelated consequences: Arabic got a written literature apart from the Quran, grammar developed as a field of inquiry, and language underwent specific changes.[10] What these three developments have in common is writing: writing, specifically books, effectively restructured consciousness.[11] In a recent book on the history and impact of paper in the Islamic world, Jonathan Bloom describes this very same transformation as a "shift" too, which he describes as "fateful."[12]

The most important scholar of the changes occasioned by the presence of paper, writing and books on Arab Islamic culture has been Gregor Schoeler who, in a series of influential articles and books, has insisted on a distinction – first made by Sprenger in a study of the life of Muhammad[13] – between *syngramma*, an actual book, a literary work with all the rules of definitive, or nearly definitive redaction on the one hand, and *hypomnēma*, private notes to be committed to memory.[14] Schoeler's focus has primarily been writing undertaken in the religious sciences and in the disciplines arising from the study of language; he has by and large not pronounced on the *udabā'* though his latest book on writing and oral transmission in early Islam includes a brief chapter on literature and the court ("Cour et littérature").[15] Several scholars have, it is true, written about orality and literacy in classical Arabic poetry and in literature.[16] Overall, however, remarks about the impact of literacy and textuality have, until recently, been brief.[17] The exceptions are Schoeler's works,[18] Sebastian Günther's study of Abū al-Faraj's *Maqātil al-Ṭālibiyyīn* [Martyrdoms of the Talibids],[19] and a significant collection of papers presented at a conference on 'Voix et Calame en islam médiéval' at the Collège de France in 1993 and published as articles in two fascicules of *Arabica* in 1997.[20] The article by Albert Arazi on Ibn Abī Ṭāhir in the latter includes important remarks about Ibn Abī Ṭāhir as literary historian and critic.

Ibn Abī Ṭāhir was born in Baghdad in 204/819 to a family of Iranian origin and died on Tuesday night 27 Jumādā I (= 14–15 August 893), during the caliphate of al-Muʿtaḍid.[21] He was buried in his own neighborhood,[22] in the Bāb al-Shām Cemetery, where "personages of note" were buried.[23] Ibn Abī Ṭāhir is an important precursor and representative of what I am arguing is a new kind of *adīb*, a practitioner of writerly culture. He flourished roughly 225–275/840–890 and thus belongs to the second, possibly the third, generation of authors writing during the transition to an increasingly textualized, writerly environment. Indeed, he seems to have worked and operated in ways different from writers of preceding generations. Unlike al-Madā'inī (d. 228/843), for example, his prolific output was not that of a genealogist-antiquarian. He is also quite different from his contemporaries al-Jāḥiẓ (d. 255/868) and Ibn Qutaybah (d. 276/889), two writers who in many ways represent the pinnacle of patronized, "traditional" literary scholarship and accomplishment, even if they are quite different themselves the one from the other. Ibn Abī Ṭāhir was, moreover, not associated with the court of any caliph and does not appear to have been patronized. The increasingly important role of paper, books, and readerships had a direct impact on Ibn Abī Ṭāhir in ways that it did not (and could not) on writers, contemporary or of preceding or following generations, who "resisted" or were as yet unaffected by the transformations heralded by the shift away from memory toward the written word. Ibn Abī Ṭāhir's chosen professions – teacher, tutor, bookman, storyteller, author, anthologist, and critic – illustrate this. So too the character of his literary output: Ibn Abī Ṭāhir was neither primarily a poet, like his celebrated teacher Abū Tammām (d. *c.* 231/845), nor primarily a writer of prose like al-Jāḥiẓ and Ibn Qutaybah – he was both a poet and prose-writer. And, unlike al-Mubarrad (d. 285/898), or Ibn Qutaybah, he appears to have been unconcerned with creating or sustaining a cult of Arabic linguistic and cultural purity.

Ibn Abī Ṭāhir is primarily remembered by posterity as the first author of a history of Baghdad, the six-volume *Kitāb Baghdād* [Book of Baghdad], only part of one volume of which survives. The few surviving manuscripts, the titles of his lost works, and the countless anecdotes reported on his authority in such works as Abū al-Faraj al-Iṣbahānī's *Kitāb al-Aghānī* [Book of songs] and al-Ṣūlī's literary-historical collections, among others, testify to his wide-ranging interests and his considerable contacts with literary personalities of his day. Ibn Abī Ṭāhir is the first writer to devote a book to writers, the *Kitāb al-Mu'allifīn* [Book of authors/ writers].[24] The *Kitāb al-Manthūr wa-al-manẓūm* [Book of prose and poetry] is the first attested multi-author anthology of poetry, epistles and, significantly, prose writing. *Balāghāt al-nisā'* [The (instances of the) eloquence of women], one of the surviving volumes of the *Book of prose and poetry* is an early attempt to draw attention to the eloquent role of women in the use of the classical language. The *Kitāb Sariqāt al-shu'arā'* [Book of the borrowings/plagiarisms of the poets] is one of the first three works – possibly the first outright – to address the plagiarisms of poets from one another. Although all of Ibn Abī Ṭāhir's books on poetic borrowing are lost, extracts and references do survive in later works. The *Kitāb Sariqāt Abī Tammām* [Book of the borrowings/plagiarisms of Abū Tammām] may be part of the preceding work or a discrete one. Whatever the case, it is the first work to deal with the *sariqāt* (poetic borrowings, plagiarisms) of Abū Tammām, a question that was to become one of the burning issues in literary criticism from the third to fifth/ninth to eleventh centuries. This work, and the *Kitāb Sariqāt al-Buḥturī 'an Abī Tammām* [Book of the borrowings/plagiarisms of al-Buḥturī from Abū Tammām], also appear to be the first to be written about living poets. Ibn Abī Ṭāhir's *Book of Baghdad* is the first work devoted to that city. Ibn Abī Ṭāhir's numerous anthologies are either the only attested ones of their kind (e.g. of the poetry of al-'Attābī [d. 208/823 or 220/835], and Bakr ibn al-Naṭṭāḥ [d. 227/ 837]), or the first to be produced (e.g. Ibn Harmah [d. *c.* 176/792]). The foregoing makes clear Ibn Abī Ṭāhir's originary role as writer and editor, roles for which he was ideally poised in an environment in which writing and writerly sensibilities began to occupy first rank. (For a complete catalogue of Ibn Abī Ṭāhir's works, see chapter 4 below.)

The importance of books in general, and of Ibn Abī Ṭāhir's works in particular, cannot be emphasized enough. The following anecdote illustrates the high regard the lexicographer and scholar Ibn Durayd (d. 321/933) had for one of Ibn Abī Ṭāhir's works, *Qalaq al-mushtāq* [The disquiet of the yearnful]:[25]

> *I read in the* Book of elegant composition (*Kitāb al-Taḥbīr*), *and this was also authoritatively recounted to me by al-Sharīf Iftikhār al-dīn Abū Hāshim 'Abd al-Muṭṭalib ibn al-Faḍl ibn 'Abd al-Muṭṭalib al-Hāshimī: Abū Sa'd al-Sam'ānī quotes, authorized by licentia* [ijāzatan] *if not by certificate of audition* [samā'an]*: I heard the amīr Abū Naṣr ibn Aḥmad ibn al-Ḥusayn ibn Aḥmad ibn 'Ubaydallāh ibn Aḥmad al-Mīkālī*[26] *say*: We were one day talking about pleasure-grounds (*al-mutanazzahāt*) and Ibn Durayd was present. Someone said, "The most pleasing of all places is the Damascus Oasis." "No," another said, "surely it's the Ubullah Canal." "Samarqand, rather," said another. Yet another said, "No, Nahrawān." "Bawwān Gorge, in Fārs," said another, while yet another said, "The Barmakid Temple of Balkh."
>
> "These are pleasure-grounds for the eyes," responded Ibn Durayd. "What are your views on the pleasure-grounds of the heart?"

"And what are they, O Abū Bakr?" we replied.

"The *Quintessential accounts* (*ʿUyūn al-akhbār*) of al-Qutaybī," he said, "the *Flower* (*al-Zahrah*) of Ibn Dāwūd, and the *Disquiet of the yearnful* (*Qalaq al-mushtāq*) of Ibn Abī Ṭāhir."[27] And then he recited the following:

> Let others see their recreation
> In beautiful songstresses and wine,
> What we offer are literary gatherings and books
> As recreations of the mind.[28]

In the *ʿUyūn al-akhbār* [Quintessential accounts], which survives,[29] Ibn Qutaybah anthologized a wide range of material with which he expected educated Muslims (and especially administrators) to be familiar. The anthology of love poetry and theory, *Kitāb al-Zahrah* [Book of the Flower] by Ibn Abī Ṭāhir's student Ibn Dāwūd (d. 294/907), also survives;[30] Ibn Abī Ṭāhir's *Qalaq al-mushtāq* [Disquiet of the yearnful], very probably an anthology of love poetry, does not.[31]

The conspicuous neglect of certain writers, such as Ibn Abī Ṭāhir, can only partially be explained by the loss of his works. For example, his extant introductory remarks about the famous pre-Islamic poems, the *Muʿallaqāt*, in a surviving volume of the fourteen-part anthology, *Book of prose and poetry*, significant as they are about the process of collection and the identity of its collectors, have gone largely unnoticed and unacknowledged by historians of literature, both medieval and modern: M. J. Kister (1969) and Seeger A. Bonebakker (1970) are two early exceptions, and Albert Arazi is a recent one (1997).[32] One of the purposes of my work is to remedy that neglect and to demonstrate that there were other intervening writers of signal importance, such as Ibn Abī Ṭāhir, who helped to shape the corpus of Arabic literature and to define the role of, and the directions that would be taken by, *adab* and the *adīb*. They accomplished this through their poetic and prose output, their critical works, and their anthologies.

Several Western scholars have, it is true, acknowledged Ibn Abī Ṭāhir as a significant participant in the cultural and literary scene and history of third/ninth century Baghdad, but again, with the exception of the 1908 study by Hans Keller of the *Book of Baghdad* – where the focus is primarily the extent of al-Ṭabarī's reliance on Ibn Abī Ṭāhir – until recently remarks have been brief.[33] Franz Rosenthal's short but excellent 'Ibn Abī Ṭāhir' entry in the *Encyclopaedia of Islam* (1971)[34] and D. M. Dunlop's paragraph in *Arab Civilization to AD 1500* (1971)[35] were matched neither by Bosworth's 1995 entry in *Encyclopedia Iranica*, which references earlier scholarship but relies on very little of it,[36] nor by the *Cambridge History of Arabic Literature*, where Ibn Abī Ṭāhir is only briefly mentioned,[37] nor by R. A. Kimber's 1998 *Encyclopedia of Arabic Literature* entry, which is content to characterize Ibn Abī Ṭāhir as "a literary dilletante".[38]

Non-Western treatments have tended to be more elaborate. It is in the Arab world that (most of) the contents of the three extant volumes of Ibn Abī Ṭāhir's

Book of prose and poetry were edited and published; and Muḥsin Ghayyāḍ's 1977 introduction to his edition of the volume on poetry from the latter is the lengthiest overall discussion of Ibn Abī Ṭāhir in Arabic, surpassing Shawqī Ḍayf's analysis of a few years earlier.[39] Ḍayf's treatment did have the virtue of considering Ibn Abī Ṭāhir a poet – an important aspect of Ibn Abī Ṭāhir's professional life with which others have little concerned themselves, or which they have outright ignored.[40] Brahim Najar did include Ibn Abī Ṭāhir in his recent project of anthologizing the "minor poets" (he calls them *al-shuʿarāʾ al-mansiyyūn*, "forgotten poets") of the second/eighth and third/ninth centuries, but regrettably includes only one selection.[41] Until 1998, the 1988 entry devoted to Ibn Abī Ṭāhir in the Persian Islamic encyclopedia was the most critical comprehensive discussion to date in any language.[42] Āzartāsh Āzarnūsh there culled the sources and highlighted Ibn Abī Ṭāhir's numerous contacts, though the discussion of his professional affiliations is limited. Āzarnūsh also catalogs much of Ibn Abī Ṭāhir's poetic output, identifying source and rhyme-letter.[43]

Ibn Abī Ṭāhir is by no means unique. He is not the only author whose life and career is linked to the written word. But he is unusual in that he combined several distinct vocations and avocations and distinguished himself in all of them: poetry, prose, history (literary, cultural, and political), anthology, storytelling (like his poetry, an ignored aspect of his output), and literary criticism. His is thus the legacy of an important, but understudied, polymath of the third/ninth century. Saïd Boustany recognized the importance of Ibn Abī Ṭāhir as an *adīb* of the new type in his 1967 study of Ibn al-Rūmī (d. *c.* 283/896), an acquaintance, possibly even a friend of Ibn Abī Ṭāhir's, when he wrote:[44]

> Diʿbil, Abū Tammām and al-Buḥturī were content just to compose poetic anthologies. Others, such as Ibrāhīm ibn al-Mudabbir, Aḥmad Ibn Abī Ṭāhir or Ibn al-Muʿtazz, illustrated the ideal which al-Hamadhānī would extol in the following century, by endeavoring to show their mastery not only in the composition of poetry, but also by writing works in prose treating of *adab*, history, and literary criticism.

A more nuanced understanding of someone like Ibn Abī Ṭāhir can only complicate – in the very best sense – our understanding of Arabic literature and writerly culture in the third/ninth century.

1

FROM MEMORY TO WRITTEN RECORD

The rise of Arabic writing

The various stages of the postulated shift in Arabic literary culture from memory to written record, that is, from the predominantly oral-aural to the increasingly writerly, were complicated and sometimes imperceptible. There is no specific point in time that can meaningfully be isolated or identified as the moment when such a transition takes place. Even at the high point of oral usage of Arabic – pre-Quranic Arabia, i.e. before *c.* 17/640 – writing and texts were certainly already present.[1] Although writing was not unknown in that period, it was principally the privilege of Jewish and Christian scholars and of those individuals in contact with the Greek- and Persian-influenced Ghassānid and Lakhmid courts, notably the Lakhmid capital of al-Ḥīrah. Indeed, scribes who wrote in Arabic already began to be employed in the Sasanian period, as a sixth-century CE inscription attests.[2]

During the prophethood of Muḥammad (*c.* 610–32 CE), the Arabic script was elaborated,[3] a small Arabic writerly culture developed, and correspondence in Arabic circulated.[4] Authority proper, however, lay with the Prophet. His (spoken) word was regarded as God's command. This perception by and large also held true of the following two caliphs, Abū Bakr (r. 11–13/632–4) and ʿUmar (r. 13–23/634–44), whose status in the community of believers gave their word considerable authority. During his governorship of Syria (*c.* 21–41/*c.* 640–60), and his caliphate (41–60/660–80), the fifth caliph, Muʿāwiyah, adapted his bureaucratic apparatus to foreign models.[5] The language of administration was initially Greek, retaining what was already in place, and many bureaucratic procedures were indebted to Sasanian administrative practices.[6] By the time of Yazīd I (r. 60–4/680–3), bureaucratization of the Islamic polity was well under way; there remained now only the matter of Arabization.

Yazīd I's cousin, the caliph ʿAbd al-Malik (r. 65–86/684–705), was the ruler responsible for substituting Arabic for Greek and Persian in the imperial bureaux in 78/697.[7] With this change, there arose an Arabophone secretarial class, and also an Arabic epistolary tradition. The change planted, as J. D. Latham put it, "the seeds of all future developments in the field of Arabic secretarial literature."[8]

Whereas oral commands had once held sway in administration, letters composed in the chancery now performed that function.[9] Indeed, whereas it had taken several centuries after the development of the Greek alphabet for Hellenic culture to fully interiorize writing, in Arabic such an interiorization took only generations, no doubt largely due to the accelerated needs of the new administrators and the new administration. With Arabic, as with Greek, alphabet, writing, and easier scripts freed the mind for more abstract and textualized thought.[10]

With the new organizational models – letters, formularies, and the attendant exigencies of the page, and of sequenced pages – came new meanings and new sets of meanings. Administrative activity acted as a bridge between oral activity and textual activity, and as a mirror of the changes occasioned by the importance of the written record. Records become more detailed (e.g. in revenue collection),[11] the kind of information recorded more varied (e.g. budgets, land-grants, notary documents), and the qualifications for secretaryship (*kitābah*, lit. writing) more "literate." The growth of the secretarial class, known as the *kuttāb* (lit. writers, sing. *kātib*) and in the number of writers also resulted in an explosion of writing, by them and for them, especially administrative manuals of right secretaryship, e.g. Ibn Qutaybah's *Kitāb al-Maʿārif* [Book of essential knowledge], or his *Adab al-kātib* [Conduct of the secretary].[12]

M. T. Clanchy adduces the explosion in output of notarial and administrative documents in England from 1066 to 1307 as evidence of the growth of literacy.[13] A similar growth in the number of documents in the Arabic context also occurred. The sources frequently mention the numerous letters produced in the burgeoning chanceries; even jurists kept their own archives.[14] But, unlike fifth/eleventh- and sixth/twelfth-century England, very little in the way of Umayyad and Abbasid official administrative documents survive. In this regard, the extant volumes of Ibn Abī Ṭāhir's *Kitāb al-Manthūr wa-al-manẓūm* [Book of prose and poetry] are an invaluable source, preserving, among others, letters by ʿAbd al-Ḥamīd al-Kātib (d. 132/750), who alone is credited with a thousand folios worth of epistles.[15] A close textual analysis of letters from different periods may reveal something about changes brought about by the increased documentation. R. B. Sergeant undertook this, to some extent, in his comparison of first/seventh and second/eighth century prose, sermons, and letters, but was constrained by the late compilation of the material.[16] Similarly useful would be a comparison of early and later *shurūṭ* (document drafting) literature.[17]

Large-scale book production, technical expertise based on the written word (and also on reckoning, which allowed administrators to register, count, value and survey),[18] and the consequent proliferation of writing, all meant that one needed to write more quickly. This need was met by the creation and standardization of rapid scribal hands, such as the *naskh* or *qalam al-nussākh*,[19] scripts which would be perfected in the fourth/tenth and fifth/eleventh centuries thanks to the efforts of the calligraphers Ibn Muqlah (d. 328/940) and Ibn al-Bawwāb (d. *c.* 413/1022).[20] Knowledge of the scribal hand(s) was initially restricted to craftsmen (*warrāqūn*, sing. *warrāq*; *nussākh*, sing. *nāsikh*), whom others hired for the writing of letters or other written documents. This is what Eric Havelock has, in the context of classical Greece, termed "craft literacy."[21]

Arabic and literacy

The transition, or shift, as I have suggested above, was not *sensu strictu* from oral to written or from nonliterate to literate, but rather from predominantly oral to combinations of oral and written. Jonathan Bloom dates the shift also to the ninth century but posits that the watershed was later, by "the twelfth century, when the general availability of paper allowed early patterns of oral transmission and authority to be altered."[22] It is certainly true that only with the growth of literate, textual *mentalités* did matters and modes change. And though there is no fixed point that marks the beginning of these changes, they began to take place earlier with the availability and widespread use of paper, with the resulting increased reliance on written as opposed to oral/aural transmission of knowledge, and with the influx of ideas and values from other writerly traditions, notably Greek, Indian and Persian.

In philosophy and medicine, the so-called foreign sciences, which came into Arab–Islamic culture textually, that is principally through translations, orality was easily superseded by texts. In Hadith scholarship, the ideal was to collect and recollect as many Hadiths as possible. There was no getting away from the combination of profoundly and persistently oral sensibilities with the new and "intrusive" literate sensibilities. Statements such as "There is no one who holds in his hand an inkwell or a sheet of paper who is not deeply indebted to al-Shāfiʿī [d. 204/820]," attributed to Aḥmad ibn Ḥanbal (d. 241/855), however, give lie to the perception of purely *orally* functioning Hadith scholars (*muḥaddithūn*).[23] Even the Hadith collector al-Bukhārī (d. 256/870), whose prodigious memory is legendary – he is reputed to have memorized 600,000 Hadiths – wrote down the material he collected.[24] But there was considerable debate about writing among the scholars of Hadith[25] – to cite but one objection, al-Samʿānī reports the view that written Hadiths were considered suspect because they might be mistaken for Quran.[26] As Hadith scholars began to react against the popular and folk elements in the Prophet Muḥammad's biography, the *sīrah*, and tried to apply concepts of source criticism to the material,[27] an equilibrium resulted wherein oral and written forms divided responsibilities.[28] Oral transmission on the one hand and written collections on the other thus made for a mixed orality. And in law, a notarial tradition developed, but the oral retained its primacy, in witnessing for example; the increased use of documents did, however, force the question about which was better evidence, a person's word or written record. More importantly, the question of how oral testimony was to be evaluated against written testimony when the two were in conflict also had to be addressed.[29]

As for *adab*, in its meaning of "writerly culture," it is no accident that it developed *after* the arrival of paper, the rise of a scribal class, and the development of the notions that equated literacy and eloquence with refinement (e.g. *ẓarf*, elegance, and *adab*, in its meaning of appropriate conduct).[30] If literacy and eloquence were equated with refinement, illiteracy – properly non-literacy – was correspondingly equated with commonness. As Brian Stock has observed:[31]

> Everywhere, the presence of texts forced the elements of culture embedded in oral discourse to redefine their boundaries with respect to a different type of human exchange. This invariably resulted in contrasts between the "popular" and the "learned" which were themselves byproducts of literate sensibilities.[32]

The Arabic of the non-literate Bedouin was, it is true, prized above all else. Philologists would quiz the Bedouin about the etymologies and exact meanings of words, a very "textual" desire on the part of the philologists, which the Bedouin would have no doubt found curious in the late second/eighth century. The grammarian Sībawayhi (a Persian [d. *c.* 177/793]) is reported to have been shamed by losing an argument with his rival al-Kisāʾī (d. 189/805) over a point of Bedouin Arabic grammar.[33] Pre-literates were, however, by and large judged il-literate and were lumped into the (vulgar) commonalty, the *ʿāmmah.* Accusations of incorrect grammar levelled at literates thus became a way to devalue and demean (see chapter 3 below). When these accusations were directed at speakers of non-Arab origin, whose errors were explicable as a function of their foreignness, the accusations acquired classist and racist overtones. Conversely, non-Arabs who perfected their Arabic found in it, and especially in the study of Arabic grammar and syntax, a facilitator of social mobility. Indeed, literacy in general was (and still is) a factor in social mobility.

Literacy implied social superiority, and was tied to the idea that things of the mind are higher than things of the body.[34] Mistakes in grammar came to be associated with the masses (*al-ʿāmmah*). The *laḥn al-ʿāmmah* genre, comprising books devoted to "errors of language made by the common folk," constitutes its own branch of lexicography.[35] Ironically, though purporting to correct the mistakes of the common people, these works actually addressed mistakes made by schooled individuals; *ʿāmmah* ("masses," "common folk") in the phrase *laḥn al-ʿāmmah* ("language errors of the common folk") was a cacophemism for *khāṣṣah* ("the elite," "the learned," "the elect"). Al-Ḥarīrī, for one, opted truthfully to entitle his work in the *laḥn al-ʿāmmah* genre *Durrat al-ghawwāṣ fī awhām al-khawāṣṣ* [Diving the depths for errors by adepts],[36] and al-Jāḥiẓ notes in a passage in the *Kitāb al-Bayān wa-al-tabyīn* [Book of elegant expression]:

> When you hear me mention the common folk (*ʿawāmm*), I do not mean the peasants, the rank and file, the artisans, and the tradesmen, nor do I mean the mountain Kurds ... the Berbers, the northerners [...] The common folk from among our people, our religion, our language, our culture and our moral character, are a class whose intellectual faculties and personal qualities are superior to those other peoples', even if they

do not attain the level of our own elite (*khāṣṣah*). This is the case, bearing in mind that the elite are also divided into strata.

The appearance of texts and textuality

Textuality – increased attention to and reliance on texts – occasioned a growing intellectualism.[37] If in medieval Europe the entire oral tradition had come to be identified with illiteracy, the notion of archaism had been introduced, and a culture of learning and the learned (versus the popular) had been fashioned,[38] the situation in classical Arab–Islamic society, on the other hand, was not analogous. Things dating from before Islam and the time of the Prophet Muḥammad continued to be prized, in spite of the supposed animus against the Jāhiliyyah (up to the late sixth century CE), that (theological construct of a) time when the Arabs were thought of as being unlearned, non-literate, even "ignorant."[39] The poets of the Jāhiliyyah, for example, were long perceived as superior, both as poets and as speakers of Arabic. It is in this context that the purported illiteracy (*ummiyyah*) of the Prophet Muḥammad developed, a position that subsequently came to form a hallowed part of belief about him.[40] Indeed, the cult of his illiteracy sustained a culture of orality even while his own example and the "book" he disseminated, the Quran spoke to the need for textuality, writing, and the written.[41] In many of its formulations, the Quran uses textual metaphors, including Q 96:4, regarded by Muslims as the first revelation, to cite but one example.[42] If the Quran accepted and embraced textuality, however, it took a different position vis-à-vis poets and poetry: just as Plato wished to exclude poets from his ideal Republic where formulae and clichés were outmoded and counterproductive, the Quran too prefigured a chirographically styled noetic world preferably without poets.[43] And it is perhaps only the deep attachment to Arabness – one that was to some extent defined, and definable, by the Arab poetic tradition – that provided any sort of counterpoint to this anti-poet attitude.[44]

By the middle of the third/ninth century, the written word, though it admittedly directly affected a small number of people, was nevertheless widely adopted as a basis for discussions of cultural activity and as a standard of cultural progress. Legitimacy increasingly depended upon written or textual precedents and evidence, in spite of continued ambivalence about the status of texts. As Rosenthal observes:[45]

> In the ninth century it was frankly admitted that all branches of literature relied for their preservation on written fixation.

One of the curious effects of writing is that it does not reduce orality but, rather, enhances it by organizing the principles by which it is practiced into an art; in Greece, this gave rhetoric. This was partly the result of assumptions that oral verbalization was the same as written verbalization. Only gradually did writing become composition in writing. Horace noted that the conquest of Greece had backfired, with Rome assimilating rapidly into wider Hellenistic culture rather than vice-versa.[46] This assimilation occasioned the rapid development of Learned Latin into a literary language. Two of the many developments – Walter Ong has called them "special major developments" – deriving from and affecting the interaction of orality and literacy in the West were academic rhetoric and Learned Latin.[47]

Similar claims might be made for Arabic. Indeed, the burden of the transfer – from oral verbalization to written composition – was assumed by people of non-Arab cultural background, i.e. those already immersed in a chirographic world of literate sensibility. The conquest of Sasanian Iran also "backfired," as it were. Arabic literary culture was, at least in part, assimilated into Iranian literary culture. Adapting Henri Marrou, it might plausibly be suggested that this emulation/assimilation of Iranian – and also Greek and Indian – cultural elements prepared the way for a cultural *lingua franca*, an *adab*, which was then used to transmit a tradition generally recognized as having an essential superiority over all others.[48] Although we can continue to talk of Arabic – classical, and learned – as the medium of this new cultural *lingua franca*, it is only properly definable more broadly, encompassing non-Arab elements. Even the Quran, the quintessential Arab–Islamic text, contains a large number of foreign words.[49]

Classical Arabic was a direct result of writing. Those who wrote it could speak it but there were no purely oral users.[50] Paradoxically, the textuality that kept Classical Arabic rooted in its eloquent (*faṣīḥ*) Quranic and pre-Islamic origins (and kept Learned Latin rooted in classical antiquity) also kept it rooted in orality.[51] Its grammar came from the old oral world as did its vocabulary. But Classical Arabic, like Latin, had its *base* in academia and scholarship, which were overwhelmingly the preserve of men.[52] It goes without saying that there were women who used Classical Arabic: al-Khansāʾ (d. after 23/644) and Layla al-Akhyaliyyah (d. *c*. 85/704), to name but two early poetesses; and countless other instances of women's eloquence, such as are preserved in Ibn Abī Ṭāhir's *Balāghāt al-nisāʾ* [The (instances of the) eloquence of women]. The point is not that women did not use the classical language at all but that they did so in a way dictated by an already male-empowered discourse.[53] Nancy Roberts has in fact argued that in *The (instances of the) eloquence of women* Ibn Abī Ṭāhir is no champion of women but rather an author exploiting their low station to give more sting to his own criticisms of particular individuals or groups.[54] She believes that Ibn Abī Ṭāhir is thereby able to make known views he may otherwise not have been able to express. Although Roberts overstates the case somewhat for an empowered but simultaneously disempowering male discourse, her reading of the Umm Kulthūm, ʿArwah bint al-Ḥārith, and Umm al-Banīn accounts she selects is suggestive and her larger point certainly worthy of further investigation. In any event, use of the classical language *was* gender-linked: it was a language written and spoken primarily by males, and by women prepared for and inducted into the male environment of the classical language, principally women scholars, singing-girls and poetesses.[55] And, as Ong notes about Learned Latin, Classical

Arabic, Rabbinic Hebrew, Sanskrit, Classical Chinese and Byzantine Greek, these languages were no longer used as a mother tongue (i.e. by mothers raising children): they were controlled by writing and learned from writing.[56]

Classical Arabic was thus learned outside the home, in a scholarly/scholastic, or sometimes quasi-tribal, setting. Although there is evidence in the sources that Ibn Abī Ṭāhir taught in a "public school" (*kuttāb*), and also privately,[57] where he himself trained is not specified. In the early third/ninth century though, someone in search of learning could find it in many places. Ibn Abī Ṭāhir almost certainly attended a *maktab/kuttāb* for his primary/preparatory education, where he would have first been exposed to the pre-Islamic *Muʿallaqat* poems, as his introductory remarks to the volume on poetry in his *Book of prose and poetry* attest.[58] Some scholars, typically future administrators, apprenticed in the chanceries,[59] but one could learn in more traditional ways. Mosques were an early site of knowledge transmission, especially because initially the knowledge imparted was religious, the so-called Islamic or religious sciences, encompassing the Quran, which was memorized in part or in its entirety, and Hadith. These were complemented by the study of grammar, lexicography and any other science that facilitated the learning, transmission, and commentary of religious sciences. Poets also met in the mosques where they apprenticed, vied, exchanged ideas, and criticized one another's work. Certain mosques were known for their poetical meetings and soirées. During the caliphate of al-Mahdī (r. 158–69/775–85), for instance, the al-Ruṣāfah mosque was an important meeting-place.[60] And in the mosque of al-Manṣūr, the *qubbat al-shuʿarāʾ*, or poet's dome, was reserved for the poets;[61] it was there in fact that the future court poet Abū Tammām first became known to the Baghdad literary world.[62] Lectures in literary studies were held in mosques too but the norm was to attend the study circles (*ḥalaqāt*, sing. *ḥalqah*) and lectures of masters, both publicly, and privately in their homes,[63] even though private studies could be very expensive. Another way of acquiring knowledge was to listen to storytellers and preachers. The influence of the latter – in particular the proto-Ḥanbalī preachers[64] – who educated and influenced the masses, occasionally inciting them to violent action, led to two caliphal bans which also extended to booksellers (see chapter 2 below).

Books and book-places

The advent of paper and paper-related technologies and the increased availability of books and written materials irrevocably changed the nature of learning and the literary environment. New centers of learning and study included the private homes of munificent patrons or of fellow-scholars, both publicly-funded and private libraries and, later, *madrasahs*,[65] all of them places where books could be consulted, and thus all of them dependent on the existence and availability of books.

The most famous and important public library of the third/ninth century was the one in the *Bayt al-Ḥikmah* (lit. house of wisdom) in Baghdad, actively supported by the caliph al-Maʾmūn (r. 198–218/813–33), and possibly modeled on the Academy at Jundishapur (Gondēshāpūr) credited with passing the Nestorian heritage of the Greek learning of Edessa and Nisibis to Baghdad.[66] A. I. Sabra has argued that the interest in translation (from Greek *inter alia*) which occasioned its founding was linked to writing and scribal or book-based culture, and heralded a cultural explosion.[67] A predecessor of the *Bayt al-Ḥikmah* appears to have existed since the time of al-Maʾmūn's own predecessor, Hārūn al-Rashīd (r. 170–93/786–809). If it later became an academy or institute, it was most likely only a library at the time of Hārūn, whence the other name by which it is known, the *Khizānat al-Ḥikmah* (lit. Storehouse, or Library, of Wisdom). On the strength of this name, and on the use of the term *khizānah* to describe Sasanian royal libraries and archives, Dimitri Gutas has argued that the *Bayt al-Ḥikmah* was not ever a translation academy, but he does concede that the existence of such a "bureau" contributed to an environment conducive to translation.[68] Even if it was undertaken there, official patronage of translation would certainly not have been confined to the *Bayt al-Ḥikmah*. The likes of Sālim (fl. second/early eighth century) and Ibn al-Muqaffaʿ (d. *c.* 142/759), among others, also translated numerous Persian works into Arabic, especially those pertaining to right government and in the Sasanian *Fürstenspiegel* tradition.[69] Ibn Abī Ṭāhir's *Kitāb Tarbiyat Hurmuz ibn Kisrā Anūshirwān* [The education of Hurmuz ibn Kisrā Anūshirwān] is no doubt to be situated within the context of this (and possibly also evening storytelling [*samar*]) activity. Ibn Abī Ṭāhir's work, like many works by Ibn al-Muqaffaʿ, may thus have been translations or adaptations (see chapters 5 and 7 below).

Wealthy patrons also put together private libraries. The courtier ʿAlī ibn Yaḥyā Ibn al-Munajjim (d. 275/888–9) collected a large personal library for the minister and fellow book-lover al-Fatḥ ibn Khāqān (d. 247/861).[70] In his personal library,[71] which he called the *Khizānat al-Ḥikmah* possibly after the then defunct caliphal library of the same name, ʿAlī ibn Yaḥyā provided stipends and free materials for people from all over (*yaqṣiduhā al-nās min kull balad*) who wished to use his vast private collection.[72] The scholar, courtier and chess master Muḥammad ibn Yaḥyā al-Ṣūlī (d. *c.* 335/946) also collected an outstanding library on which he prided himself and his learning.[73] The following century the Shiite Būyid vizier Sābūr ibn Ardashīr (d. 416/1025) established a superb private library known as the *Dār al-ʿIlm* (House of knowledge) or *Dār al-Kutub* (House of books) in the Bayn al-Surayn suburb of Baghdad.[74] In 395/1005, the Fatimid caliph al-Ḥākim had founded a library-institute in Cairo called the *Dār al-Ḥikmah*, apparently inspired by its predecessors, given its name.[75] Wealthy patrons supported original literary production through these libraries, and also directly. It is in such a context, that is the context of material and economic support of writerly culture, that the books of such writers as Ibn Abī Ṭāhir, al-Jāḥiẓ and others emerged, circulated, and functioned.

One of the biggest changes of all was the appearance of another new center of learning and study – the bookshop. By the early third/ninth century, there were as many as one hundred shops in Baghdad's Bookmen's Market (*sūq al-warrāqīn*),[76] and there would no doubt have been a like number of *majālis* [sing. *majlis*], communities of scholars brought together by an interest in learning, in books, and in culture in general. Bookshops were not only places where one could read books, in private – and inexpensively – but also places where one could buy them. Enterprising and entrepreneurial copyists did not simply copy single works – they had been doing this ever since writing had developed into a commercial activity – they were now able to sell the books that they, or others, copied on a large scale. Publishing technology was not yet mechanized: booksellers often relied on contract copyists who charged by the page or by the copy, depending on the nature of the work or request. But publishing was organized, and mass production had begun: the bookseller was now able effectively to provide the reading public with multiple copies of a wide range of written works.

Bookshops account to a considerable extent for the impressive learning of a number of individuals, of which al-Jāḥiẓ is a classic and famous example (see chapter 2 below). The autodidacticism that bookshops facilitated, that is the possibility of accomplishing one's training in *adab* through self-teaching, resulted in an inevitable drop in the reliance on oral/aural transmission of knowledge and information, and increased dependence on books and written materials. The published literary (literally) artifact – tangible, reproducible, ownable, and in the public domain – gained importance in an environment that was being populated by a growing writerly audience, including autodidacts.[77] The availability of easily circulated, authenticated books was in effect both a function of, and a catalyst for, the changes in methods employed in the transmission of learning.

In the pre-readerly environment of Arab–Islamic scholarship, a sign of learning was the successful acquisition (often simply memorization) of knowledge. In order to learn something, one had to learn everything; in order to know something, one virtually had to "know everything," learning what one did not need to know in order to learn what one did need to know.[78] Learning conferred authority. One needed to demonstrate mastery of a discipline through knowledge of meticulous detail and obscure variants. If someone knew only a little, he might often be quoted by the learned, but was not considered learned himself. A little learning was thus dangerous – and unauthoritative.

Transmission of the "literary" heritage

Information obtained from direct scholarly contact with lecturers, professors, and colleagues continued to play an important – in some cases central – role in transmission. What "writings" survive by such "writers", survive essentially because their own students recorded their (spoken) words. It is only in the latter half of the second/eighth century that even *pre-Islamic* poetry began to be codified *ne varietur.*[79] The caliph al-Mahdī (r. 158–69/775–85) was influenced by the tendency of the philologists to fix meaning and text. This is why he applauded al-Mufaḍḍal al-Ḍabbī (d. *c.* 163/780) for respecting the integrity of a fixed "text" while decrying the transmitter Ḥammād al-Rāwiyah (d. after 163/

780) for continuing to indulge in an oral, pre-textual model of transmission. In his biography of Ḥammād, Abū al-Faraj al-Iṣbahānī records the following decree, made on the caliph's orders:[80]

> O men of learning present here, the Commander of the Faithful makes known to you that he has rewarded Ḥammād the poet with 20,000 dirhams on account of the excellence of his poetry – but he [Ḥammād] has corrupted his reliability as a transmitter of poetry by adding his own fabricated verses to the poetry of others. And he [al-Mahdī] has given 50,000 dirhams to al-Mufaḍḍal on account of his honesty and reliability as a transmitter of poetry. So, whosoever wants to hear excellent modern poetry, let him listen to Ḥammād; and whosoever wants a reliable transmission [of ancient poetry], let him listen to al-Mufaḍḍal.

The gathering asked for an explanation for this decree, whereupon the following story was recounted:[81]

> Al-Mahdī said to al-Mufaḍḍal when he had summoned him and they were alone together: "I see that Zuhayr ibn Abī Sulmā [d. 609 CE] began his ode with 'Leave this, and turn your words instead to Harim,' without preceding it with anything. What was he telling himself to leave off? "Commander of the Faithful," al-Mufaḍḍal replied, "I have heard nothing on this matter, except that I suspect he was thinking about something else; or he was reflecting on some verses to recite then desisted in favor of praising Harim and so said 'Leave this'; or he was thinking about some affair of his, left off doing so, and said 'Leave this,' that is, 'Leave off what your thoughts are engaged in and tell instead of Harim,' and so refrained from doing so. Then the Caliph summoned Ḥammād, and asked him the same question he had asked al-Mufaḍḍal. "That, Commander of the Faithful," Ḥammād replied: "is not how Zuhayr opened his poem." "How then?" he asked, and Ḥammād recited: "To whom belong the dwelling-places on the summit of al-Ḥajr. . ." Al-Mahdī cast down his eyes for a time, then approached Ḥammād and said to him: "The Caliph has heard a report about you which makes it necessary to have you take an oath." He then made him swear by his oath of allegiance to the Caliph, and by every other solemn oath, that he would give truthful answers to all questions, and bound him by his oath to these. Then he said, "Tell me the truth about these verses: who added them to Zuhayr's poem?" He then revealed to him that he had himself composed the verses. He [the Caliph] accordingly ordered for him and for al-Mufaḍḍal what he ordered based on their reputations and his disclosure.

As Rina Drory notes, the caliph sees Ḥammād's professional competence "to be at most that of a poet [that is, from the world of orality] and by no means that of a "faithful transmitter," i.e. a scholar [that is, from the world of texts], who, unlike traditional tribal transmitters, does not dare tinker with the original version of the poem."[82] And as Suzanne Stetkevych pertinently notes about this same anecdote, "what is really at issue here is the transition from an oral to a literary poetic corpus . . . Ḥammād preserves the prerogatives of a live tradition," whereas for al-Mufaḍḍal the tradition "has become a cultural artifact that must be preserved intact and with which it is sacrilege to tamper."[83] Al-Manṣūr is said to have asked al-Mufaḍḍal, tutor to his son, the future caliph al-Mahdī, to produce an anthology of *muqillūn* poets, that is, those who composed only a small number of poems. Al-Mufaḍḍal then compiled the *Kitāb al-Ikhtiyārāt* [Anthology] or *Kitāb al-Mukhtārāt* [Choice selections], which later came eponymously to be known as *al-Mufaḍḍaliyāt*.[84] The story may be apocryphal, but it nonetheless gives al-Manṣūr at least an invisible hand in determining al-Mahdī's preference of al-Mufaḍḍal's "procedure" over Ḥammād's.

The "editing" of experience presaged the importance of editing as a procedure and process. In Hadith, editing gave scholars the possibility of producing defined and definitive (canonical) collections, where some verified material was included and other dubious or less reliable material excluded. And the fact of Hadith compilation created a whole class of people whose lives were ordered not only by the need to evaluate, transmit and interpret the Hadith, but also by the very ethical precepts they were preserving and transmitting. This was in all likelihood true also of the exemplary life (*sīrah*) of Muḥammad which, when written and recorded, could begin to order and organize the lives of religious scholars (*ʿulamāʾ*) and, by presenting the *sīrah* as an exemplar, the lives of some of the believers.[85] The "mirrors for princes" works, translated and adapted for the benefit of the leaders of the community (primarily the caliphs), similarly, provided textual models. The Quran also provided a model as text, though it managed to retain in large measure its orality, underscored by its very name which evoked "recitation" rather than "reading." By the second/eighth century, it was authoritatively taught by Quran-reciters (*qurrāʾ*), and thought to be preserved only in the "hearts" of the believers. And yet, its standardization did make for an edited version as it were.[86]

Poets and *rāwīs* (transmitters), such as al-Mufaḍḍal al-Ḍabbī, Abū Tammām (d. 231/845), and, of course, Ibn Abī Ṭāhir, by producing poetry collections (*dīwāns*) and anthologies, effectively edited the poetic and biographical tradition.[87] The oral "canon" was, it is true, an open one. "Selections" from it were not perceived as disembodied parts of it. But with conscious *ikhtiyār* (selection/choice), the agency of the selector/editor acquired added and canonizing importance. Ibn Abī Ṭāhir represents the crystallization of this activity, an activity that he would extend also to include the anthologizing of prose. Like Ibn Abī Ṭāhir, al-Ṣūlī would later also distinguish himself in selecting and anthologizing poetry from diverse poetry collections, and in the editing of poetry collections of individual poets.[88]

2

THE PRESENCE AND INSISTENCE OF BOOKS

The importance of books

The oral/aural contact that earlier predominantly accounted for the transmission of literary and scholarly material was supplemented, not supplanted, by the reliance on books and written evidence. A look at the *akhbār* (accounts, sing. *khabar*) reported in fourth/tenth-century works of *adab* reveals that although a good deal of information is taken from books, anecdotes preceded by the transmission formulae *dhakara* ("he mentioned"), *qāla* ("he said") and *ḥakā* ("he recounted"), for instance, a great deal is also still obtained through oral testimony, as the formulae *akhbaranī* ("he informed me") and *ḥaddathanī* ("he told me") attest.[1] In spite of the increasingly pervasive presence and influence of books, book culture did not supplant oral intellectual culture but complemented it, creating an interdependence. Writers of the late second/eighth and early third/ninth centuries did not rely all that much on available written sources. Walter Werkmeister has shown, for instance, that the majority of the material used by Ibn ʿAbd Rabbihi (d. 328/940) was obtained from *majālis* (sing. *majlis*, discussion sessions, class sessions) and *ḥalqah*s (study circles), and not from written sources.[2] Jurists did not rely greatly on written materials either. As Jeanette Wakin has noted, "jurists never modified their attitude toward written documents and managed to avoid the Quranic injunction [to draft written documents under certain circumstances] by interpreting it as a simple recommendation."[3] Behind the principle that oral testimony deserved more credence than written evidence lay "the correct assumption that numerous documents used in legal claims ... were forgeries.... The technology of written record was insufficiently advanced to be efficient or reliable."[4]

The downturn in importance of personal scholarly contact for transmission and for authentication of that transmission did, however, culminate in an increased reliance on written works. There were two channels of transmission for a scholarly work: one oral, that is, directly from the author or one authorized to transmit; and one written. If one happened upon an autograph copy of a work, one still needed to obtain an *ijāzah* (license to transmit) to transmit it further, but there could be considerable separation in time and place between the (original) author and the latest reader. In spite of the possibility of finding a master with whom one could read the written work, and who would then certify this with a *samaʿ* (certificate of audition), the *ijāzah* did remain extremely important in scholarly transmission as an ideal. That this method remained in place for centuries is clear from statements to that effect by later scholars throughout the sources. This may help explain why volume fourteen of Ibn Abī Ṭāhir's *Kitāb al-Manthūr wa-al-manẓūm* [Book of prose and poetry] was already "out of print" in Ibn al-Nadīm's time. Its author had died a century earlier, the work's "print run" had probably been low, it was long, and it most likely had not been memorized – this because it was a lengthy anthology (fourteen volumes), because it was produced at a time when memorization was less of an exigency, and because, not having been produced under oral/aural circumstances, it was also not transmitted that way. Attention to genre is also important here: the fact that Ibn Abī Ṭāhir is a writer producing "outside" the Islamic sciences or those ancillary to it is doubtless a factor to be considered in explaining the loss of his works. It would have been well-nigh impossible completely to lose something as central as Thaʿlab's grammar book, *al-Faṣīḥ* [Eloquent (grammar)], which was short, often quoted, often used, often memorized, and duly transmitted. The copyist Muḥammad al-Arzānī (d. 415/1024), for example, earned his keep exclusively by (re)producing the *Faṣīḥ* daily.[5]

Yet, in spite of its continuity, the oral/aural method began increasingly (and inescapably) to be undermined by the written text. By not transmitting his work on grammar, *al-Kitāb*, (lit. "the book") to anyone, the grammarian Sībawayhi (d. *c.* 177/793) is one of the first individuals who can be described as having undermined the system of oral/aural transmission – and with one of the earliest texts to have been composed as a *book*.[6] But that literacy and orality were interdependent is clear from the fact that certain habits and modes of communication associated with orality persisted in the textual environment, such as the continued adherence to orally sanctioned norms in the transmission of books on a teacher's authority. Orality thus retained its functions within a system of graphic representation.[7] On the other hand, scholars of literacy and orality have shown that when texts are introduced into communities that have no writing, unprecedented perceptual and cognitive possibilities arise. Texts, in restructuring consciousness, delivered a new technology of the mind.[8] "Abstractly sequential, classificatory, explanatory examination of phenomena or of stated truths," notes Walter Ong, "is impossible without writing and reading. Human beings in primary oral cultures ... learn by apprenticeship ... by discipleship, which is a kind of apprenticeship, by listening, by repeating what they hear, by mastering proverbs and ways of combining and recombining them, by assimilating other formulary materials, by participating in a kind of collective retrospection."[9] Analytic, chirographic thinking, on the other hand, resulted in categories. These categories made things memorable. To this shift may be credited such works as anthologies and *ṭabaqāt* (class/ification) works.

Ambivalence toward the "text"

Although the written no longer merely recorded but could now also dictate the principles of coherence and inner meaning, a clear indication of the changed environment, as Stock has noted about Latinate Europe, was "the ambivalence with which many textual models were greeted by the medievals themselves."[10] In general, until the textual and the writerly would be fully interiorized by Arab–Islamic culture, the credence given to writing and written records remained low. Oral transmission was deemed more credible, because ear- and eye-witnesses could (if still alive) be challenged to defend their statements in a way that written texts could not, and because the Arabic script could be defective.[11] The fear of the threat posed by the existence of books proper (Schoeler's *syngrammata*), i.e. not just the threat of circulating ideas, resulted on some occasions in full-fledged censorship and bans. In 279/892–3, for instance, copyists were prohibited from copying books on certain subjects. This ban is the very first event mentioned by al-Ṭabarī under the year 279 Ḥijrī in his chronicle. He describes it as follows:[12]

> Among them [the events taking place that year], was the authorities' decree that it be announced in Baghdād that no storyteller/preacher, no astrologer and no fortune-teller may sit [and practice their trade] in the streets or in the Friday Mosque. And the booksellers were sworn not to trade in books of theology, dialectics, or philosophy.

Al-Ṭabarī would have been an adult witness to this ban, likewise Ibn Abī Ṭāhir who died a few months later. Al-Ṭabarī reports a similar ban in Jumādā II, 284 [July–August 897].[13] The sources do not state whether this ban was issued because it had earlier been rescinded and needed to be re-applied, or because it had been ineffective in the first instance. But texts endure. There is no way of refuting a text effectively because even after such a refutation the offending text continues to exist, offending and unchanged. This is one reason why books are burned or expurgated. Another reason that attempts are made to destroy books (or parts of them) is ambivalence about the very role of texts (and text), principally ambivalence about the way they order knowledge and lives. Given the ambivalence about texts, the censorship decreed by al-Muʿtaḍid comes as no great surprise.

For his part, Ibn Abī Ṭāhir does not appear to display ambivalence, unless his reluctance to attribute authorship to some of the letters he anthologizes in the *Book of prose and poetry* is interpreted as an indication of ambivalence.[14] His remarks display comfort with writing, with texts, and with textuality; for instance, he writes matter-of-factly in the *Book of prose and poetry* that:

> These are selections of compilation (*ta'līf*), composition (*taṣnīf*), and classification/categorization (*al-tafarruq fī abwāb*), chosen from epistles written by secretaries/writers (*kuttāb*), both early and recent.[15]

Elsewhere in the same anthology, in the volume devoted to the eloquence of women, Ibn Abī Ṭāhir is explicit about his reliance on books:[16]

> I found this in a book: I did not learn it through oral transmission from anyone.

For al-Jāḥiẓ (d. 255/868), writing contemporary with or a generation before Ibn Abī Ṭāhir, books have already made great inroads. He opines as follows in his treatise on teachers:[17]

> Those who read books by good authors and thumb through wise men's works in order to make use of the ideas they contain are on the right track.

And yet, there is evidence in the very same work, that he also still thinks about words in an oral way:[18]

> The right way is to have words spinning in one's ears, echoing in one's heart and fermenting in one's breast.

By the time of Aḥmad ibn Muḥammad al-Bushtī (d. 348/959), a century later practices have changed. Of his *Takmilat Kitāb al-ʿAyn* [Supplement to (al-Khalīl ibn Aḥmad's) 'Kitāb al-ʿAyn'] al-Bushtī writes:[19]

> What I have put in this book of mine, I have derived from these [above-mentioned] books. . . . And for doing so, some might be vexed by this and wish to rebuke and disparage me, seeing as I have attributed the contents of the books to those scholars without having a certificate of audition (*samāʿ*).
>
> Indeed, my transmission on their authority (*ikhbārī ʿanhum*) is in fact a transmission on the authority of their writings (*ʿan ṣuḥufihim*). This will not be rejected by anyone who knows thin (*al-samīn*) from thick (*al-ghathth*), and who can distinguish what is sound (*al-ṣaḥīḥ*) from what is sickly (*al-saqīm*).

Al-Bushtī goes on to cite illustrious antecedents:[20]

> Abū Turāb [d. 275/888], the author of the *Kitāb al-Iʿtiqāb [fī al-lughah]*, did as much when he cited, on the authority of al-Khalīl ibn Aḥmad, Abū ʿAmr ibn al-ʿAlāʾ and al-Kisāʾī, though there was an interval of time between his period and theirs; likewise al-Qutaybī [= Ibn Qutaybah], who cited, on the authority of Sībawayhi, al-Aṣmaʿī and Abū ʿAmr [ibn al-ʿAlāʾ] without having seen a single one of them.

In Abū Bakr Muḥammad ibn Yaḥyā al-Ṣūlī (d. *c*. 335/947),[21] also from the fourth/tenth century, we encounter someone who is evidently very comfortable with writerly culture, but whose own ambivalence is nevertheless revealed and exemplified in his comments about Ibn Abī Ṭāhir in the context of an anecdote reported by the latter. The anecdote, in the *Akhbār al-shuʿarāʾ* [Accounts of the poets] and also to be found in the extant portion of Ibn Abī Ṭāhir's *Kitāb Baghdād* [Book of Baghdad], recounts an exchange between Aḥmad ibn Yūsuf (d. 213/828) and the caliph al-Maʾmūn on the latter's desire to appoint Ghassān (d. after 205/821) governor of Sind.[22] The anecdote is introduced by al-Ṣūlī with the words: *Taḥaddatha Aḥmad Ibn Ṭayfūr anna* ... ("Aḥmad Ibn Ṭayfūr said that..."). The unusual use of *taḥaddatha* ("said") here as a transmission term is explained by al-Ṣūlī himself in a lengthy gloss to the anecdote, where he also points out that the account reported is in fact about the caliph Hishām:[23]

> *Abū Bakr [= al-Ṣūlī] writes:* This is actually a report (*khabar*) about Hishām ibn ʿAbd al-Malik. Asad ibn ʿAbdallāh al-Qasrī asks about Naṣr ibn Sayyār, and he responds with the same answer. Hishām then says what he [= Ibn Abī Ṭāhir] claims al-Maʾmūn said, reciting it in verse, except that in [the] Asad [report] the verses are [more] numerous.

Al-Ṣūlī continues:[24]

> I [= al-Ṣūlī] have reported it according to the transmissions of reliable authorities (*bi-asānīd al-thiqāt*), and from several sources, but Ibn Abī Ṭāhir attributes it to al-Maʾmūn and Aḥmad ibn Yūsuf without naming an authoritative source. This is because he is someone who gets his knowledge from books (*ṣaḥafī*), someone who does himself harm by speaking too much (*ḥāṭib layl*[25]). He imposes as a condition the selection of good poetry for inclusion in his anthologies but he actually includes bad poetry (*al-radīʾ*). And he claims to be picky and careful. Furthermore, he relates untruths and makes mistakes in his dating and in his attribution of poetry.
>
> *Abū Bakr* [= *al-Ṣūlī*] *writes*: I saw him in Basra in 277 [890/91];[26] Aḥmad ibn ʿAlī al-Mādarāʾī had summoned him there. I took down in writing two or three of his [Ibn Abī Ṭāhir's] lectures but when I realized he was a *ṣaḥafī*, in whom I saw nothing I wanted, I left him. I am sorry that I have to speak ill of and belittle a littérateur (*aḥad min ahl al-adab*) but I have no choice but to speak the truth and state matters as they are.

A *ṣaḥafī* (also *ṣuḥufī*) was someone who relied on books and on libraries for his knowledge rather than on memory and on oral and direct acquisition from others. The word derives from the word *ṣaḥīfah* (leaf or page of a book, piece of writing, and by extension letter or book), but the same root *Ṣ-Ḥ-F* also yields *taṣḥīf* (corrupt speech). The meaning "someone who errs while reading, or writing" is also attested in the lexica for *ṣaḥafī*.[27] The connection between the meaning "someone who relies on books" and the meaning "someone who errs when reading" is, of course, significant in a context where the precise value of book and book-related knowledge has not yet been settled.

*Ṣaḥafī*s were evidently not held in high regard in the third/ninth and fourth/ tenth centuries. In a section devoted to knowledge based solely on texts and attendant solecisms in the *Muḥāḍarāt al-udabā' wa-muḥāwarāt al-shuʿarā' wa-al-bulaghā'* [The ready replies of the littérateurs and the conversations of poets and prose stylists] al-Rāghib al-Iṣbahānī includes as the first aphorism: "Neither get your learning from a *ṣaḥafī*, nor your Quran-recitation from a *muṣḥafī*."[28] A *muṣḥafī* was someone whose knowledge of the Quran was based on the written text and not on study with a *qāri'* or *muqri'* (Quran-reciter).[29] The whole attitude toward *ṣaḥafī*s and *muṣḥafī*s is encapsulated in a line of verse cited by al-Rāghib at the very beginning of the section on solecisms:[30]

> When other people prop their reports with real *isnād* chains,
> His prop is books and inventions.

Al-Ṣūlī was well-known for his reliance on books. It is curious, therefore, to find him expressing the negative judgment quoted above about another scholar who relies on books. Al-Ṣūlī was himself criticized for this reliance, and even lampooned to this effect by, among others, Abū Saʿīd Muḥammad ibn ʿAmr al-ʿUqaylī (d. 322/934):[31]

> Al-Ṣūlī is a Master most knowledgable,
> Or, at any rate, his library is.
>
> If we ask him for knowledge,
> Seeking his superior analysis,
>
> He says, "Young men, then bring me
> such-and-such a ream or thesis.

By recording, in writing, all the knowledge he acquired from his many distinguished teachers,[32] and by relying heavily on books, al-Ṣūlī amassed an enormous library. One of al-Ṣūlī's students, Abū Bakr ibn Shādhān (d. 376/986), is quoted as saying:[33]

> I saw a large room of al-Ṣūlī's filled with books, stacked on shelves, their bindings in different colors. Each bookshelf was one color; one shelf was red, another green, another yellow, and so on. . . . Al-Ṣūlī used to say, 'All these books are my certificates of audition'."

Al-Ṣūlī was proud of his library – which he generously allowed others to use – and also of his book-based learning. Al-Ṣūlī was thus himself a product of the book-based culture for which he so comprehensively criticizes Ibn Abī Ṭāhir.

In later times, reliance on books would become *pro forma*. Two generations later, the bibliophile and bookseller Ibn al-Nadīm would open countless entries in the *Fihrist* [The Catalog] with the words "I read in the hand of . . .," "I read in . . .," or other such locutions.[34] It is Ibn al-Nadīm who notes that al-Ṣūlī, in addition to being criticized for excessive reliance on books, was guilty of plagiarism, noting that he was able to identify entire passages of the *Kitāb al-Shiʿr wa-al-shuʿarāʾ* [Book of poetry and poets] of Abū Aḥmad ibn Bishr al-Marthadī (d. 286/899) in al-Ṣūlī's *Kitāb al-Awrāq* [Book of folios].[35] And Ibn al-Nadīm suspects that al-Ṣūlī's rescension of the poetry of Ibn Harmah (d. *c.* 176/792) is a fabrication but, as Stefan Leder points out, this cannot be confirmed.[36] Ibn Abī Ṭāhir's *Akhbār Ibn Harmah wa-mukhtār shiʿrihi* [Accounts of Ibn Harmah and selections of his poetry] would have been useful in this regard, but is not extant.

Corroboration of al-Ṣūlī's allegedly flawed reliance on the written word over the spoken is provided by a *khabar* reported by al-Khaṭīb al-Baghdādī:[37]

> Muḥammad ibn al-ʿAbbās al-Khazzāz wrote: I attended [a lecture of] al-Ṣūlī's where he transmitted a tradition of the Prophet, [the one that begins] "Man ṣāma Ramaḍāna wa-atbaʿahu sittan min Shawwāl. . ."[38] [But] he [= al-Ṣūlī] said [instead] ". . . wa-atbaʿahu *shayʾan* min Shawwāl," so I said, "Professor, put the two dots that are beneath the letter *yāʾ* above it." But he didn't understand what I meant, so I said, "It's '*sittan* min Shawwāl'." Thereafter, he transmitted it as he had said it.

Al-Ṣūlī here supplies the wrong pointing to the sequence of letters to give the meaning "something of" (*shayʾ*) instead of "six days of" (*sitt*).

Ambivalence toward texts is also illustrated by the reluctance to give credence to manuscripts that have been "found" (sometimes after an author's death).[39] This was because

> A book which one has not made one's own, in the form of direct transmission through competent members of a chain going back to the author, is only owned as *wijādah*: it has been 'found' but not heard and received in authentic form.[40]

Use of and reliance upon such manuscripts on their own authority was initially regarded as unacceptable but eventually works discovered by family members, associates, or pupils began to gain acceptance and to be considered authoritative. It is not difficult to imagine enterprising copyists (*warrāqūn*) undertaking the same kinds of search, looking for manuscripts the ownership or copying of which meant lucrative business. This is not to say that writers, poets, and scholars were not already freely associating with *warrāq*s or, indeed, with the profession (*wirāqah*).[41]

Cultivating such friendships could only stand the writer in good stead. It meant access to all the materials and privileges connected with books: paper, ink, copyists, letters, handlists and booklists, librarians, and books themselves.

There were, of course, book-lovers long before the bibliographer-bibliophiles, Ibn al-Nadīm and al-Ṣūlī. Ibn Abī Ṭāhir's associate and friend, the poetry-transmitter and lexicographer Abū Hiffān (d. 257/871), makes the following observation in the mid-third/ninth century:[42]

> The three greatest lovers of books and learning I have ever seen or heard are al-Jāḥiẓ, al-Fatḥ ibn Khāqān, and the judge Ismāʿīl ibn Isḥāq.
>
> Al-Jāḥiẓ never let a book pass through his hands without reading it from cover to cover, no matter what it was. He would even rent the shops of the *warrāq*s, and spend his nights there, poring over them.[43]
>
> Al-Fatḥ ibn Khāqān[44] used to attend the audiences of al-Mutawakkil and whenever he needed to excuse himself, he would take a book out of his sleeve or boot and begin to read it while still in the presence of al-Mutawakkil and until he would return to him, and even in the latrine itself.
>
> As for Ismāʿīl ibn Isḥāq,[45] never have I visited him without finding him poring over a book, rummaging through books, or dusting them off.

This anecdote draws attention to the fact that the books so prized by the three erudites are in fact material objects, ones that can literally be handled: Al-Jāḥiẓ has books passing through his hands, al-Fatḥ keeps them in his sleeve, and Ismāʿīl rummages through them and dusts them. Moreover, these individuals are representive of three significant consumers of books: men of letters, men of state, and men of law, respectively. They, and their relationships to the books, demonstrate how much texts and books have become interiorized, and constitutive of book culture and writerly culture.

Moreover, reading, dialogue, and the absorption of texts led to the rise of "textual communities," groups of people whose "social activities are centered around texts or a literate interpreter of them."[46] And where there are texts, there are also groups to study them.[47] Writers began, for example, to organize literary salons and soirées (*majālis, asmār*). These kinds of communities contributed to the growth in importance, and eventual primacy, of books. A professional textual community appeared consisting of copyists/booksellers/publishers.

The process of learning and reflection that the growth of communities organized around the existence and proliferation of texts occasioned inevitably influenced the relationship of the communities to those texts. Although the author/ized study of books and transfer and transmission of information became decreasingly oral, books still needed to be bought, lent, discussed, and copied, which ensured the persistence of the social aspect of the scholarly enterprise. Paradoxically, literacy and book-based activity, in addition to (and, sometimes, rather than) promoting readerly communities, also promoted isolated activity. One could, after all, do as al-Jāḥiẓ did and read alone, or as al-Ṣūlī is alleged to have done and rely on books alone.

Notions of Authorship

In oral/aural transmission, the authorized text relied on a chain of "authors" who certified to the authenticity of the utterance.[48] Author/ization changed radically with the arrival of editor or author, an "independent" for whom transmission was writing. Authors could now claim books as their own. In primarily oral societies, "words" are common public property. Authorship and the existence of the written word, however, generated feelings of private ownership of words.[49] Indeed, one of the clearest consequences occasioned by textuality was proprietary notions about texts. With writing, there arose an increasing resentment of plagiarism.[50] As a whole range of critical methods for using texts as evidence developed, forgery, and resentment of it, also followed. This underscored the ambivalence felt by so many about texts. Forgery depended on texts, textual antecedents, and attribution – in short, textuality. Forgers were not occasional deviants on the periphery but rather "experts at the centre of literary and intellectual culture."[51]

Forgery is attributing to someone else something you have written yourself. Plagiarism is attributing to yourself something that someone else has written, and is in a sense the obverse of forgery.[52] The need to attribute correctly is writerly and post-oral because it tries to counteract forgery, itself a feature of writerly culture. Expertise in it and its denunciation are also a feature of writerly culture. The need intentionally to misattribute is also writerly and post-oral because it relies on the force of a written precedent. Borrowing, which is usual in an oral culture, and acceptable, can become plagiarism in a written culture.

The decision to write books exposing plagiarism is therefore a "literary" or writerly one. So too is anthologizing, as it implies (but may sidestep) an interest in questions of attribution.[53] By the fourth/tenth century, a compilation such as Abū al-Faraj al-Iṣbahānī's *Book of songs* which had as its initial focus the "top one hundred" songs, would turn into a massive (over thirty printed volumes) celebration of anthology and canonization.[54] It is thus not surprising that this classic text of writerly culture gives pride of place to a denunciation of forgery in its opening pages. Ḥammād ibn Isḥāq (fl. early third/ninth century) is quoted to the effect that the bulk of the book that also went by the name *Book of songs* that was then circulating in Baghdad was not in fact by his father at all:[55]

> *Muḥammad ibn Khalaf Wakīʿ reported to me saying*: "I heard Ḥammād ibn Isḥāq say, 'My father never composed any such book, nor did he ever see it. The proof of this is that most of the verses which are collected in it and assigned to accompanying stories were in fact never sung by

anyone, that most of the attributions to the singers are wrong, and that what my father himself compiled (*allafahu*) from his own repertoire of songs points to the falsity of this book. In fact, it was one of my father's *warrāq*s who put it together after his death, all except for "al-Rukhṣah," which is the first part of the book. My father – may God have mercy on him – himself composed it, as all the *akhbār* in it emanate from us'." *This is what I heard directly from Abū Bakr [= Wakīʿ], and which I memorized, though there may be a word more or a word less here and there.*

Aḥmad ibn Jaʿfar Jaḥẓah told me that he knew the warrāq *who wrote it, that he was called Sanad [ibn ʿAlī], and that his booth was at the Dung Market [Khān al-zibl] in the Sharqiyyah Quarter. He was a copyist of Isḥāq ibn Ibrāhīm. He and a partner of his agreed to put it together.*

The very phrasing of this account illustrates the shift from a predominantly oral/aural tradition of scholarly and intellectual transmission to an increasingly scribal, text-based and writerly one. The need to specify "I heard this account from Abū Bakr, which I memorized, though I may add or omit a word here and there" is born of an impulse that can only exist in a fixed-text-based tradition. It has little meaning in an oral one, and reflects anxiety about preserving the (purportedly) greater degree of reliability or oral transmission.

Intentional misattribution, forgery, and imitation were, to judge by the comments of al-Jāḥiẓ and others, common, or at any rate lucrative. In his 'Risālah Fī faṣl mā bayna al-ʿadāwah wa-al-ḥasad' ['An epistle on distinguishing the difference between enmity and enviousness'] al-Jāḥiẓ writes:[56]

> I cannot be certain – may God preserve me – that these books, which I write at the cost of so much toil, and which I rack my brains to compose, will not be presented to you by someone who has donned the garb of perfidy by claiming to to produce their like. That he will not attribute to himself the ability to produce their equal – as similar as cousins, if not as similar as brothers – and attribute to himself the knowledge of subjects similar to them, and get his boastful fill from something with which God did not provide him.

Al-Jāḥiẓ later in the same work tackles the issue of authorship in the following famous passage, treating of imitation in the first paragraph (the divisions are mine), of forgery (which turns out to be intentional misattribution) in the second, and of both intentional misattribution (which turns out to be a kind of plagiarism) and anonymity in the third:[57]

> I have on occasion written a solid and thorough book on religion and law, epistolography and biography, sermons, the land tax, on legal principles, or some other field of learning, and published it under my

> own name, whereupon it has been furiously and maliciously assailed by a group of scholars, motivated by their innate feelings of envy, even though they were well aware of the book's excellence and distinction. This is all the more likely when the book has been written for a prince with the power to advance an author or degrade him, to exalt or to humble, and to inspire hope and fear. They rail against the book, like camels in heat; and if there is any possible way of denigrating the book to the patron, they make straight for him, he's the one they need. If, however, the patron is experienced and intelligent, skilled and discerning, astute and sharp-witted, such that they cannot employ this ruse, then they simply steal the ideas out of the book, rewrite them, add some filler, and then present their pirated version to some other prince in order to win his favor. Of course, when [the original book] had my name on it, all they could do was denigrate and abuse it.[58]
>
> I would also on occasion write a second book, inferior in ideas and in language [to the one I attacked], signing it with a name other than mine, and attributing it to authors of a preceding generation, such as Ibn al-Muqaffaʿ, al-Khalīl, Salm, Director of the "House of Wisdom," Yaḥyā ibn Khālid, al-ʿAttābī, or similar writers.[59] Then the very same people who criticized my first and better book would come to me begging me to let them have copies of the second inferior one. They would ask to study it under my guidance, and copy it in their own handwriting, making of it a model to be emulated. They would discuss it among themselves, model themselves on it by using its phraseology and ideas in their own books and lectures, teach it to their students on my authority in the relevant discipline, thereby gaining preeminence for themselves and establishing a school of imitators. All this simply because my name does not appear in it anywhere and because no-one attributes it to me.
>
> Often a book of mine has appeared as firm and polished as the back of a smooth stone, its ideas subtle and tightly intertwined, and its language lofty and eloquent. I feared the censure of the envious if I admitted its attribution to me; just as I could not bear attributing its splendid structure and fine expressions to someone else. So I would bring it out as an anonymous work – one of many works by unknown authors. These people would then fall eagerly on it like a deluge of sand, and race to read it like horses on race day, straining toward the finish line.

Everything al-Jāḥiẓ describes is a function of textuality and is dependent on notions of authorship, attribution and proprietarinesss. It is of interest that someone such as al-Jāḥiẓ would misattribute his own work; what is more, he is not the only one to have done so. False attribution is not unacceptable yet.

In the fourth/tenth century, Ibn al-Nadīm is highly critical of anonymous and pseudonymous works. This is to be expected from one writing at a time when works are being regarded as "property." For Ibn al-Nadīm, not to establish and claim authorship is simply inexplicable, as the following passage attests:[60]

> I say, however, that for an eminent man to sit down and take all the trouble to write a book containing two thousand pages, the composition of which plagues his mind and thoughts, then to trouble his hand and body with copying these things, and then afterwards to attribute all this to another man, whether real or fictitious, is sheer folly.

Variants/variance

The issue of authorship raises an important question: What was the effect of oral transmission on textual fidelity and textual variance? This issue may conveniently be illustrated by looking at one anecdote and its variants:[61] an anecdote involving Ibn Abī Ṭāhir is apposite. The anecdote in question is an account describing a ploy devised by Abū Hiffān (d. 257/871) and Ibn Abī Ṭāhir to raise money by pretending that one of them has died and then seeking funds for the cost of a burial shroud. In al-Tawḥīdī (d. after 400/1009) the events unfold as follows:[62]

> *Abū Hiffān writes:* I was staying in the vicinity of al-Muʿallā ibn Ayyūb and Ibn Abī Ṭāhir was staying with me. We were both in mighty straitened circumstances so I said to Ibn Abī Ṭāhir, "Are you up to doing something unobjectionable? Let me wrap you in a white cloth and then go to the house of al-Muʿallā. I'll tell him that a friend of mine has died, and I'll get us the money for the burial shroud. We can make that last a few days till God favors [us again]." "I'll do it," he replied. *Now, al-Muʿallā had appointed an agent to arrange for the shrouding of all those who had died and had not left enough [money] behind for the shroud, the rate being three dinars.*
>
> *Abū Hiffān writes:* So I went to al-Muʿallā's house, told him what had happened, and his agent came along to verify the report. He entered my house and uncovered Ibn Abī Ṭāhir's face. He had some doubts about him so he rapped him on the nose whereupon Ibn Abī Ṭāhir farted. The agent turned to me and asked, "What's this?" to which I replied, "What's left of his spirit.... It hated the smell of his breath so it left through his arse (*karihat nukhatahu wa-kharajat min istih*)." He laughed till he fell to the ground. Then he payed me the three dinars, saying "You two are gallants and debauchees indeed [*antum ẓurafāʾ mujjān*]! Spend it on whatever you need!"

Al-Raqīq al-Nadīm (d. 417/1026) records the account as follows in a section entitled 'Akhbār al-shuʿarā' wa-al-mujjān' [Accounts of the poets and the debauchees] in a work on the joys of wine, the *Quṭb al-surūr fī awṣāf al-khumūr* [The pole of pleasure on descriptions of liquor]:[63]

> Aḥmad Ibn Abī Ṭāhir and Abū Hiffān drank till they exhausted what they had. They were in the vicinity of al-Muʿallā ibn Ayyūb so Ibn Abī Ṭāhir said to Abū Hiffān: "Play dead so I can petition al-Muʿallā for [the price of] your burial shroud." So he wrapped him in a garment and went off to see al-Muʿallā and said: "God preserve you! We are staying in your vicinity and we find ourselves in need of you. Abū Hiffān has died and has no burial shroud." So he [al-Muʿallā] said to his agent, "Go with him to witness the body, then pay him the cost of the shroud." When he got to him, he found him wrapped in a cloth. He hit him on the nose, whereupon he [Abū Hiffān] broke wind. "What's this?" he asked, and Ibn Abī Ṭāhir said, "God preserve you! The pressure of the grave has caught up with him early because he died with debts on his head (*ʿujjilat lahu ḍarṭat al-qabr li-annahu māt wa-ʿalayhi dayn*)." He [the agent] laughed and ordered that they be given some dinars.[64]

Here, it is Ibn Abī Ṭāhir who suggests the ploy and Abū Hiffān who plays dead.[65] In the account preserved in the *Jamʿ al-jawāhir fī al-mulaḥ wa-al-nawādir* [The collected jewels of tales and jokes (about fools)] of al-Ḥuṣrī (d. 433/1061), the anecdote reprises the al-Raqīq al-Nadīm version up until Ibn Abī Ṭāhir says "God preserve you!". It then reads:[66]

> "What's left of his spirit. It hated the smell of his breath so it left through his behind (*dubrih*)." He informed al-Muʿallā who laughed and ordered that they be given many dinars"

The Ḥuṣrī version uses the punchline from the Tawḥīdī version (and changing "istihi," "his anus" to "dubrihi," "his behind") before then "returning" to the Raqīq ending, but not before making al-Muʿallā, as opposed to his agent, the grantor of many, as opposed to some, dinars.

These accounts, in spite of the similarity of the outcome, are nevertheless different. Whereas in the Tawḥīdī version, which is likely the earliest, it is Ibn Abī Ṭāhir who plays dead at Abū Hiffān's suggestion, in the Raqīq and Ḥuṣrī versions, it is the other way around. Only in the Raqīq version is the anecdote occasioned by the fact that they have spent everything they have on drink. This is to be expected from an anecdote in a work on wine. In the other two versions, on the other hand, no mention of drinking is made and the focus is rather on an unexplained indigence. When al-Muʿallā's agent hits the dissimulator on the nose and he breaks wind, the agent naturally expresses wonder. In the Tawḥīdī and Ḥuṣrī versions, the breaking of wind is humorously explained but the explanation in no way draws on the other circumstances to explain the faux pas. The agent is tickled pink, and characterizes (in the Tawḥīdī version alone) the two characters as gallant and debauched (though it does in Raqīq occur in the section devoted to the gallant and the debauched). In the Raqīq version however, Ibn Abī Ṭāhir explains – in this version he is the "living" character – that the "pressure of the grave" has caught up with the dead man because of his debts. This explanation relies on other information within the anecdote. By referring to debts, it plays on the fact that they are broke. By referring to an early grave/ death, it plays on the fact of the false death. Although the other versions include explanatory information, it is the Raqīq version that narratively exploits the material more effectively, including a description of receipt of the money in the first person.

The divergences in the wording of the anecdotes, and the differing roles played by those enacting the events described, illustrates a very common feature of early transmission (*riwāyah*), namely that numerous transmitters were particularly concerned with the spirit of an anecdote, and far less concerned with the letter.[67] To adapt Bernard Cerquiglini: in an oral environment anecdotes do not produce variants, they are variance.[68] This is best demonstrated by the Ḥuṣrī version, likely the latest, and the one most revealing of a writerly impulse, where he does not even cite the source of his information. The preoccupation in the tradition of oral transmission was not narrative originality, but the managing of a particular interaction with one's audience, as in the Raqīq version which better exploits the story for his (wine-related) purposes. Al-Ḥuṣrī is (merely) recording, in writing, an interesting account, before moving on to the next account.

Al-Raqīq al-Nadīm may have been aware of the story from either an oral or a written source but his recension is a (necessarily) written reconstruction of the "story," which retains the outcome, but not quite the same punchline, and retains the principal actors, though they are in different roles. For Goody and Watt, inferring from examples such as these, "In literate traditions, the meaning is in the text; in oral traditions, the meaning is in the context."[69]

The creation of a readership and market

Wherever texts appeared, relations between authors, listeners, readers, and the real or imagined public changed. If we can speak of the emergence of the author, we can also speak of the emergence of the reader. But for precisely what readers and readerships the authors were writing is difficult to establish with any certainty. It is evident that early compilations of material, such as name-lists, were produced in the context of antiquarian scholarship. Antiquarian scholars engaged in a kind of corporate reflection upon the past. This was not for them an "itemized terrain, peppered with verifiable 'facts'," but, rather, the domain of the ancestor, hence the need to rehearse and repeat genealogies.[70] In oral cultures, once knowledge is acquired, it must be constantly repeated or else it is likely to be lost.

Now, writers from any given group or class were often read by and writing for others of the very same group, or for those aspiring to be part of that group – this, to a certain extent, is true even today. The early sustained prose – the epistles and treatises of Ibn al-Muqaffaʿ and Sālim for instance – were evidently directed at rulers and later came to be read also by administrators and by other writers in search of written models to emulate. Sībawayhi, a grammarian, came to be read by other grammarians; al-Madāʾinī, an antiquarian, to be read by other antiquarians; al-Shāfiʿī, a legal scholar, by other legal scholars, and so on.

Outside of the coteries and social circles in which moved the patronized writers, and apart from the autodidacts, there was a readership interested in popular literature, stories, and romances, that is, in works that entertained.[71] Stories from the *Alf laylah wa-laylah* [Thousand and One Nights] until very recently remained excluded from the school curriculum in most Arabic-speaking countries and were regarded as inferior literature, if they were regarded as literary at all. Indeed, the importance of curriculum (then, as now) cannot be underestimated. As long as a work was worthy of study, whether in a structured learning environment (e.g. *maktab*, or *majlis*), or by autodidacts, it continued to be copied and circulated. If it was only of interest to a small group of specialists, its print run might be low and it might not necessarily find its way far afield. If the work was for popular consumption, its print run might be high but it had little chance of surviving the ravages of time because it was usually cheaply produced. Sometimes merchants, unaware of the value of the works in their possession, sold them piecemeal, thereby almost ensuring their destruction.[72] It is also probable that works written primarily for a basically literate readership were held in low regard – another reason why these kinds of works (e.g. romances) do not, and perhaps could not – survive. Even today, on the streets of Cairo or in the train-stations of Lahore, popular, cheap books are sold for mass consumption. Durability and quality are of little concern. Often these books are available for rent or resale in used bookshops, as would have been the case in ninth-century Baghdad.[73]

Titles of numerous such works are attested but in very few cases do texts survive.[74] Copyists and popular authors might rely on the production of such works – cheap and with a high circulation – to earn their bread and stew. Such works were not regarded as serious and would often be kept short, or divided into small parts, in order to be produced and reproduced rapidly. And they would be produced with and on inexpensive materials to keep the price low (and the volume of sales high). However, use of inferior, or at any rate less durable, materials resulted in a very short life (and shelf-life). In contrast, the books of Ḥunayn ibn Isḥāq (d. 264/877), for example, dedicated to patrons and destined for libraries, are said to have endured because they were produced on such thick paper, chosen, according to Ibn Abī Uṣaybiʿah, so that they might fetch a higher price.[75] Today, academic presses produce books on high quality paper at high cost to themselves and, to make the publication economically feasible, at high cost to the libraries and individuals acquiring them. Print runs may be low but they are widely disseminated and can be consulted at all major institutions of learning. Trade publishers produce popular novels, sometimes in the millions. But they are often produced on paper of inferior quality. So, although they find their way into countless bookshops and homes (of the literate but non-specialist public), they "disappear" rapidly and anyway are not durable.

The *Kitāb al-Hudhaliyyah wa-al-Makhzūmī* [The Hudhalī woman and the Makhzūmī man] by Ibn Abī Ṭāhir's fellow fabulist Sahl ibn Hārūn (d. 215/830), to cite one of countless lost works, was in all likelihood produced for, and addressed to, a literate but popular, non-specialist readership.[76] Some scholars, basing themselves on known titles, have suggested that works of this type must have been the product of idle intellects. It is certainly possible that works of the *faḍāʾil* (virtues of ...) precedence genre (discussed in chapter 5 below), for example, were rhetorical exercises, but it is not very likely that they would be produced without an intended audience, and, given the work involved and costs (admittedly sometimes minimal) associated with production, without some expectation of payment.[77] We know altogether too little about popular literature, its reach, and its readership, but, judging from the sheer number of titles and the calibre of writers associated with such writing,[78] we can infer that the readership – or the demand at any rate – was significant.

The motivation for writing was certainly connected to demand. There was the demand created by a growing readership that now extended beyond the narrower elite to encompass an increasingly literate public, beginning with a so-called sub-elite (merchants, lawyers, aspiring littérateurs, the wealthy, and foreign or visiting scholars),[79] and extending into the emerging bourgeoisie of Baghdad (landowners, small business folk, civil servants, teachers, and so on). Authors, publishers and booksellers had an economic incentive to market works for which there was a demand that might mean wide circulation. This (partly) explains Ibn al-Muʿtazz's characterization of Ibn Abī Ṭāhir's writings as follows:[80]

> His poetry is so famous among the elite and the common folk that we need not record any of it in this book of ours. He has not just one book [but many] composed on the [different] branches of *adab* (literature), *akhbār* (historical accounts), and *ayyām* (battledays) which have [all] reached East and West.

Al-Jāḥiẓ's books are described in similar terms: they are said to have been circulated by people who had read them and recognized their merit.[81] Evidently, once a book or pamphlet or story succeeded on the market, it would capture readerships and generate new demand. Such material thus found its way into writerly culture at both scholarly and popular level, a distinction that is to some extent discernible in the taxonomy of Ibn al-Nadīm's *Catalog* (completed in 377/987–8), a catalog of all works written in Arabic, or translated into Arabic. Ibn al-Nadīm divides his work into ten sections (*maqālāt*) as follows:

1. Languages and scripts; the scriptures of Muslims and other people of the book [35 published pages]
2. Grammar and lexicography (*naḥw*, *lughah*) [51 pages]
3. History (*akhbār*), belles-lettres (*ādāb*), biography (*siyar*), genealogy (*ansāb*) [73 pages]
4. Poetry (*shiʿr*) [22 pages]
5. Scholastic theology (*kalām*) [47 pages]
6. Law (*fiqh*) and Tradition (*ḥadīth*) [38 pages]
7. Philosophy (*falsafah*) and the "ancient sciences" (*al-ʿulūm al-qadīmah*) [62 pages]
8. Stories (*asmār*), legends (*khurāfāt*), romances (*gharāʾim*), magic (*siḥr*), conjuring (*shaʿbadhah*) [17 pages]
9. Doctrines of the non-monotheistic creeds [32 pages]
10. Alchemy [9 pages]

What I have tried to sketch in this and the preceding chapter is that – with the writing down, and study of, the Quran; with the growth of scribal culture, that is, the proliferation of scribes and books, and the perfection of script; with further book-based contact with the cultural institutions of other civilizations, notably Sasanian and Hellenic; with the canonization of Hadith; with the widespread availability of affordable paper; with the anthologizing of the literary heritage; with the development of education and educational institutions at all levels; and with the concomitant rise in levels of literacy – an important transformation took place. The scholarly and literary milieux were now ones that had to reckon with the permanent and irrevocable presence of books and writerly culture.

In the following chapter, I focus on three of Ibn Abī Ṭāhir's activities: the composition of poetry, the transmission of poetry, and storytelling, activities that we might preliminarily term pre-writerly.

3

RECITING POETRY, TELLING TALES

Ibn Abī Ṭāhir, Poet

Many modern scholars who view Ibn Abī Ṭāhir primarily as a historian and anthologist altogether ignore his poetic output. In a 1996 *Encyclopaedia Iranica* article, for instance, C. E. Bosworth does not even mention Ibn Abī Ṭāhir's verse in spite of the fact that one of his key references, a Persian encyclopedia entry, is explicit about it and catalogs it.[1] Indeed, the earliest extant notice devoted to Ibn Abī Ṭāhir – one page long in the published version – is in the *Ṭabaqāt al-shuʿarāʾ al-muḥdathīn* [Classes of modern poets] of Ibn al-Muʿtazz (d. 296/908).[2] Ibn al-Muʿtazz, whose ill-fated caliphate lasted just one day, was a fine poet, perceptive critic, and was also the author of the *Kitāb al-Badīʿ* [Book of novel expression], the first work to address expression(s) of the "modern," the "new" and the "novel."

Although he uses the word *ṭabaqāt* in the title of his collection – after the *Ṭabaqāt fuḥūl al-shuʿarāʾ* [The Classes of great poets (lit. stallions)] of Ibn Sallām al-Jumaḥī (d. *c.* 232/847), which concentrates on Arab poets of the pre-Islamic and very early Islamic period – Ibn al-Muʿtazz eschews the comparative, classifying method of Ibn Sallām, and concentrates instead on individual poets of merit.[3] Iḥsān ʿAbbās has plausibly suggested that in the literary tradition *ṭabaqāt* came to refer to notable poets and no longer designated preference or precedence.[4] The *Classes of modern poets* comprises one hundred and thirty-two poets followed by six poetesses; Ibn Abī Ṭāhir is placed one hundred and twenty-fourth.[5] That he appears "late" in the collection is not in itself significant given that the book is neither organized hierarchically nor chronologically. Thus, Abū Tammām appears fifty-second and al-Buḥturī one hundred and eighth, to name just those two. If there is an underlying raison d'être to Ibn al-Muʿtazz's sequencing, it has so far eluded scholarly analysis; however, the relative positioning of Ibn Abī Ṭāhir's notice vis-à-vis the notices of Abū al-ʿAynāʾ (123rd), al-Qiṣāfī (122nd), al-Tammār (120th), and Abū Hiffān (119th), all of which immediately precede his, does appear to be siginificant and is discussed in chapter 7 below.

The Ibn Abī Ṭāhir notice, like many of the other notices in the *Classes of modern poets*, does not provide the type of information usually found in a biographical notice per se, such as dates of birth and death, scholarly or literary pedigree (i.e. the names of teachers and students), and genealogy or full name. But what information it does supply is instructive. Though contact between Ibn al-Muʿtazz and Ibn Abī Ṭāhir is unlikely, it is not impossible, and so the information may be based on first-hand knowledge. The notice is tripartite, consisting of one anecdote, one attribution, and a brief biographical conclusion. It reads as follows:[6]

[1] Al-Tamīmī Aḥmad ibn Mundhir related to me [= Ibn al-Muʿtazz] saying, I heard Aḥmad Ibn Abī Ṭāhir say, "I recited to Abū Ḥakīmah[7] an elegy on my tool, in which appear the following two verses:[8]

Ayrī ʿalayya maʿa ʾz-zamā-
ni fa-man adhummu wa-man alūmū
Ash-shaʾnu fī ayrī yuqa-
wwamu li ʾl-qiyāmi fa-lā yaqūmū.

My penis is in cohoots with time against me
So who am I to blame, and whom to criticize?

The thing about my penis is
Though designed to get erect, it doesn't want to rise.

Abū Ḥakīmah said, 'By God, I have no equal in this art (*fann*) and through it have distinguished myself peerlessly. God strike me down,' he said, 'should I say anything after this on that subject!'" He [Ibn Abī Ṭāhir] said, "Abū Tammām used to say [to me] after that, 'How are you, O one who made Abū Ḥakīmah repent of his misdeeds?'"

[2] And Ibn Abī Ṭāhir is the one who said:

Idhā ʾl-yadu nālathā bi-ḍighnin tawaqqarat
ʿalā ḍighnihā thumma ʾstafādat min ar-rijli

If the hand accosts it [= the cup] with hatred,
it treats that with aplomb, and then goes on
to seek vengeance on the foot."[9]

This line has been transmitted as part of a poem by Abū Tammām[10] but the line is Ibn Abī Ṭāhir's.

[3] His poetry is so famous among the elite and the common folk that we need not record any of it in this book of ours. He has not just one book [but many] composed on the [different] branches of *adab* (literature),

> *akhbār* (historical accounts), and *ayyām* (battledays) which have [all] reached East and West.

The one anecdote Ibn al-Muʿtazz has chosen to include in the Ibn Abī Ṭāhir notice is unmistakably a humorous one. It has Abū Ḥakīmah declaring that Ibn Abī Ṭāhir cannot be surpassed in his elegy on the penis. That the lines are an elegy on such a subject, rather than on a kinsman, murdered heroes, or a patron, is particularly amusing. It was in fact common for the *muḥdath* (modern/ist) poet to write on newer subjects or for them to engage in parody. Though he overstates matters somewhat, Abu Deeb captures the newness of the modern(ist) poets when he writes:[11]

> Here, for the first time, we witness the involvement of poetry in everyday life, in experiences by which older standards were mundane and outside the domain of poetry. Here also we see the dominance of a modern sensibility. But, perhaps more significantly, we also see an excellent representation of the work and lives of poets who were genuine rebels, total outsiders. . . .

The humor of the anecdote does not appear intended in any way to debase the poetic abilities of Ibn Abī Ṭāhir. Indeed, it, and the notice generally, may be read in light of Abu Deeb's comments as an illustration of the modern sensibility of both Ibn al-Muʿtazz as anthologist and Ibn Abī Ṭāhir as a modern/ist poet.

The opinion of the famous modern/ist panegyrist Abū Tammām (d. 231/845), quoted for his congratulation of Ibn Abī Ṭāhir on having composed the verses, confers upon Ibn Abī Ṭāhir further "prestige." It is also evidence of the association between Abū Tammām and Ibn Abī Ṭāhir, an association that is later confirmed by the court-companion and anthologist al-Ṣūlī (d. 335/946) in the *Akhbār Abī Tammām* [Accounts of Abū Tammām]. Abū Tammām is in fact himself the subject of two important works by Ibn Abī Ṭāhir, the *Kitāb Sariqāt al-Buḥturī ʿan Abī Tammām* [The borrowings/plagiarisms of al-Buḥturī from Abū Tammām] and the *Kitāb Sariqāt Abī Tammām* [The borrowings/plagiarisms of Abū Tammām]. Both these works are lost but references to and very short passages from the former are quoted in later works (see chapter 4 below).

Ibn al-Muʿtazz's esteem for the literary abilities of Ibn Abī Ṭāhir is clear from the latter's inclusion in his collection. Those abilities are underscored in the second part of the notice. Here, Ibn al-Muʿtazz dispels the misconception that a particular line is attributable to Abū Tammām, asserting that it is in fact by Ibn Abī Ṭāhir. Just as there is no mistaking the humor in the anecdote at the beginning of the notice, so there is no mistaking the implication of this correction: that Ibn Abī Ṭāhir's verse is good enough to be attributed to the great Abū Tammām. It is worth noting that the misconception/misattribution dates from the time of Ibn al-Muʿtazz's writing. There is scholarly disagreement about the date of composition of the *Classes of modern poets*, but after 285/898, or some time between 293/905 and 296/908, are the most likely.[12] The misattribution, presumably of the transmitters, thus persisted until forty years after the death of Abū Tammām (231/845), and several years after the death of Ibn Abī Ṭāhir (280/893). The date of composition of the *Classes of modern poets* is also significant in connection with the fame attributed by Ibn al-Muʿtazz to Ibn Abī Ṭāhir's poetry in his closing passage. Ibn al-Muʿtazz states clearly that Ibn Abī Ṭāhir's poems are very popular, so popular, in fact, that Ibn al-Muʿtazz does not see the need to record any of them. He makes a similar statement regarding Abū Nuwās, quoting only those verses little known to the ordinary readership (*al-ʿawāmm*):[13] there is thus no reason to read this statement as a literary conceit or a way to dismiss Ibn Abī Ṭāhir's poetry.[14]

That Ibn Abī Ṭāhir was regarded a modern/ist poet is established by his presence in the *Classes of modern poets*. That he was a popular poet is stated outright by Ibn al-Muʿtazz. Judging from the two extracts Ibn al-Muʿtazz quotes – and indeed from much of Ibn Abī Ṭāhir's other poetry – it was probably a combination of the wit he displayed in his verses and his modern(ist) sensibilities that guaranteed them wide circulation. Indeed, his verse is widely quoted in later *adab* works, notwithstanding an admittedly limited output.[15]

Ibn Abī Ṭāhir does not appear in the other major extant biographical collection of poets of the third/ninth century, the *Kitāb al-Shiʿr wa-al-shuʿarāʾ* [Book of poetry and poets] by the secretary/encyclopedist Ibn Qutaybah (d. 276/889).[16] Although Ibn Qutaybah argues in his famous introduction to this work for the importance of the merits of individual poets and about intrinsic criteria in the evaluation of poetry, he evidently has his own agenda and is concerned with a particular kind of poetry:[17]

> I have mainly concentrated on the famous poets known to the majority of the men of letters and those whose verses are cited as authorities to explain rare usage, grammar, and the Book of God and the Hadith of the Prophet. As for those whose names are unheard of, who are little-cited, whose poetry does not move briskly on the market (*wa-kasada shiʿruhu*), and who are known only to a few specialists, I mention very few of this category as I know very little about them myself and have little information to add about them.

Thus, although the *Book of poetry and poets* was composed at a time when, on the strength of Ibn al-Muʿtazz's statements, Ibn Abī Ṭāhir was already well-known, Ibn Qutaybah either did not know him or did not consider him worthy of inclusion. Indeed, of the one hundred and twenty-seven poets discussed by Ibn al-Muʿtazz, only twenty-five figure in Ibn Qutaybah's work. The excluded poets are all avowedly modern/ist (*muḥdath*) but other moderns do find their way into Ibn Qutaybah's collection. One prominent poet omitted by Ibn Qutaybah is Abū Tammām. The precise motives for Ibn Qutaybah's exclusions,[18] including Ibn Abī Ṭāhir – if Ibn Qutaybah considered him a poet at all – cannot be confirmed.[19] One explanation may be that whereas Ibn al-Muʿtazz was a poet and a specialist of literature, Ibn Qutaybah, by his own admission ("I mention very few of this category as I know very little about them myself and have little information to add about them"), was not. He was, rather, a conservative bureaucrat with a special interest in religious matters. This explains why poets whose verses are helpful in scriptural exegesis are of particular interest to him. Ibn Qutaybah's so-called reconsideration of the status of poetry, giving primacy to the poetry rather than to the personalities, is thus more complex an issue than it first appears.[20]

Al-Masʿūdī (d. 345/946), who is the only writer to preserve Ibn Abī Ṭāhir's elegy on the crucified Shiite rebel, Abū al-Ḥusayn Yaḥyā ibn ʿUmar, calls Ibn Abī Ṭāhir a poet outright ("the poet, Aḥmad Ibn Abī Ṭāhir").[21] Al-Marzubānī (d. 384/994), for his part, devotes an entry to Ibn Abī Ṭāhir in his works on poets and their output, *al-Muwashshaḥ fī maʾakhidh al-ʿulamāʾ ʿalā al-shuʿarāʾ* [The Embroidered (treatise) on the scholars' borrowings from poets].[22] Al-Khaṭīb al-Baghdādī (d. 463/1071), and Yāqūt (d. 626/1229) reprising him, write that Ibn Abī Ṭāhir was "a man of eloquence, a poet, and a transmitter/narrator, someone endowed with understanding and celebrated for knowledge" (*aḥad al-bulaghāʾ al-shuʿarāʾ al-ruwāt min ahl al-fahm al-madhkūrīn bi-al-ʿilm*).[23] In *Siyar aʿlām al-nubalāʾ* [Lives of the noble notables], al-Dhahabī (d. 748/1348) drops the identification *rāwī* (which is curious as Ibn Abī Ṭāhir is most certainly a transmitter/narrator), retaining man of eloquence and poet, and cites two verses.[24] In *al-Iʿlān bi-al-tawbīkh li-man dhamma al-taʾrīkh* [The public castigation of those engaged in History's fustigation], al-Sakhāwī (d. 902/1497), who includes Ibn Abī Ṭāhir because of his history of Baghdad, immediately draws attention to his poetic and prose abilities in the micro-biography he reserves for him late in the work, calling attention to his accomplishment both in poetry and in prose by describing him as "one of the master poets and of the leading prose writers" (*aḥad fuḥūl al-shuʿarāʾ wa-aʿyān al-bulaghāʾ*).[25] Al-Sakhāwī then goes on to cite the same two verses as al-Dhahabī (on whom he likely relied).

Ibn al-Nadīm (d. 385/995), who is an early and informative biographer of Ibn Abī Ṭāhir, does not, however, identify Ibn Abī Ṭāhir as a poet. On the contrary, the first anecdote he cites in his notice on him includes the opinion of the celebrated poet al-Buḥturī that Ibn Abī Ṭāhir was unable to craft a single line of adequate verse, that he was a plagiarist, and that his language and diction were ungrammatical and corrupt:[26]

> I have never seen anyone as famous as he [Ibn Abī Ṭāhir] because of the books he composed and because of the poetry he recited whose speech was more corrupt (*akthar taṣḥīfan*), whose mind was more slow-witted (*ablad ʿilman*), and whose language was more ungrammatical (*alḥan*). He recited some poetry to me about Isḥāq ibn Ayyūb and made grammatical errors in it in more than ten places. What is more, no-one plagiarised more than he did (*asraq al-nās*), half a line, or even a third of a line.

None of Ibn Abī Ṭāhir's poetry that survives reveals any of the imputed corruptions; the biographers uniformly refer to him as eloquent; and it is fairly clear that he made a career of writing and teaching. But, as there was no love lost between al-Buḥturī and Ibn Abī Ṭāhir, the credibility of the allegations can be called into question. Indeed, Ibn Abī Ṭāhir leveled similar accusations at al-Buḥturī and even wrote a satire on the subject when al-Buḥturī accused him of plagiarism.[27]

No *dīwān* of Ibn Abī Ṭāhir exists and none is mentioned in the sources.[28] Ibn al-Nadīm, who is in general well-informed about exisiting *dīwān*s and about Ibn Abī Ṭāhir, makes no mention of one in *The Catalog*. On the other hand, Ibn Abī Ṭāhir's friend and associate Abū Hiffān, described by Ibn al-Muʿtazz as widely and often cited, and whose poetry is described as widely disseminated (*mawjūd fī kull makān*), also left no *dīwān*.[29] In the case of poets whose *dīwān*s either do not survive or did not exist, it is fortunate that later, and sometimes contemporary, writers anthologised them. Examples of such anthologies are the *Kitāb al-Zahrah* [Book of the Flower] of Ibn Dāwūd (d. 297/909), the *Kitāb al-Tuḥaf wa-al-hadāyā* [Book of gifts and bequests] of the Khālidī brothers (d. 380/990 and 391/1001), and *al-Maṣūn fī al-adab* [The Well-grounded (book) on literature] of Abū Aḥmad al-ʿAskarī (d. after 382/993). The poetry of Ibn Abī Ṭāhir caught the attention of these other anthologists. In this regard, the *Kitāb al-Zahrah* [Book of the Flower] is particularly valuable: were it not for that collection – significantly, by someone who was in scholarly contact with Ibn Abī Ṭāhir[30] – seventy nine of the extant lines of Ibn Abī Ṭāhir's poetry would not have survived, as those seventy nine lines are preserved in the *Book of the Flower* alone.

The anthologist al-Ḥusayn ibn Muḥammad al-Rāghib al-Iṣfahānī (d. early fifth/eleventh century) quotes Ibn Abī Ṭāhir extensively (twenty-nine selections) in his florilegium, *The ready replies of the littérateurs*, and even praises his poetry.[31] Al-Rāghib's critical appreciation was echoed by a number of prominent medieval literary critics. The anthologist and critic Abū Hilāl al-ʿAskarī (d. after 395/1005), for example, quotes four lines of verse by Ibn Abī Ṭāhir in the section on *taṭrīz* (poetic embroidery) in his famous handbook of rhetoric for aspiring writers, the *Kitāb al-Ṣināʿatayn al-kitābah wa-al-shiʿr* [Book of the two crafts: prose and poetry].[32] The short introduction preceding Ibn Abī Ṭāhir's lines reads as follows:[33]

> It [= *taṭrīz*] is when words of equal measure occur in the consecutive lines of verse. The embroidery in the poem is then like the embroidery in clothing. This device is rare in poetry. The best examples of it, though, are the words of Ibn Abī Ṭāhir:

Idhā Abū Aḥmada jādat lanā yaduhu
    lam yuḥmadi ʾl-ajwadāni al-baḥru wa ʾl-maṭaru
wa-in aḍāʾat lanā anwāru ghurratihi
    taḍāʾala ʾl-anwarāni: ʾsh-shamsu wa ʾl-qamaru

Wa-in maḍā ra'yuhū aw ḥadda ʿazmatuhu
ta'akhkhara 'l-māḍiyāni 's-sayfu wa 'l-qadaru
Man lam yakun ḥadhiran min ḥaddi ṣawlatihi
lam yadri mā 'l-muzʿijāni 'l-khawfu wa 'l-ḥadharu

When Abū Aḥmad extends
generosity to us, openhanded
Even the two benefactors, Rain and Sea are bestèd.

When we,
by his blazon are illuminated
Even the two great blazes, Sun and Moon, are eclipsèd.

And when his views are honed
and his sharp resolve and will expressed
The two blades, Sword and Fate, are far surpassèd.

Whoever is unwary
of the sheer blade-edge of his force
Goes unwarned of the two arousers, Fear and Dread.

Al-ʿAskarī quotes the same lines in the section on panegyric (*madīḥ*) in his *Dīwān al-maʿānī* [Anthology of motifs], a collection of elegant and original expressions and motifs in both poetry and prose. They are in turn quoted by Aḥmad ibn ʿAbd al-Wahhāb al-Nuwayrī (d. 732/1332) in the *Nihāyat al-arab fī funūn al-adab* [The Desire of the hearts in culture's arts].[34]

The major fourth/tenth century critic Ibn Ṭabāṭabā (d. 322/934) was also impressed by these lines. He cites them as an example of "Poetry which hones understanding and alleviates worry" in his influential *ʿIyār al-shiʿr* [The Gauge of poetry]:[35]

> Poetry such as this [referring to a preceding example], and the problems from which it suffers, clouds [lit. rusts] understanding and causes distress [also: makes things obscure], unlike the following by Ibn Abī Ṭāhir, which strengthens [lit. hones] understanding and alleviates worry.

After the verses, Ibn Ṭabātabā adds, "This poetry is limpid and free of contamination (*lā kadar fīh*)".

At the close of the section entitled "On the description of horses" (*Fī ṣifāt al-khayl*) in the *Anthology of motifs*, al-ʿAskarī quotes three other lines by Ibn Abī Ṭāhir.[36] The anthologist has just quoted several descriptions in prose (e.g. by al-Naẓẓām and Jaʿfar ibn Yaḥyā) and poetry (by Ibn Munādhir[37]) but then adds Ibn Abī Ṭāhir's lines:

Juʿiltu fidāka qad amsā ḥimārī
lahū sarjun wa-laysa lahū lijāmū
Ka-mithli ʾl-ʿāṭili ʾl-ḥasnāʾi amsat
lahā ḥalyun wa-laysa lahā niẓāmū

Oh, might I be made your ransom! My donkey is jaded.
He has a saddle, but has no rein.

Just like a beauty bereft. In her twilight
She has pearls, but has no chain.

In his anthology, the *Khizānat al-adab* [The repository of culture] ʿAbd al-Qāhir al-Baghdādī (d. 486/1093), citing al-Ṣūlī, writes that Ibn Abī Ṭāhir is a poet who ably uses the value of a particular individual's friendships after having tested others' as a motif in his poetry. Ibn Abī Ṭāhir's lines are:[38]

Balawtu ʾn-nāsa fī sharqin wa-gharbin
wa-mayyaztu ʾl-kirāma min al-liʾāmī
Fa-raddaniya ʾbtilāya ilā ʿAliyyi b-
ni Yaḥyā baʿda tajrībī ʾl-anāmī

I put to the test
People from the East and West
And I distinguished the noble from the rest.

But my testing only
Sent me back to ʿAlī
After examining all of humanity.

Al-Baghdādī makes no explicit critical pronouncements about the lines in question, but does imply that they are a fine example of the use of the motif.

Judging from what has survived of the poetic output of patronized poets over six thousand lines of al-Buḥturī's verse are extant, for example, it would appear that it was not only ability that was an indicator of one's success, but that success may also have been an indication of one's ability. In the case of "majors," such as Abū Tammām, Abū Nuwās and al-Buḥturī, their position is evidently a function of the high quality of some of their poetry in spite of verdicts – in the case of Abū Tammām, centuries-long debate – to the contrary. In the case of "minors," however, the absence of long and lucrative associations with benevolent patrons can help explain their minor status. This, and other questions relating to patronage, such as the relationship to it, if any, of fame, success, and literary survival, have yet to be adequately examined.[39] The very distinction major/minor reflects issues around the constitution of canon.[40]

What is clear about Ibn Abī Ṭāhir, and other poets like him, is that their poetry does not constitute an exclusive source of livelihood – they are not professional, patronized poets.[41]

The possibility of otherwise earning one's keep obviated the need to produce poetry for patrons. This did not prevent their poetry from becoming known, quoted and commented upon; and it did not prevent these poets from rubbing shoulders with the established, patronized ones. But it does appear to mean that their *dīwāns* had less chance of survival; and also that this could create animosities between the "major" poets, and the "minor" ones, the former finding the latter objectionable, in their choice of language, of subject, and of occasion.

Ibn Abī Ṭāhir, Transmitter/Narrator

Ibn Abī Ṭāhir is described by most biographers as a *rāwī* (reciter/transmitter of poetry; transmitter; narrator; pl. *ruwāt*). Al-Khaṭīb al-Baghdādī writes in the opening phrase of his notice that he is to be counted as "one of the eloquent prose stylists, poets, and transmitter/narrators" (*aḥad al-bulaghāʾ al-shuʿarāʾ al-ruwāt*); Yāqūt repeats this verbatim.[42] Other biographers omit this identification. Al-Sakhāwī has only "one of the premier poets and leading prose stylists" (*aḥad fuḥūl al-shuʿarāʾ wa-aʿyān al-bulaghāʾ*).[43]

Ibn Abī Ṭāhir does recite and transmit the verse of other poets, e.g. al-Nābighah al-Dhubyānī (fl. sixth centuy CE) and Abū Nuwās (d. *c.* 198/813) in al-Marzubānī's *The Embroidered (treatise)*,[44] but that recitation is more often than not evidential. The one noteworthy exception is in the *Book of the Flower*, where Ibn Dāwūd quotes Ibn Abī Ṭāhir's transmissions of Abū Tammām nine times, and of Majnūn, Ṭufayl al-Ghanawī, Abū Diʿāmah, ʿUbaydallāh ibn ʿAbdallāh ibn Ṭāhir, Abū Hiffān, and Ibrāhīm ibn al-ʿAbbās once each.[45] An example of evidential citation is illustrated by the following anecdote:[46]

> A [certain] poet used to call upon Yazīd ibn Mazyad every [single] year, so Yazīd said to him, "How much do you require per year?" "Such and such," he replied. Yazīd then said, "Stay at home and it will be despatched to you: don't weary yourself coming here." When Yazīd died, he elegized him with the following lines; the poet is Muslim ibn al-Walīd. *He [al-Juʿfī] said:* Abū al-Ḥasan ibn al-Barāʾ said: Ibn Abī Ṭāhir said to me, "The poet is [in fact] al-Taymī."

The de-emphasis on recitation proper on the part of the transmitter (*rāwī*) is to be expected. El Tayib has observed that the early poets left the elucidation of the meaning of their verses to the *rāwī*s, who acted as commentators to supply detail and the necessary background.[47] In the later case of Ibn Abī Ṭāhir, it seems that this role as a commentator-*rāwī* exceeded and overtook his role as a transmitter-*rāwī*. Put differently, his oral/aural role was transformed into a more writerly one, essentially that of literary historian, literary critic, and biographer. This fundamental role, that of literary biographer and historian, was one assumed also by one of Ibn Abī Ṭāhir's close associates, Abū Hiffān, who compiled an *Akhbār Abī Nuwās* [Accounts of Abū Nuwās], which survives. Ibn Abī Ṭāhir is, for example, an important source of information on Abū Tammām for all later critics; this is especially true for the *Accounts of Abū Tammām* of al-Ṣūlī. And Ibn Abī Ṭāhir is, for example, the sole authority cited for information about the otherwise unknown ʿAlī ibn Wahb al-Muzanī.[48]

In their roles as *rāwī*-commentators, individuals such as Ibn Abī Ṭāhir evinced other related interests. Ibn Abī Ṭāhir's own writerly pursuits extended to include three overlapping areas, (1) anthology (*ikhtiyār*), (2) biography (*akhbār*), and (3) plagiarism (*sariqah*). This is borne out by surviving works and extracts, and by the titles of his lost works. Besides the *Book of prose and poetry* his anthologies include the *Kitāb Ikhtiyār ashʿār al-shuʿarāʾ* [The selection of the poetry of (various) poets], and several selections, seven by individual poets – Imruʾ al-Qays (fl. sixth century CE), Bakr ibn al-Naṭṭāḥ (d. 222/837), al-ʿAttābī (d. after 208/823), Manṣūr al-Namarī (d. 190/805), Abū al-ʿAtāhiyah (d. 211/826), Muslim ibn al-Walīd (d. *c.* 207/823), and Diʿbil (d. 246/860) – and one of *rajaz*-metre verse.[49]

In the case of some poets, Ibn Abī Ṭāhir combines biography and anthology, e.g. the *Kitāb al-Jāmiʿ fī al-shuʿarāʾ wa-akhbārihim* [The compendium on poets and accounts about them]. He produced similar works on Bashshār ibn Burd (d. *c.* 167/864), Marwān (d. *c.* 182/798) and the Marwānids, Ibn Harmah al-Qurashī (d. 176/792), and Ibn Qays al-Ruqayyāt (d. *c.* 80/699). On Ibn Mayyādah (d. 146/763), Ibn Munādhir (d. *c.* 199/814), Ibn al-Dumaynah (fl. second/eighth century), and Abū al-ʿAynāʾ (d. *c.* 283/896) he produced *akhbār*-only works, that is accounts without the accompanying poetry.[50] Needless to stress, the *Book of Baghdad* and numerous other works are works consisting primarily of historical and literary accounts (*akhbār*). It is in works such as these that Ibn Abī Ṭāhir's role as *rāwī* in its meaning of *akhbār*-transmitter is evident. His works on borrowings include the general work, *Kitāb Sariqāt al-shuʿarāʾ* [The Borrowings/Plagiarisms of the poets], and specific works about the borrowings/plagiarisms of Abū Tammām, and of al-Buḥturī from Abū Tammām.

Ibn al-Nadīm does not identify Ibn Abī Ṭāhir as a narrator/transmitter (*rāwī*) per se in his notice in *The Catalog*, but he has already characterized the individuals in the section to which Ibn Abī Ṭāhir is assigned as "the narrators of accounts, the genealogists, and the chroniclers and biographers" (*al-akhbāriyyīn wa-al-nassābīn wa-aṣḥāb al-aḥdāth wa-al-āyāt*).[51] This subsumes *rāwī*, underscoring in particular its meaning as "narrator." In his modern notice, Āzarnūsh calls Ibn Abī Ṭāhir an *akhbārī*.[52] And, indeed, it is in this sense – and via *akhbār* collections – that he has come to be identified as a historian. However, Ibn Abī Ṭāhir is also an important transmitter of *akhbār* transmitted by others, as al-Ṣūlī's *Accounts of Abū Tammām* shows. In the section devoted to what Abū Tammām transmitted in al-Ṣūlī's work, twenty-one out of twenty-three transmissions are on Ibn Abī Ṭāhir's direct authority.[53] Al-Ṣūlī also quotes a report in which Ibn Abī Ṭāhir asks Abū Tammām whether he has someone specific in mind when he composed a certain verse: this is, of course, in keeping with the role of the commentator-*rāwī*.[54] Arazi has recognized Ibn Abī Ṭāhir's importance as *rāwī*, averring:[55]

> Ibn Abī Ṭāhir Ṭayfūr can be considered to be the *rāwiyah* who, more than any other, defined the elements constitutive of a classical approach, one of the most important stimuli of the massive movement of written redaction. He is part of the third generation of transmitters, the generation after al-Aṣmaʿī, one of poetic codification and of the appearance of theoretical works.

As I adumbrated in chapter 1 above, the decision to write books exposing plagiarism is a "literary" or writerly one. It would seem that by the time Ibn Abī Ṭāhir was writing, *sariqah* had been transformed from a term implying literary borrowing to one implying theft and plagiarism proper.[56] This change was occasioned by writerly and book-based concerns such as unambiguous attribution and the proprietorship of words.[57] Indeed, Ibn Abī Ṭāhir appears to be the first critic to address Abū Tammām's and al-Buḥturī's plagiarisms[58] and thus may mark the starting point of the comparison between them[59] – a comparison that would engender a tremendous amount of discussion and epitomize the struggle within the literary-critical establishment to come to terms with the two kinds of poetry each represented. The views developed in this context were then developed further and applied to al-Mutanabbī (d. 354/965), which in part explains the existence of works dealing with his "plagiarisms." The close relationship of al-Mutanabbī's poetic output to the poetry and plagiarisms of Abū Tammām and al-Buḥturī is apparent in later works on al-Mutanabbī, such as the *Ṣubḥ al-munabbī ʿan ḥaythiyyat al-Mutanabbī* [The prophecy of the bright morning on al-Mutanabbī's high standing] of Yūsuf al-Badīʿī (d. 1073/1662). The first two short sections are about al-Mutanabbī and the next two about al-Buḥturī's first encounter with Abū Tammām and their relations. Even the opening line of the section entitled "Views of Learned Men about the Poetry of Mutanabbī" is expressed in terms of the earlier poets.[60]

One of the earliest uses of the word *sariqāt* in a work devoted to the subject is in the *Kitāb Sariqāt al-Kumayt min al-Qur'ān* [The Borrowings of al-Kumayt from the Quran] of Ibn Kunāsah (d. 207/823).[61] As plagiarism implies an attempt to pass something off as one's own, the term *sariqāt* in Ibn Kunāsah's title must mean, rather than plagiarism, the borrowing of phrases and motifs, which anyone with knowledge of the Quran would be able to discern; it is unlikely that al-Kumayt was trying to pass off Quranic expressions and motifs as his own. The title would thus best be rendered "The creative literary borrowings from the Quran of the poet al-Kumayt." Wolfhart Heinrichs has shown that the translations "plagiarism" for *sariqah* and "plagiarisms" for *sariqāt* with respect to the poetry of the modern poets (*muḥdathūn*) is also inadequate given that that poetry's "most basic prerequisite is intertextuality," and "reference … to predecessors in the literary past."[62] For Heinrichs, *sariqah* is perhaps best understood as a "raid," sometimes illicit and sometimes incognito, but often legitimate, warranted, and in the open. Heinrichs' observation about the acceptability of the raid should be reconsidered as an important characteristic of the literary culture. Raiding a superior camp may, for instance, confer prestige on one's own.[63]

In Arabic literary critical terminology there is a distinct term for a "borrowing" (*akhdh*) as opposed to outright plagiarism (*sariqah*). Writing about a line by Abū Nuwās, said by Muhalhil ibn Yamūt (fl. fourth/tenth century) to be borrowed (*ma'khūdh*; "indebted to"?) from another line by Kuthayyir (d. 105/723), al-Jurjānī observes "Should we say it is borrowed from him or should we consider it plagiarism?" (*A-kunnā naqūl innahu ma'khūdh minhu aw kunna naʿudduhu sariqah*).[64] Some writers were, in effect, perfectly content to borrow the words of others. In one anecdote, the secretary Saʿīd ibn Ḥumayd uses the motifs and language of Ibn Abī Ṭāhir in a letter he is composing to Ismāʿīl ibn Bulbul.[65] Ibn Abī Ṭāhir himself is reported to have observed, "Were Saʿīd's speech and poetry to be told, 'Go back to where you came from [lit. to your people],' Saʿīd would be left with nothing at all."[66]

Ibn Abī Ṭāhir, teller of tales

How the narrator/transmiter (*rāwī*) went from simply being a transmitter/commentator of poetry to becoming *also* a collector/transmitter of other kinds of accounts has been discussed earlier. Leaving Hadith collectors and transmitters aside (that is, persons interested only or primarily in Prophetic traditions), it is easy to see how collectors of biographical, historical, and literary information, such as Ibn Abī Ṭāhir, Abū Hiffān and others, begin to acquire multiple roles and developing multiple narrative interests.

Ibn Abī Ṭāhir demonstrates just such interests. His interest in history was not purely the interest of a chronicler but that of a cultural and literary historian. Added to this was an interest in his own native culture, that of Iran in general, and Khurāsān in particular. The surviving portion of *Book of Baghdad*, covering the caliphate of al-Ma'mūn, dwells at length on the Khurasanian Ṭāhirids. Ibn Abī Ṭāhir includes the text of a letter from al-Ṭāhir ibn al-Ḥusayn to his son ʿAbdallāh in this account, one that has rightly been described as an early "mirror for princes" work.[67] The presence of a *Fürstenspiegel* work in the *Book of Baghdad* comes as no surprise. Ibn Abī Ṭāhir's interest in Iranian culture and wisdom literature is corroborated by another professional activity of his, namely storytelling.[68]

Ibn Abī Ṭāhir's storytelling activity has, however, attracted the attention of no medieval or modern biographer – including the meticulous Iranian scholar Āzarnūsh – in spite of Ibn al-Nadīm's explicit identification of Ibn Abī Ṭāhir as one of the persons who wrote fables (*khurāfāt*) and evening stories (*asmār*):[69]

> [T]he bookmen composed and made up fictional stories. One of the persons who did this (*yaftaʿilu*) was a man known as Ibn Dallān/Dīlān.

> Another was known as Ibn al-ʿAṭṭār, and there were others. We have already mentioned above those who composed (*kāna yaʿmalu*) fables and evening stories told through the mouths of animals and other creatures [e.g. humans, *jinn*]. They are Sahl ibn Hārūn, ʿAlī ibn Dāwūd, al-ʿAttābī, and *Aḥmad Ibn Abī Ṭāhir.*

This passage appears in the first part (*fann*) of the eigth section (*maqālah*) of *The Catalog.* The section is entitled "Accounts of the scholars and titles of the books they composed" (*Fī akhbār al-ʿulamāʾ wa-asmāʾ mā ṣannafūhu min al-kutub*) and the first part is entitled "Accounts of the evening storytellers and fabulists and the titles of (evening) story and fable books" (*Fī akhbār al-musāmirīn wa-al-mukharrifīn wa-asmāʾ al-kutub al-muṣannafah fī al-asmār wa-al-khurāfāt*). Ibn Abī Ṭāhir may be grouped with altogether four other named individuals. In addition to Sahl ibn Hārūn, ʿAlī ibn Dāwūd, and al-ʿAttābī from the passage quoted above, Ibn al-Nadīm names Ibn al-Muqaffaʿ in an earlier passage.[70]

That this section of *The Catalog* has not been mined extensively for the information it contains is regrettable. Macdonald scrutinized it in a 1924 article, and the titles of the books mentioned in this section (and elsewhere) in *The Catalog*, were briefly analyzed by M. F. Ghazi in a 1957 article.[71] Ghazi lists altogether two hundred and forty-two works of imaginative literature, including romances, and names about twenty authors of such literature, omitting Ibn Abī Ṭāhir (and al-ʿĀttābī) even as he identifies the others with whom Ibn Abī Ṭāhir is grouped by Ibn al-Nadīm:[72]

> According to the *Fihrist*, fables flourished at the hands of three authors: ʿAbdallāh Ibn al-Muqaffaʿ, Sahl ibn Hārūn and ʿAlī ibn Dāwūd.

Ghazi does write that:[73]

> other writers of far more modest backgrounds also cultivated this imaginative literature ... *warrāq*s, copyists and booksellers, a greedy lot in search of paltry profits and whose zeal can obviously be explained by their love of lucre.

It is true that Ibn al-Nadīm's phrase, "*wa-ṣannafa al-warrāqūn wa-kadhabū ... wa-mimman yaftaʿilu*," conveys disapproval of the copyists' activities. The *taṣnīf* (composition, compilation; also invention) of the bookmen is decried by others too, as is their *kadhb* (lie, fabrication; also fiction?).[74] The use of *iftaʿala* also signals a negative evaluation. It is a verb usually used in connection with *kadhib* (lie), as in "*iftaʿala ʿalayhi kadhiban*," meaning "he forged a lie against him," and is to be found in the phrase "*al-khuṭūṭ tuftaʿal*," "handwritings are forged or falsified."[75] But it is also the origin of such sayings as "*aʿdhab al-aghānī mā ʾftuʿila*," "the sweetest song is the one composed with originality, not in imitation," and "*aẓraf al-shiʿr mā ʾftuʿila*," where the implications are clearly not negative.[76]

Pellat is correct in observing that Ibn al-Nadīm contrasts *khurāfah* and *samar*, but Ibn al-Nadīm also specifically pairs the two terms. In Ibn al-Nadīm's usage, *khurāfah* does seem to suggest fictitiousness or fictionality but it is also used to translate the Persian *afsāna* (tale, fable). Ibn al-Nadīm writes:[77]

> The first people to compose fables (*khurāfāt*), put them into books, and store these in libraries, were the early Persians. They later composed these fables with talking animals. The next people to become absorbed by fables were the Ashkanian [= Parthian] kings, the third dynasty of Persian rulers. This [interest] grew and became more widespread in the time of the Sasanian kings. The Arabs translated them into Arabic whereupon masters of literary style and eloquence took them up, improving upon them and refining them, and composing similar works on this subject. The first book written on this subject was the *Hazār Afsāna* which means *A Thousand Fables.*

Khurāfah is said to have been the given name of a man from pre-Islamic times who claimed to have been carried off by demons. When he told stories of his adventure nobody believed him and the phrase "*ḥadīth Khurāfah*" (story [worthy] of Khurāfah) came into being, meaning "utterly fictitious talk."[78] The Prophet Muḥammad, however, vouched for the existence of the character and the veracity of his accounts.[79] Khurāfah may also simply derive from the verb *kharifa*, meaning "to be senile" or "to talk nonsense." If *khurāfāt* later unequivocally meant *anything* fictitious, it is clear that in the fourth/tenth century usage of al-Masʿūdī and Ibn al-Nadīm, it meant something quite specific. Al-Masʿūdī uses *khurāfah* both to translate the Persian *afsāna* in his passage on the *Thousand and One Nights* and uses it also to indicate pagan/pre-Islamic myths.[80] The terms *ḥikāyah*, *ḥadīth*, and *khabar* were, it is true, interchangeable by the eighth/fourteenth century in the broad meaning of story.[81] But in earlier times, the terms, as well as the vocations of the collectors, were different, often discrete. The diversity of storytelling terms is an indication that "tales, legends and stories of all kinds were in vogue [in the first centuries] and that they were distinguished from one another with great precision."[82]

Samar (pl. *asmār*) means soirée, evening story, evening entertainment, night session. From it derive words such as *sāmir*, companion,[83] its plural *summār*, evening companions,[84] *musāmirūn*, evening storytellers, *musāmarāt*, evening discourse,[85] and *tasāmur*, exchange of evening stories.[86] The nature of the *samar* is captured in a number of remarks made by eminent patrons and writers and in the titles of certain classic works of *adab*. Al-Ṣāḥib Ibn ʿAbbād is reported to have said, "We are the sovereign by day, but by night we are brothers all,"[87] underscoring the egalitarian atmosphere that obtained. This suggests that a broad spectrum of people attended the night sessions. Al-Tawḥīdī's *Kitāb al-Imtāʿ wa-al-muʾānasah* [Delight and entertainment] is purportedly a "record" of conversations held on such evenings.

Abbott long ago cautioned against the (scholarly) tendency to consider the night sessions trivial or worldly, thereby overlooking "the fact that from the start some statesmen and scholars devoted part of the night to serious literary and religious discussions."[88] Ibn al-Nadīm himself points out:[89]

> The fact is – God willing – that the first person to devote the night to evening stories was Alexander. He had a group (*qawm*) who made him laugh and listen to fables. He did not do this for amusement alone, but also for the sake of preserving [them]. In this way, some of the kings who came after him also used the *Hazār Afsāna* which included a thousand nights, but less than two hundred stories as each story was told over several nights. I have seen it in its entirety several times. It is truly a shabby and stupid book.

Ibn al-Nadīm continues:[90]

> Al-Jahshiyārī, the author of the *Book of ministers* (*Kitāb al-Wuzarā'*), began compiling a book for which he selected a thousand evening stories (*asmār*) from the stories of the Arabs, Persians, Greeks, and others. Each division (*juz'*) [= night? story?] was self-contained, unconnected with any other section. He convoked the evening storytellers and obtained from them the best of what they knew and in which they excelled. He [also] selected whatever he found agreeable in books devoted to evening stories (*asmār*) and fables (*khurāfāt*). He was [an] accomplished [scholar] and was able to assemble four hundred and eighty of the nights. Each night corresponded to one complete evening story consisting of more or less fifty pages. But death overtook him before he was able to accomplish his goal of collecting a thousand nights. I saw a number of sections/stories in the handwriting of Abū al-Ṭayyib, the brother of al-Shāfi'ī.[91]
>
> Before this, those who composed evening stories and fables told through the mouths of people, birds, and beasts consisted of a group that included 'Abdallāh Ibn al-Muqaffa', Sahl ibn Hārūn (ibn Rāhiyūn) [sic], and 'Alī ibn Dāwūd, the secretary of Zubaydah, among others. We have dealt with the accounts of these authors and what they composed in appropriate sections of this book.

Al-Jahshiyārī died in 331/942, and thus probably collected from the *musāmirūn* late in the third/ninth and/or early in the fourth/tenth centuries. Al-Jahshiyārī's collection, which Ibn al-Nadīm says he saw in one recension, is not extant. Of al-Jahshiyārī's works, only the *Kitāb al-Wuzarā' wa-al-kuttāb* [Book of ministers and secretaries] survives: sections of this work are quoted in other works, e.g. by Yāqūt in the Ibn Abī Ṭāhir notice in the *Irshād al-arīb* [The guide for the intelligent].[92]

It is not known whether al-Jahshiyārī knew, or had even met, Ibn Abī Ṭāhir who was much his senior, but certainly probable that the latter was anthologized by al-Jahshiyārī as Ibn al-Nadīm appears to name only the most accomplished and well-known storytellers.

Ibn al-Nadīm also records the titles of the storytellers' books. In so doing, he provides us with the titles of books he had read, seen, heard, or read about, and those in, or originally in, Arabic. He does not name any soirée or fable books by Ibn Abī Ṭāhir in section eight of *The Catalog*, but he does, in the Ibn Abī Ṭāhir notice, mention the following four works:[93]

1 *Kitāb Tarbiyat Hurmuz ibn Kisrā Anūshirwān*
[The education of Hurmuz ibn Kisrā Anūshirwān];
2 *Kitāb Khabar al-malik al-ʿālī fī tadbīr al-mamlakah wa-al-siyāsah*
[The account of the great king and the management and administration of the kingdom];
3 *Kitāb al-Malik al-muṣliḥ wa-al-wazīr al-muʿīn*
[(The story of) the virtuous king and the supportive vizier]; and
4 *Kitāb al-Malik al-bābilī wa-al-malik al-miṣrī al-bāghiyayn wa-al-malik al-ḥakīm al-rūmī*
[(The story of) the two tyrannical Babylonian and Egyptian kings and the wise Byzantine king].

These may be what Ibn al-Nadīm has in mind when he refers to Ibn Abī Ṭāhir's fables and evening stories. If Ibn Abī Ṭāhir did recount these stories during evening storytelling sessions, there is no record of it. For Ibn al-Nadīm, these are manifestly books, *written* compositions which were circulated and sold. I shall return to Ibn Abī Ṭāhir and storytelling in chapter 5 below. I turn in the next chapter to Ibn Abī Ṭāhir's other writerly occupations.

4

BEING A BOOKMAN

A contention of this study is that the constitution of the littérateur (*adīb*) of the mid- to late third/ninth century was increasingly influenced and mediated by the new dominance of writerly and book culture. Books and writing were making inroads such that littérateurs now operated in a milieu permeated by the written word. In this chapter I focus on Ibn Abī Ṭāhir as I attempt to show that writing, books and writerly culture influenced the littérateur's professional activities, that is, his trade, occupation, employment, and pursuits.

Ibn Abī Ṭāhir, Teacher

The only known categoric statement about Ibn Abī Ṭāhir's professional activities is one made by Jaʿfar ibn [Muḥammad ibn] Ḥamdān (d. 323/935) in the lost *Kitāb al-Bāhir fī (al-ikhtiyār min) ashʿār al-muḥdathīn* [Book of splendor on (selections of) the poetry of the moderns], quoted by Ibn al-Nadīm in the *Catalog* notice devoted to Ibn Abī Ṭāhir. The passage in question reads as follows (the divisions in square brackets are mine):[1]

> [1] *Innahu kāna muʾaddiba kuttābin ʿāmmi[yya]n* [2] *thumma takhaṣṣaṣa* [3] *wa-jalasa fī sūq al-warrāqīn fī al-jānib al-sharqī*

This passage poses a number of problems. That it emanates from someone possibly hostile to Ibn Abī Ṭāhir need not detain us as there is no reason to assume that the facts have been falsified. At issue, rather, is the precise meaning of the passage in light of the multiple, sometimes technical, discrete meanings of the words *muʾaddib*, *kuttāb*, *ʿāmm/ʿāmmiyyan*, *takhaṣṣaṣa*, and *jalasa*. The slipperiness of this phrase has not escaped scholars, and their translations, interpretations, and decisions reflect some of the different ways in which the constituent words and the statement as a whole may be understood. MacGuckin de Slane translates the passage as follows:[2]

> [He] commenced his career as a low schoolmaster and *kātib*. He then rose to considerable eminence and opened a shop in the book-bazar on the west side of the Tigris.

Clément Huart is more expansive:[3]

> [He] was first of all a teacher, then a private tutor in wealthy families and finally followed the trade of a copyist of manuscripts, for which he opened a shop in the *Sūq al-Warrāqīn*.

Bayard Dodge is more literal and leaves no term untranslated:[4]

> He was first a teacher in a common school, but later did private work, being established at the Paper Workers' Bazaar on the East Side.

And Franz Rosenthal summarizes the passage, as follows:

> He started out as a teacher and eventually took up residence in the bookmen's bazaar in the Eastern quarter of Baghdad.[5]

Literally, a *muʾaddib* is anyone who instructs, technically in proper behavior. As the active participle of *addaba*, it also means one who instructs or imparts *adab*. Notwithstanding Makdisi's suggestion that *muʾaddib* was completely interchangeable with the terms *mukattib* and *muktib* (one who teaches writing), the term *naḥwī* (grammarian), and the term *muʿallim* (one who imparts knowledge [*ʿilm*] = teacher),[6] *muʾaddib* is used almost exclusively to refer to tutors. What kind of teacher/tutor is meant in Ibn Abī Ṭāhir's case is complicated by the fact that *muʾaddib* is in construct with *kuttāb*.

Kuttāb (pl. *katātīb*) means elementary school or writing school.[7] In this meaning it is used interchangeably with *maktab*, also elementary school, but the term *kuttāb*, in this meaning, pre-dates *maktab*.[8] The *kuttāb* was "the most specifically designated institution of learning for subjects of *adab*," a Quran school, a grammar school, a grade school and secondary school, most especially a school where writing was taught and where learning was "dispensed at a higher level than what is normally understood in modern times as elementary."[9] The *maktab/kuttāb* was thus a preparatory school. This preparation began at a young age, around seven years.[10] Further training would take the form of an apprenticeship, private tuition, autodidacticism, and travel.

In his work on teachers, the *Kitāb Ādāb al-muʿallimīn* [On the proper conduct of teachers], Ibn Abī Ṭāhir's contemporary, the North African Ibn Saḥnūn (d. 256/870), identifying the subjects to be studied in a *maktab*, writes:[11]

> They [students] ought to be taught arithmetic, but it is not required ... and poetry, rare words, classical Arabic, penmanship and all of grammar.... The inflection of the Quran is obligatory, so too its vocalization, spelling, beautiful calligraphy, measured reading, and recitation. All these are required. There is no harm in teaching them

> the poetry – free of obscenity – of the early Arabs, and the stories of their deeds, but this is by no means required.

Talas suggests that in Abbasid times educators were divided into two groups, one specializing in Quran instruction, the other in language and literature. This is possible but there is no explicit statement to that effect in the sources.[12] That poetry was in fact taught at the primary/elementary level is confirmed by Ibn Abī Ṭāhir himself. He writes in the introduction to volume twelve of his *Book of prose and poetry* that one reason he does not include the complete texts of the *Muʿallaqāt* poems is their renown, and another reason is that they are the "first thing the children (*al-ṣibyān*) are taught in school."[13] It is probable that he knew this first-hand and actually taught the poems.

If we read the description of Ibn Abī Ṭāhir as "*mu'addiba kuttābin ʿāmmiyan*," *ʿāmmiyyan* modifies *mu'addib*,[14] and thus describes an ordinary or regular tutor (or teacher), very likely one who teaches in a public rather than a private school, perhaps one with numerous students rather than just a select few. If we read "*mu'addiba kuttābin ʿāmmin*," *ʿāmmin* modifies *kuttāb*, and so describes the school rather than the teacher, again a public school rather than a private school, an ordinary rather than a specialised one. In either case, the general sense is similar. De Slane's translation "a low schoolmaster..." reads more commonness into the word *ʿāmm* than is indicated by the phrase, but many disparaging remarks are in fact recorded in the sources about the teaching profession. A few examples will suffice: when he is accused by Ibn Saʿdān of being a Rāfiḍī, the wit Abū al-ʿAynā' calls him "a mere schoolteacher;"[15] an accusation of lack of eloquence on the part of the celebrated grammarian Thaʿlab (d. 290/904) is framed as follows: "[His] method is the method of elementary school teachers (*madhhab al-muʿallimīn*);"[16] and in an early fifth/tenth century collection of popular proverbs, "*Aḥmaq min muʿallim kuttāb*," "Stupider than a schoolteacher," is recorded. In these and other cases, it is *muʿallim*s, teachers, who are being singled out, and not *mu'addib*s, tutors. Ahmed notes this when he points out that it was the teacher, not the tutor (*mu'addib*), who was held in low regard.[17] This underscores the fact of a (qualitative) difference between school teaching and tutoring. Muḥammad ibn Ḥabīb (d. 245/860) disliked both teaching and private tutoring, leaving both professions maintaining that teaching children affected one's mind, even if they were caliphs or their children.[18] But Ibn al-Nadīm is aware of the distinction between *muʿaddib* and *muʿallim*. When describing the littérateur al-Washshā' (d. 325/937), for instance, Ibn al-Nadīm writes "*wa kāna naḥwiyyan muʿalliman li-maktab al-ʿāmmah*,""he was a grammarian, a teacher in a public school."[19]

The juxtaposition of *ʿāmmiyyan/ʿāmmin* with the verb *takhaṣṣaṣa*, and the use by Ibn al-Nadīm (and others) of *ʿāmmī* and *khāṣṣī* to mean Sunni and Shiite respectively, has led some scholars to another reading of "*mu'addib kuttāb ʿammīyan*." In fact, al-Khāqānī, in a two-volume history of the poets of Baghdad, understands the passage in question to refer expressly to Ibn Abī Ṭāhir's sectarian affiliation: "He was a Sunnī schoolteacher and then became a Shiite," where *ʿāmmiyyan* has become *sunniyyan*, and *takhaṣṣaṣa* become *tashayyaʿa*.[20] Ghayyāḍ adopts the same reading and, although it is his own interpretation, imputes this to Ibn al-Nadīm.[21] It is true that Ibn al-Nadīm understands *ʿāmmī* to mean Sunni, and *khāṣṣī* to mean Shiite, but such readings are reserved by him for *fuqahā'* and are unlikely in Ibn Abī Ṭāhir's context (see chapter 5 below).[22] I (along with de Slane, Huart, Dodge and Rosenthal) take "*thumma takhaṣṣaṣa*" to mean that Ibn Abī Ṭāhir "then specialised." This could mean that he became a private tutor and/or that he concentrated on only a few subjects and students. In any event, a transition from the public to the private, and from the general to the specialized, is indicated.

Some scholars have argued that in many instances *khāṣṣah* and *ʿāmmah* imply elite and sub-elite as opposed to elite and the masses respectively.[23] The sub-elite are those people occupying the echelons immediately below those occupied by the caliph, senior military leaders, and government officials. This would include, but would not be limited to, merchants, lawyers, aspiring littérateurs, the wealthy, and foreign or visiting scholars: in short the literate, or would-be literate, bourgeoisie, and the intellectuals. The use of *ʿāmm* in the Ibn al-Nadīm passage would then not refer to the common people but rather to a sub-elite, and *takhaṣṣaṣa* would still refer to the elite. Adopting either of those readings, Dodge's "but later did private work" is admissible (the "but" is unnecessary). Huart believes that Ibn Abī Ṭāhir taught the children of the wealthy. He does not indicate whether this is his interpretation of Ibn Abī Ṭāhir's profession pre- or post-"specialization."[24]

One meaning of *takhaṣṣaṣa* is "to excel" or "to distinguish oneself."[25] De Slane's "He then rose to considerable eminence" depends on this meaning but what he intends by it is unclear. Is he suggesting that Ibn Abī Ṭāhir became well-known and sought after, and that is why he then moved to the Bookmen's Market? Or does he mean that he came to be highly regarded *tout court*? I view Ibn Abī Ṭāhir's "specialization" as coinciding in pertinent ways with his move to the Bookmen's Market: *takhaṣṣaṣa* can, for example, be taken to mean that Ibn Abī Ṭāhir gave specialized instruction in writing. This would include, but not be limited to, the drafting of official correspondence, papers, public speeches, and training in the writing of prose.[26] Another plausible meaning is that Ibn Abī Ṭāhir first taught at a preparatory level and then moved on to what Makdisi calls "graduate studies."[27] In any event, the move and the specialization underscore Ibn Abī Ṭāhir's connection to writing and writerly culture.

It is not clear how much the teacher in a *kuttāb* earned probably somewhere in the range of two and a half to three dinars a month.[28] Often, the teacher's salary consisted of the fees he received from the families of the students. It is possible that he charged different amounts to different families, that he charged one fee, or that it was determined by market forces. The reputation of a teacher permitted him to charge a premium but certainly not as much as a private tutor. Ibn al-Sikkīt (d. *c.* 243/867) taught the children of the poor, then tutored for ten dirhams a lesson.[29] And Hishām ibn Muʿāwiyah (d. 209/824) was paid ten dinars per month to tutor the son of an official.[30] Chancery clerks and private tutors earned far more. The monthly starting salary at a *dīwān* in the mid-third/ninth century was on the average between 10 and 15 dinars.[31] For everyone but the wealthy, living in Baghdad in the third/ninth century was financially burdensome. Sabari estimates that at the beginning of the third/ninth century, one dinar per month had sufficed to maintain an average family whereas one dinar per day was necessary for subsistence by the end of the century. The high cost of living that century is to be noted, especially in 201/822 and 251/865, during the siege of Baghdad, and during the war between al-Mustaʿīn and al-Muʿtazz; in 260/873, the year in which rising prices affected the whole Islamic world; and in 272/885, the year of a price increase caused by al-Ṭāʾī, the farmer-general of revenues, who knowingly obstructed the re-stocking of Baghdad.[32]

Now, Ibn Abī Ṭāhir is described as having *jalasa* in the Bookmen's Market. *Jalasa* means 'to sit,' and from it derive several words connected with educational and literary activity.[33] The one with widest application is *majlis* [pl. *majālis*],[34] the numerous meanings of which include gathering, session, course, literary circle, and academy.[35] In the context of *adab* there were two important types of *majlis*: both were held in the homes of poets and writers,[36] and also in the shops of merchants, namely literary salons, and study-sessions. *Majlis* in fact designated the session (class), the place where that session was held (class 'room'), and the subject of the session and its participants (class/course), who might, by virtue of continued association with a professor or lecturer, turn into a côterie. Examples of *majālis* abound: three examples will suffice. The poet Ibrāhīm Ibn Lankak used to sit (*jalasa*) in the Basra Congregational Mosque where a group of common people (*qawm min al-ʿāmmah*) used to sit with him (*jalasa ilayhi*).[37] The North African poet ʿAbbās ibn Nāṣiḥ al-Thaqafī (d. *c.* 238/852) describes a *majlis* at the home of Abū Nuwās as follows:[38]

> I found al-Ḥasan [= Abū Nuwās] seated (*jālisan*) in a lofty seat surrounded by the aspiring men of letters (*muʾaddibīn*)[39] of Baghdad. . . . I greeted him and took a place (*jalastu*) (=sat) at the edge of the gathering (*majlis*).

Ibn al-Rūmī used to sit (*kāna yajlisu ʿindanā*) in ʿAbdallāh ibn Waṣīf al-Nāshī's shop in Baghdad.[40] The use of the verbs *jalasa maʿa* and *jalasa ʿinda*, like *jalasa ilā* in the passage in *The Catalog* about Ibn Abī Ṭāhir, imply more than just being seated and, as is attested in other instances of the use of *jalasa*, imply circumstances specifically related to the professions of teaching and bookselling. Ibn Abī al-Azhar (fl. third/ninth century) reports:[41]

> I was one day at the *majlis* of Bindār ibn Lirrah al-Karkhī, in the vicinity of his home on ʿAbd al-Raḥīm al-Razzāmī Lane in a shop of one of the *abnāʾ* when a group of his students were present.

For de Slane, a rise in eminence not only accounted for Ibn Abī Ṭāhir's professional move "to the book-bazaar," but also prompted him to open a shop.

Interpreting *jalasa* to mean "he opened a shop" – Huart does so too – is conjectural but attractive because it establishes that Ibn Abī Ṭāhir had a bookshop. Rosenthal's "took up residence" is also attractive because it establishes Ibn Abī Ṭāhir's place of residence, but is also conjectural. Dodge is more circumspect, opting for "being established at the Paper Workers' Bazaar." Although Ibn Abī Ṭāhir may have lived in the Bookmen's Market at some point, the only explicit information in the sources about his place of residence puts him elsewhere. Al-Ṣūlī writes:[42]

> Sawwār ibn Abī Shurāʿah reported to me, saying: "Aḥmad Ibn Abī Ṭāhir came to me one day and said: 'I would like you to thank al-Buḥturi for me. He met me in al-Mukharrim and said to me: '*Did you come from your home in Bāb al-Shām* up to here on foot?'"

Now, if Ibn Abī Ṭāhir did live in the Bookmen's Market and *jalasa* does mean that he held *majālis*, or has some other cognate professional meaning, then Ibn Abī Ṭāhir could have *jalasa* in his home. But even if Ibn Abī Ṭāhir's move was (only) a professional one he may well have held *majālis* at his bookshop.

Indeed, Ibn Abī Ṭāhir's connection to the Bookmen's Market is a fact that has attracted the notice of virtually every biographer and student of his career. Whereas it is nowhere explicitly stated that he became a copyist/bookseller, it has become the opinion of many scholars that he was one.[43] Certainly a move there is most easily explained by a desire to become a bookman (*warrāq*).

Ibn Abī Ṭāhir, Bookman

The word *warrāq* (pl. *warrāqūn*) from *waraqah*, a sheet, describes the individual who engaged in *wirāqah*, that is, who transcribed professionally.[44] By extension, it is the word used to denote scribe, copyist, bookbinder and bookseller, meanings attested in the medieval dictionaries and in *adab* works of the third/ninth century. In the meaning of copyist it is synonymous with the terms *nāsikh* and *nassākh*, both from *nasakha*, to copy. *Warrāq* is also occasionally a synonym for the term *kātib* in the meanings "writer" and "writer of artistic prose."

Paper was introduced some time after 133/751.[45] Its widespread use in government circles has been dated to the time of Barmakid ascendancy, 158–69/775–85, and an operational paper mill is attested for Baghdad by 178/794. Attempts on the part of the caliph al-Muʿtaṣim to manufacture paper in Samarra in 221/836 did not, however, meet with success.[46] By the late second/eighth century – at the very earliest – and certainly by the third/ninth century, the Bookmen's Market of Baghdad, the *sūq al-warrāqīn*, could boast one hundred shops.[47] Le Strange summarizes the various sources as follows:

> From the Ḥarrānī Archway up to the New Bridge over the Ṣarāṭ Canal both sides of the roadway were occupied by the shops of the papersellers

> and booksellers, whose market was in this quarter [= Sharqiyyah], as also on the bridge itself; and this market was called after them the Sūq al-Warrāqīn, more than one hundred booksellers' shops being found there.

By 274/888, the Market was well established. Upon Jaʿfar ibn Aḥmad al-Marwazī's death in Ahwāz that year, his books were brought to Baghdad and sold, Ibn al-Nadīm reports, in the Ṭāq al-Ḥarrānī.[48] In this market, located in the fief or suburb (*qaṭīʿah* or *rabaḍ*) of Waḍḍāḥ, north-east of Karkh,[49] many of the *udabāʾ* would meet to exchange ideas and information, and socialize.[50]

*Warrāq*s who were copyists only were also available for hire and for contract-work and could find employment in several quarters. They were employed by the caliph, not only as employees in government (chancery) service, and in the academies and institutes, such as the *Bayt al-Ḥikmah*, but also for more mundane work. They are specifically mentioned in the budget of the caliph al-Muʿtaḍid (r. 279–89/892–902).[51] A number of writers also had their own personal copyists. Ḥunayn ibn Isḥāq employed a copyist by the name of al-Azraq.[52] Al-Kindī employed a group of copyists (all of whose names followed the same pattern).[53] Al-Jāḥiẓ (d. 285/898), who is credited with an epistle in praise of copyists (*Fī madḥ al-warrāq*) and another censuring them (*Fī dhamm al-warrāq*),[54] had his own copyist.[55] Similarly, the philologist Ibn Durayd (d. 322/934) had a *warrāq* who came to be known as al-Duraydī, after his employer.[56]

Although some booksellers were themselves copyists, others employed copyists to work for them when they received orders for books. Ibn Abī Azhar (fl. third/ninth century) reports that a young neighbor of his, al-Fayruzān (fl. third/ninth century), worked as a copyist in the shop of ʿAllān al-Warrāq al-Shuʿūbī (fl. third/ninth century), sometime copyist in the *Bayt al-Ḥikmah*. Al-Fayruzān was a *warrāq* himself and had a shop in which he sold books and transcribed (*yansakhu*).[57] The *warrāq*'s shop, stall, or booth was called a *dukkān* or *ḥānūt*.[58] The sale of books in the bookshops was usually done "over the counter" but also by auction (*nidāʾ*);[59] potential buyers sat in a circle and bid for the book. In some cases, the bookseller operated a family business.[60] This may have been the case with Ibn Abī Ṭāhir, though the occupation of his son, Abū al-Ḥasan ʿUbaydallāh (d. 313/925), who wrote a continuation of his father's *Kitāb Baghdād*, is not explicitly indicated in the sources.[61]

Not surprisingly, the early *warrāq*s were Quran copyists; in the first century after the death of the prophet Muḥammad, all were traditionists.[62] These *warrāq*s, known in Medina as *aṣḥāb al-maṣāḥif*, 'the people of scripture/codices,' made the Qurans available in codex form.[63] The late second/eighth century, however, saw an increase in the demand for books, both in the religious and non-religious spheres. The *warrāq*s, who once dealt only in Quran- and Hadith-related materials, and who were by default the only real stationers, now found themselves part of an environment in which books about the past (*ayyām* and *taʾrīkh*), about poets (*ṭabaqāt*), books of poetry (*dīwān*s), and *adab* works, were in increasing demand. This demand was occasioned by the arrival of paper and the paper industry, and brought with it changes. Books came to be copied, bought, and sold. In fact, the early Iraqi scholars in the fields of language and literature became known as *aṣḥāb al-kutub*, book men. *Warrāq*s also began to compose their own books, including volumes of stories and fables. Ibn al-Nadīm writes that[64]

> Evening stories (*asmār*) and fables (*khurāfāt*) were much sought after and enjoyed in the days of the ʿAbbāsid caliphs, especially in the days of al-Muqtadir [r. 295–320/908–32].[65] Accordingly, the bookmen (*warrāqūn*) composed (*ṣannafa*) and made up [fictional] stories (*kadhabū*).

An oft-cited passage in the opening pages of the *Book of songs* refers to the treachery of *warrāq*s.[66] And al-Masʿūdī, who warns unscrupulous writers and copyists not to plagiarize or alter his work,[67] records the following anecdote involving Abū al-ʿAynāʾ:[68]

> One day he [Abū al-ʿAynāʾ] attended the gathering (*majlis*) of a certain vizier. The subject of the Barmakids, their generosity and their liberality was broached, so the vizier turned to Abū al-ʿAynāʾ – he had heaped high praise upon them, their patronage, and their favor – and remarked, "You overstated their qualities and exaggerated your descriptions of them. That was just the invention of the bookmen (*taṣnīf al-warrāqīn*) and the fabrication/fiction of writers (*kadhb al-muʾallifīn*)." "Why is it that the bookmen don't lie about you, your excellency?" retorted Abū al-ʿAynāʾ. The vizier fell silent and the onlookers were surprised indeed by Abū al-ʿAynāʾ"s audacity.[69]

Indeed, copyists, like teachers, were sometimes held in low regard. As Abbott notes:

> The rank and file of students, young scholars and laymen had to be content with the indifferent commercial advantage of the average copyists or booksellers, for whose services and stock of books there was ever-increasing demand.[70]

And like the teacher, the *warrāq* was often not well-off. Abū Hiffān once asked a *warrāq* how he was doing, and he replied:

> My life is more constricted than an inkwell, my body more delicate than a guide-sheet, my standing more fragile than glass, and my face blacker in people's eyes than ink mixed with vitriol. My [measly] lot is more negligible than the pen's [fine] slit, my hands are weaker than a reed, my food is more bitter than gall, my drink more acrid than ink, and my misfortune more insistent than glue.[71]

In 232/845, a large papyrus sheet for official correspondence cost one-twelfth of a dinar (two dirhams). Copying cost one-tenth of a dirham per page, or two hundred and forty pages per dinar.[72] For most copyists, therefore, copying seems to have only been enough to provide subsistence, especially those who only copied and did not, or could not, compose works of their own. Marc Bergé, writing about al-Tawḥīdī's first profession, observes that copying "was no menial calling; it was often the prerogative of a highly educated elite of men of learning *but [of] no private means* who could be relied upon to produce an accurate text."[73] Al-Tawḥīdī himself writes:

> The reason I left ʿIrāq and came to this [= Ibn ʿAbbād's] door, and sought refuge in the company of those [seeking patronage] here, was to be delivered of the brutal misery [of my profession], since the market for copying in Baghdad was bad.[74]

The question of income was mediated by the exigencies of the market. The copy of a scientific work by someone with expertise in that field would fetch a higher price than the work of a copyist in the field of *adab*, one whose work might easily be accomplished by other competent technicians. Most of the copying was done by self-employed copyists, whose work as such was their sole means of livelihood, either because they had no other choice, or because they chose to do so in order to avoid compromising their dignity and morality by working for government officials (whose sources of income were believed by many to be of dubious origin).[75] Some copyists were authors in their own right.

Most biographers emphasize the fact that Ibn Abī Ṭāhir was a *balīgh* (pl. *bulaghāʾ*), literally "an eloquent," more accurately "an eloquent master of prose style" – this mastery is one of the principal reasons why accusations of incorrect and ungrammatical speech leveled at Ibn Abī Ṭāhir must be taken with a grain of salt. Indeed, Ibn Abī Ṭāhir's eloquence is usually mentioned *first* in biographical descriptions of him. Being identified as a *balīgh* often referred to the fact that one was a writer of prose.[76] Being a *balīgh* (noun), as opposed to *balīgh* (adjective) demonstrated that one was competent/qualified to compose in prose. The *bulaghāʾ* were consequently individuals gifted and/or well-trained in the writing of prose.[77] Hence Rosenthal's decision to render al-Sakhāwī's characterization of Ibn Abī Ṭāhir as *balīgh* with "an outstanding stylist."[78] The kind of writing to which this at first referred was epistolary (*rasāʾil*) but it also accommodated other kinds of prose, such as works in the *naṣīḥat al-mulūk* (advice to rulers) genre, and works of ethics, argument, and debate, in short, works of *adab*. This, as well as the foregoing points, are illustrated by three lists produced by Ibn al-Nadīm. The first identifies forty-three *bulaghāʾ* [eloquent prose stylists],[79] the second names the top ten.[80] All the individuals are *kātib*s, secretaries, of one kind or another, and all flourished before or in the early third/ninth century. Ibn al-Nadīm gives no indication why later *bulaghāʾ*, such as Ibn Abī Ṭāhir potentially, do not figure on the list, but there is a third list, the 'modern men of eloquence' (*al-bulaghā' al-ḥadath*), consisting of only three names: Ibrāhīm ibn al-ʿAbbās al-Ṣūlī, al-Ḥasan ibn Wahb, and Saʿīd ibn ʿAbd al-Malik.[81] All three are *kātib*s.

Ibn Abī Ṭāhir, Author

The words *kātib* and its plural *kuttāb* designate directors, secretaries, and clerks in government service in the chanceries, of all ranks up to and including Secretary of State, and thus broadly denote all civil servants.[82] From *kataba,* to write, *kātib* also means "writer, scribe, expert in writing."[83] References in various sources to Ibn Abī Ṭāhir as a *kātib* are, therefore, either an indication that he was attached to a chancery in a professional capacity, or that he worked as an independent writer, letter-writer and author. By independent, I mean neither attached to a government institution nor retained by private individuals. His access to documents of state, as cataloged, for example, in the section on *rasā'il* (letters, epistles) in the *Book of prose and poetry*, cannot be adduced as strong evidence for government employment as letters were often circulated outside of chanceries. Such was the case, for example, of the letter of Ṭāhir ibn al-Ḥusayn to his son ʿAbdallāh.[84] And Ibn Abī Ṭāhir's associate Abū ʿAlī al-Baṣīr for example, is described by Ibn al-Muʿtazz as "*kātiban risāliyyan*," "a letter-writer," which letters Ibn al-Muʿtazz describes as numerous, and widely and well-known.[85] This last statement is an indication that letters were composed for a wider readership, circulating beyond the (two) correspondents. Indeed, the letter and epistle in Arabic, as in many other literary traditions, became a literary form and conceit through which one could instruct, inform, announce, and criticize.

Ibn al-Muʿtazz, Ibn al-Nadīm, and Yāqūt, who might be termed Ibn Abī Ṭāhir's "literary" biographers, make no reference whatsoever to the fact that he was a *kātib*.[86] On the other hand, al-Khaṭīb al-Baghdādī, al-Dhahabī, and al-Sakhāwī, who might be termed Ibn Abī Ṭāhir's "non-literary" biographers, call him "*al-Kātib*." When the latter do so, however, it is not within the descriptive part of the notice, but as a constitutive part of Ibn Abī Ṭāhir's name, e.g. "Aḥmad Ibn Abī Ṭāhir, *al-Kātib* Abū al-Faḍl."[87] The "literary" biographers do not use the designation "*al-Kātib*," but either name Ibn Abī Ṭāhir's many works (Ibn al-Nadīm, Yāqūt) or mention the fact of their number and popularity (Ibn al-Muʿtazz). Conversely, the "non-literary" biographers do use the designation "*al-Kātib*" but only mention one work, *Book of Baghdad*. And no notice or anecdote makes any reference to chancery employment of any kind. This suggests that "*al-Kātib*" is meant to function as a *laqab* (honorific, nickname) and not as a professional designation. Use of the nickame "*al-Kātib*" thus becomes a way for the name as a whole to draw attention to Ibn Abī Ṭāhir as a writer. "*Al-Kātib*" is thus better rendered "Author," "Writer," or even "Learned Writer."[88] Significantly, when al-Mīkālī (d. 436/1044) identifies the poets he is including in the introduction to his anthology *al-Muntakhal*, he includes Ibn Abī Ṭāhir in the section on modern poets (*al-muḥdathūn*) and not in the section on ministers and state secretaries (*al-wuzarā' wa-al-kuttāb*).[89]

One anecdote which explicitly identifies Ibn Abī Ṭāhir as one of three *kātib*s met by Abū al-Yusr Ibrāhīm ibn Muḥammad al-Shaybānī (d. 298/911), a Baghdādī scholar visiting al-Andalus, reads as follows:[90]

> The travelers who came to al-Andalus from the East include: Abū al-Yusr Ibrāhīm ibn Muḥammad al-Shaybānī from Baghdād, who lived in Qayrawān and was known as al-Riyāḍī. He had certificates of audition from the majority of the Hadith scholars, jurists, and grammarians of Baghdad, among whom he met al-Jāḥiẓ, al-Mubarrad, Thaʿlab and Ibn Qutaybah. Among poets, he met Abū Tammām, al-Buḥturī, Diʿbil and Ibn al-Jahm; and *among the kātibs* [secretaries/writers] he met Saʿīd ibn Ḥumayd, Sulaymān ibn Wahb and *Aḥmad Ibn Abī Ṭāhir*, among others.

Sulaymān ibn Wahb and Saʿīd ibn Ḥumayd are explicitly identified as chancery *kātib*s in the sources, and both held high office.[91] There is, however, no direct evidence that Ibn Abī Ṭāhir was in government employment. If it is curious, that two of the members of the trio would be such well-known government servants and one not, it is equally curious that al-Jāḥiẓ would be in a trio with Ibn Qutaybah and Thaʿlab.[92] I would argue that here, again, *kātib* means writer in Ibn Abī Ṭāhir's case, and not secretary. The conflation is explained by the fact that he wrote letters, taught *kātib*s, and associated with prominent *kātib*s. The conflation may be said to hold true also for Saʿīd ibn Ḥumayd: he was a *kātib* in government service but is also remembered as an accomplished private writer of letters and epistles. The three do not in fact form such a surprising trio. Considerable contact is attested between Ibn Abī Ṭāhir and Saʿīd ibn Ḥumayd, and to a lesser extent, between Ibn Abī Ṭāhir and the Wahb family.

Michael Carter has suggested that the "average *kātib*, far from existing in the rarefied atmosphere of philology, calligraphy and literature, live[d] and breathe[d] in a much more practical element, namely money," and that he was for the most part engaged in accounting and in financial management.[93] This view and the further view that "the *kātib* evidently lived with money and thought about little else," are overstated.[94] Also to be revisited is Carter's contention that "the ideal *kātib* portrayed in the sources, especially the *adab*-writers, is a fiction and a literary cliché."[95] There is, however, considerable anecdotal evidence for the affluence of *kātib*s. Ibn Abī Ṭāhir's associate Abū Hiffān, whom al-Khaṭīb al-Baghdādī describes as having occupied a position of literary eminence (*kāna lahu maḥall kabīr*), on seeing several *kātib*s riding by, once declaimed:[96]

> Oh Lord, the vilest of the vile ride
> while my feet are bloody from trodding the ground.
>
> If only You would carry me, like You do them,
> Or else, at least (agree to) carry me the second-time round!

Abū Hiffān is complaining that *kātib*s can afford to ride whereas he himself cannot because of the financial burden.

Ibn Abī Ṭāhir also experienced financial difficulty. One anecdote, mentioned above, shows this, and it is the same Abū Hiffān who is his companion in penury.[97] That anecdote clearly points to the fact that Ibn Abī Ṭāhir was not wealthy; this may explain why he was staying with Abū Hiffān,[98] for whom indigence is attested.[99] It is interesting, and significant, that they looked to obtain money by employing a ruse (that was bound eventually to backfire) to get a few dinars, rather than seek the money directly from al-Muʿallā or another "patron." The decision of Ibn Abī Ṭāhir and others like him to criticize and satirize, and even to "make prominent enemies,"[100] may have contributed to his inability to support himself better. What it certainly strongly suggests is that individuals such as Ibn Abī Ṭāhir were not dependent on patrons or patronage. And it also supports the contention that *kātib* in Ibn Abī Ṭāhir's case means writer, not civil servant.

Ibn Abī Ṭāhir was the author of approximately sixty works, everything from letters to multi-volume critical studies, from editions of poetry to verse anthologies, but very little of his output survives. There can be no one satisfying explanation for the survival of some works and not of others. In the case of a good many writers and compilers, both well-known and not so well-known, no works of theirs survive. In other cases, even works that had very wide currency in their own time or shortly thereafter were soon lost to posterity. Al-Masʿūdī (d. 345/956) speaks, for example, of the no longer extant *Kitāb al-mulūk wa-akhbār al-māḍīn* [Book of kings and accounts of the past] of ʿAbīd/ʿUbayd ibn Sharyah (fl. late second/eighth?) as being widely known and circulated.[101] And as early as the time of the writing of *The Catalog*, in 367/977, Ibn al-Nadīm observes that the last volume of Ibn Abī Ṭāhir's fourteen-volume *Book of prose and poetry* is already lost.[102] Loss of works was certainly common. Indeed, the movement of books was not always benevolent or beneficial to the author or posterity. Merchants, for example, might sell multi-volume works for a profit, thereby often dispersing the work irretrievably.[103]

Information about Ibn Abī Ṭāhir's works may principally be obtained from the two main notices devoted to him, namely the bio-bibliographical entries in *The Catalog* of Ibn al-Nadīm (d. after 985) and the *Guide for the intelligent* of Yāqūt (d. 1229). Yāqūt states that he is citing Ibn al-Nadīm's list and, in effect, deviates from it in only a few cases. These deviations are in any case typically alternatives to titles furnished by Ibn al-Nadīm. Nonetheless, five titles reported by Ibn al-Nadīm are not to be found in Yāqūt.[104] Some titles, which do not form part of the Ibn al-Nadīm/Yāqūt list, are mentioned in literary and literary-critical sources of the fourth/tenth century. Most of these are either alternative titles for ones already attested, or names of sections, chapters, or constituent parts of known works. In a few cases, they are altogether different works.

The only erstwhile critical bibliography of Ibn Abī Ṭāhir's works is that of Muḥsin Ghayyāḍ in the introduction to his 1977 edition of the first part of the twelfth volume of the *Book of prose and poetry*.[105] Ghayyāḍ duplicates Yāqūt's list and supplements it with comments about the deviations of the latter from Ibn al-Nadīm's list. He comments at length on Ibn Abī Ṭāhir's originality and does include a few titles indicated in other sources,[106] but his division of Ibn Abī Ṭāhir's works into two groups, historical (*ta'rīkhiyyah*) and literary (*adabiyyah*), is insufficiently nuanced and does not account for works that may overlap the two rubrics, including for example the *Book of Bahgdad*, which is characterized by a great deal of emphasis on matters cultural too. The following listing of titles of works is organized (speculatively) into likely generic clusters.[107] Translations of the titles into English are followed by attested variant titles (and their translations).

1
Kitāb Tarbiyat Hurmuz ibn Kisrā Anūshirwān[108]
Book of the education of Hurmuz ibn Kisrā Anūshirwān

Variant titles: (a) *Kitāb Marthiyat Hurmuz ibn Kisrā Anūshirwān* [Elegy on Hurmuz ibn Kisrā Anūshirwān (d. 590 CE)];[109] (b) *Kitāb Martabat Hurmuz ibn Kisrā Anūshirwān* [The high rank of Hurmuz ibn Kisrā Anūshirwān][110]

2
Kitāb Khabar al-malik al-ʿālī fī tadbīr al-mamlakah wa-al-siyāsah
Book of the story of the great king and the management of the kingdom and its administration

Variant title: *Kitāb Khabar al-malik al-ʿānī fī tadbīr al-mamlakah wa-al-siyāsah* [The story of the distressed king and the management of the kingdom and its administration][111]

3
Kitāb al-Malik al-muṣliḥ wa-al-wazīr al-muʿīn[112]
Book of [the story of] the conciliatory king and the supportive vizier

4
Kitāb al-Malik al-Bābilī wa-al-malik al-Miṣrī al-bāghiyayn wa-al-malik al-ḥakīm al-Rūmī
Book of [the story of] the two tyrannical Babylonian and Egyptian kings and the wise Byzantine king

Variant title: *Kitāb al-Malik al-Bābilī wa-al-malik al-Miṣrī al-bāghiyayn wa-al-malik al-ḥalīm al-Rūmī* [The story of] the two tyrannical Babylonian and Egyptian kings and the gentle Byzantine king

5
Kitāb al-Ḥijāb[113]
Book of chamberlainship[114]

6
Kitāb al-Maʿrūfīn min al-anbiyāʾ
Book of known prophets

Variant title: *Kitāb al-Muʿriqīn min al-anbiyāʾ* [Noble prophets][115]

7
Kitāb Jamharat Banī Hāshim
Book of collected [genealogies] of the Banū Hāshim

8
Kitāb al-Khayl, kabīr
Book of horses, unabridged

9
Kitāb al-Ṭard
Book of the hunt

10
Kitāb al-Mukhtalif min al-muʾtalif[116]
Book of differences between similar [names]

11
Kitāb Asmāʾ al-shuʿarāʾ al-awāʾil
Book of names of the first poets

12
Kitāb Alqāb al-shuʿarāʾ wa-man ʿurifa bi-al-kunā wa-man ʿurifa bi-al-ism
Book of the nicknames of poets, and of those [poets] known by their agnomens, and of those known by their given names[117]

13
Kitāb Man anshada shiʿran wa-ujība bi-kalām
Book of those who recited poetry and were answered in words

14
Kitāb Maqātil al-fursān
Book of murdered heroes[118]

15
Kitāb Maqātil al-shuʿarāʾ
Book of murdered poets

16
Kitāb al-Jāmiʿ fī al-shuʿarāʾ wa-akhbārihim
The compendium on poets with accounts about them[119]

17
Kitāb Ikhtiyār ashʿār al-shuʿarāʾ
Book of selections from the poetry of [various] poets

Variant titles: (a) *Kitāb Ikhtiyārāt ashʿār al-shuʿarāʾ* [Selections of poetry by (various) poets]; (b) *Kitāb Fī ikhtiyārāt ashʿār al-shuʿarāʾ* [Book of selections of poetry by (various) poets]

The following are either parts of # 17 above,
possibly part of # 36 below, or discrete works

18
Kitāb Ikhtiyār shiʿr Imraʾ al-Qays
Book of selections from the poetry of Imruʾ al-Qays [d. *c.* 565 CE]

19
Kitāb Ikhtiyār shiʿr al-rajaz
Book of selections of *rajaz*-meter poetry

20
Kitāb Ikhtiyār shiʿr Bakr ibn al-Naṭṭāḥ
Book of selections from the poetry of Bakr ibn al-Naṭṭāḥ [d. 222/837]

21
Kitāb Ikhtiyār shiʿr al-ʿAttābī
Book of selections from the poetry of al-ʿAttābī [d. 208/823 or 220/835]

22
Kitāb Ikhtiyār shiʿr Manṣūr al-Namarī
Book of selections from the poetry of Manṣūr al-Namarī [d. 190/805]

23
Kitāb Ikhtiyār shiʿr Abī al-ʿAtāhiyah
Book of selections from the poetry of Abū al-ʿAtāhiyah [d. 211/826]

24
Kitāb Ikhtiyār shiʿr Muslim
Book of selections from the poetry of Muslim [d. 207/823]

25
Kitāb Ikhtiyār shiʿr Diʿbil
Book of selections from the poetry of Diʿbil [d. 246/860]

26
Kitāb Akhbār Bashshār wa-ikhtiyār shiʿrihi[120]
Book of accounts about Bashshār [d. *c.* 167/784] and a selection of his poetry

Variant titles:(a) *Kitāb Ikhtiyār shiʿr Bashshār* [A selection of the poetry of Bashshār]; (b) *Bashshār wa-al-ikhtiyār min shiʿrihi* [Bashshār and a selection of his poetry]

27
Kitāb Akhbār Marwān wa-Āl Marwān wa-ikhtiyār ashʿārihim
Book of accounts about Marwān [ibn Abī Ḥafṣah] [d. *c.* 182/798] and the House of Marwan and selections from their poetry[121]

Variant title: *Marwān wa-al-ikhtiyār min shiʿrihi wa-akhbār Āl Marwān* [Marwān, selections from his poetry, and accounts about the House of Marwan]

28
Kitāb Akhbār Ibn Harmah wa-mukhtār shiʿrihi
Book of accounts about Ibn Harmah [d. *c.* 176/792] and selected poetry[122]

29
Kitāb Akhbār wa-shiʿr ʿUbaydallāh Ibn Qays al-Ruqayyāt
Book of accounts and poetry of ʿUbaydallāh Ibn Qays al-Ruqayyāt [d. *c.* 80/699]

30
Kitāb Akhbār Ibn Mayyādah
Book of accounts about Ibn Mayyādah [d. *c.* 136–46/753–63]

31
Kitāb Akhbār Ibn Munādhir
Book of accounts about Ibn Munādhir [d. *c.* 199/814]

32
Kitāb Akhbār Ibn al-Dumaynah
Book of accounts about Ibn al-Dumaynah [d. early second/eighth *c.*]

33
Kitāb Sariqāt al-shuʿarāʾ
Book of the borrowings/plagiarisms of the poets[123]

The following works are either sections of #33 above, or possibly discrete works

34
Kitāb Sariqāt Abī Tammām
Book of the borrowings/plagiarisms of Abū Tammām [d. *c.* 232/845][124]

35
Kitāb Sariqāt al-Buḥturī min Abī Tammām[125]
Book of the borrowings/plagiarisms of al-Buḥturī [d. 284/897] from Abū Tammām

36
Kitāb al-Manthūr wa-al-manẓūm. 14 vols
Book of prose and poetry

Variant title: *Kitāb al-Manẓūm wa-al-manthūr* [Book of poetry and prose][126]
Volumes 11, 12 and 13 are extant and published piecemeal[127]

37
Kitāb al-Mu'allifīn
Book of authors

Variant title: Akhbār al-mu'allifīn (Accounts concerning authors)[128]

38
Akhbār al-mulūk
Accounts concerning rulers[129]

39
Kitāb Baghdād[130]
Book of Baghdad

Variant titles: (a) *Ta'rīkh Baghdād* [History of Baghdad]; (b) *Akhbār Baghdād* [Accounts concerning Baghdad];[131] (c) *Ta'rīkh akhbār al-khulafā'* [Chronicle of accounts concerning the caliphs]; (d) *Akhbār al-khulafā'* [Accounts concerning the caliphs][132]
Most of volume 6 is extant and published.[133]

40
Kitāb Faḍl al-ʿArab ʿalā al-ʿAjam
Book on the superiority of the Arabs over the Persians

41
Kitāb Mufākharat al-ward wa-al-narjis
Book of the boasting-match between the rose and the narcissus

Variant title: *Kitāb Faḍā'il al-ward ʿalā al-narjis* [Book on the superiority of the rose to the narcissus]

42
Kitāb al-Hadāyā
Book of gifts

43
Kitāb al-Jawāhir
Book of gems

44
Kitāb al-Muwashshā
Book of the adorned (or embroidered)

45
Kitāb al-ʿIllah wa-al-ʿalīl[134]
Book on affliction and the afflicted

Variant title: *Kitāb al-Ghullah wa-al-ghalīl* [Burning thirst and ardent desire]

46
Kitāb al-Ḥilā [or Ḥulīy]
Book of ornament and raiment

Variant title: *al-Ḥalī wa-al-ḥulal*[135]

47
Kitāb Akhbār al-mutaẓarrifāt[136]
Book of the accounts of women displaying/affecting [wit and] elegance.[137]

48
Kitāb al-Mughramīn
Book of those infatuated

49
Kitāb al-Mu'nis
Book of amusement

50
Kitāb al-Muzāḥ wa-al-muʿātabāt
Book of [love-] play and reproaches

Variant title: *Kitāb al-Mizāj wa-al-muʿātabāt* [Temperament and reproaches][138]

51
Kitāb Lisān al-ʿuyūn
Book of the language of the eyes

52
Kitāb Qalaq al-Mushtāq
Book of the disquiet of the yearnful[139]

53
Kitāb al-Muʿtadhirīn
Book of those who make apologies in verse

54
Kitāb Iʿtidhār Wahb min ḥabqatihi[140]
Book of the apology of Wahb on breaking wind

Variant title: Kitāb Iʿtidhār Wahb min ḍartatihi[141] [Book of the apology of Wahb on farting]

55
al-Risālah fī al-Nahy ʿan al-shahawāt
Epistle on the restraint of lusts

56
Risālah ilā Ibrāhīm ibn al-Mudabbir
Epistle addressed to Ibrāhīm ibn al-Mudabbir [d. 279/893][142]

57
Risālah ilā ʿAlī ibn Yaḥyā I[143]
Epistle addressed to ʿAlī ibn Yaḥyā [d. 275/888 or 889], I

58
Risālah ilā ʿAlī ibn Yaḥyā II[144]
Epistle addressed to ʿAlī ibn Yaḥyā, II

59
Risālah fī dhamm Ibn Thawābah
Epistle in censure of Ibn Thawābah [d. 273/886 or 277/890][145]

60
Risālah ilā Abī ʿAlī al-Baṣīr fī hijāʾ Ibn Muk(ar)ram wa-thalbihi
Epistle addressed to Abū ʿAlī al-Baṣīr [d. after 252/866], in satire of Ibn Muk(ar)ram [fl. third/ninth century][146]

61
Kitāb Akhbār Abī al-ʿAynāʾ
Book of accounts about Abū al-ʿAynāʾ [d. *c*. 283/896]

Ibn Abī Ṭāhir was a bookman par excellence, evincing wide-ranging interests in subjects cultural, literary, and literary-critical, and writing about them in works of which, alas, few survive. What was Ibn Abī Ṭāhir's stake in these matters, if any? I broach that question in the next two chapters.

5

NAVIGATING PARTISAN SHOALS

In the preceding two chapters I explored the connections between professional activities and writerly culture, suggesting that paper and writing influenced *adab* and the professional choices of *udabā'* in new ways. In this chapter I focus on ethnicity, doctrine, and party in an attempt to show that such attachments played a decreasingly important role in the constitution of *udabā'* in the new writerly environment.

The contention that one's Shiism, for example – or indeed any ideological position to the extent that it is readily identifiable[1] – played a determining role in the *formation* of the littérateur needs to be re-examined when considering the writerly culture of third/ninth century Baghdad. A particular ethnic, doctrinal, or partisan affiliation might appear to have ensured someone a position in the secretariat, or blacklisted him from it; might appear to have secured a poet patronage in some quarters, and excluded him from others; and it might appear to have granted some access to certain individuals, institutions, and materials, and close doors to others. The argument that al-Ma'mūn, for example, sought the company and support of Muʿtazilites, or vice versa, or that al-Mutawakkil, for example, sought the company of individuals who were anti-Shiite, or vice versa,[2] may be true, but the mechanisms of that identification and disidentification need to be scrutinized. Admittedly, religious or sectarian disagreements were often inseparable from personal rivalries;[3] and religious and sectarian alignment were also often connected to professional necessity and self-interest. Patronized writers and poets evidently catered to their patrons. Even as (purportedly) free a spirit as al-Jāḥiẓ pandered to his patron:[4]

> Since you do me the honour of giving [my books] your attention, and in case it is not possible for you to delve into them and acquaint yourself with them thoroughly because of the responsibilities which overcome you, I ask you, in the name of your shining magnanimity and abundant virtue to content yourself with the general outlines, and to acquaint yourself rather with the subjects of the various chapters by leafing through the first few pages.

Uncertainty about someone's doctrinal affiliation was common. This uncertainty was additionally complicated with regard to Shiism because of the practice of *taqiyyah*, concealing one's Shiism in unfavorable circumstances.[5] Individuals were therefore sometimes quizzed about their doctrinal or sectarian affiliations by peers and patrons. Al-Mutawakkil once said to the wit Abū al-ʿAynāʾ, "I hear you are a Rāfiḍī [lit. someone who rejects (the first two caliphs)]. . . ?", i.e. a Shiite, to which Abū al-ʿAynāʾ replied:[6]

> Commander of the Faithful, how can I be a Rāfiḍī when my origin is Basra, my home its Friday Mosque, my teacher al-Aṣmaʿī, and my neighbors the Bāhilah (tribe)?

Yet, Abū al-ʿAynāʾ, who is not identified by Sunni biographers as Shiite, or particularly pro-Shiite for that matter, is included in the section on poets of the Prophet Muḥammad's noble family (*Baʿḍ shuʿarāʾ ahl al-bayt*) by the Shiite scholar Ibn Shahrashūb (d. 588/1192) in his *Maʿālim al-ʿulamāʾ* [The guideposts of the learned guides] in the sub-section describing those who concealed their Shiism by practising *taqiyyah*. Ibn Shahrashūb also includes Abū Tammām and al-Ṣūlī in this sub-section: these are poets who praised the family of the Prophet Muḥammad, rather than Shiite themselves.[7] It is reasonably clear that by including poets who were not necessarily Shiite in their catalogs, Ibn Shahrashūb and others were claiming well-known figures as Shiite.

The poet al-Buḥturī was blatant about the fact that he went whichever way the prevailing wind blew when it came to doctrinal affiliation. In one anecdote, al-Kajjī (d. 292/905), citing an early verse of al-Buḥturī, asks him whether that does not effectively show him to be a Muʿtazilite.[8] Al-Buḥturī replies:

> "That was my religion in the reign of al-Wāthiq, then I repudiated it in the reign of al-Mutawakkil." So I [al-Kajjī] said: "That's a pretty doctrine that changes with the ruler."

Ibn Abī Ṭāhir, 'son of a Persian noble'?

Ibn Abī Ṭāhir's full name was Abū al-Faḍl Aḥmad Ibn Abī Ṭāhir Ṭayfūr al-Marwarrūdhī. His *nisbah* (ethnic or relator name) al-Marwarrūdhī shows that he was from Marw al-Rūdh, a town on the Murghāb river in Khurāsān,[9] the large north-east Iranian province that first came under Muslim influence and control *c.* 31/651 and played a critical role in the Abbasid overthrow of the Umayyad caliphate. Ibn Abī Ṭāhir's father's given name (*ism*), *Ṭayfūr*, confirms the family's Khurasanian origins, as it is overwhelmingly attested for individuals from Khurasan and its environs[10] (and only attested in the post-classical Islamic period[11]). Nothing else is known about Ibn Abī Ṭāhir's father and paternal line. Abū al-Faraj does mention that the *nisbah* of the first cousin (mother's sister's son) of one "Abū al-Faḍl al-Kātib" is al-Ṭūsī.[12] If this Abū al-Faḍl is Ibn Abī Ṭāhir –

which appears likely as Abū al-Faraj does refer to Ibn Abī Ṭāhir in this way elsewhere in the *Book of songs*[13]– and Ṭūs being a town in Khurasan, it may be supposed that Ibn Abī Ṭāhir's mother was also from Khurasan.

Ibn al-Nadīm notes specifically that Ibn Abī Ṭāhir was "*min abnā' Khurāsān min awlād al-dawlah*."[14] The *abnā' Khurāsān* were the descendants of the original *ahl Khurāsān* army who became the backbone of support for al-Ma'mūn within the walls of Baghdad.[15] They were, consequently, members of the Abbasid aristocracy. Their status was based not only on their membership (or forbears' membership) in the loyal Khurasanian regiments that brought the Abbasids to power, but also on their possible descent from Persian nobility.[16] In the *Book of Baghdad* Ibn Abī Ṭāhir himself describes the *abnā'* as being either *muwalladūn* (of mixed Arab/Persian parentage), or the sons of *dihqān*s (Persian notables/nobles).[17] The ethnic breakdown of the *abnā' Khurāsān* has been the subject of some debate. Some maintain that it designates the largely Arab military regiments loyal to the Abbasid cause, others that it denotes a mixed Khurasanian population of *mawālī* (non-Arab Muslims affiliated to Arab Muslims) and Arabs, which may or may not have had military status. Part of the confusion stems from the distinction that must be made between *abnā'/ahl Khurāsān* regiments loyal to al-Ma'mūn and *abnā'/ahl Khurāsān* regiments loyal to his brother al-Amīn during their war.[18] In his exhortation to his (mixed) *abnā'* troops as they faced the predominantly Persian troops of Ṭāhir ibn al-Ḥusayn (d. 205/821), the caliph al-Amīn's (r. 193–8/809–13) general, ʿAbd al-Raḥmān ibn Jabalah al-Abnāwī, addressed them as follows: "O People of the Abnā', O Sons of Kings."[19]

As with the *abnā' Khurāsān* in Ibn al-Nadīm's description, the precise connotation of *awlād al-dawlah* is also difficult to fix.[20] Brockelmann has understood *awlād al-dawlah* to mean that Ibn Abī Ṭāhir was "descended from a princely family."[21] Ghayyāḍ has questioned this interpretation.[22] Indeed, "*al-dawlah*" here would seem rather to be the Abbasid state, suggesting, in turn, membership in the *ahl Khurāsān* rather than in a princely family. Ibn Abī Ṭāhir therefore appears to be from a Khurasanian family of possibly noble descent. Clément Huart's conjecture that the name *Ṭayfūr* (*ṭay-fūr*) derives from the Pahlavi *taka puthra*, "children/sons of the dynasty," would, if true, provide corroborating evidence for Ibn Abī Ṭāhir's noble Persian background, and correspond to Ibn al-Nadīm's *awlād al-dawlah*,[23] though some, such as Dodge, take this a step further to imply that he was an Abbasid official.[24] The Old Iranian *visō puthra*, "the son of the house," i.e. prince, however, was more prevalent than *taka puthra*, and there is no evidence that Ibn al-Nadīm knew Pahlavi, his remarks about the Persian script notwithstanding.[25] For his part, de Slane suggests that Ibn Abī Ṭāhir was the son of a Khurāsānī slave, but this too is an unsupported claim.[26]

Ibn Abī Ṭāhir and Doctrine

No medieval biographer or writer pronounces on the question of Ibn Abī Ṭāhir's doctrinal affiliation, nor does Ibn Abī Ṭāhir make a statement about it himself.

The only textually supportable argument in favor of Ibn Abī Ṭāhir's possible Shiism is his fourteen-line elegy on Abū al-Ḥusayn Yaḥyā ibn ʿUmar, a Shiite rebel killed in battle in Kufa in Rajab 250/August 864 on the order of the caliph al-Mustaʿīn (r. 248–52/862–6)[27] – an argument that has been advanced by Shawqī Ḍayf, who believes that both Ibn Abī Ṭāhir and Abū ʿAlī al-Baṣīr were Imāmī Shiites who concealed their Shiism for fear of reprisal.[28] Saïd Boustany believes that Ibn al-Rūmī practised this kind of concealment too.[29] Ibn Abī Ṭāhir's poem was possibly recited in Samarra, where Yaḥyā's head was displayed, or else before the large crowds that are known to have gathered in Baghdad.[30] In the elegy Ibn Abī Ṭāhir attacks the Sunni caliphal family for its usurpation of the rights of the House of ʿAlī. Al-Masʿūdī (d. 345/946), who is credited with an active sympathy for the family of the Prophet and for the Shiites – and who was probably himself an Imāmī, born in Kufa to Shiite parents[31] – is the only author to mention Ibn Abī Ṭāhir's poem or to preserve any part of the text. He does not identify his source for Ibn Abī Ṭāhir's poem, but it was no doubt one of the many written works on which he relied in his own composition (one hundred and sixty-five in the case of the *Murūj al-dhahab* [Meadows of gold] alone), or else notes from the lectures of any of his numerous professors: these included al-Ṣūlī and Ibn Durayd, both of them well acquainted with the works of Ibn Abī Ṭāhir.[32] The elegy opens as follows:[33]

> Farewell Islam, for it is departing with the Prophet's departing family, farewell.
>
> Losing them means losing all glory and splendor, and seeing the thrones of benevolence crumble.
>
> Can eyes close in sweet repose when the Prophet's own ancestors' repose is underground?
>
> The Prophet Muḥammad's home has been deserted by Faith and by Islam; it is now abandoned.

Salāmun ʿalā ʾl-islāmi fa-hwa muwaddaʿun
idhā mā maḍā ālu ʾn-nabīyi fa waddaʿū
Faqadnā ʾl-ʿulā wa ʾl-majda ʿinda ʾftiqādihim
wa-aḍḥat ʿurūsh al-makrumāti taḍaʿḍaʿū
A-tajmaʿu ʿaynun bayna nawmin wa-madjaʿin
wa-li ʾbni rasūlillāhi fī ʾt-tarbi madjaʿū
Fa-qad aqfarat dāru ʾn-nabīyi Muḥammadin
min ad-dīni wa ʾl-islāmi fa ʾd-dāru balqaʿū

Al-Masʿūdī mentions that many elegies were written for Yaḥyā ibn ʿUmar and that he has recorded some of these in his *Kitāb al-Awsaṭ* [The middle book],[34] but in the *Meadows of gold* it is to the elegy by Ibn Abī Ṭāhir that he gives pride of place.

Boustany has suggested that the poet Ibn al-Rūmī's (d. 283/896) strong Shiite (and Muʿtazilite) sentiments came out into the open with the recitation/publication of his elegies on the very same Yaḥyā ibn ʿUmar elegized by Ibn Abī Ṭāhir.[35] But, as al-Maʿarrī (d. 449/1058) observed centuries before Boustany, the imputing of Shiite beliefs to Ibn al-Rūmī – and by extension to any poet – is open to serious question:[36]

> The Baghdadis insist that [Ibn al-Rūmī] was a Shiite and invoke as evidence of this his poem rhyming in the letter *jīm* [= elegy on Yaḥyā ibn ʿUmar]. To my mind, his practice is no different from that of any other poet (*wa-mā arāhu illā ʿalā madhhab ghayrih min al-shuʿarāʾ*).

For al-Maʿarrī then, this sort of Shiism is nothing more than a conceit, a Shiism of poets, as it were. Indeed, even Boustany concedes that there are no indications, apart from this elegy to Yaḥyā, that Ibn al-Rūmī was in fact Shite.[37]

In an anecdote reported by Abū al-Faraj al-Iṣbahānī (d. 356/967) on the authority of his uncle al-Ḥusayn in both the *Book of songs* and the *Kitāb Maqātil al-Ṭālibiyyīn* [Book of murdered Ṭālibids] Ibn Abī Ṭāhir describes being in the home of one of his friends in the company of Abū ʿAbdullāh Muḥammad (ibn ʿAlī) ibn Ṣāliḥ ibn ʿAlī al-Ḥasanī.[38] Abū ʿAbdallāh (d. 255/869) was an ʿAlid poet who was imprisoned by al-Mutawakkil in 240/854 for three years.[39] He spent some time in Samarra where he befriended Saʿīd ibn Ḥumayd; it is possibly the latter's home that is described in the anecdote. Ibn Abī Ṭāhir writes that Abū ʿAbdallāh remained indoors until the middle of the night and that when he was to leave Ibn Abī Ṭāhir feared for his safety, in spite of the fact that he was carrying a sword.

Abū ʿAbdallāh is one of numerous Shiites with whom Ibn Abī Ṭāhir was in contact. But, as with Ibn Abī Ṭāhir's elegy to Yaḥyā ibn ʿUmar, it is not possible to adduce this contact as evidence of his Shiism, or Shiite sympathies. It is true that Ibn Abī Ṭāhir praised ʿAlī ibn Yaḥyā al-Munajjim and Ismāʿīl ibn Bulbul for example, prominent Shiites both. On the other hand, many of Ibn Abī Ṭāhir's professional and personal contacts included Sunnis, his close friend Abū Hiffān for instance. There is, in short, nothing to suggest a predisposition by him to or against anyone because of his doctrinal, or presumed doctrinal, affiliation, and certainly nothing to suggest that others were predisposed one way or another toward him for doctrinal reasons either.

Ibn Abī Ṭāhir and Persia

Ibn Abī Ṭāhir was from Khurasan and of Persian origin. But that someone was Persian and Khurasanian does not perforce reveal anything about that individual's doctrinal affiliation. The equation of Khurasanian origin with Shiism is incorrect. As Heinz Halm has noted, "It must be borne in mind that the Shia originated in the Arabian milieu of Kufa and may thus be understood neither as an expression of Iranian mentality – as has long been believed – nor yet as the revenge of Aryan Iranianism on Islam and the Arabs."[40] On the other hand, one's Persian origin could have implications. In the case of Ibn Abī Ṭāhir his Persianness appears to have played a significant role in his literary activity and output.

The role of Persian culture in the elaboration of Arab–Islamic culture has long been recognized. This role is illustrated by an anecdote reported by Ibn Abī Ṭāhir himself in the *Book of Baghdad*.[41] In it, the littérateur Abū ʿAmr Kulthūm ibn ʿAmr al-ʿAttābī (d. 208/823 or 220/835) is at the court of Muḥammad ibn Ṭāhir ibn al-Ḥusayn (d. 259/873) in Raqqah and addresses a certain Yaḥyā ibn al-Ḥasan in Persian. The Persian-speaking Yaḥyā responds by saying:[42]

> 'Abū ʿAmr, what's with you and this gibberish?' He said, 'He answered me saying, "I've gone to that country of yours three times and copied the Persian books that are in the library in Merv." The books were brought there and added to the holdings by Yazdajird; they have remained there to this day. Then he said, "I copied what I needed, and then traveled to Nishapur. I had traveled ten *farsakh*s to a village known as Dhūdar,[43] when I remembered a book I had not yet finished with. So I returned to Merv and spent several months there."' He said, 'So I said, "Abū ʿAmr, why did you transcribe Persian books?" and he replied, "Are ideas (*maʿānī*)[44] and eloquence anywhere but in the books of the Persians? We may have the medium (*lughah* [= language, i.e. Arabic]), but they have the import (*maʿānī*)."' After that, we would [often] trade gems of Persian literature and converse at length in Persian.

Al-ʿAttābī was an Arab littérateur of Northern Syria who moved to Baghdad, where he became known as an administrator and letter-writer, a witty courtier, and an accomplished poet.[45] He had had to flee the court of Hārūn al-Rashīd, where he was a sometime poet and evening storyteller, possibly because of his attachment to the Barmakids; Aḥmad al-Najjār credits al-ʿAttābī's interest in matters Persian to this closeness to the Barmakids.[46] Al-ʿAttābī managed to return to Baghdad later and flourished during the caliphate of al-Maʾmūn. His poetry was highly regarded by his contemporaries and by posterity. The only attested edition of al-ʿAttābī's poetry is in fact a selection made by Ibn Abī Ṭāhir, the *Kitāb Ikhtiyār shiʿr al-ʿAttābī* [A Selection of the Poetry of al-ʿAttābī].

Ibn al-Nadīm includes al-ʿAttābī in his list of the (forty-three) most eloquent men (*asmāʾ al-bulaghāʾ*), where he is also described as learned.[47] He appears to have been an autodidact, obtaining his knowledge from books.[48] Indeed, al-ʿAttābī's consultation of Persian manuscripts in Merv and Nishapur may have been in order to glean from them material for his stories and other works. Cejpek believes that the single works adapted into Arabic were selected "with great care, preserving in this way the best and most interesting samples" from the Sasanian period.[49] A great portion of what was preserved of Middle Persian literature passed over into Arabic literature, and helped form "a special kind of literature, known as *adab*, namely instruction on correct and successful behaviour in any given situation."[50] Regrettably the titles of none of al-ʿAttābī's works hint explicitly at his interest in Iranian culture (or at his storytelling [discussed below]), except perhaps the *Kitāb al-Ādāb* [On Proper Conduct].[51]

The incident that prompts al-ʿAttābī to address Yaḥyā ibn al-Ḥasan in Persian is an exchange between the latter and a servant of his. Several decades later, al-Ṭabarī would hear verses declaimed in Persian in Marāghā, the capital of Azerbaijan. It is certainly not surprising that Persian continued to be spoken in areas where Arabization did not completely take root, and where people of Persian descent, language, and culture continued to dominate. As Rypka observes:[52]

> A hundred-and-fifty years after the Arab invasion we find in Transoxania, Nishapur and Tukharistan a swarm of men of letters who no longer write exclusively in Arabic, but also in Persian or only in Persian.

This situation is attributed by Rypka to the patronage of the Ṭāhirids (205–59/820–72), who, he believes, could not and did not take such an indifferent or hostile attitude towards the Persian language as is frequently supposed.[53] The importance of the Ṭāhirids in Ibn Abī Ṭāhir's mind is demonstrated by the fact that he devotes a substantial portion of the surviving volume of the *Book of Baghdad* to them.[54]

As for Ibn Abī Ṭāhir's knowledge of Persian, there is no explicit statement to the effect that he knew or spoke it. As the child of first-generation Khurāsānī inhabitants of Baghdad, he may reasonably be expected to have spoken Persian as a mother tongue. But even if he did not speak it natively, the fact that he reports anecdotes that include Persian exchanges may indicate that he learned Persian, like al-ʿAttābī and others. Indeed, as suggested above, the possibility that his fables were translations from, or adaptations of, Persian texts cannot be excluded, especially in light of the considerable volume of translation undertaken in the second/eighth and third/ninth centuries.

If they were not translations from Persian, several of Ibn Abī Ṭāhir's works were certainly inspired by Persian models. The adoption of Persian literary models and adaptation of Persian material were not necessarily cases of direct written transmission, but could have also been acquired through oral tradition. Stephen Belcher, developing B. E. Perry's argument, argues, for example, that the *Book of Sindbād* is not of Indian origin but a product rather of medieval Near Eastern fiction. Belcher alerts us to:[55]

> the possibility that Sindbād was *not originally composed in Persian (or Pahlavi) at all, but in Arabic,* and that what is meant when Ibn al-Nadīm, for

instance, says that such a book is Persian [= *Fihrist*, p. 186, line 6] is that *the story is Persian*, although *the redaction may be Arabic*, or that *the Arabic redaction represents a compilation of a variety of written Persian sources* (such as single-episode romances and the tradition of *andarz*).

Interest in Persianate material of this kind has been attributed specifically to the influence of the attachment to Persian ideas and ideals of the new Abbasid administrative class, the secretaries (*kuttāb*). Because of these administrators' interest in right government, the argument goes, there is an attendant interest in Persian stories illustrating right government.

There was undoubtedly also a *popular* interest in past Persian glories and proper kingly behavior. There were in fact numerous tales dealing with kings, wise men and philosophers.[56] The characters in these traditions and tales were based on historical figures, Sasanian emperors such as Ardashīr, Bahrām Čūbīn, and Khusraw I Anūshirwān, and wise ministers, notably Buzurgmihr. Ardashīr (incidentally the person credited with the founding of Ibn Abī Ṭāhir's hometown, Marw al-Rūdh[57]) and Anūshirwān are remembered for organizational initiatives within government, for their testaments, and for their actual, or literary, debates with heretics and adherents of religious sects.[58] As for Hurmuz IV (r. 579–90), although Byzantine historians portray him as a proud man of mediocre intelligence, in al-Ṭabarī's account for instance, he is compassionate toward the common folk, severe with his nobles and the Zoroastrian clergy (which led to their revolt and his execution), and just, surpassing even the legendary justice of his father Anūshirwān (r. 531–79). These figures generated fictionalized personae that became a vehicle in the third/ninth century for edifying tales. These also generated a number of stories and stories within stories, including those in the "education of princes" genre, called in Arabic *naṣīḥat al-mulūk*, literally "Advice for rulers" (*Fürstenspiegel* [mirrors for princes]).[59] Cognate works consisted of testaments to heirs, advising them on matters of state, ethics, power and justice, and often included aphorisms and sentences.

It is undoubtedly the case that the "advice for rulers" literature appealed to the secretaries, counsellors, courtiers, and writers in the late Umayyad and early Abbasid periods.[60] But it is also true that Persian and other kinds of Near Eastern works provided models for other kinds of writing with a wider appeal, such as historical narratives and chronicles, romances, and debate and disputation literature.[61] When al-Masʿūdī writes in an oft-cited remark that he was shown a book written in 113/731 based on works in the collections of Persian Kings, he is providing evidence for continued interest in transmitting this material well into second/eighth century.[62] Translated into Arabic from Persian for the caliph Hishām (r. 105–25/724–43), this book contained information on Persian history, science, and architecture, and included portraits.[63] Zoroastrian works were also copied and translated into the third/ninth century.[64]

This generic variety is evident in Ibn Abī Ṭāhir's oeuvre. One of his lost works unambiguously illustrates his interest in Persian "advice for rulers" literature, namely his *Kitāb Tarbiyat Hurmuz ibn Kisrā Anūshirwān* [Book of the Education of Hurmuz ibn Kisrā Anūshirwān]. This work may have been based on the *Kitāb Anūshirwān*, the *Kitāb al-Kārnāmaj fī Sīrat Anūshirwān* [Book of Deeds from the Life of Anūshirwān], or the *Kitāb Khwadāy-Nāmag* [The Book of Kings], all mentioned by Ibn al-Nadīm.[65] Many of these were translated into Arabic from the Pahlavi by Ibn al-Muqaffaʿ (d. *c.* 139/756), al-ʿAttābī, and others,[66] possibly even Ibn Abī Ṭāhir himself. There were, in addition to translated Persian wisdom works, Arabic chronicles and histories based on, or inspired by, Persian *siyar al-mulūk* (lives of kings) works, almost all of which were written by Persians. Al-Dīnawarī, Ibn Abī Ṭāhir and al-Ṭabarī, to name only three, were able to draw from the *Khwāday-Nāmag/Khudāynāma* and similar works.[67] Parallel to the development of a prose tradition which sought inspiration in the lore and legends of India, Iran, Mesopotamia, and Greek Antiquity,[68] narrative prose developed also out of the kernel of the *khabar*.[69] In this form, the antecedents of prose writing include not only extra-Arabian traditions, but also the traditions of pre-Islamic verse and Arabian antiquity.[70] *The Book of Baghdad* may also defensibly be read as a reworking of the Islamic past – and present – in the style of the Persian historical/legendary tradition, including accounts of rulers' exchanges with their advisors and counsellors.[71] The testamentary letter from al-Ṭāhir ibn al-Ḥusayn to his son ʿAbdallāh upon his appointment to the governorship of Khurasan is preserved there.[72]

Persian stories

H. A. R. Gibb is undoubtedly correct in observing that it is impossible to *isolate* Persian elements in Arabic literature and Arabic culture because of the confluence of many divergent strands.[73] But the contribution of Persians (and Persophiles) to the development of Arabic culture is undeniable, even if precious little of Persian traditional literature translated into Arabic has survived.[74] There is in fact a manifest link between Persianness/Persophilia and evening storytelling and fable-writing. A great number of the stories originate, or get their inspiration, from Persian models, and the writers Ibn al-Nadīm ties to evening-stories and fables underscore that Persian connection: all those he names are themselves either Persian or Persophile.

There is not a great deal of information about *asmār*-storytellers (evening storytellers = *musāmirūn*, *quṣṣāṣ*) and fabulists qua storytellers in the sources.[75] This is not altogether surprising. Abbott suggests that like their counterparts, the *quṣṣāṣ*-storytellers (*quṣṣāṣ* = preachers),[76] evening-storytellers (*musāmirūn*) were not held in high regard, consequently, little of their literary output survives, and little information therefore finds its way into biographical and bibliographic sources.[77] The low esteem in which storytellers were held was caused by the nature of the material they related, in spite of (because of?) diverse content which would have included religious discussions and exhortations blended with stories of the prophets and their deeds (*qiṣaṣ al-anbiyā'*); battle-accounts of the pre-Islamic Arab past (*ayyām al-ʿArab*); stories connected with the life of the Prophet Muḥammad (*sīrah, ḥadīth*) and the first few caliphs (*akhbār, ḥadīth*?); stories about the Umayyad and Abbasid caliphs (*akhbār, Alf laylah*?); stories from legend (*khurāfāt*); and adaptations of legends and fables of Persia (*khurāfāt, asmār, siyar al-mulūk*). It is certainly easy to see how an amalgamation of these stories and themes at the hands of storytellers and copyists, and in the polemic of the preachers, might have transformed storytelling.[78]

There had, ever since the rise of Islam and on into its first three centuries, been an animus against stories from outside, in particular from the Persian tradition. Indeed, the Quran's *asāṭīr al-awwalīn* (tales of the ancients) and *lahw al-ḥadīth* (idle narrative), may refer to stories of Iranian origin.[79] Ibn Hishām attributes these stories to the Meccan al-Naḍr ibn al-Ḥārith (d. *c.* 2/624), a merchant who may have traveled to Persia, and who is credited with challenging Muhammad by saying, "I know better stories than you, I know the stories of Rustam and Isfandiyār".[80]

Persian motifs and stories did not come to Arabic through Iranian or Persophile writers alone. The Lakhmids, as vassals of the Sasanians, and patrons of culture at al-Ḥīrah, also showed interest in this material. It may be, therefore, that al-Naḍr ibn al-Ḥārith learned his stories in al-Ḥīrah, probably in the early 600s CE. That there was a difference between sanctioned stories and forbidden ones, and that such a distinction persisted, is clear from al-Ḥarīrī's defence of his own *Maqāmāt* in the sixth/twelfth century. He maintained that his compositions were useful stories (*ḥikāyāt*), such as the stories found in *Kalīlah and Dimnah*, and not the false stories forbidden by Islam – presumably the Quran's *asāṭīr al-awwalīn* (tales of the ancients).[81]

Although the entry devoted to Ibn Abī Ṭāhir in *The Catalog* is not in the section devoted to individuals who translated works from Persian, he is, as mentioned above, clustered by Ibn al-Nadīm elsewhere in *The Catalog* together with four such translators, namely al-ʿAttābī (d. after 208/823), ʿAlī ibn Dāwūd (fl. late second/eighth century), Ibn al-Muqaffaʿ (d. *c.* 137/756), and Sahl ibn Ḥārūn (d. 215/830). I have discussed al-ʿAttābī above. ʿAlī ibn Dāwūd is described by Ibn al-Nadīm as "one of the eloquent prose stylists (*bulaghāʾ*) who in his compositions (*taṣnīfāt*) followed the method (*ṭarīqah*) of Sahl ibn Hārūn," and names as works *Kitāb al-Jurhumiyyah wa-Tawkīl al-niʿam* [The Story of the Jurhumī woman and Tawkīl al-niʿam], *Kitāb al-Ḥurrah wa-al-Amah* [The Story of the freedwoman and the slavegirl], and *Kitāb al-Ẓirāf* [On Elegant (Men)].[82] This last title is similar to Ibn Abī Ṭāhir's *Kitāb Akhbār al-mutaẓarrifāt* [Book of women displaying/affecting (wit and) elegance] (also attributed to Ibn Abī Ṭāhir's son ʿUbaydallāh). Little else is known about ʿAlī.[83]

Ibn al-Muqaffaʿ's works include a book on the life of Anūshirwān, and translations and adaptations of the *Khwādāy-Nāmag*,[84] and numerous fables. While not the originator of imaginative literature in Arabic, Ibn al-Muqaffaʿ was certainly the first to popularize and bring attention to it, specifically with his versions of *Kalīlah and Dimnah*,[85] fables told through the mouths of animals, and

Bilawhar wa-Yūdāsaf, an Arabic tale based on a Sanskrit legend of the Buddha.[86] Ibn al-Muqaffaʿ also wrote important works in the "advice for rulers" genre. In his *Risālah fī al-Ṣaḥābah* [Epistle on caliphal companions] perhaps addressed to the caliph al-Manṣūr (r. 136–58/754–75), he saw the caliph as the only source of both religious and political authority and advised him to use it to impose religious and legal uniformity.[87] Ibn al-Muqaffaʿ's imperial, neo-Sasanian vision – including a caliphal corps of religious scholars, a respected military, an aristocratic civil service, and the exclusion of menials from authority[88] – does not, however, explicitly draw on Kisrā, Buzurgmihr or anything Persian.[89]

Like Ibn al-Muqaffaʿ, the writer, translator and poet Sahl ibn Hārūn ibn Rāhawayh (d. 215/830) was of Iranian origin.[90] Like al-ʿAttābī, Sahl was a secretary of Yaḥyā al-Barmakī (d. 187/803), the vizier of Hārūn al-Rashīd (r. 170–93/786–809). And like al-ʿAttābī, he survived the fall of the Barmakids and became close to Hārūn. It is unclear whether he retained under al-Amīn (r. 293–98/809–13) the office of *ṣāḥib al-dawāwīn* (director of chanceries) conferred upon him by Hārūn, but in the caliphate of al-Maʾmūn (198–218/818–33) he was attached to al-Ḥasan ibn Sahl (d. 236/850) and served as chief director and librarian of the library, the *Khizānat* (or *Bayt*) *al-Ḥikmah*.[91]

Ghazi's suggestion that Sahl might have been the "faithful disciple" of Ibn al-Muqaffaʿ is a little far-fetched given their dates, but Gabrieli is almost certainly right in suggesting that Ibn al-Muqaffaʿ set in motion a virtual myth, and that a whole generation of writers, including Sahl, modeled their own literary output on his.[92] He was also an orator of great style and sophistication. Indeed, both Sahl's name and words became proverbial.[93] One of Sahl's admirers was al-Jāḥiẓ, who heaped upon him and his books considerable praise.[94] This affection may have derived, in part at least, from Sahl's attachment to the Muʿtazilite cause. He is also explicitly identified as "a partisan of the *Shuʿūbīs*, with strong anti-Arab views" by Ibn al-Nadīm who goes on to note that many of Sahl's works dealt with the claims by non-Arabs of equality with or superiority to Arabs (see below).[95] Sahl is also credited with a treatise on miserliness – though the attribution has been called into question – his ridicule of Arab ideals having been suggested as a motive for his writing it. This praise for frugality was apparently then used against him by his anti-*Shuʿūbī* opponents.[96]

Some titles and extracts of fables by Sahl, modeled on Persian *andarz* or wisdom literature, survive. These are moralizing stories told through the speech of birds, animals, or even humans (usually archetypal or legendary). Excerpts survive from *Kitāb Thaʿlah wa-ʿAfrah (or ʿAfrāʾ)* [Book of Thaʿlah and ʿAfrah], which Ibn al-Nadīm says Sahl modeled on *Kalīlah and Dimnah*.[97] His *Kitāb al-Hudhaliyyah wa-al-Makhzūmī* [Book of the Hudhaylī Woman and the Makhzūmī (Man)] does not survive, but the *Kitāb al-Namir wa-al-Thaʿlab* [Book of the panther and the fox] exists in an abridged version. It is not possible to say whether Sahl translated from Pahlavi originals or composed the stories himself. But the imprint of Middle Persian literature is indelible. It is not surprising, therefore, that Sahl came to be known as the "Buzurgmihr of Islam." Buzurgmihr was the wise counsellor and

Minister to Anūshirwān who was not only the direct inspiration for several important works but also the model for other king/counsellor works. These include Pahlavi originals and also Arabic analogs, the most famous example of which is Hārūn al-Rashīd/Jaʿfar the Barmakid, in the *Thousand and One Nights*, for instance.[98] The fall of the Barmakids may even have been responsible for reviving interest in the literary topos of the great king and his counsellor.

Ibn Nubātah mentions that Sahl wrote a *Sīrat al-Ma'mūn* [Biography of al-Ma'mūn] the only book known explicitly to treat this caliph alone. It was more than likely written in the Persian *siyar al-mulūk* tradition of royal biography and may have have been the source of many later accounts of al-Ma'mūn, possibly also Ibn Abī Ṭāhir's *Kitāb Baghdād.*[99] Alhough Ibn al-Nadīm does not mention the *Sīrat al-Ma'mūn*, he does mention a *Risālah fī al-Qaḍā'* [Epistle on judgeship], addressed/dedicated to a *qāḍī* of Persian origin (ʿĪsā ibn Abān [d. 220/835]); several romances, including the *Kitāb al-Wāmik wa-al-ʿAdhrā'* [Book of the solicitous lover and the virgin], and *Kitāb Nadūd wa-Wadūd wa-Ladūd*[100] [Book of Nadūd, Wadūd and Ladūd]; and also the *Kitāb Adab Ashk ibn Ashk* [The conduct of Ashk son of Ashk].[101]

Although the royal biography (*siyar al-mulūk*) literature, *Kalīlah and Dimnah*, other animal fables, and other Persian models had an obvious formal and original impact on Arabic prose, important also were other examples of wisdom literature assimilated into Arabic literature from the Greek, Indian, and Ancient Near Eastern traditions.[102] These include such stories as those about the relationship between Alexander, the model of kingship and rule, and Aristotle, the model of counsel and ethical advice. This strand might have contributed to the composition of more generic titles, such as Ibn Abī Ṭāhir's *Book of (the story of) the conciliatory King and the supportive vizier*, or *Book of (the story of) the great King and the management of the kingdom and its administration*. This title bears a close resemblance to the *Kitāb Tadbīr al-mulk wa-al-siyāsah* [Book of the management and administration of the realm] by fellow storyteller and fabulist, Sahl ibn Hārūn.[103] In the case of *Book of [the story of] the two tyrannical Babylonian and Egyptian kings and the wise Byzantine king*,[104] also by Ibn Abī Ṭāhir, it is reasonably clear that the protagonists are archetypal.[105] This may therefore have been a debate or dispute text. In such texts, when the contenders are human they are usually representatives of a particular group rather than ordinary folk (see chapter 6 below).

Ibn Abī Ṭāhir and the Shuʿūbiyyah

In life as in prose, the relationship of non-Arabs to Arabs became prominent in discussion in the third/ninth century. The movement knows as the *Shuʿūbiyyah* comprised the parties of those who claimed equality of non-Arabs with, or their superiority to, Arabs.[106] H. A. R. Gibb suggested that the original *Shuʿūbīs* were the Kharijites, who "on religious grounds maintained the doctrine that no race or tribe enjoyed inherent superiority," Persians included.[107] The word *Shuʿūbiyyah* itself goes back to a Quranic proof text (Q 49/13) which states that humankind was created in peoples and tribes, and does not seem to have been used pejoratively. On the contrary, it was a name that acquired force from scripture.

In the wake of conquest of non-Arab areas and conversion of non-Arab peoples, Islam's teaching of the brotherhood and equality of all Arabs was understood to be a teaching of the equality of all peoples under God's law. This is why, in some quarters, *Shuʿūbiyyah* thinking called for equality (*taswiyah*) between Arabs and non-Arabs, and why they were also known as *ahl al-taswiyah* [the people/party of equality]. In other quarters, however, *Shuʿūbiyyah* thinking categorically denied any significance whatsoever to the Arabs. The latter view was no doubt prosecuted mainly by the Persians and Turks who needed right away to understand and establish their position in the various new communities of which they were now part, and indeed in the *ummah* at large.[108] H. T. Norris has described it as a widespread movement in the new middle class of influential secretaries, which had as its aim the remolding of political and social institutions, indeed the whole spirit of Islamic culture, according to Sasanian institutions and values.[109]

The group which prosecuted the *Shuʿūbiyyah* cause did so mainly in writing. Indeed, some scholars have been skeptical about the political reality of the *Shuʿūbiyyah*, suggesting that the Arab/non-Arab rivalry is an exaggeration and that "the only real manifestations of the *Shuʿūbiyyah* were ... simply literary ones."[110] But others maintain that the *Shuʿūbiyyah* represented a reawakening of Persian national consciousness.[111] In any event, the *Shuʿūbiyyah* was most likely not a threat to established political order. As Gibb notes:[112]

> Their aim was not to destroy the Islamic empire but to remold its political institutions and values, which represented in their eyes the highest political wisdom.

This is underscored by the fact that those known to be partisans of the *Shuʿūbiyyah* were all educated, and were mostly administrators and writers (i.e. *kātib*s).[113] The *Shuʿūbiyyah* was, therefore, principally the product of the literary activity of writers and scholars, and not of the unhappiness of disgruntled mobs.

The rise of the Persian secretarial *kātib* class had brought with it attention to matters Persian, e.g. Persian models of kingship; Arabic philologists prosecuted a distinctly Arabic humanities. And both groups advanced their visions using Arabic prose. Gibb saw the conflict between the two cultural traditions as the cause of the *Shuʿūbiyyah* movement, especially as non-Persian members of the increasingly literate middle class began to occupy positions of importance in the administration. This view has recently been revised by Susanne Enderwitz, who suggsts that:[114]

> It was not simply a question of the triumph of one cultural tradition over another; rather, it was a matter of *status*. At risk was not just the

reputation of the Persian court literature but the *social privileges* of the secretaries who followed its tradition. Meanwhile, the Arab and Islamic literature was not simply a product of isolated philologists and jurists but reflected the world-view of the new citizens.

The *Shuʿūbiyyah* provided a stimulus for the study of genealogy. This resulted in works such as *Kitāb Asmāʾ baghāyā Quraysh fī al-Jāhiliyyah wa-man waladna* [The names of the whores of the Quraysh in pre-Islamic times and those they bore].[115] The Abbasid caliphs – only three of whom were the sons of free mothers, viz. al-Saffāḥ, al-Manṣūr, and al-Mahdī – had undermined, as it were, the whole notion of genealogy, and rendered maternal descent dynastically irrelevant.[116] This resulted in an impulse to buttress the importance of genealogy, and of the caliphate, and generated a rise in the number of works devoted to both. There also developed a trend of teaching traditions that recommended and required respect for the Arabs. It is traditions such as these that Ibn Qutaybah records in his anti-*Shuʿūbī* tract, the *Kitāb al-ʿArab*.[117] Persian lineage could also be valuably deployed, in the case of *dihqāns* (Persian princes, nobility) for example, descendants of old noble Persian families, whose own nobility was contrasted with – and posited as superior to – pure Arab parentage. Writers of Persian ethnicity also occasionally claimed royal Sasanian descent, Abū Hilāl al-ʿAskarī, for example. *Shuʿūbī* philologists studied Arab genealogies in order to expose fabricated and falsely attributed ones.[118] The *kātib* Saʿīd ibn Ḥumayd (d. after 252/866), an extreme *Shuʿūbī* and someone said to be descended from *dihqāns*, often criticized the vainglorious claims of Arabs to noble descent in critiques that were the hallmark of *Shuʿūbī* writing. Regrettably, his *Kitāb Intiṣāf al-ʿAjam ʿalā al-ʿArab* [Book of the parity of the Persians with the Arabs, or Meting out of Justice of the Persians over the Arabs, or Vindication of the Persians in the face of the Arabs], also known as The *Kitāb al-Taswiyah* [Book of equality] is lost.[119]

Predictably, the *Shuʿūbiyyah* generated a rich comparative literature which weighed Arab virtues against Persian vices and Persian virtues against Arab vices. Much of this literature was produced in the *faḍāʾil* (excellences) genre, in which quality or precedence were demonstrated and praised.

The earliest *faḍāʾil* works were in praise of the Quran. *Faḍāʾil* works on individuals or groups were followed by those in praise of cities. But evidently the latter rapidly came to be nothing more than collections of sayings attributed to Muḥammad and his Companions to political and regional ends. Some were likely not meant to be taken at face value, the *Faḍl al-kilāb ʿalā kathīr mimman labisa al-thiyāb* [Book of the superiority of dogs over many of those who wear clothes], by Ibn Abī Ṭāhir's student, Ibn al-Marzubān (d. 309/921), which survives and is clearly ironic.[120] Ibn Abī Ṭāhir's son ʿUbaydallāh (d. 313/925) is credited with a *Kitāb al-Sikbāj wa-faḍāʾilihā* [Book of Sikbāj stew and its virtues].[121] The titles of such works – many are attested – suggest they were written in reaction to and/or imitation of *faḍaʾil* works. They would have combined humor, critique, social criticism, and perhaps obscenity. Ibn al-Nadīm credits Abū al-ʿAnbas al-Ṣaymarī (d. 275/888), who writes about the lucrativeness of writing about *sukhf* (obscenity), with a *Kitāb Faḍl al-surm ʿalā al-fam* [Book of the superiority of the anus to the mouth],[122] and also with a *Faḍl al-sullam ʿalā al-darajah* [The superiority of the ladder to the staircase].[123]

The earliest known philological "rejoinder" to the *Shuʿūbiyyah* on the part of those valuing Arab virtues has been identified as the *Kitāb al-Ishtiqāq* [Book of the Derivation (of Proper Names)] by Ibn Durayd (d. 321/933);[124] Ibn Durayd's pupil, Abū Aḥmad al-ʿAskarī (d. 382/992), wrote a treatise entitled *al-Risālah fī al-tafḍīl bayna balāghatay al-ʿarab wa-al-ʿajam* [Epistle on the comparison between the eloquence of the Arabs and the eloquence of the Persians].[125] It has been characterized as pro-Arab on the basis of the fact that Ibn Durayd states in his introduction that he is refuting those who attack Arabic, and the etymologies of Arabic names. But Ibn Durayd does not name the people he is refuting and it is not unequivocally clear that these people need be *Shuʿūbīs*. As for Ḥamzah al-Iṣfahānī (d. 350/961), who prided himself on his Persian descent,[126] and who wrote works intended to "put the Iranian past into the foreground of Muslim consiousness," he did not display one of the primary *Shuʿūbī* tendencies, namely a sense of prejudice against Arabs and Arabness.[127] This may explain his decision to write an epistle on the noble qualities of Arabs, *al-Risālah al-muʿribah ʿan sharaf al-Aʿrāb* [The clear epistle on the nobility of the Arabs].

Indeed, one's ethnic or doctrinal affiliation was not necessarily related to one's position in the *Shuʿūbī* debate. More importantly, works began to appear which broached the debate, and might even take a particular position out of literary interest without being veritably partisan. This helps explain why some scholars have rejected attribution of the *Kitāb Faḍāʾil al-Furs* [The Virtues of the Persians] of Abū ʿUbaydah (d. after 209/824–25) to *Shuʿūbiyyah.*[128] Abū ʿUbaydah may have been motivated not by partisan tendencies, or by his high opinion of the Persians and low opinion of the Arabs, but by interest in the subject.[129]

The foregoing suggests that a title attested for Ibn Abī Ṭāhir, the *Kitāb Faḍl al-ʿArab ʿalā al-ʿAjam* [Book of the superiority of the Arabs over the Persians], while it may have resembled Ibn Qutaybah's *Kitāb al-ʿArab* [Book of the Arabs] which al-Bīrūnī felt compelled to point out as being particularly hostile to the Iranians,[130] might just as easily have been similar to Abū ʿUbaydah's *Kitāb Faḍāʾil al-Furs* [Book on the Virtues of the Persians] that is, a work written not as a contribution to the *Shuʿūbiyyah* debate but as one evincing interest in the virtues of the Arabs per se. The possibility that Ibn Abī Ṭāhir's *Book of the superiority of the Arabs over the Persians* was a friendly rejoinder to Saʿīd ibn Ḥumayd's *Book of the parity of the Persians with the Arabs* cannot be excluded either (or vice-versa, for that matter). The two were friends and there is no reason why their exchanges in verse and letters could not extend to the writing of entire works. As Sellheim cautiously concludes about works in praise of Arab virtues:[131]

> To what extent anti-*Shuʿūbī* tendencies play a part in these works, as seems to have been the case with Aḥmad ibn Abī Ṭāhir Ṭayfūr's (d. 280/893) *Kitāb Faḍl al-ʿArab ʿalā al-ʿAjam* [. . .], *has not been clarified.*

Ibn Abī Ṭāhir was evidently interested in relative virtues. In the next chapter I look at literary debate, another area in which this interest manifested itself.

6

PRECEDENCE AND CONTEST

Rose vs Narcissus

Partisans of the *Shuʿūbiyyah*, the movement that sought recognition of the equality of non-Arabs with Arabs, wrote works that echoed the earlier *mufākharah* genre, including both self-praise and derision. *Mufākharah* was a form of boasting or vaunting that was sometimes used to end a quarrel between two people.[1] An impartial umpire would be appointed as judge and forfeits deposited with him. The outcome depended, of course, more on skill than on principles of justice. Variants of the *mufākharah* included the *munāfarah*, *mukhāyalah*, *munājadah*, and *muḥājāh*. In the *muḥājāh* (satiric exchange) it was the public who decided, based on the satires, which of two enemies would prevail.[2] The term *mufākharah* came to be used in conjunction with works in the contest genre of debate literature (*munāẓarah*), works such as Ibn Abī Ṭāhir's *Book of the boasting-match between the rose and the narcissus*.[3] Ibn Abī Ṭāhir's work may have been one of the earliest literary debates (*munāẓarah*) in Arabic. The *munāẓarah* between the Spring and Fall attributed to al-Jāḥiẓ is in all likelihood the work of a much later author.[4] Al-Jāḥiẓ is well-known for his praise/censure and virtues/faults works, but in all cases the debates are conducted by advocates and not by the subjects themselves: properly speaking, debate per se only took place in works where the subjects themselves spoke and vied.[5] Regrettably, it is not extant; it is therefore not possible to determine whether it fulfilled the generally accepted criteria of the Near Eastern literary debate, namely two or more persons, things, or abstractions *personally* putting forward claims of superiority. Dispute between inanimate objects seems to have originated with a poem by al-ʿAbbās ibn al-Aḥnaf (d. after 193/808) which has the eye and the heart accusing one another of afflicting the poet with love. Here it is not a question of precedence or excellence but of censure and blame.

Although it is no longer extant, al-Tanūkhī (d. 384/994) writes in the fourth/tenth century that he saw a copy of Ibn Abī Ṭāhir's *Book of the boasting-match between the rose and the narcissus*, calling it by its variant title, "Book of the superiority of the rose to the narcissus." There is no reason to doubt that the same work is meant. But to judge by the titles alone, different kinds of work are suggested, one praising the excellences of the rose over the narcissus, the other providing both sides of the argument. Confusion about the title may stem from the generic similarities between the *mufākharat* and *faḍā'il* genres; or from the work's similarity to Ibn Lankak's *Risālah fī Faḍl al-ward ʿalā al-narjis* [Epistle on the superiority of the rose to the narcissus] – even though Ibn Abī Ṭāhir's book is, according to al-Tanūkhī, "a larger and more extensive and useful work than Ibn Lankak's book."[6] What is more, Ibn Abī Ṭāhir and Ibn Lankak knew one another.

The two most prominent proponents of these two flowers in the third/ninth century were Ibn al-Muʿtazz (d. 296/908), who preferred the rose, and Ibn al-Rūmī (d. 283/896), who favored the narcissus. It should be noted that Ibn al-Muʿtazz's exclusion of Ibn al-Rūmī from the *Classes of the modern poets* is attributed by some scholars to the former's dislike of the latter's Shiite sympathies.[7] But Diʿbil (d. 246/860), another vocal Shiite, is not similarly excluded by Ibn al-Muʿtazz. It is possible that Ibn al-Rūmī's *hijā'* (satire) of Ibn al-Muʿtazz lies at the root of this silence, just as it is possible that the rose/narcissus dispute between Ibn al-Muʿtazz and Ibn al-Rūmī also played a role: The latter's poem, often referred to as "Tafḍīl al-narjis ʿalā al-ward" ["The superiority of the narcissus to the rose"], is said to have prompted several responses.[8]

It is not known whether Ibn Abī Ṭāhir's work was intended as a response to Ibn al-Rūmī, whether Ibn al-Rūmī's was a response to Ibn Abī Ṭāhir's, or if the two works were produced independent of one another.[9] The first of these seems likely: in the first place, the debate was a prominent one; in the second place, one of the arguments adduced by Ibn al-Rūmī for the superiority of the narcissus to the rose is the fact that people are named Narcissus (Narjis) but that no-one is named Rose,[10] and the brief surviving extract of Ibn Abī Ṭāhir's work, quoted by al-Tanūkhī in *al-Faraj baʿd al-shiddah* [Relief after distress] refutes that claim by listing names of women named 'Rose.'[11] What is known about contact between Ibn Abī Ṭāhir and Ibn al-Rūmī is limited to the satires they exchanged. In spite of the virulence of many of these, it is possible that the two were friends, perhaps facilitated by their shared dislike for al-Buḥturī.[12] They certainly had numerous personal contacts in common, e.g. Ibn Thawābah, Ibrāhīm ibn al-Mudabbir, Ibn Bulbul, and especially ʿAlī ibn Yaḥyā ibn al-Munajjim. On the other hand, reverses in attention led Ibn al-Rūmī later to belittle many of these individuals. Ibn Abī Ṭāhir might have thereby become an associated target of Ibn al-Rūmī's invective, if he was not a direct one himself. Ibn al-Rūmī was apparently easily provoked, especially by rival poets, disagreements with whom he often aired in his verse. The animosity felt by some individuals for others is widely recorded – recall al-Buḥturī's views on Ibn Abī Ṭāhir, and also Ibn Kaysān's observation:[13]

> Those who,
> when confronted with the hostility of an envious rival
> Shed blood through the spearheads of their pens.

And the biographer, al-Ṣafadī, observes of Ibn Abī Ṭāhir's associate, Abū al-ʿAynāʾ, that "one day, he passed by the home of an enemy of his."[14]

Some exchanges, such as those between Ibn Abī Ṭāhir and Ibn al-Rūmī below, may admittedly have have been purely for literary purposes. One of Ibn al-Rūmī's satires of Ibn Abī Ṭāhir reads as follows:[15]

'Why do you bark at the moon,' I asked Ibn Abī Ṭāhir,
'when it shines full?'

'It towers high above humanity,' he replied,
'and I envy what makes it beautiful.'

'Why do you bark only at the moon,' I said,
'when the sun offers the same?'

'Its light blinds me,' he replied, 'But my eyes
find the moonlight tame.'

The following isolated line recorded by al-Mīkālī may have been part of Ibn Abī Ṭāhir's response to that satire:[16]

I was like a dog who appeared to be barking at the moon.
But (tell me), does the barking of a dog do harm to the moon?

Wa kuntu ka ʾl-kalbi uḍḥī nābiḥan qamaran
wa hal yaḍurru nubāḥu ʾl-kalbi bi ʾl-qamarī

But barking is also mentioned in two other satires, and so the line mentioned above may have been a response to one of those. The first of those reads:[17]

Those who seek
information about things
asked me why dogs bark at the moon, but no one can tell.

No-one knows
why they bark at it,
except one man who was a dog like them for a spell.

He's known by
his late father's name,
Ṭāhir, the chaste but, by God, he's far from chaste.

Ask him why
he barks at it and,
if he takes to you, he'll fill you in and give you a taste.

The other satire reads:[18]

Enough of you, Ibn Abī Ṭāhir,
May I never again see such a poet.

You are neither hot nor cold,
What's in the middle but the lukewarm and tepid?

Like the one who's always about
to spit up a thick, clotted mass of vomit.

Your 'art' vacillates
between the arts, neither 'urban' nor 'desert.'

I saw you bark at me the way
You barked at the moon, like a nitwit.

No harm done to the moon,
Just the over-eager dog's habit.

My bows are strung
their strings thick, sound and tight,

My arrows, sharp
as your fear of the avenger's threat.

But your refuge from its damage
is the lowness of your worth in everyone's eyes.

So fear not my arrows when I take aim,
But don't feel secure from one shot aimlessly.

The following satire by Ibn al-Rūmī shares similarities with the one above:[19]

Enough of you,
Ibn Abı Ṭāhir, my hope is
never to see the likes of you before I dine.

The heat of your verse
is not the heat of fire,
The frigid verse you write is still not cool as wine.

As I suggested above, it is quite possible that these satires were occasioned by the publication of Ibn Abī Ṭāhir's work on the precedence of the rose over the narcissus.

Al-Washshā' (d. 325/937), who devotes a section of his *Kitāb al-Muwashshā* [Book of the embroidered] to the excellence of the rose,[20] states that its virtues "are more numerous than can be enumerated," and that the *ahl al-ẓarf* (people of elegance) preferred roses above all other flowers.[21] Ibn Abī Ṭāhir is the author of a *Book of women affecting wit and elegance (= mutaẓarrifāt)* and also a *Book of the embroidered*, both lost. Ibn al-Nadīm reports that the former (as well as the *Book of the language of the eyes*) are said to have been put together by Ibn Abī Ṭāhir's son, 'Ubaydallāh; 'Ubaydallāh is also credited with a separate volume on people affecting elegance, the *Kitāb al-Mutaẓarrifāt wa-al-mutaẓarrifīn* [Book of women and men affecting wit and elegance].[22]

The opposition rose/narcissus was evidently a well-known one in the century Ibn Abī Ṭāhir was writing. But why the narcissus, as opposed to any other flower, is singled out for comparison to the rose has not been explained either by medieval critics or by modern scholars of Arabic literary debate.[23] Al-Washshā' does quote several sentiments in prose and verse to the effect that myrtle (*ās*) is superior to the rose because it is long-lasting; indeed, al-Washshā' identifies as the prime rival of the rose the myrtle, not the narcissus.[24] Perhaps the origin for the various preferences is rooted in the following statements attributed to the Prophet Muḥammad:[25]

> The white rose was created from my sweat on the Night of the Ascension [*Mi'rāj*], the red rose was created from the sweat of Gabriel, and the yellow rose was created from the sweat of Burāq.
>
> Adam was cast down from the Garden with three things: with a myrtle tree, which is the chief aromatic of the world; with an ear of wheat, which is the chief food of the world; and with a date, which is the chief fruit of the world.

It certainly seems likely that the monopoly imposed by al-Mutawakkil on roses occasioned discussions, or further discussions, about the relative merits of different flowers. Al-Nawājī (d. 859/1455) reports in his work on wine, the *Ḥalbat al-kumayt* [The racecourse of the bay]:[26]

> Al-Mutawakkil said, 'I am the sovereign power, the rose is the sovereign flower (*anā malik al-salāṭīn wa-al-ward malik al-rayāḥīn*), and we are all better in the company of equals,' and forbade the people roses. He monopolized them, saying 'They do not suit the common folk (*al-'āmmah*).'

The precise connotation of al-Mutawakkil's statement is not clear. It may, for example, echo the contest that al-Tanasī (d. 899/1494) believes is the origin of the contest between the rose and the narcissus, namely a conversation between two Sasanian kings.[27]

Citing the admittedly much later *al-Jawhar al-fard fī munāẓarat al-narjis wa-al-ward* [The Unique Jewel: The debate between the narcissus and the rose] of ʿAlī ibn Muḥammad al-Māridīnī (fl. ninth/fifteenth century), Mattock finds it curious and unclear that "the rose simply asserts its God-given superiority over all the other flowers."[28] He also does not understand how the narcissus can make good its threat to break the roses' thorns; the rose had claimed to be able to control the narcissi with them. In the context of al-Mutawakkil's decree, however, these sentiments acquire some meaning: the rose becomes the caliph, the narcissus becomes the Persianate elements around the caliph. This also helps clarify the rose's disparaging remarks about other flowers and its claim to be able to control them by virtue of its thorns, and also on the narcissus's counterclaims. That the dispute is sent to the patron for arbitration does not undermine the residual correspondences I am suggesting. In al-Jāḥiẓ's *Kitāb Mufākharat al-jawārī wa-al-ghilmān* [Book of the boasting match between slavegirls and slaveboys], for instance, there is also an arbiter (*ṣāḥib*).[29] For Mattock, however, the absence of any "actual referent" makes the arguments "largely irrelevant, frequently obscure and sometimes almost meaningless," and the dispute one with "no real substance in it."[30]

The influence of Persian elements in the Abbasid caliphal court is documented. So too the importance of rivalries between these elements. Subsequently self-adduced attributes of the rose support the interpretation of rose as caliph and narcissus as Persian secretary or courtier. For example, the rose sits, while the narcissus stands. The rose leaves a valuable legacy, the narcissus none. The narcissus connects yellow to gold and shows it to be superior to red by a reference to fire. The connection of fire to Persian (pre-Islamic) religious practices is well-known. And its comment about the rose being short-lived is trenchant if it refers to the short-lived rules of all but one of the caliphs from al-Wāthiq to al-Muhtadī. The one long rule was al-Mutawakkil's and the shortest-lived rule (one day) was, uncannily, Ibn al-Muʿtazz's.

The entire question of the superiority of the rose to other flowers may have been occasioned by simple rhetorical argument. If so, this would not quite be in the tradition of the *munāẓarah* (altercation, *Rangstreit*) genre because the objects do not themselves speak and because the poet or author takes a particular position. Some scholars have noted that the contest may have had more than a surface or literary significance, "that there may underlie them some reflection of political, social, perhaps even religious tensions."[31] Heinrichs, who focuses on the rose and narcissus *munāẓarah*, disusses possible underlying meanings too. He plumbs the *Kitāb Kashf al-asrār ʿan ḥikam al-ṭuyūr wa-al-azhār* [*Revelation of the Secrets of the Birds and Flowers*] of Ibn Ghānim al-Maqdisī (d. 678/1279?) and concludes that not even any mystical meaning is apparent.[32] But Mattock, for one, believes that it is difficult to find such motives in many of the debates, "*particularly* between the rose and the narcissus."[33] He concludes that the majority of *munāẓarāt* must therefore have been composed for their own sake. And yet, the fact is inescapable that the debate between the rose and the narcissus is the one that has most frequently been taken up in later centuries.

The debate about the merits of these two flowers persisted into the fifth/eleventh century in al-Andalus (Spain), where Aḥmad ibn Burd al-Aṣghar (d. 445/1053–54) wrote an epistle in defence of the rose, and Abū al-Walīd al-Ḥimyarī (d. 440/1048) one of the narcissus.[34] Heinrichs has shown that Aḥmad ibn Burd's epistle does presuppose a contest even if it is not strictly speaking a debate.[35] Of special interest, as far as this text is concerned, is that a political interpretation does seem to impose itself.[36] The affinities al-Māridīnī's debate shares with Aḥmad ibn Burd's earlier one underscore the correspondences I am suggesting. Indeed, in al-Ḥimyarī's refutation of Aḥmad ibn Burd (in which he favors the narcissus), he is explicit about the fact that the rose was chosen for the caliphate (*al-khilāfah*).[37] Applying this interpretation to the earlier context, Ibn al-Muʿtazz's rose becomes "caliphal" and Ibn al-Rūmī's narcissus "non-caliphal." In fact, Boustany for one, interprets this preference politically, arguing for a Sunni/Shiite polemic.[38] This has been refuted by Schoeler.[39] Heinrichs concurs with Schoeler, but, by noting that Ibn al-Rūmī's preference for the narcissus "*seems* to have been just a matter of personal predilection," shows that he is still willing to admit a symbolic motive and interpretation.[40] About the Andalusian epistles of Ibn Burd and Abū al-Walīd, Heinrichs concludes:[41]

> Whether [they]can be read as *romans à clef*, as it were, with each flower corresponding to an actual personage on the political scene is doubtful.... *That they are political documents is, however, immensely probable.*

It seems to me possible to extend that political interpretation and possibly apply it more generally to other rose/narcissus contests too.

The Abu Tammām/al-Buḥturī question

Another debate of tremendous importance in the third/ninth century, and one on which Ibn Abī Ṭāhir pronounced, was the comparison between the poets Abū Tammām and al-Buḥturī. No single literary figure generated as much discussion and polarization from the third/ninth to fifth/eleventh centuries as the poet Abū Tammām. At issue was a comparison of Abū Tammām's modern poetry with the neo-classical poetry of his star student, al-Buḥturī. A preference for – or simple acceptance of – Abū Tammām's poetry implied an acceptance that his novel form of expression (*badīʿ*) was effective and appropriate.[42] Such an acceptance implied also that the new poetry was on par with classical poetry, an ideological position the acceptance or rejection of which went on to color the judgments of philologists, poets, and critics who pronounced on the issue.[43]

A preference for Abū Tammām over al-Buḥturī, or for al-Buḥturī over Abū Tammām, was of particular importance not only to the medieval critics of Arabic poetry who wrote comparative books about the two, but also to biographers and scholars as it permitted them to characterize someone according to the position they took in the "debate." Sources thus often state whether a given person was pro- or anti-Abū Tammām. In the notice on al-Battī (d. 406/1015) in Yāqūt's *Guide for the intelligent*, for example, the description of his leanings and tendencies is not confined to remarks about his theological preferences (that he followed the thinking of the Muʿtazilites and that he inclined toward Ḥanafite jurisprudence), and tribal allegiances (that he was also strongly biased [*taʿaṣṣub*, lit. clannishness] in favour of the Ṭā'ī clan).[44] It also notes that "he preferred al-Buḥturī to Abū Tammām."[45]

Al-Masʿūdī is one of many writers to characterize the two camps, those who excessively favor, and those who excessively disdain, Abū Tammām:[46]

> People (*al-nās*) are of two opposing camps regarding Abū Tammām. Those who are partial to him (*mutaʿaṣṣib lahu*) give him more than his due, elevate him to a rank far above his worth, and consider his poetry better than any other poetry. Those of the other camp oppose him, denying him any merit, finding fault with what is good, and finding his beautiful and unique expressions repugnant.

Al-Masʿūdī's teacher, al-Ṣūlī, recognized that views about Abū Tammām's poetry were, more often than not, a function of ideological motivations, having little or nothing to do with literary critical norms.[47] In his epistle to Muzāḥim ibn Fātik, prefixed to his *Accounts about Abū Tammām*, al-Ṣūlī writes:[48]

> Others go to excess and put [Abū Tammām] in a class of his own, outstripping the rest, unequalled . . . [Another] group . . . finds fault with him and discredits much of his poetry, citing the authority of certain scholars. Their opinion is based on tradition and on unproven assumptions, since there is no sound evidence against him and no argument that supports their position. Nevertheless, I have seen both of these types and no one of either group can be relied upon in his treatment of Abū Tammām's poetry or his explanation of its meaning. Moreover, they do not even venture to cite a single *qaṣīdah* of his, since that would inevitably force upon them information that they had not transmitted, [and] metaphors that they had never heard. . .

Abū Tammām was born some time between 172/788 and 192/808 in Jāsim, Syria, to Christian parents.[49] His father ran a wine-shop in Damascus where he may have worked. At an unknown date, he converted to Islam, changed his name, and pretended descent form the Ṭā'ī tribe. He became a weaver's assistant for a time, then left for Egypt where he sold water in a mosque and studied poetry, between the years 211/826 and 214/829. His first significant panegyric was to the caliph al-Ma'mūn *c.* 215/830 after his return to Syria, probably in Ḥimṣ. But it was the patronage of al-Muʿtaṣim in Samarra that propelled Abū Tammām into the highly charged atmosphere of the court. Abū Tammām was also panegyrist to al-Wāthiq and many prominent ministers and notables. He died in

231/845 or 232/846 in Mosul, where he had recently been sent as Postmaster-General. In addition to his poetry, he left an indelible mark on Arabic literature and *adab* in general with the compilation of *al-Ḥamāsah* [Bravery], an anthology of pan-tribal poetry heavily influenced by his own poetics.[50]

Abū ʿUbādah al-Walīd ibn ʿUbayd (Allāh) al-Buḥturī (d. 284/897) was born in the Arab-stock town of Manbij, where he is reputed to have perfected his flawless Arabic.[51] After his training at the hands of Abū Tammām,[52] al-Buḥturī was poised to, and did, occupy first rank on his teacher's death in 231/845 (of which he was accused by many of not having sufficiently lamented). He was not, however, known for his wit, repartee, or extempore composition.[53] Nor is his personality described in positive terms by many biographers. He is described by many as mercenary and unprincipled. Indeed, in spite of the fact that most of the literary-critical works favor him over Abū Tammām, his biographers portray him in less than flattering terms. One report, for example, has him burning five hundred separate *dīwāns* to ensure that the poets would never become famous and that their good qualities and lives would never be widely publicized.[54] And Ibn Rashīq describes al-Buḥturī as very taken with his own poetry.[55]

Al-Buḥturī belonged to the tribe from which Abū Tammām claimed descent. Two verses by Ibn Abī Ṭāhir about the 'genealogies' of al-Buḥturī and Abū Tammām are preserved by the critic al-Ḥātimī (d. 388/998) in a study of al-Mutanabbī's poetry:[56]

Seeking Buḥturī's kinship in "Buḥtur"
Is like looking for Abū Tammām's in the Thu'al tribe.

Both conjecture their kinships
And their hearts are frightened at the kinships they ascribe.

Al-Buḥturiyyu idhā fattashta nisbatahū
fī buḥturin ka-Ḥabībin fī Banī Thuʿalī
Kilāhumā yataẓannā ʿinda nisbatihī
wa qalbuhū min taẓannīhi ʿalā wajalī

This verse is adduced by al-Ḥātimī as evidence for Ibn Abī Ṭāhir's pro-Abū Tammām leanings. But establishing that Ibn Abī Ṭāhir favored the poetry of his teacher Abū Tammām over that of al-Buḥturī is not as simple as it at first appears.

It is true that Ibn Abī Ṭāhir wrote a book detailing the borrowings/plagiarisms of al-Buḥturī from Abū Tammām (*Kitāb Sariqāt al-Buḥturī min Abī Tammām*), the first work to address this issue, and perhaps the progenitor of that subgenre of medieval Arabic literary critical works comparing the two poets, a subgenre that culminated in efforts such as al-Āmidī's in the *Muwāzanah bayna al-Buḥturī wa Abī Tammām* [Weighing between al-Buḥturī and Abū Tammām], and later replicated in works evaluating al-Mutanabbī's poetry, such as those of al-Jurjānī and al-Ḥātimī. Al-Āmidī (d. 371/987), who had access to Ibn Abī Ṭāhir's book – he quotes from it and mentions that Ibn Abī Ṭāhir lists numerous lines plagiarized by al-Buḥturī from Abū Tammām – also had recourse to Abū al-Ḍiyā''s work.[57]

The citation in al-Āmidī is in a section of his work comparing Abū Tammām and al-Buḥturī.[58] And forty-six of the lines Ibn Abī Ṭāhir considers plagiarisms by Abū Tammām are also preserved in the *Weighing* and sub-divided by al-Āmidī into three categories: unambiguous plagiarism (31 lines); ambiguous plagiarism, because the motif is in the public domain or archetypal (6 lines); and incorrectly attributed plagiarism (9 lines).[59] In defining *sariqah* (poetic borrowing, plagiarism), al-Āmidī writes:[60]

> I found that Ibn Abī Ṭāhir had condemned the plagiarisms of Abū Tammām. He was correct in some cases but mistaken in others, because he mixed personal motifs with those that are common among the people, and the use of such motifs does not constitute plagiarism.

Stetkevych concludes from this that for al-Āmidī, the use of traditional imagery does not constitute plagiarism. More importantly, it suggests that for Ibn Abī Ṭāhir, immunity was not afforded by the use of traditional imagery – about which there could hardly be consensus – when it came to plagiarism.

Ibn Abī Ṭāhir was certainly well known for having produced his work on al-Buḥturī's plagiarisms, and is cited often by later authors on this matter. Al-Marzubānī, for example (relying in large part on Ibn Abī Ṭāhir), states matter-of-factly in the late fourth/tenth century that "the plagiarisms of al-Buḥturī from Abū Tammām are numerous," and that "[Literary scholars] say: Were solecisms to be [more carefully] sought in [al-Buḥturī's] poetry, many more than these [enumerated above] would be discovered."[61] When al-Marzubānī feels that he may appear biased against al-Buḥturī, he writes that he does not mention al-Buḥturī's poetic borrowings out of prejudice, especially as he considers the poet gifted, but rather because he wants to clarify the true situation to those from whom it might otherwise be hidden.[62] Comparisons of poets, their talents and their plagiarisms had existed for a long time. What was new was the appearance of literary-critical books on *sariqāt*: these works came to map the theoretical landscape of plagiarism.[63]

Significantly, Ibn Abī Ṭāhir also wrote a *Book of the plagiarisms of Abū Tammām*.[64] Indeed, the fact that he wrote the latter might suggest that he was more interested in identifying and evaluating poetic borrowings/plagiarisms *in general* than in determining whether Abū Tammām or al-Buḥturī was superior. This is borne out by his *Book of the plagiarisms of the poets*, one of the first three works – probably the first outright – to address generally the plagiarisms of poets from one another.[65] Short passages from this work are quoted by al-Baghdādī and al-Marzubānī.[66] And al-Ḥātimī quotes Ibn Abī Ṭāhir's views on literary borrowings in the *Ḥilyat al-muḥāḍarah* [Adornment of conversation].[67]

It is clear that even if he thought Abū Tammām was superior to al-Buḥturī, Ibn Abī Ṭāhir was not blind to the infelicities of the former's poetry.[68] These infelicities were not lost on his associates either. Abū Hiffān, for example, appalled by the popularity of Abū Tammām, said to him one day, "What's the matter with you, Abū Tammām? You rely on pearls which you then you hurl into a filthy sea. Who but you is going to retrieve them!"[69]

Ibn Abī Ṭāhir's opinion of al-Buḥturī is revealed in a satire of al-Buḥturī only the opening lines of which survive:[70]

> When I leafed (*taṣaffaḥtu*)
> through his poetry
> I found that in his verses he'd defecate.
>
> In some he babbles (*lāḥin*)
> ignorantly (*jāhil*), in others is plagiarist's banditry (*sāriq*)
> and in others yet, all he does is imprecate.
>
> *Fa-lammā* taṣaffaḥtu *ashʿārahū*
> *idhā huwa fī shiʿrihī qad kharī*
> *Fa-fī baʿḍihā* lāḥinun jāhilun
> *wa fī baʿḍihā* sāriqun *muftarī*

It is of additional interest as it is lexically similar to an indictment by al-Buḥturī of Ibn Abī Ṭāhir quoted by Ibn al-Nadīm (d. 385/995):[71]

> I have never seen anyone ... whose speech was more corrupt (*akthara taṣḥīfan*), whose mind was more slow-witted (*ablada ʿilman*), and whose language was more ungrammatical (*alḥan*) ... [N]o-one plagiarized more than he did (*asraq al-nās*).

Ghayyāḍ believes that it is Ibn Abī Ṭāhir's book on the plagiarisms of al-Buḥturī from Abū Tammām that provoked the antagonism between the two.[72] While this is plausible, there is no evidence for it. On the other hand, given that the accusations are lexically similar – as the following oppositions show: *alḥan/lāḥin*, *ablada ʿilman/jāhil*, *asraq/sāriq* – it is likely that one exchange inspired or occasioned the other.[73] There is one qualitative difference, however: Ibn Abī Ṭāhir's opinion is formulated as a satire whereas al-Buḥturī's is formulated as a verdict.

An anecdote recounted on the authority of Sawwār ibn Abī Shurāʿah (fl. early fourth/tenth century) also shows al-Buḥturī's animosity for Ibn Abī Ṭāhir, which, again, might have been in response to the latter's criticisms:[74]

> Sawwār ibn Abī Shurāʿah reported to me, saying: "Ibn Abī Ṭāhir came to me and said: 'I would like you to thank al-Buḥturi for me. He met me in al-Mukharrim and said to me: 'Did you come here from your home in Bāb al-Shām on foot?' I said, yes [I had]. He said, 'You distress

me with this [news]. It would be more fitting for us to treat each other nicely now that we have reached this age'."

'So I [Sawwār] went to al-Buḥturī and thanked him and told him what he [Ibn Abī Ṭāhir] said, and he said: "What did he think [I meant, that] son of a bitch?"

I said, "He thought you were concerned [for his welfare]". He [al-Buḥturī] said, "It's not what he thinks. It irked me that he still had the strength to walk from Bāb al-Shām to al-Mukharrim!".' [Sawwār] said: 'Ibn Abī Ṭāhir said to me [later], "Did you thank al-Buḥturī?" And I replied, "I thanked him. Be kind to him"...'

It is important to bear in mind, however, that although Ibn Abī Ṭāhir had a low personal opinion of al-Buḥturī, reports transmitted by Ibn Abī Ṭāhir also portray Abū Tammām in an unflattering light, as al-Ṣūlī makes abundantly clear.[75]

Notwithstanding his low opinion of Ibn Abī Ṭāhir and his uneasiness with reports recounted on his authority, al-Ṣūlī relies heavily on Ibn Abī Ṭāhir. In the section devoted to anecdotes reported by Abū Tammām ("*Mā rawāhu Abū Tammām*") in his *Accounts about Abū Tammām* twenty-one of the twenty-three anecdotes included by al-Ṣūlī are on the authority of Ibn Abī Ṭāhir.[76] This is due largely to the fact that Ibn Abī Ṭāhir is an important transmitter (*rāwī*) of Abū Tammām. Perhaps it is also a function of the fact that Ibn al-Muʿtazz, who was evidently partial to both Abū Tammām and Ibn Abī Ṭāhir, was al-Ṣūlī's teacher,[77] and influenced his literary tastes. Seeger Bonebakker believes that Ibn al-Muʿtazz's *Kitāb al-Badīʿ* [Book on novel expression] was written specifically because of the Abū Tammām controversy.[78] Indeed, Ibn al-Muʿtazz is also credited with a *Risālah Fī maḥāsin shiʿr Abī Tammām wa masāwiʾihi* [Epistle on the merits and faults of Abū Tammām's poetry]. Al-Ṣūlī's own partiality for Abū Tammām emerges from his reaction to a report he includes elsewhere in the *Akhbār Abī Tammām* on Ibn Abī Ṭāhir's authority. Al-Ṣūlī writes that this report is adduced by detractors of Abū Tammām who maintain that he was an unbeliever.[79] Al-Ṣūlī quotes Ibn Abī Ṭāhir in one other place regarding Abū Tammām, from a written work. The work may have been *The compendium on poets with accounts about them*, an extract from which is preserved by Ibn Ḥajar al-ʿAsqalānī.[80]

Ibn Abī Ṭāhir does not fall easily into either of the two "camps" described by al-Masʿūdī and others above, but rather espouses a position that I believe reflects an interiorization of new writerly sensibilities. These new sensibilities recognize the parity of the New poetry with the Ancient. This is why, and how, the very notion of a plagiarism by a neo-classical poet such as al-Buḥturī from a modern poet such as Abū Tammām is even possible in his eyes, and why it is of such great interest to him. Like Ibn Abī Ṭāhir, his contemporary Abū al-Ḍiyāʾ also wrote borrowings/plagiarism works, such as the *Kitāb Sariqāt al-Buḥturī min Abī Tammām* [Book of the borrowings/plagiarisms of al-Buḥturī from Abū Tammām]. Like

Ibn Abī Ṭāhir, he evinces these new writerly sensibilities; Yāqūt describes him Abū al-Ḍiyā' as "very cultured littérateur" (*adīb kathīr al-adab*).[81] Indeed, the new *udabā'* appear to have been more concerned with what might be termed literary critical issues than in 'proving' the correctness of their particular subjective position. It must be noted, however, that even in writers of later centuries, the debate about the relative merits of al-Buḥturī and Abū Tammām remained a domain of serious contention.

Contest

'Contest,' evidently a common feature of Arabic literary culture, did not necessarily appeal to all writers. Ibn Abī Ṭāhir, however, seems to have had a special interest in it. In addition to the *Boasting-match between the rose and the narcissus*, and the *(Instances of) the eloquence of women* volume of his *Book of prose and poetry*, which contains numerous contest accounts – the most celebrated of which is the one between Hind bint al-Khuss and Jumʿah bint Kuthayyir at ʿUkāẓ[82] – al-Sarakhsī's (d. 286/899) account of a discussion with Ibn Abī Ṭāhir about a debate he had attended, between those favoring heterosexuality and those favoring pederasty, is quoted at length in ʿAlī ibn Naṣr's *Jawāmiʿ al-ladhdhah* [*Encyclopaedia of Pleasure*].[83] The passage in question, about fifteen pages long, begins as follows:[84]

> Speaking of pederasty, Ahmad Ibn al-Ṭayyib said that Ahmad Ibn Abī Ṭāhir told him that some disputes between some men in favour of pederasty and others in favour of heterosexuality had taken place. When he asked Ibn Abī Ṭāhir to tell him how those disputes had taken place and which of them had won, he said that he would tell him that which he remembered. Then he told him that once he had attended a meeting in which both pederasts and heterosexuals had been present. Before he arrived, they had had a hot discussion and then they continued their dispute. Then Aḥmad Ibn Abī Ṭāhir quoted the following parts of their dispute which he had attended.

The material Ibn Abī Ṭāhir remembers is considerable. The account closes as follows:[85]

> When Ibn Abī Ṭāhir had finished with the description, I (al-Sarakhsī) said to him: What is your opinion about what these two (the partisans of boys and the partisans of girls) have to say? He replied: A boy's jealousy of his lover is more refined than a woman's jealousy of a man because of her fellow wife. I said: But what do you say about the remarks made by either party? Tell me something that I can report on your authority with attribution to you. He said: Where they slandered each other I think they went too far, and where they praised they made untrue and unseemly statements.

Ibn Abī Ṭāhir evidently blames both sides for too much partisanship. As Rosenthal notes: "on the whole, no forceful and exclusive endorsement of any one point of view seems intended," – it is, in short, a draw.[86] This may help explain al-Rāghib al-Iṣbahānī's citation of a line by Ibn Abī Ṭāhir (about al-Mubarrad):

Yafirru min al-munāẓiri in atāhū
wa-yarmī man ramāhū min baʿīdī

When a disputant approaches him he flees
Then from a distance flings at him repartees[87]

Ibn Abī Ṭāhir was a Persian of Khurāsānian origin. This is stated by his biographers and confirmed by his father's name. It is also possible that he was descended from a noble family. His interest in Persia is illustrated by, inter alia, his storytelling (*asmār, khurāfāt*), his literary output (*andarz*-works, *siyar al-mulūk*), his probable knowledge of Persian, his interest in such dynasties as the Ṭāhirids in the *Book of Baghdad*, and by his interest in individuals such as al-ʿAttābī.

It is true that Ibn Abī Ṭāhir's *Book of the superiority of Arabs over non-Arabs* suggests that he was not a partisan of the *Shuʿūbiyyah*, rather the opposite. In the absence of the work itself, however – indeed, in the absence of but a handful of works produced in the context of the *Shuʿūbiyyah* 'debate,' it is in fact impossible to characterize Ibn Abī Ṭāhir's contribution to it. It may, for example, have been written in an ironic or satirical vein. It is not far-fetched to imagine someone such as Ibn Abī Ṭāhir finding in this 'debate' material for a book. Indeed, the material for mockery of the Arabs was legion, especially the rivalry between the northern and southern Arabs, a rivalry that continued to have far-reaching consequences.[88]

Ibn Abī Ṭāhir's partiality to matters Persian is not perforce to be understood or seen in the context of the struggle or tension between the Arab–Islamic and the Persian, or even in the context of the *Shuʿūbiyyah*. Indeed, *udabāʾ* like Ibn Abī Ṭāhir appear to have had had no theological, doctrinal, or partisan axes to grind. Of Ibn Abī Ṭāhir's sixty or so works, for example, not a single one deals with any theological or religious issue. Interest in literary criticism, interest in the mapping and anthologizing of the Arabic literary heritage, and interest in literature *qua* literature, meant that doctrinal, ethnic and partisan considerations took a back seat to a pursuit that was increasingly secular. The littérateur could no longer be – and could no longer afford to be – one-sided. It is, ironically perhaps, Ibn Qutaybah who gave these new littérateurs an epithet: many-sided.

In a number of ways, Ibn Abī Ṭāhir is illustrative of the littérateurs whose interests and literary output are not obligatorily a function of doctrine, ethnicity or party. The transformed littérateur, with access to books, writing, and the literary heritages of other cultures and civilizations, has begun to move away from the need to align ideologically with causes which claim ethnic, linguistic or doctrinal purity or superiority. This can partly be seen in the alliances and friendships he cultivated and the circles in which he moved – the subject of the next chapter.

7

THE "BAD BOYS" OF BAGHDAD

The relatively small overall number of *udabāʿ* in third/ninth century Baghdad virtually guaranteed contact between, or at the very least knowledge of, one another through *majālis* (social or literary gatherings), *andiyat al-adab* (literary salons), *ḥalqah*s (study circles), and the various processes of knowledge transmission. These *udabāʾ* were, furthermore, divided into various groups and sub-groups. It is, of course, difficult to produce a schema describing the membership of all these groups. Such alignments were, it is true, sometimes mediated by ethnic (e.g. *Shuʿūbiyyah*), doctrinal (e.g. Muʿtazilites), and political factors. And, as Bencheikh has shown, caliphal patronage could be of particular importance in this regard.[1] However, by focusing on specific individuals, contours of certain networks can be drawn, and suggestions proposed about the criteria that helped demarcate those contours. Indeed, one of the principal areas in which writerly culture made inroads was in the constitution of allegiances, alliances, friendships, rivalries, and circles of acquaintances.

In this chapter, I look at the individuals with whom Ibn Abī Ṭāhir associated, and at the individuals with whom Ibn Abī Ṭāhir is associated by others, in order to shed light on the nature of the alignments of increasingly book-based, writerly *udabāʾ* within the literary and scholarly circles of Baghdad. This chapter also sheds light on alliances and rivalries between individuals peripheral to, or outside of, the machinery of caliphal legitimation and government.

Networks

In a 1991 article, Hilary Kilpatrick first studied the function, selection and placement of anecdotes and biographical and historical accounts (*khabar*, pl. *akhbār*) in *adab* works, in particular the *Kitāb al-Aghānī* of Abū al-Faraj al-Iṣbahānī (d. 356/967).[2] An aspect of accounts discussed by her is the phenomenon of placement enhancement. Kilpatrick shows that one account may often cast into relief aspects of another account because of the two account's relative placement, that "the context in which a *khabar* or group of *akhbār* is placed enhances its meaning."[3]

A look at the accounts and other information about, or on the authority of, Ibn Abī Ṭāhir for example, suggests a different kind of relationship between accounts, one that is the direct result of author/compiler agency. 'Proximity,' the name I give this relationship, is when the author/compiler chooses to record together, or in close proximity, accounts that relate to figures who are otherwise connected. In other words, I am suggesting that the presence of certain names in an account – whether in the chain of transmission (*isnād*) or the text itself – leads the author/compiler to include other accounts that contain other individuals who, in the author/compiler's mind, are connected. These associations may even transcend the categories and divisions of a given work, such as biographical entries, or discussions of particular tropes in a work of literary criticism. Associations known to the author/compiler take hold and guide the selection of accounts. What may at first blush appear to be a random process turns out to be more mediated. The selection of item number 2 is predicated on item number 1. In some cases this process may extend to such decisions as the sequence of notices in a biographical dictionary. The link that is established gives a super-structural coherence to clusters of accounts.

That a question posed in the reader's mind about one account might be answered by another or several other proximate accounts (within the same superstructure) is not surprising, as questions that occur to the *lecteur averti* can be expected to have occurred to the compiler too. My formulation of 'proximity' in *adab* works in general thus draws upon and reworks Kilpatrick's argument, whose conclusions about the *Book of songs* are that:

> It is not often that two articles close to each other generate thematic contrasts or parallels which will enhance the meaning of both of them; rather, articles seem to exist as self-sufficient units. But within a given article the interaction between *akhbār* may add to their significance. This interaction depends on sharing a prominent feature, a linguistic marker ..., a pattern of narrators ..., motifs important to the action ..., parallel series of episodes ... or a combination of these.[4]

I am suggesting, rather – and this may be implicit in Kilpatrick – that two articles or sections or notices close together do generate parallels that enhance their meaning, and that these parallels often depend on the shared feature of associated individuals. This is of interest as it underscores association between individuals. It also allows, in the absence of explicit statements about such associations, for speculation about such associations by identifying links through 'proximity.' In the context of this study, 'proximity' serves to *confirm* associations about which we are, or may already be, aware, and to disclose associations about which we may not already be aware. As the following ten examples (there are many more examples and the number ten is arbitrary) relating to Ibn Abī Ṭāhir show, 'proximity' is a potentially useful method for ascertaining associations. One may further speculate therefore that among the processes that lead to mistaken attributions, or simple confusion, were associations made by authors and compilers because of perceived affinities and proximities.[5]

1 As I suggested in chapter three above, the specific method used by Ibn al-Muʿtazz (d. 296/908) to determine the placement of notices in his *Ṭabaqāt al-shuʿarāʾ al-muḥdathīn* [Classes of modern poets] is not known. The notices do not appear chronologically, alphabetically, thematically, or according to talent.[6] Indeed, there does not seem to be an underlying method to the sequence that places the poets Abū Nuwās thirty-fourth, Abū al-ʿAtāhiyah thirty-eighth, Abū Tammām fifty-second, and al-Buḥturī one hundred and eighth. In 'proximity,' however, may lie part of the answer.

Ibn Abī Ṭāhir is placed one hundred and twenty-fourth.[7] There is in and of itself nothing remarkable about this positioning. His is the fourth-last notice among male poets (there follow six female poets), but as the collection is not arranged in classes (*ṭabaqāt*) reflecting the skill or worth of generations of poets, this does not reveal anything *per se*. The positioning of Ibn Abī Ṭāhir's notice in relation to others', on the other hand, is quite revealing:

110 Ibn Abī Fanan
111 Abū ʿAlī al-Baṣīr
112 al-Jarjarāʾī
[.....................]
119 Abū Hiffān
120 Yaʿqūb al-Tammār
[...]
122 al-Qiṣāfī
123 Abū al-ʿAynāʾ
124 Ibn Abī Ṭāhir

As it turns out, these are all individuals with whom Ibn Abī Ṭāhir was closely associated (discussed below). This suggests that the motivation for this particular sequencing is related to Ibn al-Muʿtazz's knowledge of these poets' associations.

2 The *Kitāb al-Waraqah* [Book of the folio] of Ibn al-Jarrāḥ (d. 296/908) also reveals 'proximity.' In his notice on al-Qiṣāfī (d. 247/861), following some verses recited by Abū Hiffān, Ibn al-Jarrāḥ includes an anecdote that he quotes directly on Ibn Abī Ṭāhir's authority, describing the gift of a pot of *sikbāj* stew sent by Abū Ayyūb Ibn Ukht Abī al-Wazīr to Muḥammad Ibn Mukarram (fl. third/ninth century). This took place in the presence of al-Qiṣāfī the Younger, who declaimed two lines about the event.[8] Quoting both Abū Hiffān and Ibn Abī Ṭāhir for information on al-Qiṣāfī is not itself remarkable, but the mention of Abū Hiffān appears to have evoked for Ibn al-Jarrāḥ the others, namely Ibn Abī Ṭāhir, Abū Ayyūb, and Ibn Mukarram.[9] The connection between Abū Hiffān, al-Qiṣāfī, Ibn Abī Ṭāhir, and Abū al-ʿAynāʾ was obvious to compilers, as Ibn al-Muʿtazz's classification also suggests.

Abū Hiffān is also quoted by Ibn al-Jarrāḥ in the notice on al-Aṣmaʿī (d. 213/828?).[10] In light of 'proximity,' it comes as no surprise that Ibn Abī Ṭāhir is also mentioned there. The same is true for the notice devoted to Abū al-Janūb (fl. third/ninth century), where Ibn Abī Ṭāhir is quoted soon after Abū Hiffān.[11] In the Abū Firʿawn al-Sāsī (d. early third/ninth century) notice, Abū Hiffān is quoted for some of that poet's verses, so too Abū al-ʿAynā'.[12] Abū Hiffān makes another appearance in the notice devoted to al-Ḥumāḥimī.[13] Indeed, all the verses in this notice are reported and directly quoted by either Abū Hiffān or Abū al-ʿAynā'.

3 In the *Murūj al-dhahab* [Meadows of gold] al-Masʿūdī (d. 345/946) quotes a story on the authority of Saʿīd ibn Ḥumayd (d. after 257/870), His story leads directly into a very amusing anecdote which al-Masʿūdī introduces with the phrase "Among the witty and amusing anecdotes about profligates is one mentioned by Ibn Abī Ṭāhir. . . ."[14] The anecdote reported on Ibn Abī Ṭāhir's authority appears to have been evoked specifically because al-Masʿūdī already has in mind one of his associates, namely Abū Hiffān.

4 In the notice devoted to Ibrāhīm ibn Saʿdān (fl. mid third/ninth century) in the *Irshād al-arīb* [Guide for the intelligent] of Yāqūt (d. 626/1229), Ibn Abī Ṭāhir and Abū al-ʿAynā' make "proximate" appearances.[15] Ibn Abī Ṭāhir is quoted for the datum that Ibrāhīm was the tutor of al-Mu'ayyad, and Abū al-ʿAynā' is both the originator and subject of an anecdote, reported through al-Ṣūlī and al-Marzubānī, which has the caliph al-Mutawakkil inquire of him whether he is indeed Shiite. This is the only "proximity" concerning Ibn Abī Ṭāhir and his associates in the *Irshād* other than in the anecdotes devoted to them and their circle, and serves as a reminder of the need for a much wider sample in order to determine the value of "proximity" as a gauge of associations. In the *Kitāb al-Aghānī*, for example, al-Iṣbahānī (d. 356/967) widely quotes Ibn Abī Ṭāhir and his associates, but there is only one instance of "proximity" proper.[16]

5 Ibn al-Nadīm (d. after 385/995) writes in his introduction to the *Fihrist* [*Catalog*] that it is an index of all the books, in the Arabic language and script, of the Arab and non-Arab peoples, in all branches of knowledge, accompanied by biographical accounts of the compilers, arranged according to their classes (*ṭabaqāt*).[17] He then provides a table of contents of the ten chapters or discourses (*maqālāt*), most of which are further divided into sections (*funūn*, sing. *fann*). Ibn Abī Ṭāhir's account is in the third section of the third discourse. The section is described as comprising "accounts of the literati, court-companions, singers, buffoons and slapstick clowns [lit. slap-takers], and the names of their books" (*akhbār al-udabā' wa-al-nudamā' wa-al-mughanniyyīn wa-al-ṣafādimah wa-al-ṣafāʿinah wa-asmā' kutubihim*). The section heading adds *julasā'* (courtiers) and *muḍḥikīn* (jesters), conforming to the description in the table of contents.[18] Ibn Abī Ṭāhir is further characterized by the way in which Ibn al-Nadīm frames the sub-section into which he falls:[19]

> [Heading =] We return to the renowned authors (*al-muṣannifīn al-mushahharīn*):
>
> Muḥammad ibn Isḥāq [Ibn al-Nadīm] writes: When I mention one of these authors, I follow him with another who is similar to him (*man yuqāribuhu wa-yushbihuhu*), and if I delay [mentioning] him in favor of mentioning the one who comes after him, well, that is my methodology (*sabīlī*) in this book. God provides succor with his bounty and blessing.
>
> The accounts (*akhbār*) of Ibn Abī Ṭāhir
> His son, ʿUbaydallāh
> The Abū al-Najm Family
> Abū Isḥāq ibn Abī ʿAwn
> The accounts (*akhbār*) of Ibn Abī al-Azhar
> Abū Ayyūb al-Madīnī
> al-Taghlibī
> Ibn al-Ḥarūn
> Ibn ʿAmmād al-Thaqafī
> Ibn Khurradādhbih
> al-Sarakhsī
> Jaʿfar ibn Ḥamdān al-Mawṣilī
> Abū Ḍiyāʾ al-Naṣībī
> Ibn Abī Manṣūr al-Mawṣilī
> Ibn al-Marzubān
> al-Kisrawī
> Ibn Bassām, the poet
> al-Marwazī
> Abū Bakr al-Ṣūlī
> al-Ḥakīmī
> al-Ruḥābī
>
> Another cluster (*ṭabaqah*, lit. class/ification) of those as yet unmentioned.

The inclusion of Ibn Abī Ṭāhir's son in this cluster is explained not by the biological relationship but by the fact that his compositions were similar to his father's.[20] ʿUbaydallāh is also specifically identified in biographical notices as a principal student of Ibn Abī Ṭāhir's. Another member of this cluster, Ibn al-Marzubān, was also his student. Others in this cluster may have been so too. Evidently, for Ibn al-Nadīm, these individuals all belong together – he is explicit about the fact that he organizes his book in this way. The importance of cluster is emphasized by Ibn al-Nadīm's comment a few pages later, after the al-Ruḥābī notice, namely that the individuals that follow are members of another cluster (*ṭabaqah*).[21] Also of importance is the cluster that *precedes* the Ibn Abī Ṭāhir notice. That cluster comprises:

Isḥāq ibn Ibrāhīm al-Mawṣilī
Ḥammād ibn Isḥāq
Munajjim family members: Ābān,
ʿAlī ibn Yaḥyā [discussed below]
Yaḥyā ibn ʿAlī
Ḥārūn ibn ʿAlī
ʿAlī ibn Hārūn
Aḥmad ibn ʿAlī
Hārūn ibn ʿAlī
Ḥamdūn ibn Ismāʿīl
Aḥmad ibn Ḥamdūn
Abū Hiffān [discussed below]
Yūnus al-Mughannī
Ibn Bānah
al-Naṣabī (?)
Abū Ḥashīshah
Jaḥẓah[22]

6 In the *Kitāb al-Tamthīl wa-al-muḥāḍarah* [Book of expression of proverbs and speech] al-Thaʿalibī (d. 429/1038) provides a classic example of 'proximity.' In one section of this work, al-Thaʿālibī lists examples by the following poets in the following order:[23]

Abū ʿAlī al-Baṣīr	(p. 91)
Saʿīd ibn Ḥumayd	(pp. 91–2)
ʿAlī ibn al-Jahm	(p. 92)
Ibn Abī Fanan	(pp. 92–3)
Yazīd al-Muhallabī	(p. 93)
ʿUmārah ibn ʿUqayl	(p. 93)
Aḥmad Ibn Abī Ṭāhir	(p. 93)
Abū Hiffān	(pp. 94)
Abū Tammām	(pp. 94–6)
al-Buḥturī	(pp. 96–9)

That al-Thaʿālibī names this selection of poets (including thirty others mentioned before Abū ʿAlī al-Baṣīr) is not remarkable: he has announced in the title of the sub-section that he is dealing here with modern (*muḥdathūn*) poets. But the cluster reproduced above suggests that these individuals were associated in the author's mind and that 'proximity' played a role in the order of enumeration.

7 In a work about habitual gatecrashers (*ṭufaylīs*), al-Khaṭīb al-Baghdādī (d. 463/1071) quotes Abū Hiffān only twice.[24] Ibn Abī Ṭāhir, who appears only once in the whole work, is mentioned in a line of transmission a mere two (printed) pages from Abū Hiffān.[25]

8 Ibn Bassām al-Shantarīnī (d. 542/1147) mentions Ibn Abī Ṭāhir only once in the eight-volume *al-Dhakhīrah fī maḥāsin ahl al-Jazīrah* [The treasury of the excellent qualities of the poeple of the peninsula]. He quotes two lines of poetry by Ibn Abī Ṭāhir, which he says he is citing from one of Ibn Abī Ṭāhir's long, and highly descriptive, odes.[26] Immediately after mentioning these lines, Ibn Bassām quotes verses "along the same lines" by the poet Ibn Lankak (d. *c.* 360/970). Ibn Lankak is the author of a book on the superiority of the rose to the narcissus, likened by al-Tanūkhī to a book on the same subject by Ibn Abī Ṭāhir.[27] The similarity is, I believe, noticed by Ibn Bassām because in his mind he already links the two poets. Indeed, of the authors who cite these lines, Ibn Bassām is the only one to see a parallel between Ibn Abī Ṭāhir's verses and those of Ibn Lankak.

9 In the *Kitāb Nūr al-qabas* [Book of the light of the firebrand], al-Yaghmūrī's (d. 673/1274) abridgement of a work by al-Marzubānī, a verse attribution by Ibn Abī Ṭāhir is immediately followed by an account (*khabar*) reported by Abū al-ʿAynāʾ.[28]

10 In all of the twenty-seven volumes of *Nihāyat al-arab fī funūn al-adab* [The heart's desire in the arts of writerly culture] al-Nuwayrī (d. 732/1332) quotes verses by Ibn Abī Ṭāhir only twice: once in volume three; and once in volume ten for a nine-line passage of poetry, in a sub-section dealing with donkeys.[29] The notice preceding these lines involves al-Faḍl al-Raqāshī (d. *c.* 200/815). The one preceding that revolves around Abū al-ʿAynā''s request from a donkey-broker for a particular kind of donkey.[30] Donkeys are, of course, what link this account with the verses by Ibn Abī Ṭāhir. But I would argue further that mention of Abū al-ʿAynāʾ is what brought Ibn Abī Ṭāhir to al-Nuwayrī's mind then, and caused him to include the Ibn Abī Ṭāhir lines when and where he did.

The *Shayāṭīn al-ʿAskar*

'Proximity' is evidently very useful in identifying and delimiting networks of udabāʾ, or confirming them, but this method does have its limitations as the Yāqūt example cited above shows. Fortunately, in the case of Ibn Abī Ṭāhir and his associates two other important sources of information are available: the first is an explicit statement made by the literary historian, critic, and biographer al-Marzubānī, the second, numerous anecdotes in the sources describing literary gatherings (*majālis*). These are discussed below.

Several of Ibn Abī Ṭāhir's associates are grouped together by the literary scholar al-Marzubānī (d. 384/994) in his *Kitāb al-Muʿjam al-shuʿarā* [Encyclopedia of poets]. Abū Hiffān, Ibn Mukarram, al-Yaʿqūbī (= Yaʿqūb al-Tammār), Abū ʿAlī al-Baṣīr, and Abū al-ʿAynāʾ are all identified as "the elegant and licentious demons of al-ʿAskar" (*Shayāṭīn al-ʿAskar fī al-ẓarf wa-al-mujūn*) in the notice devoted to Muḥammad ibn al-Faḍl al-Kātib (fl. mid third/ninth century), whom al-Marzubānī describes as closely associated with (and, incidentally, as the most obscene and debauched of) the Demons of al-ʿAskar.[31] Everett Rowson has summarized *mujūn* as follows:[32]

> Libertinage, licentiousness ... *mujūn* refers behaviourally to open and unabashed indulgence in prohibited pleasures, particularly the drinking of wine and, above all, sexual profligacy. *Mujūn* literature describes and celebrates this hedonistic way of life, frequently employing explicit sexual vocabulary, and almost invariably with primarily humorous intent.

But precisely what is meant by *Shayāṭīn al-ʿAskar* is not explained by al-Marzubānī. Elsewhere in the *Encyclopedia of poets* he does write that Abū ʿAlī al-Baṣīr "wrote panegyrics of the caliphs and of the *ru'asā' ahl al-ʿAskar* [heads of the people of *al-ʿAskar*]."[33] Other authors also refer to certain poets in this way. Al-Jāḥiẓ, for instance, calls Abū al-Asad "one of the poets of *al-ʿAskar*."[34] Yāqūt (possibly quoting al-Ḥuṣrī) notes that "When ʿAlī ibn Yaḥyā al-Munajjim died [d. 275/888–9], ʿAlī ibn Sulaymān [al-Akhfash al-Ṣaghīr (d. 315/927)], one of the poets of *al-ʿAskar* elegized him."[35]

The modern critic Shawqī Ḍayf, taking *al-ʿAskar* literally, i.e. "the Army," infers that these writers associated with, and appear to have enjoyed the patronage of, leading government servants. He consequently entitles the section of his work in which he discusses Ibn Abī Ṭāhir, Abū ʿAlī al-Baṣīr and Ibn Durayd, 'Poets of the Ministers, Governers, and Commanders' (*shuʿarā' al-wuzarā' wa-al-wulāt wa-al-quwwād*).[36] Jamal Eddine Bencheikh believes that the Demons of al-ʿAskar – whom he too links with the Army, calling them "army demons" (*démons de l'armée*) – were rejectors of the prevailing patronal system and literary economy.[37] He even surmises "the foundations of a counter-culture" in the example of these poets.[38] Bencheikh appears to be correct in his characterization of this group as embodying an attitude of rejection (*refus*),[39] but argues against himself by suggesting both a connection with leading military figures and a concomitant rejection of the prevailing patronal system.

This apparent paradox might be resolved by taking *al-ʿAskar* to mean not the Army, but rather an area known as *al-ʿAskar*. There are three realistic possibilities: ʿAskar Abī Jaʿfar, a synonym for the Round City of Baghdad;[40] ʿAskar al-Mahdī, which was the earlier name of al-Ruṣāfah, a quarter of Baghdād on the Eastern banks of the Tigris;[41] and ʿAskar al-Muʿtaṣim, the earlier name of Samarra', the caliphal capital built by al-Muʿtaṣim.[42] Demons of al-ʿAskar would thus refer to the poets associated with one or other of these areas. Given the profiles of the individuals named by al-Marzubānī, it is likely that al-Ruṣāfah is meant.[43]

The links between the members and associates of the Demons of al-ʿAskar are underscored by, *inter alia*, Ibn al-Muʿtazz's placement of their biographical notices in close proximity to one another in the *Classes of modern poets*, as discussed above and as illustrated by the table below:[44]

Ibn al-Muʿtazz cluster	*Poets identified as "Shayāṭīn al-ʿAskar"*
Ibn Abī Fanan (110)	—
Abū ʿAlī al-Baṣīr (111)	Abū ʿAlī al-Baṣīr
al-Jarjarāʾī (112)	—
. . .	Ibn Mukarram
Abū Hiffān (119)	Abū Hiffān
Yaʿqūb al-Tammār (120)	al-Tammār
. . .	
al-Qiṣāfī (122)	—
Abū al-ʿAynāʾ (113)	Abū al-ʿAynāʾ
Ibn Abī Ṭāhir (124)	—
—	Muḥammad ibn al-Faḍl al-Kātib

Below, I single out and briefly characterize a few of the Demons of al-ʿAskar, a group I also call the "Bad boys" of Baghdad.

Abū Hiffān

ʿAbdallāh ibn Aḥmad ibn Ḥarb al-Mihzamī (d. 255/869 or 257/871)[45] was from Basra, but little is known of his youth or background, other than that he came from a family of transmitters, and is said to have revelled in his Arab origins. By training, Abū Hiffān was a grammarian, lexicographer, poet, and transmitter (*rāwiyah*) of considerable reputation who occupied an important place in *adab* circles.[46] As he does with Ibn Abī Ṭāhir, Ibn al-Muʿtazz, characterizes Abū Hiffān's poetry as widely known (*mawjūd fī kull makān*).[47] He was the transmitter of Abū Nuwās, about whom he wrote a volume entitled *Akhbār Abī Nuwās* [Accounts concerning Abū Nuwās], which survives.[48] None of his other works, the *Ṣināʿat al-shiʿr* [The craft of poetry] for example, is extant.[49]

All of Abū Hiffān's biographers identify al-Aṣmaʿī (d. *c.* 216/831) as one of his principal teachers,[50] and he is identified in his biographical notices as one of the principal transmitters to Ibn Abī Ṭāhir; indeed, Ibn Abī Ṭāhir is almost always the first named student.[51] How the two first met is not known, but they certainly appear together in numerous anecdotes and lines of transmission,[52] and it is evident that they became good friends. The anecdote in which they play dead in order to raise a few dinars for a burial shroud shows this.[53] So too an anecdote in which Abū Hiffān reports that he was convalescing at Ibn Abī Ṭāhir's home.[54]

Abū Hiffān's career brought him into contact with countless literary personalities. Besides Abū Nuwās, the following may be singled out: Abū Diʿāmah, al-Jammāz, al-Jāḥiẓ, ʿAlī ibn Yaḥyā al-Munajjim, Abū al-ʿAynāʾ, al-Tammār, al-Buḥturī, al-ʿUtbī, and al-Mubarrad.[55] Basing himself on Yāqūt, Nājī, surmises that al-Jāḥiẓ and Abū Hiffān were not on good terms,[56] but it seems more likely, especially in the absence of any corroborating evidence, that their relations were good. Al-Jāḥiẓ's criticisms – which do not survive – were likely tongue-in-cheek. Indeed, given al-Jāḥiẓ's well known opposing positions on most issues, it is not clear whether his views can be inferred with a high degree of accuracy. As for Abū Hiffān's relations with al-Buḥturī, suffice to mention one anecdote which recounts that they were drinking one night at the home of one of their patrons and then took their leave together.[57] Al-Buḥturī offered Abū Hiffān a ride on his riding beast and, seated behind al-Buḥturī, Abū Hiffān declaimed some scatological verses. Al-Buḥturī then pushed Abū Hiffān off and swore at him. This may well have been in good spirit, but recall Abū Hiffān's attested friendship for Ibn Abī Ṭāhir, and al-Buḥturī's antipathy toward him.

In spite of the circles in which he moved, and his importance as a transmitter, Abū Hiffān led an impoverished life, sometimes selling his clothes for food. Some authors even report that his reputation was tainted by his indigence (*ḍayyiq al-ḥāl*), and also his niggardliness (*muqattir*), drinking (*sharrāb li-al-nabīdh*),[58] and shamelessness (*mutahattik*) – the latter two being compatible with his characterization also as one of the *mujūn*-poets.[59] The sources uniformly portray Abū Hiffān as someone who lived – and had to live – by his wits, perhaps especially because of his modest means. One Nawrūz, for instance, Abū Hiffān was unable to find a gift suitable for his benefactor and friend ʿUbaydallāh ibn Yaḥyā ibn Khāqān (d. 263/877). This prompted him to compose verses explaining that the only appropriate and commensurate gift is praise.[60]

The attitude of Abū Hiffān toward reward and patronage – one that I am arguing is modified in the increasingly writerly and bookish literary environment of late third/ninth century Baghdad – is illustrated by an anecdote reported by ʿAlī ibn Muḥammad Ibn al-Aḥḍar (fl. third/ninth century) in which Abū Hiffān both satirizes his presumed potential benefactor and subverts the 'capital' in the patronal paradigm by deeming his verses an alms-tax. One ʿĪd Festival day, Abū Hiffān was leaving Samarra when he passed by the gathering of Thaʿlab.[61] When Thaʿlab asked him where he was going, Abū Hiffān answered that he was looking for Ibn Thawābah. "How do you feel about the Banū Thawābah?" Thaʿlab asked. Abū Hiffān replied as follows:[62]

> By God, I hate to satirize them on such a day as this but I'll deem my satire alms. Here goes:
>
> Kings whose splendor is like their noble descent
> And whose morals are like their refinement.
>
> The length of their horns together prevails
> And far surpasses the length of their tails.

Abū Hiffān's contact with the Thawābah family is widely attested. In one oft-repeated anecdote, reported by his cousin al-Hadādī through al-Kawkabī, Abū Hiffān encounters Aḥmad ibn Muḥammad ibn Thawābah (d. 277/890).[63] When Aḥmad Ibn Thawābah sees Abū Hiffān's mount, he reacts by observing: "Abū Hiffān ... riding a rented donkey?" Abū Hiffān immediately replies:

I ride a rented donkey as a mount
because those to whom one has recourse are not so easily found,
And because the generous are six feet underground.

Abū Hiffān is apparently referring to Ibn Thawābah's occasional refusal to reward his panegyrists. Ibn al-Rūmī, for example, enjoyed a short patronage which one day was brought to an unexplained end. Boustany surmises that this change of heart on the part of Ibn Thawābah was related to Ibn Bulbul's deteriorating relations with Ibn al-Rūmī.[64] There was, it is true, no love lost between Ibn Thawābah and Ibn Bulbul, but Ibn Thawābah owed Ibn Bulbul his senior position in the administration, a post he occupied until his death in 277/890. Sometimes even as benevolent a patron as ʿAlī ibn Yaḥyā al-Munajjim would refuse callers entry to his gathering, because of its popularity and quality. When this happened to Abū Hiffān, he rebuked ʿAlī for it in verse.[65] It is important to note, however, that the criticism is related neither to quantum nor to purse *manqué*, but rather to generosity and open-handedness as virtues further to be cultivated by ʿAlī. There is no evidence for direct caliphal patronage of Abū Hiffān in Samarra or elsewhere (a fact also noted by Nājī).[66]

Abū Hiffān associated with members of the caliph's entourage but, like Ibn Abī Ṭāhir and Abū al-ʿAynāʾ, appears to have kept his distance from the caliph's court.[67] He was in contact with prominent scholars and patrons, but did not establish the patron-client relationship of Abū Nuwās, Abū Tammām, and others. He may best described as an 'independent,' one who praised whom he willed, satirized whom he willed, and who was content to leave not the legacy of a patronized poet but rather the legacy of a transmitter and biographer.[68]

Abū al-ʿAynāʾ

Like Abū Hiffān, Abū al-ʿAynāʾ also appears to have rejected the prevailing patronal economy. Abū ʿAbdallāh Muḥammad ibn al-Qāsim ibn Khallād ibn Yāsir ibn Sulaymān seems himself to have adopted the sobriquet Abū al-ʿAynāʾ (190–282/805–896).[69] The principal notices on Abū al-ʿAynāʾ address his unusual nickname: according to many of the biographers, an ancestor of Abū al-ʿAynāʾ's had a falling out with the caliph ʿAlī whereupon ʿAlī wished blindness upon him and all his descendants.[70]

Abū al-ʿAynāʾ was born in al-Ahwāz and raised in Basra, where he studied Hadith and *adab*. He was known primarily as a reporter of accounts (*akhbārī*), a poet (*shāʿir*), and a man of letters (*adīb*). While still sighted, Abū al-ʿAynāʾ left Basra for Baghdad and Samarra; he turned blind at the age of forty. He returned to Basra where he died after narrowly escaping drowning. Al-Ṣafadī attributes the following lines to Abū al-ʿAynāʾ:[71]

God may have taken the light from my eyes
But from my tongue and my ears the light will not fade

I've a sharp-witted heart, a mind not idle at all
And in my speech is the sharpness of a priceless blade

Abū al-ʿAynāʾ's principal teachers included al-Aṣmaʿī and Abū Zayd al-Anṣārī. Important students included Jaʿfar ibn Qudāmah, Abū al-Ḥasan al-Akhfash (a close associate of the Demons of al-ʿAskar), and al-Ṣūlī.[72] Ibn Abī Ṭāhir is credited with a work consisting of accounts concerning Abū al-ʿAynāʾ entitled *Accounts about Abī al-ʿAynāʾ*;[73] both this work and a later one bearing the same title by the erudite al-Ṣāḥib ibn ʿAbbād are lost.[74]

The relations between Abū ʿAlī al-Baṣīr, known for both his poetic turn of phrase and his prose skills, and Abū al-ʿAynāʾ, master of the quick-witted repartee (*badīhah*),[75] are particularly famous.[76] Ibn al-Nadīm mentions the correspondence between them, in particular the ridicule they exchanged in satirical verses (*muhājāt*), which he describes as good-natured (*ṭayyibah*).[77] Al-Masʿūdī mentions the existence of mutual rebukes (*muʿātabāt*), correspondence (*mukātabāt*), and pleasantries (*mudāʿabāt*).[78] Abū ʿAlī al-Faḍl ibn Jaʿfar ibn al-Faḍl ibn Yūnus al-Baṣīr, descended from a Shīʿī Persian *abnāʾ* family from al-Anbār (d. *c.* 251/865),[79] was, of all the Demons of al-ʿAskar, the one with the closest patronal links, especially with caliphs (from the time of al-Muʿtaṣim on, i.e. from 218/833).[80] He is usually described as a poet of Samarra, where he spent most of his professional life, and where he died. Indeed, as a patronized poet, Abū ʿAlī al-Baṣīr's connection to wealthy patrons kept him steeped in the old oral world.[81] The following verses recorded by al-Masʿūdī reveal this attachment:[82]

Whereas the amateurs of knowledge have only
the knowledge that's to be found in a book,

I far surpass them in my zeal and effort,
with ears for an inkwell, and my heart for a notebook.

It is apparent from this selection that Abū ʿAlī al-Baṣīr displays – that is, continues to display – an attachment to the oral/aural. This attachment shows that he still participates in the 'old' patronal economy, and is underscored by the sentiments expressed by Abū ʿAlī al-Baṣīr with regard to the poetry of Abū Nuwās. In the anecdote in question, reported by al-Marzubānī and deriving ultimately from Ibn Abī Ṭāhir, Abū ʿAlī al-Baṣīr rejects outright a 'modern' taxonomy of Abū Nuwās' poetry, averring that there are, in fact, fundamentally only two kinds of poetry, panegyric and satire, and that Abū Nuwās is only good at wine poetry and hunting poetry, if that.[83]

In the noticc devoted to him in the *Fihrist*, Ibn al-Nadīm credits (*lahu*) Abū al-ʿAynāʾ with two books, one a diwan of poetry and the other a book of accounts (*akhbār*). Of the latter, Ibn al-Nadīm writes, "*Kitāb Akhbār Abī al-ʿAynāʾ ʿamilahu Ibn Abī Ṭāhir*," "The book of the accounts of Abū al-ʿAynāʾ redacted by Ibn Abī Ṭāhir."[84] Since this book is not mentioned in the notice devoted to Ibn Abī Ṭāhir, it is possible he produced the book on Abū al-ʿAynā''s behalf, perhaps after Abū al-ʿAynā' turned blind. The two were friends, so the collaboration is not remarkable. The *Accounts of Abū al-ʿAynā'* may also have simply been a compilation of anecdotes relating to Abū al-ʿAynā by Ibn Abī Ṭāhir. He is, after all, the author/compiler of seven other *akhbār*-works. In either case, *ʿamila* in the passage "*ʿamilahu Ibn Abī Ṭāhir*" would thus mean that Ibn Abī Ṭāhir was the compiler, editor, or publisher of the work. The same verb *(ʿamila)* is used to describe Ibn Abī Ṭāhir's son's possible redaction of two of his father's works.[85]

Abū al-ʿAynā' is himself responsible for putting together or editing (*waḍaʿa*) a book. This work consisted of censures of Aḥmad ibn al-Khaṣīb, extracts of which are quoted in later works.[86] Aḥmad ibn al-Khaṣīb al-Jarjarā'ī (d. 265/879), a "ministerial" member of the Demons of al-ʿAskar, held a succession of posts in the state secretariat before becoming vizier to al-Muntaṣir in 247/861. Al-Mustaʿīn banished Aḥmad to Crete in Jumādā I 248 (August 862) after having him dispossessed and paraded in chains on a donkey. He died in exile in 265/879.[87] It was he who composed the new Friday sermon (*khuṭbah*) after the assassination of al-Mutawakkil (d. 247/861), which was then circulated by Saʿīd ibn Ḥumayd. In the book put together by Abū al-ʿAynā', he reports that at one gathering of scholars (*fuḍalā'*) everyone present disapproved strongly of Aḥmad because of his ignorance, sluggishness and carelessness. Perhaps the verses by Ibn Abī Ṭāhir recorded in the following anecdote also formed part of the work.[88]

> Ibn Abī Ṭāhir wrote: "When Aḥmad ibn al-Khaṣīb rode, petitions would be handed to him and if people disputed [his decisions] with him, he would get so angry that he would take his foot out the stirrup and kick whoever answered back. So I said:
>
> "Say to the Caliph, O cousin of Muḥammad,
> 'He has gotten loose, so tether your minister.
> Upon our honor, his tongue roams freely,
> and upon our breasts, do his feet wander'."[89]
>
> *Qul li 'l-khalīfati yā 'bna ʿammi Muḥammadin*
> *shakkil wazīraka innahū maḥlūlu*
> *Fa-lisānuhū qad jāla fī aʿrāḍinā*
> *wa 'r-rijlu minhū fī 'ṣ-ṣudūri tajūlu*

Aḥmad ibn al-Khaṣīb, perhaps in response to Abū al-ʿAynā''s work, wrote a censure of Abū al-ʿAynā'.[90] But it is impossible to know whether any of the censures were intended seriously or in jest, especially given the fact that Aḥmad ibn al-Khaṣīb was also a member of the Demons of al-ʿAskar.

One of the contributors to Abū al-ʿAynā''s work in censure of Aḥmad ibn al-Khaṣīb was Ibrāhīm ibn al-Mudabbir. An epistle from Ibn Abī Ṭāhir to Ibrāhim ibn al-Mudabbir is attested but does not survive.[91] Ibrāhīm ibn al-Mudabbir (d. 279/892–93)[92] was an official of Persian descent who played an important role in matters of state. As a boon-companion and accomplished man of letters in his own right, he had the ear of of al-Mutawakkil until he was overthrown by ʿUbaydallāh ibn Yaḥyā ibn Khāqān in 240/855. He later joined the retinue and administration of the caliph al-Muʿtamid (r. 256–79/870–92). Many of his poems are dedicated to ʿArīb, the singer and poetess who was the lover of Saʿīd ibn Ḥumayd and of whom Ibrāhīm was himself enamored.

Ibrāhīm thought highly of al-Buḥturī and his poetry, perhaps because of the latter's panegyric of him.[93] In light of the fact that he liked al-Buḥturī's poetry, it comes as little surprise to learn that he was not at all favorable to Abū Tammām's poetry, given the strong feelings that underlay preference of one poet over the other. Al-Masʿūdī records the following judgement by Muḥammad ibn Abī al-Azhar:[94]

> In spite of his learning, literary skills, and erudition, Ibrāhīm ibn al-Mudabbir had a low opinion of Abū Tammām and would swear that there was not a single worthwhile thing about his poetry.

Perhaps Ibn Abī Ṭāhir's epistle to Ibrāhīm ibn al-Mudabbir revolved around the merits of Abū Tammām's and al-Buḥturī's poetry.

To return to Abū al-ʿAynāʾ, he is sometimes described as a transmitter of Hadith (*muḥaddith*) but, as al-Ṣafadī notes, he appears in the lines of transmission of very few Hadith,[95] and the majority of his transmissions (*riwāyātih*) are in fact of accounts (*al-akhbār*) and stories (*al-ḥikāyāt*).[96] This is not surprising. On the one hand, training in religious sciences remained indispensable to the education of scholars. On the other, interest in actually cultivating that knowledge professionally and participating in the preservation of Hadith competed with the other scholarly, academic, or personal avenues that became available in an environment of books and book-based learning.

Abū al-ʿAynāʾ's knowledge of Quran and Hadith was clearly impressive. He used this knowledge of scripture and Prophetic traditions primarily to formulate witticisms, defend himself, or satirize others.[97] The following exchange with another member of the Demons of al-ʿAskar, Ibn Mukarram – the two were notorious for their often public friendly attacks on one another[98] – is a case in point:[99]

> Ibn Mukarram wrote to Abū al-ʿAynāʾ: "At my place, there is a *Sikbāj* stew that is the envy of connoisseurs, conversation that delights the despondent, and your beloved friends. So do not be arrogant, but come to me." To this Abū al-ʿAynāʾ wrote in reply: "Go into it [Hell] and do not speak to me."[100]

This belies the mutual friendship and admiration of Ibn Mukarram and Abū al-ʿAynāʾ. Indeed, Ibn Mukarram considered Abū al-ʿAynāʾ a greater stylist and writer of artistic prose than even the illustrious ʿAbd al-Ḥamīd ibn Yaḥyā.[101] Abū al-ʿAynāʾ certainly excelled in prose.[102] Several lines by Ibn Abī Ṭāhir about this talent survive in al-Yaghmūrī's abridgment of al-Marzubānī's lost *al-Muqtabas*:[103]

The rhyming prose
of Abū al-ʿAynāʾ is full of profit.[104]
Damn him! And God's curse upon his prose.

It is as if the one
who hears his words
is deafened by the sland'rous rocks he throws.

Unbelief has taken possession
of his nature even though, upon
his heart, God natural skill bestows.

Do not give him
too much attention because I,
for better or for worse, cannot escape his blows.

Sajʿu Abī ʾl-ʿAynāʾi min rajʿihī
fa-laʿnatu ʾllāhi ʿalā sajʿihī
Ka-anna man yasmaʿu alfāẓahū
yuqdhafu ṣumma ʾṣ-ṣakhri fī samʿihī
Qad ṭabaʿa ʾllāhu ʿalā qalbihī
fa ʾl-kufru mustawlin ʿalā ṭabʿihī
Lā tukthirū fīhi fa-lā budda lī
asāʾa aw aḥsana min ṣafʿihī.

The sources make much of the exchanges between the members of the Demons of al-ʿAskar.[105] These exchanges could be *mudāʿabāt* (pleasantries) or satires. The latter often focused on borrowings/plagiarism (*sariqah*), and were usually in verse.[106] Indeed, around plagiarism grew important discussions about new issues such as the nature and definition of originality, and the role of writing. In a satire, the closing lines of which are recorded by al-Qāḍī al-Jurjānī (d. 392/1002), for example, Abū Hiffān says the following concerning Ibn Abī Ṭāhir:[107]

I satirized Ibn Abī Ṭāhir, but he took it very well.
Were it not for his literary thefts, all would be well.
When he recites a verse, say, "Someone has done well..."

And Ibrāhīm Ibn al-Mudabbir reports that al-Buḥturī, Abū al-ʿAynāʾ and al-Faḍl al-Yazīdī (d. 278/891) were one day gathered at his place when al-Buḥturī declaimed some blatantly sexual lines about al-Faḍl.[108] Al-Faḍl left angered by the verses and al-Buḥturī later wrote Ibrāhīm a satire of al-Faḍl, in which he mocked his parents. When Ibrāhīm read the verses to Abū al-ʿAynāʾ, the latter asked for, and got, half the purse al-Buḥturī was going to receive. Al-Buḥturī learned of this and conceded that had it not been for Abū al-ʿAynāʾ's remarks he would not have been able to produce the lines. Such borrowings were evidently very common.

Although Bencheikh includes him in a study of al-Mutawakkil's maecenate,[109] Abū al-ʿAynāʾ does not appear explicitly to have accepted the patronage of the caliph at any time, though he was close to many members of the caliph's circle. In one celebrated anecdote, Abū al-ʿAynāʾ enters al-Mutawakkil's Jaʿfarī palace in Samarra in the year 246/860, whereupon the caliph asks, “What have you to say about this, our residence?” The question is cruel as Abū al-ʿAynāʾ is blind at the time, and has been for about sixteen years. Abū al-ʿAynāʾ's characteristically quick-witted answer is: “People build homes in the world but you, you have built a world in your home.”[110] This reply prompted al-Mutawakkil to ask Abū al-ʿAynāʾ to be one of his boon-companions. Abū al-ʿAynāʾ declined. It appears that he did not wish to be tied to the court of the caliph and to everything such an attachment entailed.

Saʿīd ibn Ḥumayd

One individual for whom the question of borrowings/plagiarisms/literary thefts is particularly relevant is Saʿīd ibn Ḥumayd (d. after 257/870).[111] His borrowings are effectively the subject of numerous anecdotes and witticisms. Ibn Abī Ṭāhir, for instance, is quoted by Ibn al-Nadīm as saying that if Saʿīd's prose and poetry were asked to return to their origins, nothing would be left behind.[112] Ibn al-Nadīm, who describes Saʿīd ibn Ḥumayd as an accomplished and predatory literary thief, mentions his literary sparrings *(muṣāraʿāt)* with Aḥmad and Ibrāhīm ibn al-Mudabbir. Saʿīd is also reported by Abū Hiffān to have modeled a whole letter on one by Ibn Abī Ṭāhir, in spite of the fact that he was himself a high-ranking secretary and an accomplished writer of prose.[113] In the section on “opening greetings” in the *Anthology of Motifs*, Abū Hilāl al-ʿAskarī devotes a few pages to a discussion of letters and poetry by Ibn Abī Ṭāhir and Abū Hiffān,[114] and, after quoting *in extenso* a letter (including eight lines of poetry) from Ibn Abī Ṭāhir to Ismāʿīl ibn Bulbul,[115] writes:[116]

> *Abū Aḥmad reported to me from his father, from Aḥmad Ibn Abī Ṭāhir, from Abū Hiffān, who said:* “One Nawrūz I called upon Saʿīd ibn Ḥumayd while he was preparing to write to his associates, so I recited to him the letter and verses you [= Ibn Abī Ṭāhir] addressed to Abū al-Ṣaqr [Ibn Bulbul],” – *i.e. the letter and poetry mentioned above* – “at which point he wrote the following to al-Ḥasan ibn Makhlad,[117] with me still there: [*Text of letter…*]. He then read it to me, and I said, ‘Abū ʿUthmān [= Saʿīd]!

> I only just read you Ibn Abī Ṭāhir's use of these very same ideas!' 'And I only just successfully used them,' he replied, 'there are no formalities between us'." *I know of no equal to these two letters on this subject, neither in the delicateness of their motifs* (riqqat maʿānīhā) *nor in the beauty of their application* (ḥusn takhrījihā).

Abū al-Ṣaqr Ismāʿīl Ibn Bulbul was a *kātib* of Persian origin who pretended Arab descent.[118] He was vizier to al-Muʿtamid and al-Muwaffaq on and off from 265–78/878–91, though it was only after the removal from office in 272/885 of al-Muwaffaq's secretary Saʿīd ibn Makhlad that Ibn Bulbul acquired real administrative power, serving as vizier to both regent and caliph. His appointment of two members of the Banū al-Furāt was opposed by various secretarial families, including the Banū Wahb.[119] When al-Muʿtaḍid became regent in 278/892, the Banū Wahb came to power again: Ibn Bulbul was arrested and died soon after. He was a regular at the literary gatherings of ʿAlī ibn Yaḥyā.[120]

Majālis habitués

Descriptions of the literary gatherings (*majālis*) at the home or behest of a particular host constitute another important way of determining which individuals associated with one another. Anecdotes often list the names of individuals who attended a given gathering. In the context of Ibn Abī Ṭāhir, the Demons of al-ʿAskar, and their network of associates, the following anecdote is of particular relevance as it identifies and associates several of the Demons of al-ʿAskar (and others) as regular participants in the gatherings of ʿAlī ibn Yaḥyā ibn al-Munajjim. Significantly, it names Ibn Abī Ṭāhir first.[121] It is quoted by Yāqūt on the authority of al-Marzubānī, the author who enumerated the Demons of al-ʿAskar in his *Encyclopedia of poets*:[122]

> ʿAlī ibn Hārūn related to me on the authority of his father and (paternal) uncle: Abū al-Ḥasan ʿAlī ibn Yaḥyā ibn al-Munajjim one day held a session and *in attendance were those poets who never missed his gatherings*, such as Aḥmad Ibn Abī Ṭāhir, Aḥmad ibn Abī Fanan,[123] Abū ʿAlī al-Baṣīr, Abū Hiffān al-Mihzamī, his cousin al-Hadādī,[124] i.e. Abū Hiffān's [cousin], Ibn al-ʿAllāf,[125] Abū al-Ṭarīf, Aḥmad ibn Abī Kāmil, the maternal uncle of Abū al-Ḥasan's son [ʿAlī ibn Hārūn],[126] and ʿAlī ibn Mahdī al-Kisrawī, who was his [ʿAlī's] son's teacher (*muʿallim*)... Abū al-ʿUbays ibn Ḥamdūn[127] was [also] present....

If we compare this list with the earlier ones, namely the enumeration of the Demons of al-ʿAskar by al-Marzubānī and the sequencing of Ibn al-Muʿtazz (which I attribute to 'proximity'), and if we exclude those who only appear in one of the three lists, we get the following:

Ibn al-Muʿtazz cluster	*Poets identified as Demons of al-ʿAskar or their close associates*	*Individuals listed as regular attenders of ʿAlī ibn Yaḥyā's gatherings*
Ibn Abī Fanan	—	Ibn Abī Fanan
Abū ʿAlī al-Baṣīr	Abū ʿAlī al-Baṣīr	Abū ʿAlī al-Baṣīr
Abū Hiffān	Abū Hiffān	Abū Hiffān
al-Tammār	Yaʿqūb al-Tammār	al-Tammār
Abū al-ʿAynāʾ	Abū al-ʿAynāʾ	—
Ibn Abī Ṭāhir	Ibn Abī Ṭāhir	Ibn Abī Ṭāhir

Other than Abū ʿAlī al-Baṣīr, Abū Hiffān and Abū al-ʿAynāʾ, discussed above, and ʿAlī ibn Yaḥyā, discussed below, of the members of the gathering enumerated, the one with the closest ties to Ibn Abī Ṭāhir was Abū al-Ḥasan ʿAlī ibn Mahdī ibn ʿAlī ibn Mahdī al-Kisrawī al-Iṣbahānī (d. between 283/896 and 289/902). In fact, in the notice he devotes to al-Kisrāwī, Yāqūt relies on a Ibn Abī Ṭāhir's characterization of him as follows:[128]

> Al-Kisrawī was a refined littérateur, a repository of transmissions, and a poet especially knowledgeable in the *Kitāb al-ʿAyn* [of al-Khalīl ibn Aḥmad]. He tutored (*kāna yuʾaddibu*) Hārūn ibn ʿAlī ibn Yaḥyā al-Nadīm.

Like the scholars and authors writing in the generations after the shift from primarily oral to increasingly writerly sensibilities, al-Kisrawī was involved in teaching and tutoring. And like Ibn Abī Ṭāhir, al-Kisrawī's compositions suggest new and writerly sensibilities. Of the four works with which he is credited, one, the *Kitāb al-Khiṣāl* [Book of properties], was "an anthology comprising accounts (*akhbār*), aphorisms (*ḥikam*), proverbs (*amthāl*), and verses (*ashʿār*);"[129] and another, *Kitāb Murāsalāt al-ikhwān wa-muḥāwarāt al-khillān* [The Correspondence of brothers and the conversations of friends], appears to have consisted of written and spoken exchanges between the members of the côteries or cliques of which he formed an integral part. The cultured influence of al-Kisrāwī on his associates is recorded in verses by Ibn Abī Ṭāhir. These verses are quoted by al-Kisrawī's student, Hārūn ibn ʿAlī ibn Yaḥyā al-Munajjim in the lost *Kitāb Iṣbahān* [Book on Iṣbahān] of Ḥamzah ibn al-Ḥasan (fl. third/ninth century), and cited by Yāqūt:[130]

> [One evening] we were gathered at ʿAlī ibn Mahdī [al-Kisrawī]'s home together with Abū al-Faḍl Aḥmad Ibn Abī Ṭāhir. When we decided to leave, Ibn Abī Ṭāhir recited [the following]:
>
> Were it not for ʿAlī ibn Mahdī and his friendship we would never have been guided aright to wit and culture.[131]
>
> *Lawlā ʿAlīyu ʾbnu Mahdīyin wa-khullatuhu*
> *la-mā ʾhtadaynā ilā ẓarfin wa-lā adabi*

Numerous gatherings attended by the Demons of al-ʿAskar are described in the *Kitāb badāʾiʿ al-badāʾih* [Book of astonishing improvisations] of Ibn Ẓāfir (d. 613/1216), based on quotations from the lost *Taʾrīkh* of Ibn Abī Ṭāhir's son, ʿUbaydallāh.[132] In the first instance, Ibn Ẓāfir quotes an anecdote recounted to ʿUbaydallāh by Abū Aḥmad Yaḥyā ibn ʿAlī ibn al-Munajjim about a gathering at his father's place (i.e. ʿAlī ibn Yahyā al-Munajjim) attended by Ismāʿīl ibn Bulbul, Aḥmad ibn Abī Fanan and Ibn Abī Ṭāhir, among other littérateurs (*jamāʿah min ahl al-adab*).[133] Another gathering at ʿAlī al-Munajjim's home forms the subject of a second anecdote. This one, attended by Aḥmad Ibn Abī Ṭāhir, Abū Hiffān and Yaʿqūb al-Tammār, is also a drinking session at which Abū Hiffān improvises a panegyric of ʿAlī, to which al-Tammār and Ibn Abī Ṭāhir add some improvised lines.[134] Al-Tammār was evidently a friend of both Abū Hiffān and Ibn Abī Ṭāhir, and given the nature of these friendships, exchanged satires with them.[135] As we saw above, Ibn al-Mu'tazz places al-Tammār immediately after Abū Hiffān, and before al-Qiṣāfī, Abū al-ʿAynāʾ and Ibn Abī Ṭāhir in the *Classes of modern poets*. Ibn Abī Fanan is placed immediately before Abū ʿAlī al-Baṣīr. All are Demons of al-ʿAskar.

In another anecdote in Ibn Ẓāfir's *Astonishing improvisations* Yaḥyā ibn ʿAlī describes how he sought permission from his father to attend a particular gathering. On learning that Aḥmad Ibn Abī Ṭāhir, Abū Ṭālib ibn Maslamah, and ʿAlī ibn Mahdī al-Kisrawī are in attendance (in addition, again, to a group of littérateurs [*jamāʿah min ahl (ʿilm) al-adab*]), Yaḥyā's father gives his consent.[136] The presence of al-Kisrawī and Ibn Abī Ṭāhir (one-time tutors both) evidently reassures ʿAlī ibn Yaḥyā notwithstanding their Demons of al-ʿAskar and debauched (*mujūn*) status. This is attributable to their long and friendly association with him, one nurtured no doubt also by their shared interests in books and writerly culture.

Abū al-Hasan ʿAlī ibn Yaḥyā ibn Abī Manṣūr al-Munajjim (d. 275/888–89) was an accomplished man of letters, an able poet and prose stylist, a transmitter of accounts and of poetry, and a courtier of the caliphs al-Mutawakkil, al-Muntaṣir, al-Mustaʿīn, al-Muʿtazz and al-Muʿtamid.[137] A lucrative position at the caliphal court permitted him to explore his academic and scientific interests although his special interests were philosophy, music, and literature. ʿAlī is uniformly described as a perfect companion to the caliphs.[138] Indeed the Munajjim family was to become the most famous and distinguished family of Abbasid courtiers.

ʿAlī ibn Yaḥyā became especially well-known for having set up a library for al-Fatḥ ibn Khāqān, and for making available to the literati free materials, board, and lodging at his own library, the "Treasury of Wisdom" (*Khizānat al-Ḥikmah*), housed on one of his properties in a Baghdad suburb. ʿAlī died in Samarra in 275/889. His numerous elegists included Ibn al-Muʿtazz.[139]

ʿAlī was first introduced to the caliph al-Mutawakkil by al-Fatḥ ibn Khāqān (d. 247/861), who was favorably impressed by him and who adopted him as a boon-companion (*nadīm*). This and subsequent associations allowed ʿAlī to amass huge wealth and a great number of properties, and explains how he was able himself to patronize many poets, Abū Tammām and Diʿbil, for instance,[140] and to indulge his, and their, interests. It was to him that the celebrated translator Ḥunayn ibn Isḥāq addressed the inventory of Galen's writings,[141] and at his request that Thābit ibn Qurrah wrote a work on questions of theory and music.

The sources are explicit about the considerable contact between the Demons of al-ʿAskar and the Munajjim family. Numerous verses praising him by various poets can be found in their diwans and in *adab* anthologies. In the case of Ibn Abī Ṭāhir, two epistles by him to ʿAlī are attested but do not survive. On the other hand, several verse passages do; the following is a typical one, taken from the *Khizānat al-adab* (Treasury of culture) of ʿAbd al-Qādir al-Baghdādī:[142]

I put to the test
People from the East and the West.
And I distinguished the ignoble from nobility.

But my testing only
Sent me back to ʿAlī,
After examining all of humanity.

Balawtu 'n-nāsa fī sharqin wa-gharbin
wa-mayyaztu 'l-kirāma min al-li'āmī
Fa-raddaniya 'btilāya ilā ʿAliyyi b-
-ni Yaḥyā baʿda tajrībī 'l-anāmī

It is not surprising that Ibn Abī Ṭāhir should praise ʿAlī ibn Yaḥyā so highly. ʿAlī obviously welcomed Ibn Abī Ṭāhir and other members of the Demons of al-ʿAskar often into his gatherings. And it seems especially likely that when ʿAlī provided free room, board, and materials to the literati he was providing it for the likes of Ibn Abī Ṭāhir and Abū Hiffān. Poets who increasingly relied on books and writerly culture were no longer the typically patronized poets, and those providing occasions and environments for these poets were no longer typical patrons either.

ʿAlī ibn Yaḥyā himself composed several works, including one exposing al-Buḥturī's plagiarisms.[143] Abū Tammām's plagiarisms are also said to have been addressed in this work.[144] Regrettably, it does not survive. The modern critic al-Rabdāwī believes that the work was occasioned by a satire composed by al-Buḥturī, at al-Mutawakkil's instigation, on Ibn al-Munajjim unattractive appearance.

There seems little doubt that most of the Baghdad littérateurs (*udabā'*) knew one another. They were not overly numerous, they learned from the same relatively small number of teachers, they attended many of the same literary and social gatherings and salons (*majālis*), and study circles (*ḥalaqāt*), and they met in the bookshops and the Bookmen's Market (*Sūq al-warrāqīn*). There is ample evidence in the sources about the friendships, enmities, and rivalries nurtured or harbored by the littérateurs. In the case of *udabā'* transformed or affected by the changes in writerly culture, these very changes appear to have played a role in the nature of the alliances they formed, doctrinal, ethnic, and political affinities taking a back seat. The individuals with whom Ibn Abī Ṭāhir associated reveals the importance they, as a group, attached to books, writing, writerly initiatives, and modernist sensibilities; and the importance they attached also to a relative distancing from the patronage of the caliphal court and the patronal economy.

Ibn Abī Ṭāhir, Abū Hiffān and Abū al-'Aynā' (and others) were independents for whom the freedom to write unfettered by the conditions imposed by the patron was of paramount importance. As poets, prose-writers, anthologists, and critics, writers such as they functioned as outsiders, something that was possible because of their access to scholarship, books, and writing, outside the machinery of oral/aural transmission and outside the machinery of caliphal patronage. They did not hesitate to indulge in licentious behavior (*mujūn*), they composed books on a wide range of subjects, and were also in a position to bring to their critical pronouncements a dispassionate interest that differed from the opinions of prince-pleasers in quest of the all-important purse.

ENVOI

Revisiting Arabic literary history of the third/ninth century

In the foregoing chapters I have tried to highlight some of the implications and effects of writing and of books on the literary culture of third/ninth century Baghdad, what I have termed Arabic writerly culture. The choice of Ibn Abī Ṭāhir as a focus of the investigation is intended to provide a point of departure for the identifications of the markers of this writerly culture. These markers include, but are evidently not confined to: changes in the nature and transmission of knowledge; the range and scope of vocations and avocations available; the nature of literary output; the decreasing importance in literary and scholarly circles of doctrinal stripe or ethnic affiliation; the constitution of social and professional networks; and the adoption of creative and critical positions little mediated by the exigencies of market or prince. By identifying Ibn Abī Ṭāhir's scholarly and professional contacts, I hope I have also brought attention to an understudied network of littérateurs who are, in some ways, more typical than perennially invoked figures, such as al-Jāḥiẓ.[1]

Ibn Abī Ṭāhir and other littérateurs like him effectively displayed an individualism that I argue is connected to their unwillingness to be tied too closely, and in the case of some, at all, to the caliph or to patrons. This led them to seek occupations and livelihoods outside the environment of caliphal and patronal benevolence or whim, and outside of the patronal economy. If one functioned outside the system of caliphal legitimation, what avenues were then available to the writer? As I have suggested, the availability of paper, the rise of a middle class seeking education, and the growth of a lay readership, meant that one could support oneself as a teacher, tutor, copyist, author, storyteller, bookseller, editor, publisher, or any combination of these. These were professions in which one could engage without recourse to the court or to the indulgence of the caliph or patron. Indeed, by moving to the Bookmen's Market (*Sūq al-warrāqīn*), Ibn Abī Ṭāhir gained access to books and the professions that arose around the production, sale, dissemination, and collection of books, and joined a growing number of individuals who had become bookmen, that is, professional writers and, by extension, publishers and booksellers.

In his capacity as transmitter/narrator (*rāwī*), another avenue available to the littérateur was the production of anthologies and works devoted to a critique of the poetic tradition. The notion of an anthology, though it does not necessitate a written record, does presuppose redaction, and the possibility of dissemination in ways other than by oral/aural transmission; that way is books. By the time of al-Ṣūlī (d. 335/946), who was, it is true, still being criticized for his reliance on the written word, he and others have already recognized, even if that recognition could be ambivalent, that the nature of the literary-historical enterprise has irrevocably changed, and take pride in the accumulation of a vast number of books on which they can rely for the composition of their own works.[2] ʿAlī ibn Yaḥyā (d. 275/888–9) had two generations earlier built a personal library to which *udabāʾ* were granted free access.

The advent of paper and paper-related technologies, and the increased availability of books, changed the nature of learning and the literary environment. New centers of learning and study included homes of patrons and fellow-scholars; public and private libraries; later, *madrasahs*;[3] and, significantly, bookshops, as many as a hundred by the early third/ninth century in Baghdad's Bookmen's Market, the *Sūq al-warrāqīn* – all places where books could be consulted. One could not only buy books inexpensively from a bookshop, one could also read them there, in private. Enterprising *warrāq*s had been copying single works ever since writing had developed into a commercial activity, but now they were able to sell the books that they, or others, copied, and on a large scale too. Publishing technology was of course not yet mechanized. Booksellers often relied on contract copyists who charged by the page or by the copy, depending on the nature of the work or request. But mass production had begun. The bookseller could provide the public with multiple copies of a wide range of works.

Moreover, the availability of books made it possible to accomplish one's training in *adab* through self-teaching. This autodidacticism, which would take stronger hold in later centuries, resulted in a concomitant drop in the reliance on oral and aural transmission of knowledge and information and an increased dependence on books and written materials. This was both a function of the change in the system proper of the method employed for the transmission of learning, but also evidently a function of the availability of easily circulated, authenticated books.

A comparison between Ibn Abī Ṭāhir and al-Jāhiẓ (d. 255/868) provides a helpful way of better situating the littérateur within the writerly culture of the period. What we know of al-Jāḥiẓ is in large part based on what survives of his output, a considerable amount of material even if it only represents twenty-some works out of about two hundred and thirty.[4] But as Pellat's numerous descriptions of al-Jāḥiz's life reveal, we actually know very little with any degree of certitude. The following passages suffice to illustrate this – the emphases are mine:[5]

> Even when *he seems* from time to time to be giving free rein to original trains of thought, *it is hard to tell* whether they are really his own ideas. . . . Jāḥiẓ *probably* had little opportunity while at Baṣra of mixing in

> aristocratic Arab circles.... *It is doubtful whether* Jāḥiẓ would have found much in the way of translations from the Greek.... A man like Jāḥiẓ ... *was bound to have been* caught up in all this intellectual turmoil... Jāḥiẓ *for some reason* reacted against ... specialization ... to become instead an *adīb*... *There is no actual evidence* to support my view that this must have been due to his own turn of mind, his intellectual curiosity, and his genuine eclecticism. Nevertheless it *seems most likely* to have been ... spontaneous, *possibly helped* by some lucky chance...

Prevailing conceptions of *adab* (literary and writerly culture) are thus indebted to rather vague notions about one of its major exponents and figures. What is known is that al-Jāḥiẓ frequented the great open area of Mirbad on the outskirts of Baṣrah, where the caravans stopped and where scholars and aficionados of Arabic could quiz the bedouin on philological matters.[6] Al-Jāḥiẓ also spent time in the mosque, where the *masjidiyyūn*, individuals who spent their time in mosques for the express purpose of discussion, would meet and discuss all sorts of subjects.

At the turn of the third century Ḥijrah (the ninth century), al-Jāḥiẓ's fortunes changed. The Basran grammarian al-Yazīdī (d. 202/818) presented some of al-Jāḥiẓ's writings to the caliph al-Ma'mūn (r. 198–218/813–833) who was very impressed with al-Jāḥiẓ's views on the imāmate, the way he expressed those views, and his general argument. Al-Jāḥiẓ thereafter embarked on a career as popularizer, promoter, and defender of official doctrine. He thus made his living primarily through the dedication of his books to influential patrons, usually prominent Muʿtazilites. His *Book of animals* (*Kitāb al-Ḥayawān*), for example, is dedicated to the minister-poet Muḥammad Ibn al-Zayyāt (d. 233/847), and *Elegance of expression and clarity of exposition* (*al-Bayān wa-al-tabyīn*) to the judge and chief prosecutor of the rationalist Muʿtazilite cause, Aḥmad ibn Abī Du'ād (d. 240/854). As Pellat has noted, al-Jāḥiẓ is very much a publicist of prevailing policies:

> In a large proportion of his works, Jāḥiẓ in fact appears as an official writer, charged with announcing, publishing or explaining government decisions, vulgarizing the religious ideas of the moment and ... defending the dynasty, Islām, and the Arabs.[7]

The importance of al-Jāḥiẓ's patronage cannot be overestimated. A letter from al-Fatḥ ibn Khāqān, the Turkish favorite of the caliph al-Mutawakkil, to al-Jāḥiẓ illustrates just how important and lucrative such an association could be:[8]

> The Commander of the Faithful has taken a tremendous liking to you, and rejoices to hear your name spoken. Were it not that he thinks so highly of you because of your learning and erudition, he would require your constant attendance in his audience chamber to give him your views and tell him your opinion on the questions that occupy your time and thought.... *I went out of my way to enhance the already high opinion he has*

> *of you.... You thus have me to thank for the gain to your reputation....* Finish *The Refutation of the Christians* (*al-Radd ʿalā al-Naṣārā*), hasten to bring it to me, and endeavor to gain personal advantage from it.
>
> You will be receiving your monthly allowance: *I have arranged for you to be credited with the arrears*, and am also having you paid a whole year in advance. There is a windfall for you in this...

Al-Jāḥiẓ's *Virtues of the Turks* (*Manāqib al-Turk*), dedicated to al-Fatḥ ibn Khāqān, includes fulsome praise of this patron. It is clear that this was expected of him: as a patronized writer, he was evidently required to praise his benefactors. This is not to say he did not also rebuke them, as in the 'Epistle on Jest and Earnest' (*Fī al-jidd wa-al-hazl*), in which he takes his patron to task for showing anger toward him. But ultimately, the patron was the source of the patronized writer's keep.

The relationship between patron and patronized was so important that when the former fell into disfavor, so too did the latter. When Ibn al-Zayyāt was arrested and tortured in 233/847, al-Jāḥiẓ fled to Basra and was returned to Baghdad some time later "in a pitiful state."[9] And in 247/861, on the assassination of al-Mutawakkil and al-Fatḥ, al-Jāḥiẓ retired again to Basra. Although he may admittedly have been prompted by ill-health, the change in caliphal policy toward Muʿtazilism can reasonably be expected to have played a part in his decision.

Professionally, al-Jāḥiẓ was thus very different from Ibn Abī Ṭāhir. It is true that neither held – or is known to have held – an official position for any significant amount of time.[10] But that is all they had in common. Al-Jāḥiẓ was patronized and his dedications were his major source of revenue;[11] Ibn Abī Ṭāhir operated largely outside the patronal economy. Al-Jāḥiẓ was a promoter of prevailing Abbasid ideology; Ibn Abī Ṭāhir, by all indications, was simply a chronicler of Abbasid political and cultural history. Al-Jāḥiẓ wrote defences of the Muʿtazilites, the Banū Hāshim, ʿAlī's actions at the Battle of Ṣiffīn, and on other political and theological issues; Ibn Abī Ṭāhir wrote no such treatises.[12] Al-Jāḥiẓ compiled no poetic or poet-centered anthologies of any kind; Ibn Abī Ṭāhir produced many. Al-Jāḥiẓ's literary criticism is confined to his anthology devoted to eloquence and expression, the *Book of elegance of expression and clarity of exposition*; Ibn Abī Ṭāhir directly tackled both the issue of plagiarism and the burning literary-critical issue of the day, the modern/ancient (*muḥdath/qadīm*) and related Abū Tammām/al-Buḥturī controversies.[13] Al-Jāḥiẓ was an essayist and polemical writer of prose; Ibn Abī Ṭāhir a writer of prose *and* of poetry, an anthologist, an editor, a literary critic, and a writer of fables. Al-Jāḥiẓ was intimately connected to the court; Ibn Abī Ṭāhir was not.

Al-Jāḥiẓ also differed from Ibn Abī Ṭāhir in his attention to Arabness. It is clear from the kind of *adab* (writerly culture) he expounded that al-Jāḥiẓ believed in the cultivation of an Arabic humanities, based on the Arabic language and with the sources of its inspiration in literary and religious traditions of the Arabs (many of them collected by his Basran compatriots and teachers). In this connection, the *Book of elegance of expression and clarity of exposition* is often characterized as an attempt to prove the superiority of the Arabs to the non-Arabs in poetry and rhetoric (though whether al-Jāḥiẓ's belief in Arab literary superiority extended to a belief also in the overall superiority of the Arabs to non-Arabs is impossible to say). Writers influenced by the Persian and other literary traditions, on the other hand, drew on a heritage that included literary models and inspiration for the writing of works on right conduct, manners, and, in the case of rulers, mirrors for princes (*naṣīḥat al-mulūk*) and other wisdom literature (Persian, *andarz*). It is not surprising that al-Jāḥiẓ produced no such works. Influenced though he undoubtedly was by the intellectual heritage of Persia, he strove for an Arab literary culture and therefore seems to have avoided, or altogether ignored, works of this type.[14] Ibn Abī Ṭāhir's wisdom-literature works and his storytelling activity made him a littérateur of a different ilk from al-Jāḥiẓ.

Furthermore, al-Jāḥiẓ was not a poet; Ibn Abī Ṭāhir, as we have seen, was. Though it is true that no diwan of Ibn Abī Ṭāhir survives, even a casual glance at any of a number of significant poetical collections of the third/ninth and later centuries, e.g. the *Book of the Flower* of Ibn Dāwūd, the *Muntaḥal* [Collection] of al-Thaʿālibī, or the *Ready replies of the littérateurs* of al-Rāghib al-Iṣfahānī, demonstrate that his verses were known and widely diffused. Some eighty lines of Ibn Abī Ṭāhir's poetry can be found in the *Book of the Flower*. Al-Rāghib al-Iṣbahānī (d. early fifth/eleventh century) quotes twenty-nine selections. Their anthological-critical appreciation was echoed by literary critics such as Abū Hilāl al-ʿAskarī (d. after 395/1005),[15] Ibn Ṭabāṭabā (d. 322/934),[16] and others. Al-Masʿūdī (d. 345/946), who alone preserves his elegy on Yaḥyā ibn ʿUmar, calls him a poet outright.[17] Al-Marzubānī (d. 384/994), devotes an entry to him in the *Kitāb al-Muwashshaḥ* [Book of the ornamental belt].[18] Al-Khaṭīb al-Baghdādī (463/1071) and Yāqūt (d. 626/1229) write that he was "*aḥad al-bulaghā' al-shuʿarā' al-ruwāt wa min ahl al-fahm al-madhkūrīn bi-al-ʿilm*," one of the eloquent prose stylists, poets and transmitters, to be counted among the discerning people endowed with real knowledge.[19] The poet and critic Ibn al-Muʿtazz stated that Ibn Abī Ṭāhir's poetry was well-known among both the elite and the common folk.

Before the advent of paper and paper-related technologies, poetry flourished in the court of the caliph:

> There was no organised book trade, no wealthy publishers, so that poets were usually dependent for their livelihood on the capricious bounty of the Caliphs and his favourites whom they belauded. Huge sums were paid.[20]

In his positive description of the court of the Ḥamdānid prince Sayf al-Dawlah (d. 356/967), al-Thaʿālibī (d. 429/1038) remarks that "to a monarch's hall, as to a market, people bring only what is in demand."[21] Ibn Qutaybah uses a similar mercantile metaphor in his introduction to the *Book of poetry and poets* when he speaks of poets "whose poetry does not move briskly on the market."[22] Even in the most liberal of milieux and in the company of the magnanimous, the patronized poet was required, by convention, and as a guarantee of continued support, to praise, or at any rate, to please.[23] Failure to do so could mean ejection from the privilege of boon-companionship, stipend, or support, as the case may have been. Although Ibn Abī Ṭāhir did occasionally write verses for money, on no occasion were the verses addressed to the caliph or dependent on the fickle, unpredictable literary politics of the caliphal court. Of the few panegyric verses by Ibn Abī Ṭāhir, which do survive, many are instances of gratitude *post facto* (e.g. those addressed to ʿAlī ibn Yaḥyā), and not attempts to obtain remuneration. And many verses addressed to patron figures (that is, people who were patrons of others) are in fact satires. There is, in short, ample evidence of Ibn Abī Ṭāhir's literary association with individuals who were patrons, but no evidence of any sustained income-earning patronal relationship between him and them. One scholar of Abbasid literature has, in fact, gone so far as to characterize Ibn Abī Ṭāhir's panegyric output as outright bad, but his attempts to earn money from them as remunerative.[24] Indeed, one of the principal ways in which the transformed *adīb* differed from contemporaries or writers from preceding generations as yet unaffected by the transformations in writerly culture was, effectively, in the matter of patronage.

Ibn Abī Ṭāhir is an example of the transformed *adīb*, a scholar whose life was ruled by the existence of the written word. His move to the Bookmen's Market enabled him to have access to books and to the professions that arose around their production, sale, dissemination, and collection. In this way, Ibn Abī Ṭāhir joined the growing number of scholars who became professional writers and, by extension, publishers and booksellers. In government administration, these writers were the *kātib*s (lit. writers [of official correspondence]); in patronized circles, they were the poets, chroniclers, and apologists. Outside of officialdom, the writers were the literary critics, anthologists, chronicler-recorders (*muʾarrikhūn*), religious scholars, philosophers, and scientists. A move to the Bookmen's Market gave one access to a literary scene that was inevitably and inextricably linked to the market for, and marketplace of, *written* knowledge.

Bookmen sold paper, but "the medieval *warrāq*, like his European counterpart the 'stationer,' was much more important in the role of bookseller than in that of seller of blank paper."[25] He copied books, sometimes he forged them. He produced imaginative literature. He anthologized. He procured books on others' behalf (as a kind of book-broker).[26] He rented out his books, and sometimes his bookshop, to others.[27] He held *majālis* or *andiyat al-adab*, literary gatherings (often soirées) or salons, at his shop.[28] The bookman was also hired by authors who wanted their works to be more widely disseminated.[29] The bookman was a literary entrepreneur. He copied his own books, those of his friends and associates, or those of clients for a fee, and sold them, for a profit. This was his profession. Like the poets who vied for the patronage of this caliph or that patron, the bookman produced his works for the literate public. Just as there is no reason to separate or see as mutually exclusive the poet's "art" and his desire for reward, so too must we be careful not to separate the bookman's craft and his desire for revenue. Revenue from the sale of his own works or the works of others allowed the bookman to remain unattached to patrons or chanceries. He was often eager to keep away because of the implicit, or explicit, allegiance that this entailed. Whether it was to distance himself from the governing power, as Makdisi has characterized it,[30] to avoid compromising his morals, or simply to be independent, the evidence suggests that this was the road taken by Ibn Abī Ṭāhir.

The *adab* espoused by Ibn Abī Ṭāhir and his associates effectively represents the more secular – the term is not ideal – side of the culture.[31] It is this "secularism" that distinguished *adab* from the religiously-motivated pursuit of knowledge.[32] The possibility of drawing from non-religious sources, or sources ancillary to the religious sciences, especially in an environment where the dissemination of books was becoming increasingly easy, meant that the nature of literary production would change. Numerous new initiatives developed and new kinds of works began to be written. New poetic genres emerged. Stories from other traditions, notably Persian, Hellenistic,[33] and Indian, were translated and adapted. The *rāwī*, initially a transmitter of poems, became also a commentator, a critic, a compiler, and an anthologist. A growing number of anthologies and works devoted to a critique of the poetic tradition began to appear. This burgeoning of output, though not entirely predicated on writing, did nevertheless presuppose the possibility of dissemination in ways other than oral/aural transmission; that way was books. Books were written on a wide range of topics, sold, exchanged, and copied. Cultural history, literary criticism, science, philosophy, folklore, and conduct, initially excluded from the oral/aural institutions, now found a medium and a conduit: writers and books.

NOTES

INTRODUCTION

1 Gérard Lecomte, *Ibn Qutayba (mort en 276/889): L'homme, son oeuvre, ses idées*, Damascus: Institut français de Damas, 1965, p. vii; Brian Stock, *The Implications of Literacy: Models of Interpretation in the Eleventh and Twelfth Centuries*, Princeton: Princeton University Press, 1982, p. 5.

2 Lecomte, *Ibn Qutayba*; Fedwa Malti-Douglas, *Structures of Avarice: The Bukhalā' in Medieval Arabic Literature*, Leiden: E. J. Brill, 1958; Dominique Sourdel, *Le vizirat 'abbāside de 749 à 936 (132 à 324 de l'Hégire)*, 2 vols, Damascus: Institut français de Damas, 1959–60.

3 The important point is not the degree to which writing penetrated oral culture: it was its irrevocability: see Stock, *Implications of Literacy*, p. 17.

4 The term literacy in classical and medieval contexts has its limitations. On this, see e.g. F. H Bäuml, 'Varieties and Consequences of Medieval Literacy and Illiteracy,' *Speculum*, 1980, vol. 55(2), 237–65, and M. T. Clanchy, *From Memory to Written Record: England 1066–1307*, 2nd edn, Cambridge Mass.: Blackwell especially p. 232: "Another fundamental difference between medieval and modern approaches to literacy is that medieval assessments concentrate on cases of maximum ability, the skills of the most learned scholars (*literati*) and the most elegant scribes, whereas modern assessors measure the diffusion of minimal skills among the masses." Note, however, that literacy is distinct and different from textuality. One can be literate without using – or needing to use – texts; and one can use texts without being genuinely literate.

5 See e.g. Ibn Qutaybah's opening paragraph in *al-Ma'ārif*, ed. Tharwat 'Ukāshsah, 2nd edn, Cairo: Dār al-Ma'ārif, 1969, p. 1 [= p. 125], especially lines 6–7.

6 *Cf.* the enumeration of the middle class's constituents in Simha Sabari, *Mouvements populaires à Bagdad à l'époque 'abbasside, IXe–XIe siècles*, Paris: Librairie d'Amérique et d'Orient Adrien Maisonneuve, 1981, p. 38 ("les couches moyennes").

7 Stock, *Implications of Literacy*, pp. 7, 30, underscores "the complex interplay of orality with textual models for understanding and transmitting the cultural heritage."

8 On which see Eric A. Havelock, *The Literate Revolution in Greece and Its Cultural Consequences*, Princeton: Princeton University Press, 1982 for Greek; and Stock, *Implications of Literacy* for medieval Latin.

9 For a general discussion of the introduction of paper into the Arab–Islamic world and the history of its production, see Johannes Pedersen, *The Arabic Book*, tr. Geoffrey French, Princeton: Princeton University Press, 1984, pp. 60 ff. and Jonathan M. Bloom, *Paper before Print: the history and impact of paper in the Islamic world*, New Haven, Yale University Press, 2001, pp. 30 ff. See also Josef von Karabacek, 'Das arabische Papier. Eine historisch-antiquarische Untersuchung,' *Nationalbibliothek, Mitteilungen aus*

der Sammlung der Papyrus Erzherzog Rainer, 1887, vols 2–3, 87–178; and Clément Huart and Adolf Grohmann, 'Kāghad,' in *EI2*.

10 Beeston, 'Background Topics,' p. 7, and also 4, 14 and 23. Stock, *Implications of Literacy*, p. 3, notes that "As methods of interpretation were increasingly subjected to systematic scrutiny, the models employed to give meaning to otherwise unrelated disciplines more and more clustered around the concept of written language." Indeed, as scholars began to study, the first focus of that study was the Arabic language.

11 See Jack Goody and Ian Watt, 'The Consequences of Literacy,' in Jack Goody (ed.), *Literacy in Traditional Societies*, Cambridge: Cambridge University Press, 1968, pp. 27–68; and Bäuml, 'Varieties and Consequences.'

12 Bloom, *Paper Before Print*, p. 123.

13 Sprenger, *Das Leben und die Lehre des Mohammed*, 2nd edn, vol. 3, Berlin: Nicolai, 1869, p. xciii ff.

14 Gregor Schoeler, 'Writing and Publishing. On the Use and Function of Writing in the First Centuries of Islam,' *Arabica*, 1997, vol. 44(3), 423; *cf.* Schoeler, *Ecrire et transmettre dans les débuts de l'islam*, Paris: Presses universitaires de France, 2002, pp. 9, 153–4.

15 Schoeler, *Ecrire et transmettre*, pp. 57–70, notes at pp. 141–3.

16 See e.g. James Monroe, 'Oral Composition in Pre-Islamic Poetry,' *Journal of Arabic Literature*, 1972, vol. 3, 1–53; Michael Zwettler, *The Oral Tradition of Classical Arabic Poetry: Its Character and Implications*, Columbus: Ohio State University Press, 1978; and Manfred Fleischhammer, 'Hinweise auf schriftliche Quellen im Kitāb al-Aġānī,' *Wiener Zeitschrift für die Kunde des Morgenlandes*, 1979, vol. 28(1), 53–62.

17 See e.g. Ḥasan al-Bannā' 'Izz al-Dīn, *al-Kalimāt wa-al-ashyā': Dirāsah fī jamālīyyāt al-qaṣīdah al-jāhiliyyah*, Cairo: Dār al-Fikr al-'Arabī, 1988; Suzanne P. Stetkevych, *Abū Tammām and the Poetics of the 'Abbāsid Age*, Leiden: E. J. Brill, 1991, especially pp. 33–4.

18 Gregor Schoeler, 'Die Frage der schriftlichen oder mündlichen Überlieferung der Wissenschaften im frühen Islam,' *Der Islam*, 1985, vol. 62, 201–30; *idem*, 'Wieteres zur Frage der schriftlichen oder mündlichen Überlieferung der Wissenschaften im frühen Islam,' *Der Islam*, 1989, vol. 66, 38–67; *idem*, 'Mündliche Thora und Ḥadīṯ. Überlieferung, Schreibverbot, Redaktion,' *Der Islam*, 1989, vol. 66, 213–51; *idem*, 'Schreiben und Veröffentlichen. Zu Verwendung und Funktion der Schrift in der ersten islamischen Jahrhunderten,' *Der Islam*, 1992, vol. 69, 1–43; *idem*, 'Writing and Publishing.

19 Sebastian Günther, *Quellenuntersuchungen zu den «Maqātil al-Ṭālibiyyīn» des Abū 'l-Faraǧ al-Isfahānī (gest. 356/967). Ein beitrag zur Problematik der mündlichen und schriftlichen Überlieferung im Islam des Mittelalters*, Hildesheim and New York: Georg Olms Verlag, 1991.

20 *Arabica*, 1997, vol. 44(3) includes: Baber Johansen, 'Formes de langage et de fonction publiques: Stéréotypes, témoins et offices dans la preuve par l'écrit en droit musulman,' 333–76; Albert Arazi, 'De la voix au calame et la naissance du classicisme en poésie,' 377–406; Yūsuf Rāghib, 'La parole, le geste et l'écrit dans l'acte de vente,' in *Arabica*, 407–22; Schoeler, 'Writing and Publishing,' 423–35.

Arabica, 1997, vol. 44(4) includes: Michael Cook, 'The Opponents of the Writing of Tradition in Early Islam,' 437–530; Hugh Kennedy, 'From Oral Tradition to Written Record in Arabic Genealogy,' 531–44; Jacqueline Sublet, 'Nom écrit, nom dit: Les personnages du théâtre d'ombres d'Ibn Dāniyāl,' 545–52; Geneviève Humbert, 'Le *Kitāb* de Sībawayhi et l'autonomie de l'écrit,' 553–67.

21 *Ta'rīkh Baghdād*, vol. 4, p. 212, line 1. The *EI2* entry (see n. 34 below) has 14 March 893. This cannot be correct, as the year 280 Ḥijrī began on 23 March 893 and ended on 12 March 894: my calculation is based on the passage of 145 days from 23 March (i.e. 1 Muḥarram to 28 Jumādā I).

22 That Ibn Abī Ṭāhir lived in Bāb al-Shām is revealed in conversations he had with al-Buḥturī and al-Mubarrad: see *Irshād*, vol. 3, p. 94, line 9.

23 Guy Le Strange, *Baghdad during the Abbasid Caliphate*, Oxford: The Clarendon Press, 1900, p. 13.

24 Works on writing itself had already begun to appear, e.g. *al-Risālat al-ʿadhrāʾ* of Ibrāhīm ibn Muḥammad al-Shaybānī (d. 298/911), addressed to his friend Ibn al-Mudabbir (d. 279/892) (long mistakenly credited to the latter). By his own admission, al-Shaybānī knew Ibn Abī Ṭāhir (al-Maqqarī, *Nafḥ al-ṭīb min ghuṣn al-Andalus al-raṭīb wa-dhikr wazīrihā Lisān al-dīn Ibn al-Khaṭīb. Analectes sur l'histoire et la littérature des arabes d'Espagne par al-Makkari*, ed. Reinhart Dozy *et al.*, 2 vols, Leiden: E. J. Brill, 1855, 1861, reprint Amsterdam: Oriental Press, 1967, vol. 2, p. 92, lines 14–16), who, like al-Shaybānī, also addressed an epistle to Ibn al-Mudabbir (see *Fihrist*, p. 163, line 23).

25 *Irshād*, vol. 18, p. 142, line 4 to p. 143, line 4; included in *Dīwān Shiʿr al-Imām Abī Bakr Ibn Durayd al-Azdī*, ed. M. B. al-ʿAlawī, Cairo: Maṭbaʿah Lajnat al-Taʾlīf wa-al-Tarjamah wa-al-Nashr, 1365/1946, p. 41. Note that Yāqūt, writing in the seventh/thirteenth century, still feels the need to substantiate his "I read in the *Kitāb al-Taḥbīr*" with "and this was also recounted to me by [so-and-so]... authorized by *licentia* if not by certificates of audition."

26 This *isnād* is corrupt: it was Abū al-ʿAbbās Ismāʿīl (d. 362/973) who associated with Ibn Durayd. The title given him here, *amīr*, is possibly a reference to his appointment as *raʾīs* of Nishapur, i.e. municipal head and representative of town notables to the central government. On the family, see the 'Mīkālīs' entry in *EI2*, vol. 7, pp. 25–6, and the 'Āl-e Mīkāl' entry in *Encyclopedia Iranica*.

27 The anecdote is also recorded in al-Thaʿālibī, *Bard al-akbād fī al-aʿdād*, in *Khams rasāʾil*, Constantine: Maktabat al-Jawāʾib, 1301/1884, p. 122, in an interesting variant. Here, Ibn Durayd's answer is, "The books of al-Jāḥiẓ, the poetry of the moderns, and the witticisms (*nawādir*) of Abū al-ʿAynāʾ." The latter were presumably included in Ibn Abī Ṭāhir's lost work, *Akhbār Abī al-ʿAynāʾ* [Accounts of Abū al-ʿAynāʾ]. Al-Thaʿālibī, *Khāṣṣ al-khāṣṣ*, Beirut: Manshūrāt Dār Maktabat al-Ḥayāt, 1966, p. 69, omits the *Accounts of Abū al-ʿAynāʾ*.

28 *Wa man taku nuzhatahu qaynatun*
Wa kaʾsun tuḥaththu wa kaʾsun tuṣab

Fa-nuzhatunā wa-ʾstirāḥatunā
Talāqī ʾl-ʿuyūni wa darsu ʾl-kutub

Translation of the verses is based on George Makdisi, *The Rise of Humanism in Classical Islam and the Christian West, with special reference to scholasticism*, Edinburgh: Edinburgh University Press, 1990, p. 70.

29 *ʿUyūn al-akhbār*, 4 vols, ed. Yūsuf al-Ṭawīl, Cairo: Maṭbaʿat Dār al-Kutub al-Miṣriyyah, 1925–1930; reprint Cairo: al-Muʾassasah al-Miṣriyyah al-ʿAmmāh li-al-Taʾlīf wa-al-Tarjamah wa-al-Nashr, 1964.

30 *al-Zahrah*, 2 vols, ed. Ibrāhīm al-Sāmarrāʾī, al-Zarqāʾ: Maktabat al-Manār, 1406/1985.

31 These three books are much different, as a trio, from the four books (*arbaʿat dawawīn*) identified by Ibn Khaldūn's teachers as essential to one's education in *adab*, namely the *Adab al-kātib* [Conduct of the secretaries] by Ibn Qutaybah, *al-Kāmil* [The Perfect (compendium)] by al-Mubarrad, *Kitāb al-Bayān wa-al-tabyīn* [Book of elegance of expression] by al-Jāḥiẓ, and *Kitāb al-Nawādir* [= *Kitāb al-Amālī* (Book of dictations)] of by al-Qālī (Ibn Khaldūn, *al-Muqaddimah. Prolégomènes d'Ebn-Khaldoun*, 3 vols, ed. E. Quatremère, Beirut: Institut Impériale de France, 1858, vol. 2, p. 295, line 19 to p. 296, line 4). *Cf.* the list provided by al-Tawḥīdī, *al-Baṣāʾir wa-al-dhakhāʾir*, ed. Ibrāhīm al-Kīlānī, Damascus: Maktabat Aṭlas, 1964, vol. 1, p. 4, line 9 to p. 6, line 2, in the introduction to his *Insights and Treasures* which enumerates, among other works by

al-Jāḥiẓ, Ibn al-Aʿrābī, and others, the following: al-Mubarrad's *al-Kāmil,* Ibn Qutaybah's *al-ʿUyūn,* Thaʿlab's *Majālisāt,* "the book which Ibn Abī Ṭāhir entitled *al-Manẓūm wa-al-manthūr,*" al-Ṣūlī's *al-Awrāq,* and al-Jahshiyārī's *al-Wuzarā'.*

32 M. J. Kister, 'The Seven Golden Odes,' *Rivista degli studi orientali,* 1969, vol. 44, 27–36; Seeger A. Bonebakker, 'Poets and Critics in the Third Century AH,' in Gustav E. von Grunebaum (ed.), *Logic in Classical Islamic Culture,* Wiesbaden: Otto Harrassowitz, 1970, pp. 85–111; Arazi, 'De la voix au calame.'

33 See *Kitāb Baghdād,* ed. Keller, vol. 1, pp. i–ix. A comparison of material in Ibn Abī Ṭāhir's and al-Ṭabarī's accounts of the reign of al-Ma'mūn is the subject of the introduction to *Kitāb Baghdād,* ed. Keller, vol. 1, pp. xiii–xxvi.

34 Franz Rosenthal, 'Ibn Abī Ṭāhir Ṭayfūr,' in *EI2,* vol. 3, pp. 692–3 (1971).

35 D. M. Dunlop, *Arab Civilization to AD 1500,* London: Longman, Beirut: Librairie du Liban, 1971, p. 81

36 C. E. Bosworth, 'Ebn Abī Ṭāher Ṭayfūr,' in *Encyclopaedia Iranica,* vol. 5, ed. Ehsan Yar-Shater *et al,* Costa Mesa: Mazda, 1996, vol. 5, pp. 663–4.

37 *CHALEUP,* pp. 113, 376 (1983); *CHALABL,* p. 76 (1990).

38 R. A. Kimber, 'Ibn Abī Ṭāhir,' in *EAL,* vol. 1, pp. 306–7 (1998).

39 In *Qaṣā'id,* pp. 5–33. Several of Ghayyāḍ's conclusions and interpretations, however, need to be revisited. For Shawqī Ḍayf, *al-ʿAṣr al-ʿabbāsī al-thānī,* Cairo: Dār al-Maʿārif, 1973, pp. 419–23, Ibn Abī Ṭāhir was a poet patronized by 'Ministers, Governors and Leaders.' As I show in chapter 7, although Ibn Abī Ṭāhir did, to be sure, frequent the homes of the likes of ʿAlī ibn Yaḥyā, he remained by and large outside the patronal economy.

40 E.g. Bosworth's 'Ebn Abī Ṭāher Ṭayfūr' in *Encyclopaedia Iranica* (see n. 36 above).

41 Ibrāhīm al-Najjār, *Majmaʿ al-Dhākirah, aw Shuʿarā' ʿAbbāsiyyūn mansiyyūn. Recherches sur le corpus des poètes «mineurs» du 1er siècle du califat abbasside,* 5 vols, Tunis: Manshūrāt Kulliyyat al-Ādāb wa-al-ʿUlūm al-Insāniyyah, 1987–90, vol. 5, p. 1678. For a discussion of the theory and methodology underlying the research and inventory, see Brahim Najar [= Ibrāhīm al-Najjār], *La mémoire rassemblée. Poètes arabes «mineurs» des IIe/VIIIe et IIIe/IXe siècles,* Clermont-Ferrand: La Française d'Edition et d'Imprimerie, 1987. *Cf.* the remarks of Rypka, 'History of Persian Literature up to the beginning of the 20th Century,' in *HIL,* p. 82, who, writing about the need for a thorough approach to the study of literature, observes that it "must consist of an evaluation and linking up of separate manifestations, and that not merely in the case of the most eminent but also – and perhaps in even greater measure – of the mass of minor figures." For a discussion of the virtue of the minor/major distinction, see pp. 71–6.

42 Āzartāsh Āzarnūsh, 'Ibn Abī Ṭāhir Ṭayfūr,' in *DMBI,* vol. 2, pp. 672–6 [1988]. And see my 'Ibn Abī Ṭāhir Ṭayfūr (d. 280/893): Merchant of the Written Word,' dissertation, University of Pennsylvania, 1998.

43 See 'Ibn Abī Ṭāhir Ṭayfūr (d. 280/893),' Appendix B, pp. 336–409, to which should be added the references in n. 28 in chapter 3 below.

44 Said Boustany, *Ibn ar-Rūmī. Sa vie et son oeuvre,* Beirut: Publications de l'Université Libanaise, 1967, pp. 108–9.

1 FROM MEMORY TO WRITTEN RECORD

1 See Gregor Schoeler, 'Die Frage' and 'Writing and Publishing'; R. B. Sergeant, 'Early Arabic Prose,' in *CHALEUP,* pp. 114–53; and Nabia Abbott, *Studies in Arabic Literary Papyri,* 3 vols., Chicago: Oriental Institute/University of Chicago Press, 1957–67, vol. 2, pp. 66, and 71, n. 213.

2 Michael G. Morony, *Iraq After the Muslim Conquest,* Princeton: Princeton University Press, 1984, pp. 64–5.

3 Janine Sourdel-Thomine, 'Aspects de l'écriture arabe et de son développement,' *Revue des études islamiques*, 1980, vol. 48(1), 9–23; Sourdel-Thomine, 'Les origines de l'écriture arabe à propos d'une hypothèse récente,' *Revue des études islamiques*, 1963, vol. 31, 151–7; Sourdel-Thomine, 'Khaṭṭ,' in *EI2*; and Nabia Abbott, 'Arabic Paleography,' *Ars Islamica*, 1941, vol. 8(1–2), 65–104.

4 Muhammad Hamidullah, *Majmūʿat al-wathāʾiq al-siyāsiyyah li-al-ʿahd al-nabawī wa-al-khilāfah al-rāshidah*, 4th edn, Beirut: Dār al-Nafāʾis, 1983; Sergeant, 'Early Arabic Prose,' pp. 131–42.

5 Morony, *Iraq*, pp. 33–37, 51–79, and index; Martin Sprengling, 'From Persian to Arabic,' *American Journal of Semitic Languages and Literatures*, 1939–40, vols 56–7, 175–224 and 325–36.

6 Morony, *Iraq*, pp. 18, and 27–124.

7 Descriptions of the Arabization of the chanceries can be found in several sources, e.g. al-Jahshiyārī, *Kitāb al-wuzarāʾ wa-al-kuttāb*, ed. Muṣṭafā al-Saqqāʿ *et al.*, Cairo: Muṣṭafā al-Bābī al-Ḥalabī wa-awlāduh, 1357/1938, reprint: 1980/1401, p. 38, lines 7–20.

8 J. D. Latham, 'The beginnings of Arabic prose: the epistolary genre,' in *CHALEUP*, p. 154.

9 See Wadād al-Qāḍī, 'Early Islamic State Letters: The Question of Authenticity,' in Averil Cameron and Lawrence. I. Conrad (eds), *The Byzantine and Early Islamic Near East I: Problems in the Literary Source Material*, Princeton: The Darwin Press, 1992, pp. 215–75.

10 Havelock, *Literate Revolution*, pp. 80–8, and *idem*, *Origins of Western Literacy*, Toronto: Ontario Institute for Studies in Education, 1976. Havelock attributes the ascendancy of Greek analytic thought to the introduction of vowels into the alphabet which, for him, specifically enabled later abstract intellectual work. The relationship, if any, between the rise of the Arabic script, and attendant analytic developments, remains to be investigated.

11 E.g. the *Kitāb al-Kharāj* of Abū Yūsuf (d. 182/798) which Norman Calder, *Studies in Early Muslim Jurisprudence*, Oxford: Oxford University Press, 1993, p. 160, however, believes to be a late work, "a product of the political situation in Samarra in the years 868–70 CE."

12 One significant indicator of the influence of literate norms and principles of organization was the development of indices. As Walter J. Ong notes in *Orality and Literacy: The Technologizing of the Word*, London: Methuen, 1982, pp. 124–6, it is only in abstract, sequential analysis that headings, labels, titles, and indices serve a useful function; in an oral culture indexing is not worth the trouble – memory is more economical. Initially created for Hadith compilations (e.g. the *musnad*) to facilitate the student's task, indexing and classification of individual works outside of Hadith subsequently took root: see Franz Rosenthal, *The Technique and Approach of Muslim Scholarship*, Rome: Pontificum Institutum Biblicum, 1947, p. 40. In ninth-century Arabic writerly culture, as in twelfth-century Europe, as fact and text moved closer together, searchability inevitably shifted from memory to page layout: see Richard H. and Mary A. Rouse, '*Statim invenire*: Schools, Preachers, and New Attitudes to the Page,' in Robert L. Benson and Giles Constable, with Catherine D. Lanham (eds), *Renaissance and Renewal in the Twelfth Century*, Cambridge, Mass.: Harvard University Press, 1982, pp. 201–25.

13 Clanchy, *From Memory to Written Record*, passim.

14 See al-Khassāf, *Kitāb Adab al-qāḍī*, ed. Farhat Ziadeh, Cairo: American University in Cairo Press, 1978; and Johansen, 'Formes de langage.'

15 *Fihrist*, p. 131, lines 9–10. On the letters, see Iḥsān ʿAbbās, *ʿAbd al-Ḥamīd ibn Yaḥyā al-Kātib wa-mā tabaqqā min rasāʾilihi wa-rasāʾil Sālim Abī ʾl-ʿAlāʾ*, Amman: Dār al-Shurūq, 1988, and al-Qāḍī, 'Early Islamic State Letters.' The significance of ʿAbd al-Ḥamīd's letters is signaled in Latham, 'Beginnings of Arabic prose,' who notes on p. 166 "our

greatest debt is to Ibn Abī Ṭāhir." For other letters preserved in the sources, see Hamidullah, *Majmūʿat al-wathāʾiq*; *Jamharat rasāʾil al-ʿArab*, ed. A. Z. Ṣafwat 4 volumes, Cairo: Muṣṭafā al-Bābī al-Ḥalabī wa-awlāduh, 1356/1937; Yūsuf Rāghib, 'Lettres Arabes, I,' *Annales Islamologiques*, 1978, vol. 14, 15–35; Rāghib, 'Lettres nouvelles de Qurra ibn Sharīk,' in *Journal of Near Eastern Studies: Arabic and Islamic Studies in Honor of Nabia Abbott*, 1981, vol. 40(3), 173–87; Adolf Grohmann and Raif Georges Khoury, *Chrestomathie de papyrologie arabe: documents relatifs à la vie privée, sociale et administrative dans les premiers siècles islamiques*, Leiden: E. J. Brill, 1993; and Albrecht Noth (with the collaboration of Lawrence I. Conrad), *The Early Arabic Historical Tradition: A Source-Critical Study*, 2nd edn, tr. Michael Bonner, Princeton: The Darwin Press, 1994, pp. 76–87.

16 See Sergeant, 'Early Arabic Prose.'

17 A good starting place for such a comparison would be Jeanette Wakin, *The Function of Documents in Islamic Law. The Chapters on Sales from Ṭahāwī's Kitāb al-Shurūṭ al-Kabīr*, Albany: SUNY Press, 1972 (al-Ṭahāwī died in 321/933). See also e.g. Ibn Mughīth al-Ṭūlayṭulī (d. 459/1067), *al-Muqniʿ fī ʿilm al-shurūt*, ed. F. Javier Aguirre Sdaba, Madrid: al-Majlis al-Aʿlā li-al-Abḥāth al-ʿIlmiyyah, Maʾhad al-Taʿāwun maʿa al-ʿĀlam al-ʿArabī, 1994.

18 See Michael G. Carter, 'The *Kātib* in Fact and Fiction,' *Abr Nahrain*, 1977, vol. 11, 42–55. *Cf.* Henri-Irénée Marrou, *A History of Education in Antiquity*, tr. George Lamb, New York: Sheed & Ward, 1956, p. xvi, who notes that writing first arose "not to fix theological or metaphysical dogma . . . but for the practical needs of accountancy and administration"; and also Georges Duby, *Rural Economy and Country Life in the Medieval West*, tr. Cynthia Postan, Columbia: University of South Carolina Press, 1968, p. 7.

19 For a similar development in Latin, i.e. the rise of cursives, see Terence A. M. Bishop (ed.), *Scriptores Regis; facsimiles to identify and illustrate the hands of royal scribes in original charters of Henry I, Stephen, and Henry II*, Oxford: Clarendon Press, 1961.

20 See Abbott, *Studies*, vol. 3, pp. 13–17. See *Fihrist*, p. 12, lines 7–14 on Ibn Muqlah; pp. 10–12 on scribal hands; and p. 14, line 25 on the *qalam al-warrāqīn*. For a recent account of the rise of Arabic scripts, see Bloom, *Paper Before Print*, pp. 104–9; see also Beeston, 'Background Topics,' 10–15.

21 Havelock, *Literate Revolution*, pp. 10, 83.

22 Bloom, *Paper Before Print*, p. 123.

23 Ibn Khallikān, *Wafayāt al-aʿyān wa-anbāʾ abnāʾ al-zamān*, 8 vols, ed. Iḥsān ʿAbbās, Beirut: Dār al-Thaqāfah, 1968, vol. 4, p. 165, lines 6–7 (#558). *Cf.* Stock, *Implications of Literacy*, p. 71.

24 Ibn Khallikān, *Wafayāt*, vol. 4, p. 190, line 3 (#569); *cf.* al-Shāfiʿī, *al-Risālah*, ed. A. M. Shākir, Beirut: Dār al-Kutub al-ʿIlmiyyah, n.d., ¶ 1001.

25 See Cook, 'Opponents of Writing' and the references cited there, especially Schoeler, 'Mündliche Thora und Ḥadīṯ'; M. M. al-Aʿẓamī, *Studies in Early Hadith Literature*, Beirut: al-Maktab al-Islāmī, 1968, pp. 22–7; G. H. A. Juynboll, *The authenticity of the tradition literature*, Leiden: E. J. Brill, 1969; and M. Z. Ṣiddīqī, *Ḥadīth Literature. Its Origin, Development & Special Features*, rev. edn, Cambridge: The Islamic Texts Society, 1993, pp. 24–7. See also Abbott, *Studies*, vol. 2, pp. 13 ff.

26 al-Samʿānī, *Adab al-imlāʾ wa-al-mustamlī. Die Methodik des Diktatkollegs*, ed. Max Weisweiler, Leiden: E. J. Brill, 1952, p. 146.

27 M. J. Kister, 'The *Sīrah* literature,' in *CHALEUP*, p. 357.

28 *Cf.* Stock, *Implications of Literacy*, p. 9.

29 See Wakin, *Function of Documents*, pp. 4 ff. and 15–29; and Johansen, 'Formes de langage.'

30 For a good recent definition of *adab*, see *EAL*, pp. 54–6.

31 Stock, *Implications of Literacy*, p. 529.

32 This is not to suggest that 'popular' and 'learned' could not or did not exist as contrasts in purely oral societies too. Other contrasts or polarities emerged, e.g. custom vs law, synchrony vs diachrony, sense vs interpreted experience, and thing vs linguistic idea: see Stock, *Implications of Literacy*, p. 529. Thing vs linguistic idea is discussed in the literary theory of ʿAbd al-Qāhir al-Jurjānī (d. 471/1079) in the fifth/eleventh century: see al-Jurjānī, *Dalāʾil al-iʿjāz fī ʿilm al-maʿānī*, ed. Rashīd Riḍā, Cairo: Maktabat al-Khānjī, 1366/1946, and Kamal Abu Deeb, *Al-Jurjānī's Theory of Poetic Imagery*, Warminster: Aris & Phillips, 1979. But the tension is already evident much earlier in third/ninth century Muʿtazilī rationalist theology which sees the Quran as a created thing (a book), not as an increate linguistic idea (the co-existent word of God): see e.g. al-Shahrastānī, *al-Milal wa-al-niḥāl*, 2 vols in 1, 2nd edn, ed. Muḥammad ibn Fatḥallāh Badrān, Cairo: Maktabat Anglū-Miṣriyyah, 1956, pp. 60–131; Josef van Ess, *Theologie und Gesselschaft im 2. und 3. Jahrhundert Hidschra. Eine Geschichte des religiösen Denkens im frühen Islam*, 6 vols, Berlin and New York: de Gruyter, 1991–7, generally; and Christopher Melchert, 'The Adversaries of Aḥmad Ibn Ḥanbal,' *Arabica*, 1997, vol. 44(2), 234–53, for the 'semi-rationalists' in particular.

33 For this famous exchange, see al-Marzubānī, *Kitāb Nūr al-qabas al-mukhtaṣar min al-Muqtabas fī akhbār al-nuḥāt wa-al-udabāʾ wa-al-shuʿarāʾ wa-al-ʿulamāʾ. Die Gelehrtenbiographien des Abū ʿUbaidallāh al-Marzubānī in der Rezension des Ḥāfiẓ al-Yagmūrī*, ed. Rudolf Sellheim, Wiesbaden: Franz Steiner, 1384/1964, p. 288, lines 4–19, quoted in *Irshād*, vol. 13, p. 185, line 13 to p. 188, line 13.

34 *Cf.* Stock, *Implications of Literacy*, p. 530.

35 On *laḥn al-ʿāmmah*, see the comprehensive entry by Charles Pellat in *EI2*, vol. 5, pp. 605–10; Abbott, *Studies*, vol. 3, pp. 4–5; and the editor's prefatory remarks in Ibn Makkī (fl. fifth/eleventh century), *Tathqīf al-lisān*, ed. Umberto Rizzitano, Cairo: Centro di studi orientali della Custodia Francescana di Terra Santa, 1956.

36 al-Jāḥiz, *al-Bayān wa-al-tabyīn*, 4 vols, ed. ʿAbd al-Salām M. Hārūn, Cairo: Maktabat al-Khānjī, 1968, vol. 1, p. 137, lines 2–9.

37 *Cf.* W. J. Bouwsma, *A Usable Past: Essays in European Cultural History*, Berkeley: University of California Press, 1990, p. 372.

38 See Bäuml, 'Varieties and Consequences.'

39 Fred McGraw Donner, *The early Islamic conquests*, Princeton, Princeton University Press, 1981, pp. 11 ff. *Cf.* Ignaz Goldziher, *Muslim Studies*, vol. 1, ed. S. M. Stern, tr. C. R. Barber and S. M. Stern, London: George Allen & Unwin Ltd, 1967, p. 201–8.

40 On the Prophet Muḥammad's 'illiteracy,' see Khalil ʿAthamina, '"Al-Nabiyy al-Umiyy": An Inquiry into the Meaning of a Qurʾanic Verse,' *Der Islam*, 1992, vol. 69(1), 61–80.

41 See Daniel A. Madigan, *The Quran's Self-Image*, Princeton and Oxford: Princeton University Press, 2001, especially pp. 13–52.

42 See Madigan, *Quran's Self-Image*, *passim*. There has nevertheless also been a trend toward understanding the Quran as first and foremost an oral entity: see especially Kristina Nelson, *The Art of reciting the Qurʾan*, Austin: University of Texas Press, 1985, and William M. Graham, *Beyond the Written Word: Oral aspects of scripture in the history of religion*, Cambridge: Cambridge University Press, 1987. Graham, *Beyond the Written Word*, pp. 30–1, concurs with Ignaz Goldziher, *Die Richtungen der islamischen Koranauslegung*, Leiden: E.J. Brill, 1921, p. 20, in observing that in the early years after Muḥammad's death there reigned apparently a casual, at times even individualistic, sense of freedom concerning the actual constitution of the Quranic text, almost as if people were not overly concerned about whether or not the text was transmitted in its absolutely earliest form.

43 See Eric Havelock, *Preface to Plato*, Cambridge, Mass., The Belknap Press, 1963, pp. 3–19 and 36–60; cf. Ong, *Orality and Literacy*, p. 24.

44 The literature on the debate surrounding the Quranic view of the status of poetry and poets is considerable. A fine recent contribution is James E. Montgomery, 'Sundry Observations on the Fate of Poetry in the Early Islamic Period,' in J. R. Smart (ed.), *Tradition and Modernity in Arabic Language and Literature*, Richmond: Curzon, 1996, pp. 49–60.
45 Rosenthal, *Technique and Approach*, p. 6.
46 See Havelock, *Origins of Western Literacy*.
47 Ong, *Orality and Literacy*, pp. 108, 113.
48 Marrou, *Education in Antiquity*, p. 342.
49 See Arthur Jeffery, *The Foreign Vocabulary of the Quran*, Baroda: Oriental Institute, 1938.
50 There is a notable fourth/tenth century exception: Abū al-Qāsim Naṣr al-Khubza'aruzzī (d. 327/938), an illiterate baker-poet who sold his wares and declaimed his verses at the Mirbad marketplace in Baṣrah, and whose *dīwān*, or collected poetry, was put together by the poet Ibn Lankak (d. 360/970). On al-Khubza'aruzzī, see *GAS*, vol. 2, pp. 520–1; *Murūj*, ¶ 3531; and *Ta'rīkh Baghdād*, vol. 13, pp. 296–99 (#7271).
51 *Cf.* Ong, *Orality and Literacy*, p. 113.
52 *Cf.* Marrou, *Education in Antiquity*, p. 342, for Latin.
53 On this see Fedwa Malti-Douglas, *Woman's Body, Woman's Word: Gender and Discourse in Arabo-Islamic Writing*, Princeton: Princeton University Press, 1991; see also the critique of that position in Julie Meisami, 'An Anatomy of Misogyny?' *Edebiyât*, 1995, new series, vols 5–6, 303–15.
54 Nancy Roberts, 'Voice and Gender in Classical Arabic *Adab*: Three Passages from Aḥmad Ṭayfūr's "Instances of the Eloquence of Women",' *al-'Arabiyya*, 1992, vol. 25, 51–72.
55 See e.g. the last thirty-two entries in *Ta'rīkh Baghdād*, vol. 14, pp. 430–47 (#7800–31); al-Iṣbahānī, *al-Imā' al-shawā'ir*, ed. N. Ḥ. al-Qaysī and Y. A. al-Samarrā'ī, Beirut: Maktabat al-Nahḍah al-'Arabiyyah, 1404/1984; and *Aghānī*, *passim*.
56 Ong, *Orality and Literacy*, p. 113, and p. 114; "Learned Latin was a striking exemplification of the power of writing for isolating discourse and of the unparalleled productivity of such isolation."
57 *Fihrist*, p. 163, line 9.
58 *Qaṣā'id*, p. 37, lines 14–15.
59 Makdisi, *Rise of Humanism*, pp. 64–6, calls the chanceries 'chancery schools' because many secretaries were apprenticed there; they were not, however, separate educational institutions per se.
60 *Aghānī*, vol. 3, p. 179, lines 11–12.
61 *Ta'rīkh Baghdād*, vol. 12, p. 95, line 22; cf. vol. 13, p. 276, lines 13–14.
62 *Ta'rīkh Baghdād*, vol. 8, p. 249, line 2 to p. 250, line 13.
63 See e.g. *Inbāh*, vol. 3, p. 234, line 16 (*fī manzilih*).
64 See Sabari, *Mouvements populaires*, pp. 103 ff.
65 George Makdisi, *The Rise of Colleges: Institutions of Learning in Islam and the West*, Edinburgh: Edinburgh University Press, 1981. *Cf.* Michael Chamberlain, *Knowledge and Social Practice in Medieval Damascus, 1190–1350*, Cambridge: Cambridge University Press, 1995.
66 For Gondēshāpūr, a town in Khūzistān founded by Shāpūr I, see *EI2*, vol. 2, pp. 1119–20; Nina Garsoïan, 'Byzantium and the Sasanians,' in *The Cambridge History of Iran* vol. 3(1): *The Seleucid, Parthian and Sasanian Periods*, ed. Ehsan Yar-Shater, Cambridge: Cambridge University Press, 1983, pp. 573, and 583 ff.; and M. G. Balty-Guesdon, 'Le Bayt al-Hikma de Baghdad,' *Arabica*, 1992, vol. 34(2), 131–50 (who, on the basis of *Fihrist*, p. 118, line 12, argues that the Baghdad academy was already in existence under Hārūn al-Rashīd [r. 170–193/786–809]).

67 A. I. Sabra, 'The Appropriation and Subsequent Naturalization of Greek Science in Medieval Islam: A Preliminary Statement,' *History of Science*, 1987, vol. 25, 1–21.

68 Dimitri Gutas, *Greek Wisdom Literature in Arabic Translation: A Study of the Graeco-Arabic Gnomologia*, New Haven: American Oriental Society, 1975, pp. 53–60.

69 On Sālim, see J. D. Latham, 'Beginnings of Arabic prose,' pp. 155–64; on Ibn al-Muqaffaʿ, see Latham, 'Ibn al-Muqaffaʿ and early Arabic prose,' in *CHALABL*, pp. 48–77.

70 *Fihrist*, pp. 130, line 10, and 160, line 13. On libraries, see W. Heffening and J. D. Pearson, 'Maktaba,' in *EI2*; Y. Eche, *Les Bibliothèques arabes publiques et sémi-publiques en Mésopotamie, en Syrie et en Egypte au Moyen Age*, Damascus: Institut français de Damas, 1967; and Lutz Richter-Bernburg, 'Libraries, medieval,' in *EAL*, vol. 2, pp. 470–1.

71 R. A. Kimber suggests that al-Fatḥ's library may have provided the basis for ʿAlī ibn Yaḥyā's own library: see *EAL*, vol. 1, p. 352.

72 *Irshād*, vol. 15, p. 157, lines 7–11.

73 *Irshād*, vol. 19, p. 110: *wa-kāna li-Abī Bakr al-Ṣūlī khizānatun afradahā limā jamaʿa min al-kutub al-mukhtalifah*; Al-Marzubānī (d. 384/994) also hosted scholars in his home.

74 Yāqūt al-Ḥamawī, *Muʿjam al-buldān. Jacut's geographisches Wörterbuch*, 6 vols, ed. F. Wüstenfeld, Leipzig: F. A. Brockhaus, 1866–73, vol. 1, p. 799, lines 16–18.

75 See 'Dār al-Ḥikma,' in *EAL*, vol. 1, p. 182.

76 al-Yaʿqūbī, *Kitāb al-Buldān*, ed. M. J. de Goeje, Leiden: E. J. Brill, 1892, p. 245, lines 7–10 (*akthar min mi'at ḥānūt li-al-warrāqīn* [line 9]); cf. Ibn al-Jawzī, *Manāqib Baghdād*, ed. Muḥammad al-Baghdādī, Baghdād: Maṭbaʿat Dar al-Salām, 1392/1972, p. 26, lines 13–14.

77 Makdisi focuses on this in *Rise of Humanism*, especially pp. 217–29.

78 al-Ṣafadī, *al-Wāfī bi-al-wafayāt*, 29 vols, ed. Helmut Ritter *et al.*, Istanbul and Wiesbaden: Franz Steiner for the Deutsche Morgenländische Gesellschaft, 1931–99, vol. 1, p. 6, lines 14–15, endorsing al-Khalīl ibn Aḥmad's saying: *lā yaṣilu aḥad min al-naḥw ilā mā yaḥtāju ilayh illā baʿd maʿrifat mā lā yaḥtāju ilayh.*

79 See Régis Blachère, *Histoire de la littérature arabe des origines à la fin du VXe siècle de J.-C.*, 3 vols, Paris: Adrien Maisonneuve, 1952–66, vol. 1, pp. 112 ff., and Raif Georges Khoury, 'Pour une nouvelle compréhension de la transmission des textes dans les trois premiers siècles islamiques,' *Arabica*, 1987, vol. 34(2), 187–8. That Umayyad poets committed their poetry to writing is indicated inter alia by the fact that there was a controversy about whether the *basmalah* – the pious formula that is uttered before recitation of the Quran, before all but one Quranic chapter, and the pronouncing of which is recommended before undertaking anything – should be used when they did so: see Ibn Rashīq, *al-ʿUmdah fī ṣināʿat al-shiʿr wa-naqdihi*, 2 vols, ed. al-Nabawī ʿAbd al-Wāḥid Shaʿlān, Cairo: Maktabat al-Khānjī, 2000, vol. 2, p. 1120; *cf.* Abbott, *Studies*, vol. 3, p. 78.

80 *Aghānī*, vol. 6, p. 90, lines 5–9. *Cf.* the translation in Charles James Lyall, *The Mufaḍḍaliyāt: An Anthology of Ancient Arabian Odes, II, translation and notes*, Oxford, Clarendon Press, 1918, pp. xvii–xviii.

81 *Aghānī*, vol. 6, p. 90, line 9 to p. 91, line 8. Cf. Lyall, *Mufaḍḍaliyāt*, p. xviii.

82 Rina Drory, 'The Abbasid Construction of the Jahiliyya: Cultural Authority in the Making,' *Studia Islamica*, 1996, vol. 83(1), 47.

83 Stetkevych, *Abū Tammām*, p. 246.

84 See Lyall, *Mufaḍḍaliyāt*; Renate Jacobi, 'al-Mufaḍḍaliyyāt,' in EI2, vol. 7, pp. 306–8; and Gert Borg, 'al-Mufaḍḍalīyāt,' in EAL, vol. pp. 537–8.

85 Evidence of this is the hagiographical tendency to make the lives of pious individuals 'resemble' the life of the prophet. Emulation of Muḥammad's life also gave rise to parallels between literature and life: see e.g. James Lindsay, 'Prophetic Parallels in Abu

'Abd Allah al-Shi'i's Mission to the Kutama Berbers, 893–910,' *International Journal of Middle East Studies*, 1992, vol. 24(1), 39–56, and especially Michael Cooperson, *Classical Arabic Biography: The Heirs of the Prophets in the Age of Al-Ma'mūn*, Cambridge: Cambridge University Press, 2000.

86 In the context of the Quran, the period from *c.* 30/651 (the date of the 'Uthmānic rescension of the Quran) to 322/934 was called the period of *ikhtiyār.* During this time, the *qāri'* could choose his own reading, as long as it agreed with the consonantal text of the 'Uthmānī rescension, and with accepted rules of Arabic grammatical usage. In 322/934, Ibn Mujāhid (d. 859/936) persuaded authorities in Baghdad that a reading had also to agree with one of the seven "canonical" readings. With the acceptance of an agreed written version, the range of acceptable alternatives within the oral tradition became limited: "Variants had to fall within the possibilities allowed by the textual outline, otherwise they were *shādhdh*, 'peculiar.' Oral tradition thus became subordinate to the written text..." (Jones, 'The Qur'an-II,' p. 242).

87 See Drory, 'Abbasid Construction of the Jahiliyya.'

88 Al-Ṣūlī's edition of the poetry of Abū Nuwās is the first (extant) *dīwān* to be organized according to subject-matter instead of rhyme-letter. This represents a switch away from an aural method of classification toward one the focus of which is literary-critical analysis.

Scribes and early anthologists became "intervening transmitters." Their apparently straightforward act of copying, collating, and editing manuscripts was not free from intervention. Consequently, in their prefaces and colophons, writers often threatened scribes who introduced alterations (e.g. *Murūj*, ¶ 17). On this, see Stephen G. Nichols, 'Introduction: Philology in a Manuscript Culture,' *Speculum*, 1990, vol. 61(1), 1–11.

2 THE PRESENCE AND INSISTENCE OF BOOKS

1 This is not to imply that books could not also be transmitted through the oral/aural process: see Schoeler, *Ecrire et transmettre*, pp. 109–205. The procedure for mass publication that relied on aural transmission (*samā'*) and dictation (*imlā'*) could involve people in the tens of thousands. The lectures of 'Alī ibn 'Āṣim, for example, were reportedly attended by upwards of 30,000 students: see al-Dhahabī, *Tadhkirat al-ḥuffāẓ*, 5 vols, Hyderabad: Maṭba'at Dā'irat al-Ma'ārif al-Niẓāmiyyah, 1333–4/1914–15, vol. 1, p. 291, line 15. Grammarians would also hold such audiences/sessions, where the dictation-master (*mustamlī*) would dictate to students. On dictation see al-Sam'ānī, *Adab al-imlā'*; Max Weisweiler, 'Das Amt des Mustamlī in der arabischen Wissenschaft,' *Oriens*, 1951, vol. 4, 27–57; and Pedersen, *Arabic Book*, p. 26. On the *samā'*, see Makdisi, *Rise of Colleges*, pp. 99–105, and 140–6; Ṣiddīqī, *Ḥadīth Literature*, pp. 84–9; and *EI2*, vol. 8, pp. 1019–20.

2 Walter Werkmeister, *Quellenuntersuchungen zum Kitāb al-'Iqd al-farīd des Andalusiers b. 'Abdrabbih (246/860–328/940): Ein Beitrag zur arabischen Literaturgeschichte*, Berlin: Klaus Schwarz Verlag, 1983. See also Raif Khoury, 'Pour une nouvelle compréhension'; and Rudolf Sellheim, 'Abū 'Alī al-Qālī. Zum Problem mündlicher und schriftlicher Überlieferung am Beispiel von Sprichwörtersammlungen,' in *Studien zur Geschichte und Kultur des Vorderen Orients*, Leiden: E. J. Brill, 1981, pp. 362–74.

3 Wakin, *Function of Documents*, p. 6.

4 Clanchy, *From Memory to Written Record*, p. 262.

5 *Irshād*, vol. 20, p. 34, lines 13–16.

6 See Schoeler, 'Die Frage der schriftlichen'; Geneviève Humbert, *Les voies de la transmission du* Kitāb *de Sībawayhi*, Leiden: E. J. Brill, 1995; and Humbert, 'Le *Kitāb* de Sībawayhi et l'autonomie de l'écrit,' *Arabica*, 1997, vol. 44(4), 553–7, where she notes that the *Kitāb* constitutes an important locus for the relationship between oral and

written in the late second/eighth century. See also Monique Bernards, *Changing Traditions: Al-Mubarrad's Refutation of Sībawayh and the Subsequent Reception of the* Kitāb, Leiden: Brill, 1997.

7 *Cf.* Stock, *Implications of Literacy*, pp. 42–59 ('Orality within Written Tradition').
8 See e.g. Stock, *Implications of Literacy*, pp. 10, 12.
9 Ong, *Orality and Literacy*, pp. 49 ff.
10 Stock, *Implications of Literacy*, p. 4.
11 This characteristic gives rise to the notion of a *ṣaḥafī*, discussed below.
12 Ṭabarī, vol. 3, p. 2131: *allā yaqʿuda ʿalā al-ṭarīq wa-lā fī masjid al-jāmiʿ qāṣṣ wa lā ṣāḥib al-nujūm wa-lā-ẓājir wa-ḥullifa al-warrāqūn allā yabīʿū kutub al-kalām wa-al-jadal wa-al-falsafah. Cf.* Ibn Kathīr, *al-Bidāyah wa-al-nihāyah fī al-taʾrīkh*, 14 vols, no ed., Cairo: Maṭbaʿat al-Saʿādah, 1971, vol. 9, p. 64, line 26 to p. 65, line 1. As the ban took place under al-Muʿtaḍid, it must have occurred between October 892 and March 893 CE. It would seem that by *qāṣṣ* is meant not only the Ḥanbalī preachers but also the public storytellers. The latter are attested at the time of al-Muʿtaḍid's caliphate, e.g. the late third/ninth century itinerant storyteller, Ibn al-Maghāzilī, on whom see *Murūj*, ¶¶ 3300–4, and Shmuel Moreh, *Live Theatre and Dramatic Literature in the Medieval Arab World*, New York: New York University Press, 1992, pp. 69–70.
13 Ṭabarī, vol. 3, p. 2165, which in Rosenthal's translation (and edition) reads "it was announced in the two Friday mosques that people were forbidden to gather around storytellers and study groups were prevented from holding sessions (there)" (*The Return of the Caliphate to Baghdad*, The History of al-Ṭabarī, vol. 38, tr. Franz Rosenthal, Albany, SUNY Press, 1985, p. 47). *Cf.* Ibn Kathīr, *al-Bidāyah wa-al-nihāyah*, vol. 11, p. 76, line 24.
14 On this, see Albert Arazi and Ami Elʿad, '«L'Épître à l'Armée». Al-Maʿmūn et la seconde Daʿwa,' part 1, *Studia Islamica*, 1987, vol. 66, 28.
15 *Manthūr C*, folio 159b, lines 2–3.
16 Ibn Abī Ṭāhir, *Balāghāt al-nisāʾ*, p. 96, line 1.
17 al-Jāḥiẓ, 'al-Muʿallimīn,' in *Rasāʾil al-Jāḥiẓ*, 4 vols, ed. ʿAbd al-Salām Hārūn, Cairo: Maktabat al-Khānjī, rev. edn, 1399/1979, vol. 3, p. 40, line 15 to p. 41, line 1: *Wa-man qaraʾa kutub al-bulaghāʾ wa-taṣaffaḥa dawāwīn al-ḥukamāʾ li-yastafida al-maʿānī fa-huwa ʿalā sabīl ṣawāb.*
18 al-Jāḥiẓ, 'al-Muʿallimīn,' p. 41, lines 10–11: *fa-al-wajh al-nāfiʿ an yadūra fī masāmiʿihi wa yaghibba fī qalbih wa yakhtamira fī ṣadrih. . .*
19 Quoted by Ibn al-Qifṭī in *Inbāh*, vol. 1, p. 109, lines 13–17. On al-Bushtī, see the *Inbāh* entry (vol. 1, pp. 107–19 [#57]), and *GAS*, vol. 8, p. 195.
20 *Inbāh*, vol. 1, pp. 109, lines 17–20. On Abū Turāb's *Kitāb al-Iʿtiqāb*, see *GAS*, vol. 8, pp. 192, and 274–5.
21 On al-Ṣūlī, see Stefan Leder's entry in *EI2*.
22 *Kitāb Baghdād*, p. 131, lines 6–17; al-Ṣūlī, *Kitāb al-Awrāq: Qism akhbār al-shuʿarāʾ*, ed. J. Heyworthe-Dunn, Cairo, Maktabat al-Khānjī, 1934, p. 209, lines 3–12.
23 al-Ṣūlī, *Kitāb al-Awrāq*, p. 210, lines 1–3.
24 al-Ṣūlī, *Kitāb al-Awrāq*, pp. 210, lines 3–7.
25 *ḥāṭib layl*, literally one who gathers firewood at night, doing a good thing for himself, and who may, in inadvertently putting his hand on a viper and being bitten by it, cause a bad thing for himself. *Cf.* the proverb: *al-mikthār ḥāṭib layl* (Lane, p. 694).
26 This is the only extant passage that explicitly places Ibn Abī Ṭāhir outside Baghdad, viz. in Basra in 277 Ḥijrī (= between 25 April 890 and 15 April 891 CE). Why al-Mādarāʾī would have summoned Ibn Abī Ṭāhir there late in his life – he was seventy years old – is not explained here or elsewhere. State pressure on storytellers, authors, and copyists is not attested until two years later (see nn. 12 and 13 above), but the intellectual climate in Baghdad may have already become difficult and may have

prompted Ibn Abī Ṭāhir's departure. Ibn Abī Ṭāhir did return to Baghdad, where he died three years later, in 280/893. Abū al-Ṭayyib Aḥmad ibn 'Alī ibn Aḥmad al-Mādarā'ī (d. 303/915) was a poet about whom little is recorded: see Ibn al-Jawzī, *al-Muntaẓam fī ta'rīkh al-mulūk wa-al-umam*, 18 vols, ed. Muḥammad 'Abd al-Qādir al-'Aṭā *et al.*, Beirut: Dār al-Kutub al-'Ilmiyyah, 1412/1992, vol. 13 (#2114). Al-Marzubānī, *al-Muwashshaḥ fī ma'ākhidh al-'ulamā' 'alā al-shu'arā'*, ed. 'A. M. al-Bijāwī, Cairo: Dār Nahḍah, 1965, p. 535 (#32), reports that he wrote a satire of Ibn Thawābah, to which Ibn al-Rūmī responded.

27 See e.g. Albert de Biberstein-Kazimirski, *Dictionnaire arabe-français*, 2 vols, Beirut: Librairie du Liban, 1975, vol. 1, p. 1314: "qui commet une erreur en lisant." Al-Jāḥiẓ reports a humorous anecdote in which he overhears a teacher (*mu'allim*) recite to a schoolboy a verse, which he mangles because he has learned it from a written version: see *Muḥāḍarāt al-udabā'*, vol. 1, p. 107, lines 6–12.

28 *Muḥāḍarāt al-udabā'*, vol. 1, p. 106, line 15. See also the passage cited from a work by al-Azharī (d. 370/980) in Schoeler, *Ecrire et transmettre*, p. 121.

29 The meaning of the adjective *muṣḥafī* can be inferred from the meaning of the noun *muṣḥaf* on which it is based, but it is not separately listed in the classical dictionaries. The usual terms are *ṣaḥafī* and *muṣaḥḥafī*, which describe someone who acquires knowledge from a *ṣaḥīfah* (see e.g. Ibn Manẓūr, *Lisān al-'arab*, 6 vols, ed. 'Abd Allāh 'Alī al-Kabīr *et al.*, Cairo: Dār al-Ma'ārif, n.d., vol. 9, p. 187). A *muṣaḥḥaf* is additionally defined as an *isnād* or other text in which a name or one or more words are incorrectly transcribed: see e.g. Reinhart Dozy, *Supplément aux dictionnaires arabes*, 2 vols, Paris: G.-P. Maisonneuve et Larose, 1967, vol. 2, p. 820.

30 *Muḥāḍarāt al-udabā'*, vol. 1, p. 106, line 16:

Idhā asnada 'l-qawmu akhbārahum
fa-isnāduhū 'ṣuḥfu wa-l-hājisu.

31 *Irshād*, vol. 19, p. 111, lines 1–3:

Innamā 'ṣ-Ṣūliyyu shaykhun
a'lamu 'n-nāsi khizānah

In sa'alnāhu bi-'ilmin
nabtaghī 'anhu 'l-ibānah

Qāla yā ghilmānu hātū
rizmat al-'ilmi fulānah

– also in *Inbāh*, vol. 3, p. 236, lines 2–4, with slight variation.

32 Al-Ṣūlī's teachers included al-Mubarrad, Tha'lab, Abū al-'Aynā', Abū Dā'ūd al-Sijistānī, and for Hadith, Abū 'Abdallāh al-Ghallābī.

33 *Ta'rīkh Baghdād*, vol. 3, p. 431, line 17–20. On Abū Bakr ibn Shādhān, see *Ta'rīkh Baghdād*, vol. 5, pp. 464–5 (#3007).

34 E.g. *Fihrist*, pp. 7, line 14, 8, line 13, and 17, line 6.

35 *Fihrist*, p. 143, line 21, and p. 168, lines 3–5: *wa-hādha al-kitāb awwal fī ta'līfihi 'alā kitāb al-Marthadī fī al-shi'r wa-al-shu'arā' bal naqalahu naqlan wa intaḥalahu.*

36 Stefan Leder, 'al-Ṣūlī,' in *EI2*, vol. 9, p. 847.

37 *Ta'rīkh Baghdād*, vol. 3, p. 431, lines 10–14.

38 "Whosoever fasts the month of Ramaḍān and follows it with the six [days of superogatory fast] in the month of Shawwāl…"

39 See Abbott, *Studies*, vol. 2, pp. 76 ff.; Goldziher, *Muslim Studies*, vol. 2, p. 179; Munir-ud-din Ahmed, *Muslim Education and the Scholars' Social Status up to the 5th century Muslim Era (11th century Christian Era) in the light of Ta'rīkh Baghdād*, Zürich: Verlag 'Der Islam,' 1968, p. 99; and Dozy, *Supplément*, vol. 2, p. 791.

40 Goldziher, *Muslim Studies*, vol. 2, 179, citing Aloys Sprenger, 'On the origin and progress of writing down of historical facts among the Muslims,' *Journal of the Asiatic Society of Bengal*, 1856, vol. 25, pp. 303–29, and 375–81.

41 The jurist Aḥmad ibn Ḥanbal, for instance, wrote letters for money as a young man: see Ibn al-Jawzī, *Manāqib al-Imām Aḥmad ibn Ḥanbal*, ed. 'Abdallāh ibn 'Abd al-Muḥsin al-Turkī and 'Alī Muḥammad 'Umar, Cairo, Maktabat al-Khānjī, 1979, pp. 43–4. Abū Nuwās and Diʿbil, to name only two famous poets, were well-known for frequenting and befriending booksellers. On al-Jāḥiẓ's association with *warrāq*s, see immediately below.

42 *Fihrist*, p. 130, lines 10–15 (art. al-Fatḥ ibn Khāqān), cited in *Irshād*, vol. 16, p. 75, lines 6–14. The anecdote is recounted with slightly different wording in *Fihrist*, p. 208, lines 18–22 (art. al-Jāḥiẓ), where it is attributed to Muḥammad ibn Yazīd al-Naḥwī, not Abū Hiffān: *cf.* A. J. Arberry, 'New Material on the *Kitāb al-Fihrist* of Ibn al-Nadīm,' *Islamic Research Association Miscellany*, 1948, vol. 1, 35. On anecdotal variance, see below.

43 Malti-Douglas, *Structures of Avarice*, pp. 31–2, suggests that al-Jāḥiẓ was forced to read in bookshops and to rely on the libraries of his friends and teachers because the cost of books was high and because there were no public libraries in Basra.

44 See Sourdel, *Vizirat 'abbāside*, vol. 1, pp. 282–4; and O. Pinto, 'Al-Fatḥ b. Khāqān, favorito di al-Mutawakkil,' *Rivista degli studi orientali*, 1931, vol. 13, 133–49. Al-Fatḥ had a large personal library (see n. 73, chapter 1 above) and was a patron of poets and writers. He would, for example, receive Kufan and Basran grammarians at his home, and it was to him that al-Jāḥiẓ addressed and dedicated his *Risālah ilā Fatḥ ibn Khāqān fī faḍā'il al-Atrāk wa-'āmmat jund al-khilāfah* [An epistle to Fatḥ ibn Khāqān on the virtues of the Turks and the common soldiery of the Caliphate].

45 On Ismāʿīl (d. 282/895), chief cadi of Baghdad for 20 years, see *EI2, Supplement*, fasc. 1–2, p. 113

46 Stock, *Implications of Literacy*, p. 522.

47 These communities eventually lead to the growth of a scholastic and humanistic culture: see the works of George Makdisi, especially *Rise of Colleges*, and *Rise of Humanism*.

48 *Cf.* Stefan Leder, 'Authorship and Transmission in Unauthored Literature: The *akhbār* attributed to al-Haytham b. 'Adī,' *Oriens*, 1988, vol. 31, 67–81.

49 Locutions such as "*ṣāḥib Kitāb Baghdād*," "owner/possessor of the *Book of Baghdad*," are of interest in this regard.

50 Although it was *de rigueur* in pre-Islamic oral culture to lift from predecessors and peers and emulate them, there was still resentment of plagiarism: poets took pride in their authorship of poems. See Wolfhart Heinrichs, 'An Evaluation of *Sariqa*,' *Quaderni di Studi Arabi*, 1987–8, vols 5–6, 357–68.

51 Clanchy, *From Memory to Written Record*, p. 319. See Ibn Rashīq, *al-ʿUmdah*, vol. 2, pp. 1072–95; M. M. Haddārah, *Mushkilat al-sariqāt fī al-naqd al-ʿarabī: dirāsah tahlīliyyah muqāranah*, 2nd edn, Beirut: al-Maktab al-Islāmī, 1975; Wolfhart Heinrichs, *Arabische Dichtung und griechische Poetik*, Beirut and Wiesbaden: Franz Steiner Verlag for the Orient-Institut der Deutsche Morgenländische Gesellschaft, 1969, pp. 94–8. *Cf.* Paul Fournier, 'Etudes sur les fausses décrétales,' *Revue d'histoire européenne*, 1906, vol. 7, 33–51; and Hubert Silvestre, 'Le problème des faux au Moyen Age,' *Le Moyen Age*, 1960, vol. 66, 351–70.

A specific office for the sealing of documents (*dīwān al-khātam*) is reported to have been introduced during the caliphate of Muʿāwiyah because of an attempted forgery: see al-Jahshiyārī, *Kitāb al-Wuzarā' wa-al-kuttāb*, p. 24, line 9 to p. 25, line 2; see further *EI2*, vol. 2, pp. 304, 324.

52 For the perceptive observations of Abdelfattah Kilito on this issue, in particular *autoplagiat*, see his *L'auteur et ses doubles. Essai sur la culture arabe classique*, Paris: Editions du Seuil, 1985, pp. 11, and 37–40.

53 Abū Tammām in his collection *al-Ḥamāsah*, for example, often omits the attribution of certain lines in spite of the fact that they are by prominent poets.
54 This work has received comprehensive tretment in Hilary Kilpatrick, *Making the Great Book of Songs: Compilation and the author's craft in Abū l-Faraj al-Iṣbahānī's Kitāb al-Aghānī*, London and New York: RoutledgeCurzon, 2003.
55 *Aghānī*, p. 5, line 10 to p. 6, line 5; also in *Fihrist*, p. 158, lines 19–27 with some additional information about "al-Rukhṣah."
56 al-Jāḥiẓ, 'Faṣl mā bayn al-ʿadāwah wa-al-ḥasad,' in *Rasāʾil al-Jāḥiẓ*, vol. 1, p. 340, lines 13–16.
57 al-Jāḥiẓ, 'Faṣl mā bayn al-ʿadāwah wa-al-ḥasad,' vol. 1, pp. 350, line 7 to p. 351, line 15 (reported also in al-Masʿūdī, *al-Tanbīh wa-al-ishrāf*, ed. M. J. de Goeje, Leiden: E. J. Brill, 1894, Cairo: Dār al-Ṣāwī li-al-Ṭabʿ wa-al-Nashr wa-al-Taʾlīf, 1357/1938, pp. 66–7). *Cf.* the translation in A. F. L. Beeston, 'Jāḥiẓ "On the Difference between Enmity and Envy,' *Journal of Arabic Literature*, 1987, vol. 18, pp. 31–2, and in Abdelfattah Kilito, *The Author and His Doubles: Essays on classical Arabic culture*, tr. Michael Cooperson, Syracuse: Syracuse University Press, 2001, pp. 68, and 70.
58 *Cf.* Kilito, *L'auteur et ses doubles*, pp. 31–40, especially on the re-use of material addressed to prince(s) and patron(s).
59 Noteworthy is the fact that al-Jāḥiẓ specifically names Persians, secretaries for the most part. He may be targeting *Shuʿūbī* writers, those individuals (typically Persian) who argued for the parity between Arabs and non-Arabs: on the Shuʿūbiyyah movement, see chapter 5 below. Note also that whereas al-Jāḥiẓ mentions Sālim, in his quotation of the passage in *al-Tanbīh wa-al-ishrāf*, al-Masʿūdī names Sahl ibn Hārūn (on whom see chapter 5 below). Also of interest is the similarity of this list *pace* al-Masʿūdī to Ibn al-Nadīm's list of storytellers, namely Ibn al-Muqaffaʿ, Sahl ibn Hārūn, ʿAlī ibn Dāwūd, al-ʿAttābī and Ibn Abī Ṭāhir (*Fihrist*, p. 364, line 4, and p. 367, line 10).
60 *Fihrist*, p. 421, lines 24–6.
61 Anecdotal variance and the question of undifferentiated reports (*akhbār*) is an important focus of historiographical research. Important in this regard is Albrecht Noth, *Early Arabic Historical Tradition*, especially pp. 109–218. See also E. L. Petersen, *ʿAlī and Muʿāwiya in Early Arabic Tradition: Studies on the Genesis and Growth of Islamic Historical Writing until the End of the Ninth Century*, Copenhagen: Munksgaard, 1964; Jacob Lassner, *Islamic Revolution and Historical Memory: An Inquiry into the Art of ʿAbbāsid Apologetics*, New Haven: American Oriental Society, 1986; and A. A. Duri, *The rise of historical writing among the Arabs*, ed. and tr. Lawrence I. Conrad, Princeton: Princeton University Press, 1983. For literary history, see especially Leder, 'Authorship and Transmission,' and Hilary Kilpatrick, 'Context and the Enhancement of the Meaning of *Akhbār* in the *Kitāb al-Agānī*,' *Arabica*, 1991, vol. 38(3), 351–68.
62 al-Tawḥīdī, *al-Baṣāʾir wa-al-dhakhāʾir*, p. 27, line 13 to p. 28, line 11; quoted, with some editorial elaboration, in *Irshād*, vol. 3, p. 88, line 9 to p. 89, line 5 (where Abū Dihqān should read Abū Hiffān).
63 al-Raqīq al-Nadīm, *Quṭb al-surūr fī awṣāf al-khumūr*, ed. Aḥmad al-Jundī, Damascus: Maṭbūʿāt Majmaʿ al-Lughat al-ʿArabiyyah, 1969, p. 197, lines 3–9, quoted also (with minor variation) in al-Ḥuṣrī, *Jamʿ al-jawāhir fī al-mulaḥ wa-al-nawādir*, ed. ʿA. M. al-Bijāwī, Cairo: Dār Iḥyāʾ al-Kutub al-ʿArabiyyah, 1372/1953, p. 309, lines 1–7, on which see below.
64 This is a play on words, where "*ḍarṭat*" (breaking wind) is used for "*ḍaghṭat*" (pressure). *Cf.* Lane, p. 1793, art. *ḍaghṭah*, for the relationship between the pressure of the grave (*ḍaghṭat al-qabr*) and undischarged debts. I am grateful to Joe Lowry for pointing out use of the same phrase by Ismāʿīl ibn Yaḥyā al-Muzanī (d. 264/878) in his *Sharḥ al-Sunnah*, ed. Jamāl ʿAzzūn, Medina: Maktabat al-Ghurabāʾ al-Athariyyah, 1995/1415, p. 80. See also Lane, p. 1349, art. *S-R-Ṭ* for the expression "*al-akhdh surrayṭ*

wa-al-qaḍā' ḍurrayṭ," "taking is [like] swallowing, but giving back is [like] making the sound [with the mouth] of breaking of wind," i.e. taking a loan or borrowing is liked, but paying back the debt is disliked.

65 This is not a misidentification but rather a confusion of personages (collapsing and conflation are also common), common in (orally) transmitted material. It is attested e.g. in the Iranian heroic tradition: see Stephen Belcher, 'The Diffusion of the Book of Sindbād,' *Fabula*, 1987, vol. 28(1), p. 43, n. 44, for references.
66 al-Ḥuṣrī, *Jamʿ al-jawāhir*, p. 309, lines 1–7.
67 *Cf.* Arazi and El'ad, 'L'Epître à l'armée,' p. 31.
68 Bernard Cerquiglini, *Eloge de la variante: histoire critique de la philologie*, Paris: Editions Seuil, 1989, p. 111.
69 Goody and Watt, 'The Consequences of Literacy,' p. 27.
70 According to Ong, *Orality and Literacy*, p. 98, this explains the need for fixed and formulaic patterns of thought.
71 The tension between educating and entertaining is also underscored by the practice of al-Jāḥiẓ and others of introducing into their writing devices designed to retain the attention of readers. See *EI2*, vol. 2, pp. 536–7.
72 See *Inbāh*, vol. 3, p. 194, line 12 to p. 195, line 2.
73 M. F. Ghazi, 'La littérature d'imagination en arabe du IIè/VIIè au Vè/XIè siècles,' *Arabica*, 1957, vol. 4(2), 172–3, mentions popular Judaeo–Arabic novels circulating in Tunis
74 *Fihrist*, pp. 363–7; Ghazi, 'Littérature d'imagination,' pp. 164–76.
75 Ibn Abī Uṣaybiʿah, *'Uyūn al-anbāʾ fī ṭabaqat al-aṭibbāʾ*, ed. Nizār Riḍā, Beirut: Dār Maktabat al-Ḥayāt, 1965, p. 271, lines 1–2.
76 *Fihrist*, p. 134, line 2.
77 See Ibrahim Kh. Geries, *Un genre littéraire arabe: al-Maḥâsin wa-l-masâwî*, Paris: G.-P. Maisonneuve et Larose, 1977.
78 See *Fihrist*, pp. 263–79 (= *maqālah* [chapter] 8). *Cf.* Heinrichs, *Arabische Dichtung*, pp. 39–43.
79 *Cf.* Roy P. Mottahedeh, *Loyalty and Leadership in Early Islamic Society*, Princeton: Princeton University Press, 1980.
80 *Ṭabaqāt al-shuʿarāʾ*, p. 416, lines 13–15.
81 *Irshād*, vol. 14, 76, lines 4–5: *wa-qad tadāwalahā al-nās wa-qaraʾūhā wa-ʿarafū faḍlahā.*

3 RECITING POETRY, TELLING TALES

1 C. E. Bosworth, 'Ebn Abī Ṭāher Ṭayfūr,' *Encyclopaedia Iranica*, vol. 5, ed. Ehsan Yar-Shater *et al*, Costa Mesa, CA: Mazda, 1996, pp. 663–4; Āzarnūsh, 'Ebn Abī Ṭāher Ṭayfūr,' p. 672.
2 *Ṭabaqāt al-shuʿarāʾ*, p. 416 (15 lines).
3 Hilary Kilpatrick, 'Criteria of Classification in the *Ṭabaqāt fuḥūl al-shuʿarāʾ* of Muḥammad ibn Sallām al-Jumaḥī (d. 232/846),' in Rudolph Peters (ed.), *Proceedings of the Ninth Congress of the Union Européenne des arabisants et islamisants*, Leiden: E. J. Brill, 1981, pp. 141–52; and Adel S. Gamal, 'The Organizational Principles in Ibn Sallām's *Ṭabaqāt Fuḥūl al-Shuʿarāʾ*: A Reconsideration,' in J. R. Smart (ed.), *Tradition and Modernity in Arabic Language and Literature*, Richmond: Curzon Press, 1996, pp. 186–209.
4 Iḥsān ʿAbbās, *Taʾrīkh al-naqd al-adabī ʿinda al-ʿArab*, Beirut: Dār al-Amānah, 1971, pp. 79 ff.; *cf.* Kamal Abu Deeb, 'Literary Criticism,' in *CHALABL*, p. 345.
5 See *Ṭabaqāt al-shuʿarāʾ*, pp. 585–6.
6 *Ṭabaqāt al-shuʿarāʾ*, p. 416.
7 Abū Ḥakīmah (or Ḥukaymah), Rāshid ibn Isḥāq (d. 240/854), a poet whose elegies and other poems about his penis were widely circulated: see *Ṭabaqāt al-shuʿarāʾ*,

pp. 389–90). For examples, see *Dīwān Abī Ḥukaymah Rāshid ibn Isḥāq al-Kātib: al-Ayriyyāt*, ed. M. Ḥ. al-ʿArajī, Cologne: Manshūrāt al-Jamal, 1997.

8 *Cf.* the account in al-Tawḥīdī, *al-Imtāʿ wa-al-muʾānasah*, 3 vols, ed. Aḥmad Amīn and Aḥmad al-Zayn, Cairo: Maṭbaʿah Lajnat al-Taʾlīf wa-al-Tarjamah wa-al-Nashr, 1939–44, vol. 2, p. 55, lines 11–13, about a singing girl arousing a man by massaging his penis at a *majlis* attended by Ibn Abī Ṭāhir.

9 I.e. the effect of the wine later affects the drinker by making him unstable on his feet.

10 Abū Tammām, *Dīwān Abī Tammām bi-sharḥ al-Khaṭīb al-Ṭibrīzī*, 4 vols, ed. M. ʿA. ʿAzzām, Cairo: Dār al-Maʿārif, 1957–65, vol. 4, p. 520 (#468), verse 6:

idhā l-yadu nālat-hā bi-watrin tawaqqarat
ʿalā ḍaʿfihā thumma ʾstafādat min ar-rijli.

11 Abu Deeb, 'Literary Criticism,' p. 345.

12 Farrāj believes the work was completed before 280/892–3, but Iqbāl, an earlier editor, believes it was written late in Ibn al-Muʿtazz's life.

13 *Ṭabaqāt al-shuʿarā*, p. 211, line 15. Al-Ṣūlī uses a similar locution when describing the poetry of Abū al-ʿIbar, stating that he "finds no reason to cite him much, seeing as his poetry is widely known by the public" (cited in Najar, *La mémoire rassemblée*, p. 173, n. 1). *Cf.* al-Khālidīyān, *al-Ashbāh wa-al-naẓāʾir min ashʿār al-mutaqaddimīn wa-al-jāhiliyyah wa-al-mukhaḍramīn*, 2 vols, ed. Muḥāmmad Yūsuf, Cairo: Dār al-Maʿārif, 1958–65, vol. 1, p. 2, line 14, for a reference to poetry in the hands of the people (*fī ayday al-nās*).

14 Ibn Abī Ṭāhir does the same when referring to the *Muʿallaqāt* poems in *Qaṣāʾid*, p. 37: *wa-law-lā shuhrat hādhihi al-qaṣāʾid wa-kathratuhā ʿalā afwāh al-ruwāh wa-ismāʿ al-nās* . . .

15 See n. 28 below.

16 Ibn Abī Ṭāhir would not have appeared in the *Fuḥūlat al-shuʿarāʾ* by the lexicographer al-Aṣmaʿī (d. 213/828), given its early date.

17 Maurice Gaudefroy-Demombynes (ed. and tr.), *Introduction au "Livre de la poésie et des poètes" d'Ibn Qotaïba*, Paris: Les Belles Lettres, 1947, p. 2 (Arabic pagination); *cf.* the translation of this passage in James E. Montgomery, 'Of Models and Amanuenses: The Remarks on the *Qasida* in Ibn Qutayba's *Kitab al-Shiʿr wa'l-Shuʿara*',' pp. 25 and 45, in Robert Hoyland and Philip Kennedy (eds), *Islamic Reflections, Arabic Musings: Studies in Honour of Professor Alan Jones*, Cambridge: Gibb Memorial Trust, 2004.

18 See e.g. Seeger A. Bonebakker, 'Reflections on the *Kitāb al-Badīʿ* of Ibn al-Muʿtazz,' in *Atti del terzo Congresso di studi arabi e islamici*, Naples: Istituto universitario orientale, 1967, p. 200.

19 Al-Sayyid al-Ḥimyarī, Abān al-Lāḥiqī, and ʿAlī ibn Jahm are also excluded. See Ahmed Trabulsi, *La critique poétique des arabes jusqu'au Vè siècle de l'Hégire (IXe siècle de J.C.)*, Damascus: Institut français de Damas, 1955, p. 45. Ibn al-Muʿtazz also omits certain poets, e.g. Ibn al-Rūmī (d. 283/896). Possible reasons for this particular omission (and the debate between Ibn al-Rūmī and Ibn al-Muʿtazz about the rose and narcissus) are discussed in chapter 6 below. *Cf.* Kilpatrick, 'Criteria of Classification,' p. 151, for the view that Ibn Sallām's exclusion of ʿUmar ibn Rabīʿah, but his inclusion of ʿUmar's less well-known contemporary Ibn Qays al-Ruqayyāt, is an indication of "developed and independent taste" in the critic. Incidentally, Ibn Abī Ṭāhir composed a work entitled *Akhbār wa-shiʿr ʿUbaydallāh Ibn Qays al-Ruqayyāt* (Accounts and poetry of ʿUbaydallāh Ibn Qays al-Ruqayyāt).

20 This is taken up in Abu Deeb, 'Literary Criticism,' 343–4; in Stetkevych, *Abū Tammām and the Poetics of the ʿAbbāsid Age*, p. 94, who shows that al-Qāḍī al-Jurjānī, like Ibn Qutaybah, is "also able to begin with an apparently revolutionary declaration of the equality of the Ancients and Moderns and then proceed directly to contradict that statement . . ."; and in Montgomery, 'Of Models and Amanuenses.'

21 *Murūj*, ¶ 3025: *Aḥmad Ibn Abī Ṭāhir al-shā'ir.*
22 al-Marzubānī, *al-Muwashshaḥ*, pp. 536–7 (#34).
23 *Ta'rīkh Baghdād*, vol. 4, p. 211, lines 17–18; *Irshād*, vol. 3, p. 87, lines 4–5.
24 al-Dhahabī, *Ta'rīkh al-Islām wa-wafāyāt mashāhīr al-a'lām*, vol. 20, ed. 'Umar 'Abd al-Salām al-Tadmurī, Cairo: Dār al-Kitāb al-'Arabī, 1412/1992, pp. 255–6 (#211). The verses are:

Ḥasbu 'l-fatā an yakūna dhā ḥasabin min nafsihī laysa ḥasbuhū ḥasabuh
Laysa 'lladhī yabtadī bihī nasabun mithla lladhī yantahī bihi nasabuh

also cited in al-Tha'ālibī, *al-I'jāz wa-al-ījāz*, ed. Muḥammad al-Tūnjī, Beirut: Dār al-Nafā'is, 1412/1992, p. 171 (line 1 is in al-Tha'ālibī, *al-Tamthīl wa-al-muḥāḍarah*, ed. 'A. M. al-Ḥulw, Cairo: Dār Iḥyā' al-Kutub al-'Arabiyyah, 1381/1961, p. 93); al-Nuwayrī, *Nihāyat al-arab fī funūn al-adab*, 33 vols in 27, Cairo: Dār al-Kutub and al-Mu'assasah al-Miṣriyyah al-'Āmmah li-al-Ta'līf wa-al-Tarjamah wa-al-Ṭibā'ah wa-al-Nashr, 1923–85, vol. 3, p. 91; Ibn Ma'ṣūm, *Anwār al-rabī' fī anwār al-badī'*, 7 vols, ed. S. H. Shukr, Karbala: Maktabat al-'Irfān, 1968–9; reprint 1981, p. 110; al-Sakhāwī, *al-I'lān bi-al-tawbīkh li-man dhamma ahl al-tārīkh*, ed. Franz Rosenthal, Baghdad: Maktabat al-'Ānī, 1382/1963, p. 319; Muḥammad ibn Sayfal-dīn, *al-Durr al-farīd wa-bayt al-qaṣīd*, MS Ayasofya 3864, Süleymaniye, 109b (line 1 only).
25 al-Sakhāwī, *al-I'lān bi-al-tawbīkh*, p. 319, lines 3–4.
26 *Fihrist*, p. 163, lines 10–12; quoted in *Irshād*, vol. 3, p. 88, lines 2–7.
27 See n. 70 in chapter 6 below.
28 *Cf.* Sahl ibn Hārūn's poetry, which was highly praised, and yet survives only in fragments. The same fate befell al-Ṣūlī's *dīwān*. As for Ibn Abī Ṭāhir's surviving poetry, the references in Āzarnūsh, 'Ebn Abī Ṭāher Ṭayfūr' are supersed by the "*dīwān*" in my 'Ibn Abī Ṭāhir Ṭayfūr (d. 280/893): Merchant of the Written Word,' dissertation, University of Pennsylvania, 1998, Appendix B, pp. 336–409, to which should now be added al-Jāḥiẓ, 'Kitāb al-Hujjāb,' in *Rasā'il al-Jāḥiẓ*, vol. 2, p. 65; al-Ḥuṣrī, *al-Maṣūn fī sirr al-hawā al-maknūn*, ed. al-Nabawī 'Abd al-Wāḥid Sha'lān, Cairo: Dār Iḥyā' al-Kutub al-'Arabiyyah, 1989, p. 102; al-Azdī, *Badā'i' al-badā'ih*, p. 223; and Ibn Khallikān, *Wafayāt al-a'yān*, vol. 1, p. 110 (art. Ibn 'Abd Rabbih, to whom are also attributed the two lines quoted there).
29 *Ṭabaqāt al-shu'arā'*, p. 409, line 17. Abū Hiffān's poetry has now been collected by Nājī in 'Abū Hiffān: ḥayātuhu wa-shi'ruhu.'
30 Ibn Dāwūd uses the formulae *anshdanā* (recited to us) and *anshadanī* (recited to me) of Ibn Abī Ṭāhir often, e.g. at *al-Zahrah*, p. 211, line 14.
31 *Muḥāḍarāt al-udabā'*, vol. 1, p. 62, lines 4–6 (*wa-mā ajwada mā qāla Ibn Abī Ṭāhir. . .*)
32 Abū Hilāl al-'Askarī, *al-Ṣinā'atayn*, p. 425, and in *Dīwān al-ma'ānī*, vol. 1, pp. 47–8, al-'Askarī cites five additional verses. See also Ibn al-Shajarī, *Ḥamāsah*, pp. 402–3 (#320) (verses 1–5); Usāmah ibn Munqidh, *al-Badī' fī naqd al-shi'r*, pp. 65–6 (where the verses are unattributed); al-Tha'ālibī, *Bard al-akbād*, p. 109 (verses 1–3); al-Muḥibbī, *Janī al-jannatayn*, p. 16 (verse 1); and Muḥammad ibn Sayf al-dīn, *al-Durr al-farīd wa-bayt al-qaṣīd*, MS Fatih 3761, vol. 2, folio 182b (verse 6).
33 Abū Hilāl al-'Askarī, *al-Ṣinā'atayn*, p. 443, lines 1–2.
34 al-Nuwayrī, *Nihāyat al-arab*, vol. 3, p. 188.
35 Ibn Ṭabāṭabā, *'Iyār al-shi'r*, p. 120, line 11 to p. 121, line 1: *Fa-mithl hādha al-shi'r wa-mā shākalahu yuṣdī al-fahm wa-yūrithu al-ghamm lā kamā yajlū al-hamm wa-yashḥadhu al-fahm min qawl Aḥmad. . .*
36 al-'Askarī, *Dīwān al-ma'ānī*, vol. 2, p. 118.
37 Ibn Abī Ṭāhir composed a work about this poet (who died *c.* 199/814) entitled *Kitāb Akhbār Ibn Munādhir.*
38 al-Baghdādī, *Khizānat al-adab*, vol. 5, pp. 255–6.

39 Julie Meisami has, in *Medieval Persian Court Poetry*, Princeton: Princeton University Press, 1987, suggestively explored important aspects of the interaction between the poet and the court but her focus is (mainly) Persian poetry. A similar study for Arabic remains a pressing need but, on individual poets, see Stetkevych, *Abū Tammām and the Poetics of the ʿAbbāsid Age*, and Beatrice Gruendler, *Medieval Arabic Praise Poetry: Ibn al-Rūmī and the patron's redemption*, London and New York: RoutledgeCurzon, 2003.

40 *Cf.* Najar, *La mémoire rassemblée*, pp. 72–6.

41 For an example in verse of Ibn Abī Ṭāhir's ambivalence toward poetry and its financial reward, see *Irshād*, vol. 3, p. 93, lines 1–4:

Wa-mā 'sh-shiʿru illā 's-sayfu yanbū wa-ḥadduhū
ḥusāmun wa-yamḍī wa-hwa laysa bi-dhī ḥaddī
Wa-law kāna bi 'l-iḥsāni yurzaqu shāʿirun
la-ajdā 'lladhī yukdī wa-akdā 'lladhī yujdī.

42 *Ta'rīkh Baghdād*, vol. 4, p. 211, line 17; *Irshād*, vol. 3, p. 87, lines 4–5.

43 al-Sakhāwī, *al-Iʿlān bi-al-tawbīkh*, p. 319, lines 3–4.

44 al-Marzubānī, *al-Muwashshaḥ*, pp. 178, line 2–4, and 430, lines 6–11.

45 Ibn Dāwūd, *al-Zahrah*, pp. 368, 477, 525, 530, 531, 532, 535, 536, 606; and pp. 150, 205, 221, 271, 272, 388, 443.

46 al-Qālī, *al-Amālī*, vol. 2, p. 82, lines 10–13.

47 Abdulla El Tayib, 'Pre-Islamic Poetry,' in *CHALEUP*, p. 29 (emphasis mine).

48 al-Marzubānī, *al-Muʿjam fī asmā' al-shuʿarā'*, p. 133, lines 1–2.

49 On the *rajaz* metre, see *EAL*, pp. 645–5.

50 *Akhbār Abī al-ʿAynā'*, as has been noted above, is an edition or compilation.

51 *Fihrist*, p. 101, line 4.

52 Āzarnūsh, 'Ebn Abī Ṭāher.'

53 al-Ṣūlī, *Akhbār Abī Tammām*, pp. 249–58.

54 al-Ṣūlī, *Akhbār Abī Tammām*, p. 216, line 9 (question), line 12 (answer).

55 Arazi, 'De la voix au calame,' p. 379.

56 On *sariqah*, see *inter alia* Trabulsi, *Critique poétique*, pp. 192–213; G. E. von Grunebaum, *Kritik und Dichtkunst*, Wiesbaden: Otto Harrassowitz, 1955, pp. 101–291; and Heinrichs, *Arabische Dichtung*, pp. 82–99.

57 Islamic law does not have the notion of intellectual property.

58 For negative judgments on Ibn Abī Ṭāhir's plagiarism criticism, see al-Āmidī, *al-Muwāzanah bayna shiʿr Abī Tammām wa-al-Buḥturī*, 2nd edn, ed. Aḥmad Ṣaqr, Cairo: Dār al-Maʿārif, 1392/1972, vol. 1, p. 112, lines 2–4 and pp. 123–33, and ff.; and al-Ḥātimī, *al-Risālah al-Mūḍiḥah fī dhikr sariqāt Abī al-Ṭayyib al-Mutanabbī wa-sāqit shiʿrihi*, p. 161, line 8 (... *min ikhtilāqāt Aḥmad ibn Abī Ṭāhir*...).

59 The date of composition of Abū Ḍiyā' Bishr ibn Yaḥyā ibn ʿAlī al-Naṣībī's (d. second half third/ninth century) *Sariqāt al-Buḥturī min Abī Tammām* is not known: see *GAS*, vol. 2, p. 562).

60 Yūsuf al-Badīʿī, *Ṣubḥ al-munabbī ʿan ḥaythiyyat al-Mutanabbī*, ed. M. Y. ʿArafah, Damascus: Maktabat ʿArafah, 1350/1931, p. 101.

61 The title is recorded in *Fihrist*, p. 70, line 18. Other early *sariqāt* works include Ibn al-Sikkīt's (d. *c.* 243/857) *Sariqāt al-shuʿarā' wa-mā tawāradū [/ma 'ttafaqū] ʿalayh*; Abū Ḍiyā' work mentioned in n. 59 above; Abū Naḍlah Muhalhil ibn Yamūt's (d. 334/946) *Sariqāt Abī Nuwās* (see *GAS*, vol. 2, pp. 477, 546); and Abū al-Qāsim Jaʿfar ibn Ḥamdān al-Mawṣilī's (d. 323/935) *Kitāb al-Sariqāt*. Jaʿfar's work was unfinished at his death, and thus post-dates Ibn Abī Ṭāhir's work (*Fihrist*, p. 166, line 22; *Irshād*, vol. 7, p. 191, line 7). This is the same Jaʿfar who reports al-Buḥturī's negative opinion of Ibn Abī Ṭāhir: see *Fihrist*, p. 163, lines 10–12.

62 Heinrichs, 'An Evaluation of *Sariqa*,' p. 358.

63 For a reverse situation, see the description of the tampering and devaluing by al-Sarī ibn Aḥmad (d. 360/970) of the poetry of the al-Khālidī brother (d. 380/990 and 400/1010) by placing their verses in the *dīwān* of Kushājim, because of al-Sarī's hostility toward them: he wanted to be able to say that the al-Khālidīs had plagiarized Kushājim (d. 350/961): see *Irshād*, vol. 11, p. 184, lines 5–11.
64 al-Jurjānī, *al-Wasāṭah*, p. 209, line 11.
65 Abū Hilāl al-ʿAskarī, *Dīwān al-maʿānī*, vol. 1, p. 94, line 12 to p. 95, line 11.
66 *Fihrist*, p. 137, line 15.
67 C. E. Bosworth, 'An early Arabic mirror for princes: Ṭāhir Dhū ʾl-Yaminain's epistle to his son ʿAbdallāh (206/821).'
68 See my 'Defining *adab* by (re)defining the *adīb*: Ibn Abi Ṭāhir Ṭayfūr and Writerly Culture,' in *Defining Fiction and Adab in Medieval Arabic Literature*, ed. Philip Kennedy, Wiesbaden: Harrassowitz, 2005, forthcoming.
69 *Fihrist*, p. 367, lines 8–10 (emphasis mine).
70 *Fihrist*, p. 364, lines 24–5.
71 Duncan B. Macdonald, 'The Earlier History of the Arabian Nights,' *Journal of the Royal Asiatic Society*, 1924, 353–97. M. F. Ghazi, 'La littérature d'imagination en arabe du IIè/VIIè au Vè/XIè siècles,' *Arabica*, 1957, vol. 4(2), 164–76, is the most detailed analysis of the section as a whole but it is disappointing. Latham and Grignaschi, in their discussions of Sālim, have shown how the merest reference (*Fihrist*, p. 131, lines 14–15) can speak volumes: Latham, 'The beginnings of Arabic prose literature: the epistolary genre'; Mario Grignaschi, 'Les "Rasāʾil Arisṭāṭālīsa ilā-l-Iskandar" de Sālim Abū-l-ʿAlāʾ et l'activité culturelle à l'époque omayyade,' *Bulletin d'études orientales*, 1967, vol. 19, 8–83.
On Ibn Abī Ṭāhir's acquaintaince with Aristotle, see Seeger A. Bonebakker, 'Poets and Critics in the Third Century AH,' in Gustav E. von Grunebaum (ed.), *Logic in Classical Islamic Culture*, Wiesbaden: Otto Harrassowitz, 1970, p. 109.
72 Ghazi, 'Littérature d'imagination,' p. 174.
73 Ghazi, 'Littérature d'imagination,' p. 169.
74 *Murūj*, ¶ 17, repeated at ¶¶ 3658–60. At Murūj ¶ 1415, al-Masʿūdī describes a report (*khabar*) about Iram as unreliable because of *ṣunʿat al-quṣṣāṣ*, the invention of the storytellers (Pellat has "une invention due aux romanciers"). See also e.g. *Taʾrīkh Baghdād*, vol. 12, p. 108, lines 4–12, and *Muḥāḍarāt al-udabāʾ*, vol. 1, p. 106, lines 5–12; and, on *taṣnīf*, Schoeler, *Ecrire et transmettre*, pp. 80–90. *Cf.* Bernard of Angiers' description of the miracles of Saint Foy as popularly diffused (*vulgarium fama*) and fictional inventions (*inanis fabule commenta*): Bernardus, 'Incipit epistola ad domnum Fulbertum,' in *Liber miraculorum sancte Fidis*, ed. A. Bouillet, Paris, Alphonse Picard et Fils, 1897, p. 2, line 6.
75 Lane, p. 2420. Note the *warrāq* context.
76 Lane, p. 2420.
77 *Fihrist*, p. 363, lines 8–11.
78 *Cf.* al-Maydānī, *Majmaʿ al-amthāl*, vol. 1, p. 195 (#1028). See further Rina Drory, 'Three Attempts to Legitimize Fiction in Classical Arabic Literature,' *Jerusalem Studies in Arabic and Islam*, 1994, vol. 18, 146–64, and the references she cites.
79 Joel L. Kraemer, *Humanism in the Renaissance of Islam: The Cultural Revival during the Buyid Age*, Leiden: E. J. Brill, 1986, p. 228, writes that Miskawayh (d. 421/1030) omitted "evening gossip and fables" (i.e. *asmār* and *khurāfāt*) in his works because "the people of our time can gain experience for the tasks they face in the future only from human behavior unconnected with the miraculous."
80 *Murūj*, ¶ 3300.
81 See *EI2*, vol. 3, pp. 367–72. The fourth/eleventh century *Ḥikāyat Abī al-Qāsim* is identified by its author, Abū al-Muṭahhar al-Azdī (though it has been attributed to al-Tawḥīdī), as a *risālah*, a *qiṣṣah*, a *ḥadīth*, and a *samar* (*Ḥikāyat Abī al-Qāsim. Abulkâsim,*

ein bagdâder Sittenbild, Heidelberg: C. Winter's Universitätbuchhandlung, 1902, pp. 1–4). Al-Ḥarīrī (d. 516/1122), describing useful stories – *ḥikāyāt* such as those found in *Kalīlah wa-Dimnah* – says they were performed by *ruwāt*, here storytellers, not transmitters (*EI2*, vol. 3, p. 368). Al-Azdī's and al-Ḥarīrī's remarks speak to the polyvalence and slipperiness of storytelling vocabulary, and also to the fluid notion of "story." *Cf.* 'Abdel-'Aziz 'Abdel-Meguid, 'A Survey of the Terms Used in Arabic for "Narrative" and "Story",' *Islamic Quarterly*, 1954, 195–204. See also Stefan Leder (ed.), *Story-telling in the framework of non-fictional Arabic literature*, Wiesbaden: Harrassowitz, 1998.

82 *EI2*, vol. 3, pp. 368–9.

83 *Murūj*, ¶ 2072; see also ¶ 205.

84 See e.g. *Murūj*, ¶ 2351, where al-Masʿūdī refers to al-Mutawakkil's *summār*. These companions apparently spoke of the kings of al-Ḥīrah.

85 *Murūj*, ¶¶ 2331, 2346; *Irshād*, vol. 1, p. 216, lines 7–8, where a four-volume *Kitāb Naẓm al-sulūk wa-musāmarat al-mulūk* is credited to al-Raqīq al-Qayrawānī.

86 See e.g. *Irshād*, vol. 6, p. 296, line 12.

87 Ibn al-Jawzī, *al-Muntaẓam fī taʾrīkh al-mulūk wa-al-umam*, 18 vols, ed. Muḥammad 'Abd al-Qādir al-'Aṭā *et al.*, Beirut: Dār al-Kutub al-'Ilmiyyah, 1412/1992, vol. 14, p. 376, line 3.

88 Abbott, *Studies*, vol. 1, p. 10, n. 2.

89 *Fihrist*, p. 363, lines 17–20.

90 *Fihrist*, p. 363, line 20 to p. 364, line 5.

91 This is not the jurist al-Shāfiʿī.

92 *Irshād*, vol. 3, p. 89, line 12 to p. 90, line 6. See al-Jahshiyārī, *Kitāb al-wuzarāʾ wa-al-kuttāb*, ed. Muṣṭafā al-Saqqāʿ *et al.*, Cairo: Muṣṭafā al-Bābī al-Ḥalabī wa-awlāduh, 1357/1938, reprint 1980/1401, and *Nuṣūṣ ḍāʾiʿah min Kitāb al-Wuzarāʾ wa-al-kuttāb li-Muḥammad ibn 'Abdūs al-Jahshiyārī*, ed. Mīkhāʾīl 'Awwād, Beirut: Dār al-Kitāb al-Lubnānī, 1384/1964. Dominique Sourdel, *EI2*, vol. 2, pp. 88, disputes the attribution by some of *al-Ḥikāyāt al-'ajībah* to al-Jahshiyārī, and its identification with his *asmār* collection.

93 *Fihrist*, p. 163, lines 19–20.

4 BEING A BOOKMAN

1 *Fihrist*, p. 163, lines 9–10, cited in *Irshād*, vol. 3, p. 87, line 12 to p. 88, line 2.

2 de Slane (tr.), *Ibn Khallikan's Biographical Dictionary*, vol. 1, p. 291.

3 *EI1*, vol. 2, p. 222.

4 Dodge (tr.), *The Fihrist of al-Nadīm*, p. 320.

5 *EI2*, vol. 3, p. 692.

6 Makdisi, *Rise of Humanism*, p. 272, and Ahmed, *Muslim Education*, p. 43.

7 *Kuttāb* is also the plural of *kātib*, writer, secretary, clerk.

8 On the dispute about which term correctly applied to elementary schools, see *WKAS*, vol. 1, p. 44, art. *maktab*. On the *maktab* and *kuttāb* in general, see Makdisi, *Rise of Humanism*, pp. 48–50, and Talas, *La Madrasa Nizamiyya*, pp. 4–12.

9 Makdisi, *Rise of Humanism*, pp. 48–9.

10 Maḥmūd 'Abd al-Mawlā, 'al-Katātīb wa taʿlīm al-ṣibyān fī al-qarn al-thālith,' in Ibn Saḥnūn, *Ādāb al-muʿallimīn*, ed. Maḥmūd 'Abd al-Mawlā, Algiers: al-Sharikah al-Waṭaniyyah li-al-Nashr wa-al-Tawzīʿ, 1973, p. 63. Although the statistics provided by Richard W. Bulliett in 'The Age Structure of Medieval Islamic Education,' *Studia Islamica*, 1983, vol. 57, 105–17, concern Hadith education in Nishapur, they are nonetheless illustrative: of twenty-two cases, the average age of the beginning student was seven and a half years, and the learning career lasted on average thirteen and a half years. *Cf.* Ahmed, *Muslim Education*, pp. 143–52.

11 Ibn Saḥnūn, *Ādāb al-muʿallimīn*, p. 82, lines 7–12.

12 Talas, *La Madrasa Nizamiyya*, p. 9.
13 *Qaṣā'id*, p. 37: *wa lawla [...] annahu awwal mā yataʿallamahu al-ṣibyān fī al-kuttāb la-dhakarnāhā [= hādhihi al-qaṣā'id]* ...
14 Dodge's "a teacher in a common school," though not strictly correct, nonetheless conveys the right idea (*The Fihrist of al-Nadīm*, p. 320).
15 *Irshād*, vol. 1, p. 154, line 3. Al-Jāḥiẓ wrote an epistle entitled *al-Muʿallimīn* [On schoolmasters] of which only a few pages survive. For a wide selection of opinions about teachers and teaching, see *Muḥāḍarāt al-udabā'*, vol. 1, pp. 45–57.
16 al-Zubaydī, *Ṭabaqāt al-naḥwīyīn*, p. 143, line 21; al-Ṭālaqānī, *Risālat al-Amthāl al-Baghdādiyyah allatī tajrī bayn al-ʿāmmah*, ed. Louis Massignon, Cairo: Maktabat al-Raʿamsīs, n.d., #121.
17 Ahmed, *Muslim Education*, p. 14.
18 *Inbāh al-ruwāt*, vol. 3, p. 121, lines 4–5:

Inna 'l-muʿallima lā yazālu muʿalliman
law kāna ʿallama Ādama 'l-asmā'a
Man ʿallama 'ṣ-ṣibyāna aṣabū ʿaqlahu
ḥattā banī 'l-khulafā'i wa 'l-khulafā'a

Cf. Ta'rīkh Baghdād, vol. 14, p. 273, lines 9–11.
19 *Fihrist*, p. 93, line 21; *cf. Irshād*, vol. 17, p. 132, line 16.
20 ʿAlī al-Khāqānī, *Shuʿarā' Baghdād min ta'sīsihā ḥattā al-yawm*, 2 vols, Baghdad: Maṭbaʿat Asad, 1382/1962, p. 161. *Cf.* e.g. *Irshād*, vol. 18, p. 40, lines 11–12.
21 Ghayyāḍ, in *Qaṣā'id*, p. 6: *wa-qad dhakara Ibn al-Nadīm annahu kāna awwal amrihi ʿalā madhhab al-sunnah thumma māla ilā al-tashayyuʿ baʿd dhālik.* On Ibn Abī Ṭāhir's Shiism, see below.
22 Of Ibn Abī al-Thalj, Ibn al-Nadīm, *Fihrist*, p. 289, line 6, writes: *khāṣṣī ʿāmmī wa-al-tashayyuʿ aghlab ʿalayh.*
23 See e.g. Roy P. Mottahedeh, *Loyalty and Leadership in Early Islamic Society*, Princeton: Princeton University Press, 1980: note that the usage is not consistent across authors.
24 *EI1*, vol. 2, p. 222. This is translated as follows in the Arabic edition: *Wa kāna Ibn Abī Ṭāhir awwal amrihi mudarris mu'addib li-abnā' baʿḍ al-usar al-muthriyah thumma iḥtarafa akhīran naskh al-kutub wa ittakhadha lahu ḥānūt bi-sūq al-warrāqīn*: see *Dā'irat al-maʿārif al-islāmiyyah*, 13 vols, ed. M. Th. Houtsma, Cairo: Dār al-Shaʿb, 1969, vol. 3, pp. 205–6.
25 Lane, p. 746.
26 Extensive training in letter-writing is one of the reasons why, or perhaps how, the letter became a favorite literary device of *kātib*s. See e.g. Joel L. Kraemer, *Humanism in the Renaissance of Islam: The Cultural Revival during the Buyid Age*, Leiden: E. J. Brill, 1986, p. 209.
27 This seems to be the difference between the *majlis ʿāmm* (general session) and the *majlis khāṣṣ* (specialized session) of the professors of medicine (Makdisi, *Rise of Humanism*, pp. 60–61). *Majlis ʿāmm* was also a term applied to the Abbasid caliph's Great (or General) Audience. *Cf.* n. 35 below.
28 This figure is recorded for a teacher (*muʿallim*) in the mid second/eighth century (*Ta'rīkh Baghdād*, vol. 13, p. 332, line 2).
29 *Ta'rīkh Baghdād*, vol. 14, p. 273, line 13. Ibn Qutaybah, *ʿUyūn al-akhbār*, vol. 1, p. 221, lines 7–8 writes that one could live in Basro (a city with a lower price index than Baghdad) on 1/12th of a dinar a month on an austere coastal diet of rice-flour bread and salted fish.
30 *Inbāh*, vol. 3, p. 364, line 9.
31 Makdisi, *Rise of Humanism*, pp. 242–3. By the early fifth/eleventh century half a dinar per day was enough for Muḥammad al-Arzānī's wine, meat and fruit (*Irshād*, vol. 20, p. 34, line 16).
32 Sabari, *Mouvements populaires*, p. 40.

33 For *jalīs* (convivial companion, pl. *julasāʾ*), see e.g. *Irshād*, vol. 13, p. 168, line 6.
34 As with the Arabic *majlis*, so too did the Hebrew *yeshiva* come to designate a court in legal terminology. I thank Joe Lowry for directing me to David M. Goodblatt, *Rabbinic Instruction in Sasanian Babylonia*, Leiden: E. J. Brill, 1975, pp. 63–92.
35 See *EI2*, vol. 5, pp. 1031–3; Ahmed, *Muslim Education*, pp. 55–9; Makdisi, *Rise of Humanism*, 60–4; and Kraemer, *Humanism*, *passim*. For the meaning "humanist circle," see Makdisi, *Rise of Humanism*, p. 61. *Majālis al-uns* were social gatherings: these were often accompanied by drinking and other forms of pleasure. What protocols may have applied in other *majālis* were often absent, or suspended, there. The caliph or potentate's *majlis*, which could include singers, poets, lawyers, scholars, storytellers, and petitioners, was sometimes called *majlis al-khāṣṣah* (lit. session for the elite).
36 See Makdisi, *Rise of Humanism*, pp. 62–3; Ahmed, *Muslim Education*, pp. 135–40; Kraemer, *Humanism*, pp. 55–6.
37 al-Tanūkhī, *Nishwār al-muḥāḍarah wa-akhbār al-mudhākarah*, 8 vols, ed. ʿAbbūd al-Shaljī, Beirut: Dār Ṣādir, 1391–3/1971–3, vol. 7, p. 190, lines 2–3 (#113).
38 al-Zubaydī, *Ṭabaqāt al-naḥwiyyīn*, p. 262, line 17 to p. 263, line 2.
39 The term *mutaʾaddibūn* was also used to describe students learning privately or apprenticing in the chanceries.
40 *Irshād*, vol. 13, p. 281, lines 3–4.
41 *Irshād*, vol. 7, p. 132, lines 9–11.
42 al-Ṣūlī, *Akhbār al-Buḥturī*, p. 131, line 6 to p. 132, line 5 (#83) (emphasis mine).
43 E.g. Ghayyāḍ, in *Qaṣāʾid*, p. 7; Ḍayf, *al-Aṣr al-ʿAbbāsī al-thānī*, vol. 2, p. 419.
44 On *wirāqah*, see M. F. Jamil, 'Islamic *wirāqah*, 'stationery,' during the early Middle Ages,' dissertation, University of Michigan, 1985; Pedersen, *Arabic Book*, pp. 37–53; and al-Zayyāt, 'Ṣuḥuf al-kitābah wa-ṣināʿat al-waraq fī al-Islām,' *al-Mashriq*, 1954, 1–30, 458–88, 625–43.
45 See Bloom, *Paper before Print*, 1–47, and Pedersen, *Arabic Book*, pp. 60 ff.
46 Ibn al-Faqīh, *Kitāb al-Buldān*, ed. M. J. de Goeje, Leiden: E. J. Brill, 1885, p. 253, lines 5–7 and Pedersen, *Arabic Book*, pp. 58–9, 62. Ibn Khaldūn, *al-Muqaddimah*, vol. 2, p. 350, credits the Barmakid al-Faḍl ibn Yaḥyā with the suggestion that paper be manufactured, but this is likely apocryphal (*cf.* Franz Rosenthal [tr.], *The Muqaddimah, an Introduction to History*, 2nd rev. edn, Princeton: Princeton University Press for the Bollingen Foundation, 1967, vol. 2, p. 392, n. 208).
47 al-Yaʿqūbī, *Kitāb al-Buldān*, p. 245, lines 7–10. Le Strange, *Baghdad*, p. 92; Jacob Lassner, *Topography of Baghdad*, Detroit: Wayne State University Press, 1970, pp. 155–77; Lassner, *The Shaping of ʿAbbāsid Rule*, Princeton: Princeton University Press, 1980, pp. 194–204.
Judging from *Aghānī*, p. 6, lines 3–4 (*wa-kāna yusammā bi-Sanad al-Warrāq wa-ḥānūtuhu fī al-Sharqiyyah fī Khān al-Zibl*), *warrāq*s were not confined to the *sūq al-warrāqīn* but also to be found in the Khān al-Zibl, or Dung Market (Dodge [tr.], *Fihrist of al-Nadīm*, p. 310, has Ṭāq al-Zibl, or Dung Arch).
48 *Fihrist*, p. 167, lines 19–20. On the Ṭāq al-Ḥarrānī, see Yāqūt, *Muʿjam al-buldān*, vol. 6, p. 6.
49 In 157/773, the caliph al-Manṣūr (regn. 136–58/754–75) decided to transplant the merchants located within the city walls to a place outside of them. He chose the market town of al-Karkh, an area known to be Shiite (*Taʾrīkh Baghdād*, vol. 1, p. 79, lines 14–16). The quarter's Barāthah mosque, built so that the merchants would not need to enter the city, was destroyed by al-Muqtadir (r. 295–320/908–32) ostensibly for its Shiite activities. Al-Ṣūlī, *Akhbār al-Rāḍī wa-al-Muttaqī*, p. 261, line 18 to p. 262, line 2, reports that in 332/943, a great fire swept through al-Karkh, engulfing the areas occupied by the fishmongers, and by "the paper-sellers and shoe-sellers [*aṣḥāb al-kāghad wa-al-niʿal*]."

50 See e.g. the remarks of Abū Hiffān in his *Akhbār Abī Nuwās*, ed. ʿA. A. Farrāj, Cairo: Dār Miṣr, n.d., p. 85, line 10 to p. 86, line 2.
51 This budget reserved 36,000 dinars for jewellers, tailors, cobblers, locksmiths, embroiderers, upholsterers, perfumers and pharmacists, *copyists*, carpenters, engravers, and saddle-makers: see Sabari, *Mouvements populaires*, 25 (emphasis mine). See also Héribert Busse, 'Das Hofbudget des Chalifen al-Muʿtaḍid billah,' *Der Islam*, 1967, vol. 43, 11–36.
52 Ibn Abī Uṣaybiʿah, *ʿUyūn al-anbāʾ*, p. 270, line 30.
53 *Fihrist*, p. 320, line 18; al-Mubarrad's *warrāq*s have their own entry on pp. 65–6.
54 See *Irshād*, vol. 16, 109, lines 14–15.
55 Al-Jāḥiẓ, upset at ʿAbd al-Malik ibn al-Zayyāt for convincing him to use leather and parchment for his writing, subsequently bought paper from *warrāq*s. One of them, Abū Yaḥyā Zakariyāʾ ibn Yaḥyā, became "Warrāq al-Jāḥiẓ": see *Fihrist*, p. 209, line 30.
56 *Fihrist*, p. 67, line 2.
57 *Irshād*, vol. 12, p. 192, lines 3–6.
58 E.g. *Aghānī*, vol. 1, p. 6, line 4, and *Irshād*, vol. 4, p. 117, line 1.
59 In a famous anecdote, cited in *Inbāh*, vol. 3, p. 8, lines 8–9, as al-Jāḥiẓ is getting off a boat he hears an auctioneer selling books by the grammarian al-Farrāʾ.
60 For a book business run by a *warrāq*, his wife, and their daughter, see *Inbāh*, vol. 1, p. 39, lines 5–7.
61 *Cf.* Abbott, *Studies*, vol. 3, p. 27, line 12ff.
62 al-Samʿānī, *Kitāb al-ansāb*, 13 vols, ed. ʿAbd al-Muʿīd Khān, Hyderabad: Dāʾirat al-Maʿārif al-ʿUthmāniyyah, 1382–1402/1962–82, vol. 13, p. 300, describes the *warrāq* as "The one who produces Qurans and records Hadith and other reports; a seller of paper in Baghdad is also so called."
63 See Abbott, *Studies*, vol. 2, p. 46; Bloom, *Paper before Print*, pp. 102–8.
64 *Fihrist*, p. 367, lines 7–8. For more on Ibn Abī Ṭāhir and storytelling see below and also in chapter 5 below.
65 *Cf. Irshād*, vol. 2, p. 141, line 3.
66 *Aghānī*, vol. 1, p. 5, line 10 to p. 6, line 3, quoted in *Fihrist*, p. 158, lines 19–27, in turn quoted in *Irshād*, vol. 6, p. 57, line 2 to p. 58, line 5. The anecdote is quoted in full in chapter 2 above.
67 See e.g. *Murūj*, ¶ 17.
68 *Murūj*, ¶ 3255; *cf. Taʾrīkh Baghdād*, vol. 12, p. 108, lines 2–11, for another example of *warrāq* unscrupulousness.
69 In al-Tanūkhī's more expansive version of this story, in *Nishwār al-muḥāḍarah*, vol. 3, pp. 5–16 (#1), the *khabar* closes with an ashamed Abū Makhlad ʿAbdallāh ibn Yaḥyā al-Ṭabarī (here, the vizier is identified), and with a defense by Abū al-ʿAynāʾ of the Munajjim family, whom Abū Makhlad had earlier put down. Abū al-ʿAynāʾ's defense of the Munajjims is unsurprising as there was considerable contact between him and them.
70 Abbott, *Studies*, vol. 3, p. 12.
71 al-Ḥuṣrī, *Zahr al-ādāb wa-thamar al-albāb*, ed. ʿA. M. al-Bijāwī, Cairo: Dār Iḥyāʾ al-Kutub, 1989; *Jamʿ al-jawāhir fī al-mulaḥ wa-al-nawādir* [= *Dhayl Zahr al-ādāb*], ed. ʿA. M. al-Bajāwī, Cairo: Dār Iḥyāʾ al-Kutub al-ʿArabiyyah, 1372/1953, vol. 2, p. 512, lines 12–15; al-Thaʿālibī, *Khāṣṣ al-khāṣṣ*, p. 69, lines 12–14. For a variation on this, see *Muḥāḍarāt al-udabāʾ*, p. 106, lines 10–11.
72 *Taʾrīkh Baghdād*, vol. 17, p. 150, line 14.
73 Bergé, 'Abū Ḥayyān al-Tawḥīdī,' in *CHALABL*, p. 118 (emphases mine).
74 al-Tawḥīdī, *Akhlāq al-wazīrayn*, p. 306, lines 15–17. Ibn Shihāb al-ʿUkbarī (d. 428/1037) reports that he bought paper for five dirhams and after spending three nights copying out the poet al-Mutanabbī's diwan would sell it for between one hundred and fifty and two hundred dirhams: *Tarīkh Baghdād*, vol. 7, p. 329, line 22 to p. 330, line 1.

75 Makdisi, *Rise of Humanism*, p. 266.
76 This serves to underscore a difference between *balāghah* and *faṣāḥah*. Al-Khaṭīb al-Baghdādī (*Ta'rīkh Baghdād*, vol. 10, p. 340, line 22 to p. 341, line 1), for instance, calls ʿUbaydallāh ibn ʿAbdallāh ibn Ṭāhir "*fāḍil adīb shāʿir faṣīḥ*" but not *balīgh*. The emphasis is on his culture and poetic skills. Other such examples are to be found in the sources, namely a preference for *balīgh* to refer to skilful prose-writers and for *faṣīḥ* to refer to accomplished poets.
77 *Balāghah* also came to mean rhetoric.
78 Franz Rosenthal, *A History of Muslim Historiography*, 2nd edn, Leiden: E. J. Brill, 1968, p. 424.
79 *Fihrist*, pp. 139–40.
80 *Fihrist*, p. 140. Yāqūt reproduces this list verbatim three centuries later.
81 *Fihrist*, p. 140.
82 At the time of al-Muʿtaṣim (r. 218–27/833–42), five types of *kātib* are reported in an anecdote preserved by Ibn ʿAbd Rabbih, *al-ʿIqd al-farīd*, vol. 4, p. 258, line 16 to p. 259, line 2: secretaries in the land tax department (*kātib kharāj*), in the chancery (*kātib rasāʾil*), in the judiciary (*kātib ḥākim*), in the army (*kātib jund*), and in the police (*kātib maʿūnah* or *kātib shurṭah*).
83 *WKAS*, vol. 1, p. 44, art. *kātib*. The meaning calligrapher is also attested: see Carter, 'The *Kātib*,' p. 42.
84 Ibn Khaldūn, *al-Muqaddimah*, vol. 2, p. 141. For the text of the letter, see *Kitāb Baghdād*, ed. Kawtharī, pp. 35–53; Ṭabarī, vol. 3, pp. 1046–61 [= *Volume 32. The Reunification of the ʿAbbāsid Caliphate*, tr. C. E. Bosworth, Albany: SUNY Press, 1987, pp. 110–28].
85 *Ṭabaqāt al-shuʿarāʾ*, p. 397, line 11 and p. 398, line 6.
86 For the most part, modern scholars who have accepted Ibn Abī Ṭāhir as a *kātib* do not explain how they understand the term.
87 al-Dhahabī, *Ta'rīkh al-Islām wa-wafāyāt mashāhīr al-aʿlām*, ed. ʿUmar ʿAbd al-Salām al-Tadmurī, Cairo: Dār al-Kitāb al-ʿArabī, 1412/1992, pp. 255–6 (#211). In al-Sakhāwī, *al-Iʿlān bi-al-tawbīkh*, p. 178, line 9, the name appears as "Abū al-Faḍl Aḥmad ibn Abī Ṭāhir al-Marwazī al-Kātib" and at p. 319, lines 3–4 as "Aḥmad ibn Abī Ṭāhir Abū al-Faḍl al-Kātib al-Marwazī." See also *Ta'rīkh Baghdād*, vol. 4, p. 211, line 16.
88 *Cf.* Quran 52:68 and 52:47, where *kātib* signifies "learned man." *Cf.* Lane, p. 2590, art. *kataba*, who notes that in biographies, *kataba* means "he was a writer, or scribe, and a learned man."
89 al-Mīkālī, *Kitāb al-Muntakhal*, ed. Wahīb al-Jabūrī, 2 vols, Beirut: Dār al-Gharb al-Islāmī, 2000, vol. 1, p. 53, line 3.
90 al-Maqqarī, *Nafḥ al-ṭīb*, vol. 2, p. 92, lines 12–16 (emphasis mine).
91 On Saʿīd, see chapter 7 below. On Sulaymān, see Sourdel, *Vizirat ʿabbāside*, pp. 300–4.
92 Ibn Qutaybah, *Ta'wīl mukhtalif al-ḥadīth*, p. 60, line 9, observes that al-Jāḥiẓ is untruthful and given to falsifying Hadith.
93 Carter, 'The *Kātib*,' p. 45.
94 Carter, 'The *Kātib*,' p. 45.
95 Carter, 'The *Kātib*,' p. 45.
96 *A-yā rabbī qad rakiba 'l-ardhalū-*
na rijliya min riḥlatī dāmiyah
Fa-in kunta ḥāmilanā mithlahum
wa illā fa-arḥilnī 'th-thāniyah

(*Irshād*, vol. 12, p. 55). In *Ta'rīkh*, vol. 9, p. 370, the last line reads: *wa-illā fa-arjil banī zāniyah*, "If not, dismount, you sons of a whore."
97 See e.g. al-Tawḥīdī, *al-Baṣāʾir wa-al-dhakhāʾir*, p. 27, line 13–14 to p. 28, line 11; the anecdote is discussed in chapter 2 above. R. A. Kimber underscores this indigence in

his entry on Ibn Abī Ṭāhir in *EAL*, p. 306, but not so Philip Kennedy in his entry on Abū Hiffān in *EAL*, p. 35.

98 Ibn Abī Ṭāhir might simply have been visiting Abū Hiffān. Abū Hiffān also convalesced at least once at Ibn Abī Ṭāhir's home: see al-Qālī, *Dhayl al-Amālī*, in *al-Amālī*, 4 vols in 2, 3rd edn, ed. I. Y. Ibn Diyāb, Cairo: Maktabat al-Saʿādah, 1373/1953, vol. 3, p. 96, lines 17–20.

99 al-Suyūṭī, *Bughyat al-wuʿāt fī ṭabaqāt al-lughawiyyīn wa-al-nuḥāt*, vol. 2, p. 31 (#1355); *Irshād*, vol. 12, p. 54, line 4; Farrāj, 'Introduction,' to Abū Hiffān, *Akhbār Abī Nuwās*, pp. 7–14. He is also described as stingy.

100 This is Rosenthal's characterization in *EI2*, vol. 3, p. 693, based, it would seem, especially on anecdotes in al-Ṣūlī, *Akhbār al-Buḥturī*.

101 *Murūj*, ¶ 1415.

102 *Fihrist*, p. 163, lines 14–15.

103 Makdisi, *Rise of Humanism*, p. 82.

104 On Yāqūt as the first writer to make extensive use of the *Fihrist* in Ibn al-Nadīm's autograph, and in the edition of al-Wazīr al-Ḥusayn ibn ʿAlī al-Maghribī (d. 418/1027), see *EI2*, vol. 3, p. 896. *Cf.* Hellmut Ritter, 'Philologika I,' *Der Islam*, 1928, vol. 17, 15–23.

105 *Qaṣā'id*, pp. 11–13. See also Ferdinand Wüstenfeld, *Die Geschichtsschreiber der Araber und ihre Werke*, in *Königlichen Gesselschaft der Wissenschaften. Histor.-philolog. Classe*, 1882, vols 28–9, reprint New York: Burt Franklin, n.d., p. 27, where the titles are given in Latin. In *GAL*, *Supplement*, vol. 1, p. 210, Brockelmann lists 4 works: (1) *Ta'rīkh Baghdād*, (2) *Kitāb al-Manthūr wa-al-manẓūm*, (3) *Kitāb Balāghāt al-nisā'*, and (4) *Kitāb Faḍā'il al-ward ʿalā al-narjis*. In *GAS*, vol. 1, pp. 348–9, Sezgin mentions Brockelmann's nos 1 and 2, and adds (5) *Kitāb Fī al-nagham wa-ʿilal al-aghānī al-musammā bi-Kitāb al-Ādāb al-rafīʿah*, (6) *Kitāb al-Shuʿarā'*, and (7) *Akhbār al-mulūk*. The attribution of the *Kitāb fī al-Nagham* to Ibn Abī Ṭāhir is an error. It is in fact by ʿUbaydallāh ibn Ṭāhir. Note also that *Moslem Schisms and Sects*, tr. K. C. Seelye, New York: Columbia University Press, 1920, is not a translation of *Kitāb Baghdād* but of *al-Farq bayn al-firaq wa-bayān al-firqah al-nājiyah* by ʿAbd al-Qāhir al-Baghdādī (d. 429/1037). Sezgin inherits this error.

106 *Qaṣā'id*, pp. 14–16.

107 I make a preliminary attempt to put the works in chronological order in 'Ibn Abī Ṭāhir Ṭayfūr,' in *Arabic Literary Culture 500–925*, ed. Michael Cooperson and Shawkat M. Toorawa, Detroit: Gale, 2005, in press. A detailed discussion of Ibn Abī Ṭāhir's works and their chronology is under preparation.

108 Adopting Tajaddod's reading in *Fihrist*, p. 163, line 19.

109 *Irshād*, vol. 3, p. 91, line 3.

110 Ibn al-Nadīm, *al-Fihrist li-Ibn al-Nadīm*, ed. Gustav Flügel, Leipzig: F. C. W. Vogel, 1871–72, reprint Beirut: Maktabat al-Ḥayāt, 1966, p. 147, line 21.

111 Reading adopted by Ghayyāḍ in *Qaṣā'id*, p. 12.

112 *Irshād*, vol. 3, p. 91, line 5, mistakenly omits '*al-Malik*.'

113 Amending the (admittedly possible) *Hujjāb* ("Chamberlains") in *Fihrist*, p. 163, line 22.

114 It is possible that the account al-Jaḥiẓ quotes about Ibn Abī Ṭāhir in his 'Kitāb al-Ḥijāb,' p. 47, lines 8–12, are from Ibn Abī Ṭāhir's own *Kitāb al-Ḥijāb*.

115 Ghayyāḍ adopts this reading based on the *Irshād* manuscript: see *Irshād*, vol. 3, p. 95, n. 2.

116 The title *Kitāb Mushtaqq* (*Fihrist*, p. 163, line 16) is corrupt and arises, I believe, from a conflation of #10 and #52.

117 Ferdinand Wüstenfeld, *Die Geschichtschreiber der Araber und ihre Werke*. Göttingen: Dieterichsche Verlagbuchhandlung, 1882, p. 27: *Cognomina Poëtarum et qui praenomine inclaruerunt*.

118 Wüstenfeld, *Geschichtsschreiber*, p. 27, assumes that Persians are either meant or implied by the sequence f/r/s/ā/n, and translates the title *Caedes Persarum*.

119 The reference in *GAS*, vol. 1, p. 349 (and referred to in vol. 2, p. 95) to Ibn Ḥajar, *Iṣābah*, no ed., Calcutta: T. J. M'Arthur Bishop's Press, 1856–88, reprint Osnäbruck: Biblio Verlag, 1980–1), vol. 3, p. 1198, is to be corrected to: vol. 1, p. 1198. Trabulsi, *Critique*, p. 41, correctly translates this title as *Le Livre contenant tout au sujet des poètes et de leurs vies*, but misnames the author "Abū al-Faḍl Muḥammad ibn Ṭāhir."

120 The poet of al-Mahdī: see e.g. Ibn al-Kāzarūnī, *Mukhtaṣar*, p. 120.

121 'Alī ibn Hārūn al-Munajjim quotes 'Ubaydallāh quoting his father for information on Marwān ibn Abī al-Janūb in al-Marzubānī, *al-Muwashshaḥ*, pp 464, lines 11–14.

122 For a probable extract, see al-Ḥātimī, *Ḥilyat al-muḥāḍarah fī ṣinā'at al-shi'r*, vol. 2, ed. Ja'far al-Kitābī, Baghdad: Dār al-Ḥurriyyah/Dār al-Rashīd li-al-Nashr, 1979, p. 63, lines 5–7.

123 al-Baghdādī, *Khizānat al-adab*, ed. 'A. M. Hārūn, Cairo: Dār al-Kutub, n.d., vol. 3, p. 240.

124 al-Āmidī, *al-Muwāzanah*, vol. 2, p. 511. No biographical information is available about Shaqīq but for his father, the poet al-Sulayk ibn Salakah, see *GAS*, vol. 2, pp. 139–40, and al-Marzubānī, *al-Muwashshaḥ*, p. 120.

125 *Kitāb Sariqāt al-naḥwiyyīn min Abī Tammām* [The plagiarisms of the grammarians from Abū Tammām] in Ibn al-Nadīm, *al-Fihrist*, ed. Flügel, p. 147, line 25, is a copyist error. This is confirmed in *Choix de livres qui se trouvaient dans les bibliothèques d'Alep (au XIIIe siècle)*, ed. and tr. Paul Sbath, Cairo: Institut d'Egypte, 1946, p. 28 (#506), where the book is attested as one describing poetic borrowings by al-Buḥturī's, not by grammarians.

126 See e.g. al-Tawḥīdī, *al-Baṣā'ir wa-al-dhakhā'ir*, vol. 1, p. 240.

127 For manuscripts and publication data, see the Bibliography.

128 Al-Mas'ūdī preserves the only known extract from this work, which he identifies by its variant title, *Akhbār al-mu'allifīn*. See *Murūj*, ¶¶ 3003–10. The extract, about three pages in length in Pellat's edition, opens as follows: "*[Abū] al-Faḍl Ibn Abī Ṭāhir, in his book on the* Accounts of Authors, [has] *the following:* 'Abū 'Uthmān Sa'īd b. Muḥammad the Younger, the affiliate of the Commander of the Faithful, reported to me saying, "During al-Muntaṣir's reign a group of his companions used to revel with him, among them Ṣāliḥ b. Muḥammad, better known as al-Ḥarīrī. One day, discussion turned to matters of the heart and to passion. 'Tell me,' al-Muntaṣir asked one of the members of the gathering, 'what is the greatest and most tragic loss a soul can suffer?' 'The loss of one's friend and counterpart [*khill mushākil*],' he replied, 'and the death of one's perfect match [*shakl muwāfiq*]'" (*Murūj*, ¶ 3003). The remainder of the anecdote has the members of the gathering providing their own examples of such loss. Ṣāliḥ ibn Muḥammad and Abū 'Uthmān Sa'īd then each recount stories about their love for women who did not love them in return. In both cases, the unrequiting women are required by caliphal decree to love the men and accept them.

Sa'īd's story leads directly into a very amusing anecdote that al-Mas'ūdī also gets from Ibn Abī Ṭāhir (*Murūj*, ¶ 3011–13), which he introduces with the phrase "Among the witty and amusing anecdotes about profligates is one mentioned by Ibn Abī Ṭāhir…" Al-Mas'ūdī's familiarity with Ibn Abī Ṭāhir may be explained by his contact with his teachers Wakī' (d. 306/918) – the intervening author between al-Khaṭīb al-Baghdādī and Ibn Abī Ṭāhir in *Ta'rīkh Baghdād* – and al-Ḥasan ibn Mūsā al-Nawbakhtī (d. *c.* 310/922).

129 Ibn Abī al-Ḥadīd, *Sharḥ Nahj al-balāghah*, ed. M. A. Ibrāhīm, Cairo: 'Īsā al-Bābī al-Ḥalabī, 1960, vol. 10, p. 101.

130 Curiously, this title is omitted by the Beatty and Tonk MSS of the *Fihrist* (Dodge, tr., *The Fihrist of al-Nadīm*, p. 320, n. 59).

131 al-Azdī, *Badā'i' al-badā'ih*, p. 341 (#389); al-Mas'ūdī, *Kitāb al-Tanbīh wa-al-ishrāf*, ed. M. J. de Goeje, Leiden: Brill, 1894, p. 310; *Murūj*, ¶ 54; al-Ḥumaydī, *Jadhwat al-muqtabis fī ta'rīkh 'ulamā' al-Andalus*, ed. Ibrāhīm al-Abyārī, Cairo/Beirut: Dār al-Kitāb al-Miṣrī/Dār al-Kitāb al-Lubnānī, n.d., vol. 1, p. 168; al-Maqqarī, *Nafḥ al-ṭīb*, ed. Dozy, vol. 2, p. 118.

132 al-Sakhāwī, *al-I'lān bi-al-tawbīkh*, p. 178 [= Rosenthal, *Historiography*, p. 408]. Rosenthal (*Historiography*, p. 408, n. 6) identifies the *Akhbār al-khulafā'* as identical with *Kitāb Baghdād*, but the issue of the former's identification with the *Akhbār al-mulūk* must be resolved.

133 For MS and publication data, see the Bibliography. Ibn Abī Ṭāhir's son 'Ubaydallāh wrote a continuation of this work. In the notice devoted to him Ibn al-Nadīm explains that "He followed the example of his father in compiling and writing but he quoted less than his father did, and Aḥmad was more knowledgable, skillful and brilliant in composition. Among the books of Abū al-Ḥusayn was a supplement to his father's book about the history [*akhbār*] of Baghdad. His father wrote until the end of the period of al-Muhtadī, while Abū al-Ḥusayn added traditions about al-Mu'tamid, al-Mu'taḍid, al-Muktafī, and al-Muqtadir, which he did not complete" (*Fihrist*, p. 164, lines 9–12). A direct citation of what may be an extract from this work (Ibn al-Nadīm identifies 'Ubaydallāh's hand [*qara'tu bi-khaṭṭ*...]) is quoted in *Fihrist*, p. 241, line 18 to p. 242. line 4). It deals with the later life, capture and execution of the mystic al-Ḥallāj (d. 309/922). Ibn Khallikān, *Wafayāt al-a'yān*, vol. 6, p. 416, quotes 'Ubaydallāh's history for information on the Ṣaffārids, but in an abridged version because of 'Ubaydallāh's "prolixity." And al-Maqrīzī, *al-Mawā'iẓ wa-al-i'tibār fī dhikr al-khiṭaṭ wa-al-āthār*, Cairo: Institut Français d'Archéologie Orientale, 1911, vol. 1, pp. 263–70, preserves a long extract from 'Ubaydallāh's book or section on al-Mu'taḍid. For references to surviving passages, see *EI2*, vol. 10, pp. 761–2, to which should be added the *Fihrist* reference above; *Irshād*, vol. 5, p. 102, lines 7–9; Ibn al-Kāzarūnī, *Mukhtaṣar al-ta'rīkh*, pp. 148, 151, 170, 171; and al-Dhahabī, *Siyar a'lām al-nubalā'*, vol. 3, pp. 3–8, vol. 14, p. 55, and vol. 13, p. 200.

134 This title as given is in the *Irshād* and all the MSS of the *Fihrist*, but Flügel prefers the variant (*al-Fihrist*, ed. Flügel p. 147, line 23).

135 Reading adopted by Ghayyāḍ in *Qaṣā'id*, p. 13.

136 Rosenthal has suggested that a *khabar* in the *Kitāb al-Aghānī* (*Aghānī*, vol. 3, p. 201, line 17 to p. 202, line 7) may have formed part of the *Akhbār al-mutaẓarrifāt* [Accounts of women affecting wit and elegance] because of the mention of these women (*al-nisā' al-mutaẓarrifāt*); it could similarly have formed part of *Akhbār Bashshār wa-ikhtiyār shi'rihi* [Accounts about Bashshār and a selection of his Poetry]. The *isnād* is (1) Abū al-Faraj < his uncle, and (2) al-Ḥasan ibn 'Alī < Ibn Abī Ṭāhir, both lines from 'Abd Allāh ibn Abī Sa'd < Abū Tawbah < Ṣāliḥ ibn 'Atiyyah.

137 This title and the *Lisān al-'uyūn* were put together (posthumously?) by Ibn Abī Ṭāhir's son, 'Ubaydallāh: *wa qad qīla anna Abā al-Ḥusayn ibnahu 'amila hādhayn al-kitābayn* (*Fihrist*, p. 164, line 1). A book bearing a similar title, *Kitāb Akhbār al-mutaẓarrifīn wa-al-mutaẓarrifāt* is also attributed to Ibn Abī Ṭāhir's son, 'Ubaydallāh: see *Fihrist*, p. 164, line 12.

138 Ibn al-Nadīm, *al-Fihrist*, ed. Flügel, p. 147, lines 23–4.

139 *Irshād*, vol. 18, pp. 142–3.

140 The famous *faux pas* of Wahb ibn Sulaymān ibn Wahb, breaking wind in the presence of 'Abdallāh ibn Yaḥyā ibn Khāqān, occasioned a great deal of poetry. If it did not originate a "sub-genre," it certainly went a long way to bringing currency to the topic: see e.g. *Irshād*, vol. 5, p. 92, line 12 to p. 93, line 8; see also *Muḥāḍarāt al-udabā'*, vol. 2, pp. 274–80.

141 *Irshād*, vol. 3, p. 91, line 1.

142 "Ibrāhīm ibn al-Walīd" in *al-Fihrist*, ed. Flügel, p. 147, line 26, is a copyist error.
143 See *Jamharat rasā'il al-ʿarab*, ed. A. Z. Ṣafwat, 4 vols, Cairo: Muṣṭafā al-Bābī al-Ḥalabī wa-awlāduh, 1356/1937, vol. 4, pp. 343–4 (#224).
144 See *Jamharat rasā'il al-ʿarab*, vol. 4, pp. 344–5 (#225).
145 See *Jamharat rasā'il al-ʿarab*, vol. 4, pp. 345–7 (#226).
146 See *Jamharat rasā'il al-ʿarab*, vol. 4, pp. 347–52 (#352).

5 NAVIGATING PARTISAN SHOALS

1 Heinz Halm, *Shiism*, Edinburgh: Edinburgh University Press, 1991, pp. 29–46.
2 See Jamal Eddine Bencheikh, 'Le cénacle poétique du calife al-Mutawakkil (m. 247): contribution à l'analyse des instances de légitimation socio-littéraires,' *Bulletin d'études orientales*, 1977, vol. 29, 33–52.
3 See Christopher Melchert, 'Religious Policies of the Caliphs from al-Mutawakkil to al-Muqtadir, AH 232–295/AD 847–908,' *Islamic Law and Society*, 1996, vol. 3, 316–42.
4 al-Jāḥiẓ, 'Faṣl mā bayn al-ʿadāwah wa-al-ḥasad,' p. 337, lines 11–12.
5 For a general survey of *taqiyyah*, see *EI2*, vol. 10, pp. 134–6; *cf.* M. M. Āghā Buzurg al-Ṭihrānī, *Dharīʿah ilā taṣānīf al-Shīʿah*, vol. 4, Najaf: Maṭbaʿat al-Gharrā, 1360/1941, pp. 403–5.
6 al-Shābushtī, *al-Diyārāt*, 2nd edn, ed. Kūrkīs ʿAwwād, Baghdād: Maktabat al-Muthannā, 1386/1966, p. 89, lines 8–10.
7 Ibn Shahrashūb, *Maʿālim al-ʿulamā' fī fihrist kutub al-shīʿah wa-asmā' al-muṣannifīn minhum qadīman wa-ḥadīthan*, ed. M. K. al-Kutubī, Najaf: Manshūrāt al-Ḥaydariyyah, 1380/1961, p. 152, lines 5, 14.
8 al-Ṣūlī, *Akhbār al-Buḥturī*, ed. Ṣāliḥ al-Ashtar, Damascus: Maktabat al-Majmaʿah al-ʿIlmī al-ʿArabī, 1378/1958, p. 123 (#71). On Ibrāhīm ibn ʿAbdallāh al-Kajjī (also al-Kashshī, al-Kachchī), see *Ta'rīkh Baghdād*, vol. 6, pp. 121–4. For the verses, see al-Buḥturī, *Dīwān*, Beirut: Dār al-Kutub al-ʿIlmiyyah, 1307/1987, vol. 2, pp. 212–15.
9 *EI2*, vol. 6, p. 617: "The site seems to be marked by the ruins at the modern Afghān town of Bālā Murghāb (in lat. 35° 35′ N. and long. 63° 20′ E.)."
10 On the connection between the name Ṭayfūr and Khurasan, see my 'Notes Toward a Biography of Ibn Abi Tahir Tayfur (d. 893),' *University of Mauritius Research Journal: Social Studies & Humanities*, 1998, vol. 1, pp. 126–7.
11 Ibn Saʿd, *Kitāb al-Ṭabaqāt al-kabīr*, ed. Eduard Sachau *et al.*, Leiden: E. J. Brill, 1904–40; Ferdinand Justi, *Iranisches Namenbuch*, Marburg: N. G. Elwert'sche Verlags-buchhandlung, 1895.
12 *Aghānī*, vol. 14, p. 141, lines 4–5.
13 E.g at *Aghānī*, vol. 19, p. 311.
14 *Fihrist*, p. 163, line 8.
15 On the *abnā'*, see Ṭabarī, vol. 3, pp. 827–9, 843–5; Crone, *Slaves on Horses*, pp. 65–6; Arazi and Elʿad, 'L'Épître'; Amikam Elʿad, 'Characteristics of the Development of the ʿAbbāsid Army (Especially Ahl Khurāsān and Al-Abnā' Units) with Emphasis on the Reign of al-Amīn and al-Ma'mūn,' dissertation, The Hebrew University of Jerusalem, 1986; Lassner, *Shaping of ʿAbbāsid Rule*, pp. 133–6; Farouk Omar, 'The composition of ʿAbbāsid support in the history of the early ʿAbbāsids,' in *ʿAbbāsiyāt, studies in the history of the early ʿAbbāsids*, Baghdad: Dār al-Ḥurriyyah, 1976. For a view of the *abnā'* which ties them to the *ʿayyārūn*, see Mohsen Zakeri, *Sāsānid Soldiers in Early Muslim Society: The origins of ʿAyyārān and Futuwwa*, Wiesbaden: Otto Harrassowitz, 1995.
16 al-Khwārizmī, *Kitāb Mafātīḥ al-ʿulūm*, ed. Gerlof van Vloten, Leiden: E. J. Brill, 1895, p. 119, lines 7–10; Crone, *Slaves on Horses*, p. 66; David Ayalon, 'The Military Reforms

of the Caliph al-Muʿtaṣim: their background and consequences,' cited in Crone, *Slaves on Horses*, p. 247, n. 472; *cf.* Ṭabarī, vol. 3, p. 826.

17 *Kitāb Baghdād*, p. 42; Arazi and Elʿad, 'L'Epître,' part 1, p. 52, nn. 51 and 52; Crone, *Slaves on Horses*, pp. 64 ff.

18 See Ṭabarī, vol. 3, pp. 931–3; Crone, *Slaves on Horses*, p. 76; Arazi and Elʿad, 'L'Epître,' part 2, p. 43. For an example of the interchangeability of the terms, see the *khabar* reported by al-Jāḥiẓ in 'Dhamm akhlāq al-kuttāb,' in *Rasā'il al-Jāḥiẓ*, vol. 2, pp. 206–7.

19 Ṭabarī, vol. 3, p. 414. *Cf.* the translation in *The History of al-Ṭabarī. Volume 31: The War between Brothers*, tr. Michael Fishbein, Albany: SUNY Press, 1992, p. 81: "sons of the mission of the dynasty."

20 Crone, *Slaves on Horses*, pp. 65–6, discusses the related terms *ahl al-dawlah*, *anṣār al-dawlah*, and *abnā' al-dawlah*.

21 *GAL*, vol. 1, p. 138/144: "stammte aus einer fürstlichen Familie Ḫorāsāns."

22 *Qaṣā'id*, p. 6, where Ghayyāḍ notes that Brockelmann provides no evidence of royal lineage.

23 Clément Huart, review of *Kitāb Baghdād*, ed. Keller, in *Journal asiatique*, 1909, 10th series, vol. 13, p. 534. *Cf.* Āzarnūsh, 'Ebn Abī Ṭāher,' p. 672.

24 See *The Fihrist of al-Nadīm*, tr. Bayard Dodge, New York: Columbia University Press, 1970, p. 1107 [index], art. Ṭāhir (Abū) Ṭayfūr, where Dodge infers that this family "supplied numerous government employees."

25 G. R. Driver, *Aramaic Documents of the Fifth Century BC*, rev. edn, Oxford: Clarendon Press, 1957, p. 41; *Fihrist*, pp. 15–7.

26 *Ibn Khallikan's Biographical Dictionary*, tr. De Slane, vol. 1, p. 291, n. 7.

27 On Yaḥyā, see Ṭabarī, vol. 3, pp. 1515–24; and Ibn Kathīr, *Bidāyah*, vol. 11, pp. 5 ff.

28 Ḍayf, *al-ʿAṣr al-ʿAbbāsī al-thānī*, pp. 416 and 419, and p. 387, where he quotes the first four lines of the elegy. Given these claims, it is important to keep in mind the "fluidity" of Shiism before the mid-fourth/tenth century. Early Shiite support was not restricted to ʿAlī and his descendants. In the poetry of al-Kumayt (d. 128/744), for instance, is echoed the broad awareness that the Prophet's family comprised all the Banū Hāshim: see Wilferd Madelung, 'The Hāshimiyyāt of al-Kumayt and Hāshimī Shiʿism,' *Studia Islamica*, 1989, vol. 70, 5–26.

29 Boustany, *Ibn ar-Rūmī*, p. 122.

30 Yaḥyā's head could not be displayed in Baghdad on account of these crowds (Ṭabarī, vol. 3, p. 1522). In this same year (250/864), Shiite masses killed the wit, Abū al-ʿIbar al-Hāshimī, a member of the ruling family, by throwing him from the roof of a tavern for having slandered ʿAlī (*Fihrist*, p. 169, line 22).

31 See Devin J. Stewart, *Islamic Legal Orthodoxy: Twelver Responses to the Sunni Legal System*, Salt Lake City: Utah University Press, 1998, pp. 66–7.

32 On al-Masʿūdī, see *EI2*, vol. 6, pp. 784–9, and Tarif Khalidi, *Islamic Historiography. The Histories of Masʿūdī*, Albany: SUNY Press, 1975.

33 *Murūj*, ¶ 3025.

34 The *Kitāb al-Awsaṭ*, composed before the *Murūj al-dhahab*, does not survive; on it, see Khalidi, *Islamic Historiography*, p. 155.

35 Boustany, *Ibn ar-Rūmī*, p. 119; *cf.* p. 127.

36 al-Maʿarrī, *Risālat al-Ghufrān*, ed. Bint al-Shāṭi', Cairo: Dār al-Maʿārif, 1950, p. 477, lines 4–5.

37 Boustany, *Ibn ar-Rūmī*, pp. 118 ff.

38 al-Iṣbahānī, *Maqātil al-Ṭālibiyyīn*, ed. S. A. Ṣaqr, Cairo: Muṣṭafā al-Bābī al-Ḥalabī wa-awlāduh, 1368/1949), p. 602, line 4 to p. 603, line 5; *Aghānī*, vol. 16, p. 362, lines 6–11, and p. 362, line 7 to p. 363, line 3.

39 On Muḥammad ibn Ṣāliḥ al-ʿAlawī, see *GAS*, vol. 2, p. 647. For his poetry, of which little survives, see e.g. the entry on him in al-Marzubānī, *Kitāb al-Muʿjam fī asmā'*

al-shuʿarāʾ, ed. ʿA. A. Farrāj, Cairo: Dār Iḥyāʾ al-Kutub al-ʿArabiyyah/Muṣṭafā al-Bābī al-Ḥalabī wa-awlāduh, 1379/1960, p. 380; and Ḍayf, *ʿal-ʿAṣr al-ʿAbbāsī al-thānī*, pp. 389–92.

40 *Cf.* Wilferd Madelung, *Religious Trends in Early Islamic Iran*, Albany: SUNY Press for the Persian Heritage Foundation, 1988; and Halm, *Shiism*, p. 16.

41 *Kitāb Baghdād*, ed. Kawtharī, p. 87. *Cf.* C. E. Bosworth, 'The Ṭāhirids and Persian Literature,' *Iran*, 1969, vol. 7, pp. 104–5.

42 *Kitāb Baghdād*, ed. Kawtharī, p. 86, line 20 to p. 87, line 9.

43 A *farsakh* (also *farsang*) is between 4 and 6 kilometres. Dhūdar is probably Dīzbād: see Guy Le Strange, *The Lands of the Eastern Caliphate*, Cambridge: Cambridge University Press, 1905, p. 388.

44 On the term *maʿānī* (sing. *maʿnā*), see *EI2*, vol. 6, pp. 346–9; and *EAL*, pp. 461–2.

45 See *Ṭabaqāt al-shuʿarāʾ*, pp. 261–3; *Fihrist*, p. 134–5; *Murūj*, ¶ 2716 (and ¶¶ 2714–8 generally); *Irshād*, vol. 17, pp. 26–31; *GAS*, vol. 2, pp. 540–1; and A. M. al-Najjār, *al-ʿAttābī: adīb Taghlib fī al-ʿaṣr al-ʿAbbāsī*, Cairo: Dār al-Fikr al-ʿArabī, 1975. *Cf. Murūj*, ¶ 2534 for an anecdote where al-ʿAttābī's critical sensibilities are mocked. Line after line by Abū Nuwās is recited to him and his verdict is always that the line is plagiarized. The anecdote closes with the statement, "If Abū Nuwās's entire poetic output were brought to him, he would say, 'Plagiarized!'"

46 al-Najjār, *al-ʿAttābī*, p. 32.

47 *Fihrist*, p. 139, line 22.

48 For his attachment to books, see also *Aghānī*, vol. 13, pp. 109–25.

49 Jan Cejpek, 'Iranian Folk-Literature,' in *HIL*, p. 620.

50 Gustav E. von Grunebaum, *Medieval Islam*, Chicago: University of Chicago Press, 1983, p. 250. See also C. E. Bosworth, 'The Heritage of Rulership in Early Islamic Iran and the Search for Dynastic Connections with the Past,' *Iranian Studies*, 1978, vol. 11, 16.

51 *Fihrist*, p. 135, line 8; Ibn al-Nadīm, *Fihrist*, pp. 10–11, mentions al-ʿAttābī often in the early subsection on the virtues of books and writing implements. *Cf.* al-ʿAttābī's comments about the *kātib* in *Murūj*, ¶¶ 2716, 2718.

52 Jan Rypka, 'History of Persian Literature up to the beginning of the 20th Century,' in *HIL*, p. 116 and *cf.* pp. 141–2.

53 Rypka, 'History,' pp. 135–6. *Cf. EAL*, p. 753. See also C. E. Bosworth, 'The Ṭāhirids and Arabic Culture,' *Journal of Semitic Studies*, 1969, vol. 14, 45–79; Bosworth, 'Ṭāhirids and Persian Literature'; Bosworth, 'The Ṭāhirids and Ṣaffārids,' in R. N. Frye (ed.), *Cambridge History of Iran*, vol. 4, *The Period from the Arab invasion to the Seljuqs*, Cambridge: Cambridge University Press, 1968, pp. 90–135.

54 Ibn Abī Ṭāhir's son ʿUbaydallāh, in the lost continuation to his father's history, is similarly attentive to a Persian dynasty, the Ṣaffārids. See n. 133 in chapter 4 above.

55 Stephen Belcher, 'Diffusion of the Book of Sindbād,' p. 48 (emphases mine); B. E. Perry, 'The Origins of the Book of Sindbād,' *Fabula*, 1960, vol. 3, 1–94. See also René Basset, 'Deux manuscrits d'une version arabe inédite du recueil des Sept vizirs,' *Journal asiatique*, 1903, 10ème série, vol. 2, 43–83.

56 Boyce, 'Middle Persian Literature,' 51–61; Belcher, 'Diffusion,' 47–8.

57 Ibn al-Faqīh, *Kitāb al-Buldān*, p. 319, lines 4–9. Ibn al-Faqīh also records an anecdote in which a Khurasanian man, responding to a caliph's question (neither is identified) about peoples in the East, describes the people of Marw al-Rūdh as the most intelligent and profound (p. 320, line 2).

58 See Rypka, 'History'; C. E. Bosworth, 'The Persian Impact on Arabic Literature,' in *CHALEUP*, pp. 483–96; and *EAL*, pp. 599–601.

59 Gustav Richter, *Studien zur Geschichte der älterer arabischen Fürstenspiegel*, Leipzig: J. C. Hinrichs, 1932; A. Dawood, 'A comparative study of Arabic and Persian Mirrors for

Princes from the 2nd to the 6th century AH,' dissertation, University of London, 1965. For the European *Fürstenspiegel* tradition, see *Dictionary of the Middle Ages*, ed. J. R. Strayer *et al.*, New York: Scribner, 1982–9, vol. 8, pp. 434–6. That in many cases the emphasis is on *Realpolitik* was first underscored by Grignaschi in 'Les "Rasā'il Arisṭāṭālīsa ilā-l-Iskandar".' Belcher, 'Diffusion,' 45, believes that the Anūshirwān anecdotes generically similar to those in the *Book of Sindbād* can be viewed as "contributory details reinforcing a connection between the *Book of Sindbād* and the historical traditions of the Persians, as they were known to 9th century Arabs." For doubts about *Fürstenspiegel*'s "genuinely Persian" origin, see Franz Rosenthal, *A History of Muslim Historiography*, 2nd edn, Leiden: E, J. Brill, 1968, p. 115, n. 2.

60 The mid third/ninth century *Kitāb al-Tāj* of Muḥammad ibn al-Ḥārith al-Thaʿlabī (fl. 247/861), on which see Gregor Schoeler, 'Verfasser und Titel des dem Ǧāḥiẓ zugeschrieben sog. *Kitāb at-Tāǧ*,' *Zeitschrift der Deutschen Morgenländischen Gesselschaft*, 1980, vol. 130, 217–25, addressed to al-Mutawakkil's bibliophile courtier and commander al-Fatḥ ibn al-Khāqān, is another classic example of the *naṣīḥat al-mulūk* genre; *cf.* Franz Rosenthal, 'From Arabic Books and Manuscripts XVI: As-Sarakhsī [?] on the Appropriate Behavior for Kings,' *Journal of the American Oriental Society*, 1995, vol. 115(1), 105–10. Once held to be the work of al-Jāḥiẓ, it has been shown to be by an Arabized Persian author: see Julie S. Meisami, *Medieval Persian Court Poetry*, Princeton: Princeton University Press, 1987, 6 ff. It shares its title with Ibn al-Muqaffaʿ's translation of the accounts of the Persian kings.

61 J. N. Mattock, 'The Arabic Tradition: Origins and Developments,' in *Dispute Poems and Dialogues*, pp. 153–63, does not think it plausible to postulate a direct link between Arabic and Sumerian debate literature and believes the genre developed independently. He cites absence of evidence of any interest in "the really ancient literatures and cultures of the Near East" (p. 153). This is of course an argument *e silentio*: he accordingly cautiously notes that there is too little evidence to resolve the question of origins; see also Ewald Wagner, 'Die arabische Rangstreitdichtung und ihre Einordnung in die allgemeine Literaturgeschichte,' *Akademie von Wissenschaften und Litteratur in Mainz*, 1962, vol. 8, 437–76. Those refining this picture include Sebastian Brock, 'The Dispute Poem: From Sumer to Syriac,' *Bayn al-Nahrayn*, 1979, vol. 7(28), 417–26, and G. J. H. van Gelder, 'The Conceit of Pen and Sword: An Arabic Literary Debate,' *Journal of Semitic Studies*, 1987, vol. 32(2), 329–60.

62 *Kitāb al-Tanbīh wa-al-ishrāf*, ed. M. J. de Goeje, Leiden: E. J. Brill, 1894, p. 106, lines 5–10 and ff.

63 The interest of ʿAbd al-Malik and Hisham in Persian stories and practices is well attested: see Bosworth, 'Heritage of Rulership.'

64 See J.-P. de Menasce, 'Zoroastrian Literature after the Muslim Conquest,' in Frye (ed.), *Cambridge History of Iran*, 1968, vol. 4, pp. 543–65; Boyce, 'Middle Persian Literature.'

65 *Fihrist*, p. 364, lines 13–17: 'Names of books composed by the Persians about the Lives (*siyar*) and True Stories (*al-asmār al-ṣaḥīḥah*) concerning their Kings.' The *Kārnāmah-ī Ardashīr Papakan* survives in the Pahlavi original, ed. and tr. D. P. Sanjana, Bombay: Education Society Steam Press, 1896. It is a short prose work probably written by priests in Fārs in the late Sasanian period. See Boyce, 'Middle Persian Literature,' p. 60, and Arthur Christensen, *Les gestes des rois dans les traditions de l'Iran antique*, Paris: Librairie orientaliste Paul Geuthner, 1936, p. 78.

66 See *Fihrist*, p. 132–5; Muḥammad Muḥammadī, *al-Tarjamah wa-al-naql ʿan al-Fārsiyyah fī al-qurūn al-Islāmiyyah al-ūlā*, vol. 1, Beirut: Manshūrāt Qism al-Lughah al-Fārisiyyah wa-Ādābihā fī al-Jāmiʿah al-Lubnāniyyah, 1964; Bosworth, 'Persian Impact,' pp. 486–92; and Cejpek, 'Iranian Folk-Literature,' pp. 622–4, who cites as an example of the importance of Arabic the fact that the story of *Ārash-i Shavātīr* exists in Arabic but is not mentioned by Firdawsī (d. *c.* 411/1020).

67 See n. 84 below.
68 See e.g. Miskawayh, *al-Ḥikmah al-khālidah* [= *Jāvidān-i khirad*], ed. ʿAbd al-Raḥmān Badawī, Cairo: Maktabat al-Naḥḍah al-Miṣriyyah, 1952.
69 But *cf.* Régis Blachère, *Histoire de la littérature arabe des origines à la fin du VXe siècle de J.-C.*, Paris: Adrien Maisonneuve, 1952, vol. 1, p. 90.
70 *Cf.* Ghazi, 'Littérature d'imagination,', p. 167, n. 1. For remarks about the 'drift' of pre-Islamic myth into *akhbār*, see Jaroslav Stetkevych, *Muḥammad and the Golden Bough*, Bloomington: Indiana University Press, 1997, especially pp. 1–13.
71 But *cf.* the far more Persianate *al-Akhbār al-ṭiwāl* (Long accounts) of al-Dīnawārī (d. before 290/902–03).
72 See Bosworth, 'An early Arabic mirror for princes.'
73 H. A. R. Gibb, 'The Social Significance of the Shuubiya,' in Gibb, *Studies on the Civilization of Islam*, ed. S. J. Shaw and W. R. Polk, Boston: Beacon Press, 1962, pp. 62–73.
74 Rypka ('History,' p. 130) believes that even this would not have survived had it not been for the *Shuʿūbiyyah* movement.
75 Al-Masʿūdī mentions Ibn al-Maghāzilī, an itinerant storyteller who performed during the caliphate of al-Muʿtaḍid (r. 279–89/892–902) (*Murūj*, ¶ 3300). See also Shmuel Moreh, *Live Theatre and Dramatic Literature in the Medieval Arab World*, New York: New York University Press, 1992.
76 On *qāṣṣ* and *qiṣṣah*, see Lane, p. 2528; Johannes Pedersen, 'The Islamic preacher: *wāʿiẓ, mudhakkir, qāṣṣ*,' in Samuel Löwinger and Joseph Somogyi (eds), *Ignace Goldziher Memorial Volume*, Budapest: Globus Nyomdai Müintézet, 1948, vol. 1, pp. 231–45; and Khalil ʿAthamina, 'Al-Qasas: its emergence, religious origin and its socio-political impact on early Muslim society,' *Studia Islamica*, 1992, vol. 76, pp. 53–74. The rallying power and influence of *qaṣaṣ*-storytellers was considerable. To control public unrest, they were, on at least two occasions, banned from telling their tales: see nn. 12 and 13 in chapter 2 above. The bans appear to have been directed principally at Ḥanbalī preachers but storytellers (recounting Persianate stories?) were also targeted.
77 Abbott, *Studies*, vol. 1, p. 53, n. 9.
78 For a useful discussion of the range of narrative material produced by, and available to, storytellers, see Blachère, *Histoire*, 737–803. The influence of Arabian lore should not be underestimated. The *Kitāb al-Mulūk wa-akhbār al-māḍīn* of ʿAbīd (/ʿUbayd) ibn Sharyah, for instance, is described by al-Masʿūdī (writing in 336/947) as well-known and widely circulated (*Murūj*, ¶ 1415): see E. W. Crosby, '*Akhbār al-Yaman wa-Ashʿāruhā wa-Ansābuhā*: The History, Poetry and Genealogy of the Yemen of ʿAbīd ibn Sharya al-Jurhumī,' dissertation, Yale University, 1985, and also the recently published article in *EI2*.
79 E.g. Quran 6:25, 8:31, 31:6.
80 Ibn Hishām, *Sīrat rasūl Allāh* [*Das Leben Muhammed's*], 2 vols in 3, ed. Ferdinand Wüstenfeld, Gottingen: Dieterische Universitäts-Buchhandlung, 1858–60, vol. 1, p. 191, lines 18–20; on al-Naḍr, see *EI2*, vol. 7, pp. 872–3. *Cf.* F. Bedrehi, who has suggested, on the basis of a Hadith in ʿAbdullāh Anṣārī's *Tafsīr-i Khvājeh*, that al-Ḥārith knew the *Kalīlah wa-Dimnah* stories rather than ones about Rustam and Isfandiyār: see Michael M. J. Fischer and Mehdi Abedi, *Debating Muslims: Cultural Dialogues in Postmodernity and Tradition*, Madison: University of Wisconsin Press, 1990, p. 462, n. 3.
81 Cited in *EI2*, vol. 3, pp. 367–72, where Pellat also contrasts "edifying" *ḥadīth, qiṣṣah, khabar, nabaʾ*, and *mathal* on the one hand, with the "dangerous, frivolous" *asmār, asāṭīr*, and *ḥikāyāt* on the other. On "fictional" stories, see the arguments of Drory, 'Three Attempts to Legitimize Fiction'; *EAL*, pp. 228–30; and ʿAbdel-Meguid, 'Survey of the Terms.'
82 *Fihrist*, p. 134, lines 12–13.

83 The ʿAlī ibn Dāwūd who abets his brother, Abū ʿAbdallāh Yaʿqūb, in the revolt of Muḥammad and Ibrāhīm ibn ʿAbdallāh against al-Manṣūr in 145/762 mentioned in al-Jahshiyārī, *al-Wuzarāʾ*, p. 114, lines 3–23, may be the same individual.

84 The *Khwadāy Nāmag* [Book of kings] possibly translated into Arabic by Muḥammad ibn al-Jahm (d. after 227/842) as the *Kitāb Siyar mulūk al-ʿAjam* (see Gérard Lecomte, 'Muḥammad b. al-Ǧahm al-Barmakī, gouverneur philosophe, jugé par Ibn Qutayba,' *Arabica*, 1958, vol. 5, 263–71), focuses on the life of Zoroaster – and may have been a prototype of the *Shāhnāmeh.* See also Mary Boyce, 'Middle Persian Literature,' in Ilya Gershevitch *et al.* (eds), *Handbuch der Orientalistik*, vol. 4, *Iranistik*, 2(1): *Litteratur*, Leiden: E. J. Brill, 1968, pp. 57–60.

85 Ibn al-Muqaffaʿ's translation into Arabic of *Kalīlah wa-Dimnah* is from Burzōē's Middle Persian version (*Kalīlag u Dimnag*) of the Sanskrit *Pacatantra*: see Denison Ross, 'Ibn Muqaffaʿ and the Burzoë Legend,' *Journal of the Royal Asiatic Society*, 1926, p. 505; *cf.* Rypka, 'History,' p. 222. See also François de Blois, *Burzōy's voyage to India and the origin of the book of Kalīlah wa Dimnah*, London: Royal Asiatic Society, 1990.

86 See *EAL*, p. 150.

87 See Charles Pellat, *Ibn al-Muqaffaʿ, mort vers 140/757 "Conseilleur du calife"*, Paris: G.-P. Maisonneuve et Larose, 1976; J. D. Latham, 'Ibn al-Muqaffaʿ,' in *CHALABL*, pp. 64–72; and Said A. Arjomand, "Abd Allah Ibn al-Muqaffaʿ and the ʿAbbasid Revolution,' *Iranian Studies*, 1994, vol. 27/1–4, 9–36.

88 See Arjomand, "Abd Allah Ibn al-Muqaffaʿ'.

89 See Crone, *Slaves on Horses*, p. 70.

90 See L. A. Karp, 'Sahl b. Hārūn: The Man and his Contribution to Adab,' dissertation, Harvard University, 1992; and *EI2*, vol. 8, pp. 838–40. Ibn Abī Ṭāhir's reference in al-Ḥātimī, *Ḥilyat al-muḥāḍarah*, 1979, vol. 2, p. 45, lines 9–10, suggests a professional acquaintance with the poetry of Sahl.

91 Ibn al-ʿAbbār, *Iʿtāb al-kuttāb*, ed. Ṣāliḥ al-ʿAshtar, Damascus: Majmaʿ al-Lughah al-ʿArabiyyah, 1961, pp. 85–6.

92 Ghazi, 'Littérature d'imagination,' p. 166.

93 Ibn Bassām al-Shantarīnī, *al-Dhakhīrah fī maḥāsin ahl al-Jazīrah*, ed. Iḥsān ʿAbbās, Beirut: Dār al-Thaqāfah, 1399/1979, vol. 2, part 2, p. 729, line 12: "*takallamta bi-lisān Sahl ibn Hārūn*," "You speak with the tongue of Sahl ibn Hārūn."

94 See e.g. al-Jāḥiẓ, *al-Bayān wa-al-tabyīn*, vol. 1, p. 52, lines 1–5.

95 *Fihrist*, p. 133, lines 21–2; al-Ḥuṣrī, *Zahr al-ādāb*, vol. 1, p. 577, line 8.

96 Ibn Nubātah, *Sarḥ al-ʿuyūn fī Risālat Ibn Zaydūn*, ed. M. A. Ibrāhīm, Cairo: Dār al-Fikr al-ʿArabī, 1964, p. 244; al-Ḥuṣrī, *Zahr al-ādāb*, vol. 1, p. 577, line 9.

97 *Fihrist*, p. 134, line 2.

98 Hārūn al-Rashīd figures prominently in many of the stories of the third/ninth century (and after). This is borne out not only by his central presence in the *Thousand and One Nights* but also e.g. in the anonymous *Jawhar al-anfās fī akhbār banī al-ʿAbbās* (MS Qq-133, Cambridge University Library), in which numerous stories relate to Hārūn: see Joseph Sadan, 'Kings and Craftsmen: A Pattern of Contrasts; On the History of a Medieval Arabic Humoristic Form. Part 1,' *Studia Islamica*, 1982, vol. 56, 5–49.

99 Mohsen Zakeri believes the work on al-Maʾmūn was a possible source for al-Ṭabarī; he does not specify whether he considers Ibn Abī Ṭāhir an intermediary: *EI2*, vol. 8, p. 839.

100 *Fihrist*, p. 134, line 3 and p. 133, line 12. This title is very similar to ʿAlī ibn ʿUbaydah al-Rayḥānī's (d. 219/834) *Kitāb Warūd wa-Wadūd*: see *Fihrist*, p. 133, line 16. Ghazi, 'Littérature d'imagination,' p. 166, reads *Nadūd wa-Wadūd wa-Ladūd* but does not see (or mention) the possible connection between the titles.

101 *Fihrist*, p. 134, lines 2–5. Ashk was an Arsacid King.

102 See Miskawayh, *Ḥikmah*; Dimitri Gutas, *Greek Wisdom Literature in Arabic Translation: A Study of the Graeco-Arabic Gnomologia*, New Haven: American Oriental Society, 1975; Karel van der Toorn, 'The Ancient Near Eastern Literary Dialogue as a Vehicle of Critical Reflection,' in *Dispute Poems and Dialogues*, 1991, pp. 72, 73; J. J. A. van Dijk, *La sagesse suméro-accadienne*, Leiden: E. J. Brill, 1953, pp. 23 ff; and Helmut Brünner, *Altägyptische Erziehung*, Wiesbaden: Otto Harrassowitz, 1956, pp. 101–2.
103 *Fihrist*, p. 134, line 5. *Cf.* the stories about Ardashīr, King of Babylon, and his minister Arnūyah (*Fihrist*, p. 365, line 12).
104 See Ibn al-Dāyah, *al-ʿUhūd al-Yunāniyyah*, in ʿUmar al-Mālikī, *al-Falsafah al-siyāsiyyah ʿinda al-ʿArab*, Algiers: al-Sharikah al-Waṭaniyyah li-al-Nashr wa-l-Tawzīʿ, 1971.
105 See G. J. Reinink and H. L. J. Vanstiphout, 'Introduction,' in *Dispute Poems and Dialogues*, 1991, p. 1.
106 H. T. Norris, '*Shuʿūbiyyah* in Arabic Literature,' in *CHALABL*, p. 31. See also Roy P. Mottahedeh, 'The *Shuʿūbīyah* controversy and the social history of early Islamic Iran,' *International Journal of Middle East Studies*, 1976, vol. 7, 161–82; Gibb, 'Social Significance'; and Goldziher, *Muslim Studies*, vol. 1, pp. 137–98.
107 Gibb, 'Social Significance,' p. 69.
108 Goldziher, *Muslim Studies*, vol. 1, p. 60.
109 Norris, '*Shuʿūbiyyah*,' p. 31.
110 Gaudefroy-Demombynes (ed. and tr.), *Introduction au "Livre de la poésie et des poètes"*, 1947, p. xiii; and *EAL*, p. 717.
111 Rypka, 'History,' pp. 141–2.
112 Gibb, 'Social Significance,' p. 66.
113 *EI2*, vol. 9, pp. 513–16.
114 *EI2*, vol. 9, p. 514 (emphases mine).
115 *Fihrist*, 112, line 19.
116 *Cf.* Goldziher, *Muslim Studies*, vol. 1, pp. 115–22.
117 Edited by M. Kurd ʿAli as *Kitab al-ʿArab aw al-radd ʿala al-Shuʿubiyyah*, in *Rasaʾil al-Bulaghaʾ*, 4th edn, Cairo: Maṭbaʿat Lajnat al-Taʾlīf wa-al-Tarjamah wa-al-Nashr, 1374/1954, pp. 344–77. The anonymous author of *Raqāʾiq al-ḥilal fī daqāʾiq al-ḥiyal* [= *The Subtle Ruse: The Book of Arabic Wisdom and Guile*], tr. René R. Khawam, London and The Hague: East-West Publications, 1980, p. 15, calls the work *Faḍl al-ʿArab ʿalā al-ʿAjam.*
118 See Mottahedeh, 'Shuʿūbīyah controversy,' 164–73 for ways in which anti-*Shuʿūbī* (properly, non-*Shuʿūbī*) exegetes deployed a genealogical interpretation of the Quranic proof text to show that *shaʿb* referred specifically to *genealogical* lineage.
119 The work in defense of the Persians entitled *Manāqib al-ʿAjam* [The virtues of the Persians] is by another Abū ʿUthmān Saʿīd ibn Ḥumayd, also of Persian origin.
120 *Book of the superiority of dogs over many of those who wear clothes* by Ibn al-Marzubān, ed. and tr. G. R. Smith and M. Abdel Haleem, Warminster: Aris & Phillips, 1978 (first edited by Louis Cheikho, in *Machriq*, 1909, vol. 15, 515–31). On Muḥammad ibn Khalaf ibn al-Marzubān (d. 309/921–2), see *Fihrist*, pp. 166–67. Note that his *Kitāb Akhbār Ibn Qays al-Ruqayyāt wa-mukhtār shiʿrih* [Reports about Ibn Qays al-Ruqayyāt and a selection of his poetry], *Kitāb al-Sūdān wa-faḍlihim ʿalā al-bīḍān* [Black folk and their superiority to white folk], *Kitāb Alqāb al-shuʿarāʾ* [Nicknames of the poets], *Kitāb al-Shiʿr wa-al-shuʿarāʾ* [Poetry and poets], *Kitāb al-Hadāyā* [Gifts], *Kitāb al-Nisāʾ wa-al-ghazal* [Women and love poems], and *Kitāb Dhamm al-ḥijāb wa-al-ʿitāb ʿalā al-muḥtajab* [The censure of seclusion and the reproof of the secluded] all have titles similar to ones by Ibn Abī Ṭāhir (*Fihrist*, p. 167, lines 1, 3, 4, 5). Ibn al-Nadīm does note that Ibn al-Marzubān "follows the method of Aḥmad ibn Ṭāhir" (*Fihrist*, p. 166, line 27) by which he probably means Aḥmad Ibn *Abī* Ṭāhir. Significantly, Ibn al-Marzubān is

included in the same "section" of the *Fihrist* as Ibn Abī Ṭāhir (see chapter 7 below). Ibn al-Marzubān relied upon Ibn Abī Ṭāhir directly and indirectly for information in his works: there are three cases of direct citation in the short *Kitāb Faḍl al-kilāb* (Ibn al-Marzubān, *Book of the superiority of dogs*, pp. 13, 15, 25 [Ar. pag.]), and he is important as the link between Ibn Abī Ṭāhir and Abū al-Faraj and Abū al-ʿAynāʾ and Abū al-Faraj, as numerous lines of transmission in the *Aghānī*, e.g. vol. 1, p. 244, line 1 (art. ʿUmar ibn Abī Rabīʿah), attest.

121 *Fihrist*, p. 164, line 12.

122 *Fihrist*, p. 169, line 13; al-Ṣūlī, *Ashʿār awlād al-khulafāʾ wa-akhbāruhum min Kitāb al-Awrāq*, ed. J. Heyworth-Dunne, London: Luzac and Co., 1936, p. 325, lines 7–8.

123 *Fihrist*, p. 169, lines 12.

124 Norris, '*Shuʿūbiyyah*,' p. 44.

125 Published in *al-Tuḥfah al-bahiyyah wa-al-ṭurfah al-shahiyyah fīhā sabʿah ʿasharah majmūʿah muntakhabah tashtamil ʿalā adabīyāt muʿjibah wa-nawādir muṭribah*, no ed., Istanbul: Jawāʾib, 1302/1884–5.

126 al-Bīrūnī, *al-Āthār al-bāqiyah ʿan al-qurūn al-khāliyah. Chronologie orientalisticher Volker*, ed. C. Eduard Sachau, Leipzig: Brockhaus, 1878; reprint 1923, p. 52.

127 Goldziher, *Muslim Studies*, vol. 1, pp. 192–3; Eugen Mittwoch, 'Die literarische Tätigkeit Ḥamza al-Iṣbahānīs,' *Mitteillungen des Seminars für Orientalische Sprachen*, 1909, vol. 12, 109–69.

128 See *EI2*, vol. 1, p. 158, and vol. 2, p. 729.

129 Ibn Qutaybah, *Kitāb al-ʿArab*, in *Rasāʾil al-bulaghāʾ*, ed. Kurd ʿAlī, p. 346.

130 al-Bīrūnī, *al-Āthār al-bāqiyah*, p. 278. See Joseph von Hammer-Purgstall, 'Über die Menschenklasse welche von den Arabern Schoubijje genannt wird,' *Sitzungsberichte der Kais. Akademie der Wissenschaften in Wien, Philosophische-historische Klasse*, 1848, vol. 1, 330–87.

131 *EI2*, vol. 2, pp. 728–9.

6 PRECEDENCE AND CONTEST

1 Alfred von Kremer, *Culturgeschichte des Orients unter den Chalifen*, 2 vols, Vienna: W. Braumüller, 1875–77; reprint Aalen: Scientia Verlag, 1966, vol. 2, pp. 154 ff. See also *EAL*, pp. 186 and 284–5.

2 Goldziher, *Muslim Studies*, vol. 1, p. 57 ff., notes that the *mufākharah* (contest, or dispute, for precedence), as well as the *shiʿār* (war cry) and *taḥāluf* (tribal alliance), were manifestations of the old tribal mentality rejected by egalitarian Islam

3 In spite of his suggestions that the *Maḥāsin/Masāwī* and *Tafḍīl/Faḍāʾil* genres are rhetorical exercise, Ibrahim Kh. Geries, *Un genre littéraire arabe: al-Maḥâsin wa-l-masâwî*, Paris: G.-P. Maisonneuve et Larose, 1977, p. 22, n. 4, nonetheless believes that *Tafḍīl al-baṭn ʿalā al-ẓahr* [The superiority of the belly over the back], and *Fī dhamm al-liwāṭ* [Censure of homosexuals] "clearly indicate [al-Jāḥiẓ's] position on the subject," revealing an inconsistency in his own position.

4 Mattock, 'The Arabic Tradition,' p. 155. Al-Jāḥiẓ is, incidentally, the source for Bashshār's verse on the superiority of fire to earth, which formed part of an exchange with the poet Ṣafwān al-ʿAnṣārī: see al-Jāḥiẓ, *al-Bayān wa-al-tabyīn*, vol. 1, pp. 27, line 5 and ff.

5 On definitions of the literary debate, see Reinink and Vanstiphout, 'Introduction,' in *Dispute Poems and Dialogues*, p. 1; and H. Massé, 'Du genre littéraire 'Débat' en arabe et en persan,' *Cahiers de civilisation médiévale*, 1961, vol. 4, 137–47.

6 al-Tanūkhī, *al-Faraj baʿd al-shiddah*, vol. 4, p. 433, line 23: *aktharu qadran wa aghrazu fāʾidatan*. Ibn Lankak is the poet Abū al-Ḥusayn Muḥammad al-Baṣrī (d. *c.* 360/970).

7 *Cf.* the remarks of ʿA. A. Farrāj in *Ṭabaqāt al-shuʿarāʾ*, p. 11.
8 Ibn al-Rūmī, *Dīwān*, ed. ʿA. ʿA. Muḥannā, Cairo: Dār wa-Maktabat al-Hilāl, 1991, vol. 2, pp. 161–3 (#470).
9 Heinrichs, 'Rose versus Narcissus. Observations on an Arabic Literary Debate,' in *Dispute Poems and Dialogues*, p. 184, believes that "it all started with Ibn al-Rūmī."
10 Ibn al-Rūmī, *Dīwān*, vol. 2, pp. 161–2, lines 10–11.
11 al-Tanūkhī, *al-Faraj baʿd al-shiddah*, ed. ʿAbbūd al-Shāljī, Beirut: Dār Ṣādir, 1398/1978, vol. 4, p. 433, line 22 to p. 434, line 5.
12 On Ibn Abī Ṭāhir's dislike of al-Buḥturī, see chapter 1 above and chapter 7 below; on Ibn al-Rūmī, see Rhuvon Guest, *Life and Works of Ibn Er Rûmî*, London: Luzac & Co., 1944, p. 44; on his panegyric, see Beatrice Gruendler, *Medieval Arabic Praise Poetry: Ibn al-Rūmī and the patron's redemption*, London and New York: RoutledgeCurzon, 2003.
13 Cited in *Irshād*, vol. 17, p. 141: *Qawmun idhā khāfū ʿadāwata ḥāsidin/safakū ʾd-dimā bi-asinnati ʾl-qalāmi.*
14 Al-Ṣafadī, *Nakt al-himyān fī nukat al-ʿumyān*, ed. Aḥmad Zakī, Cairo: Maṭbaʿat al-Jamāliyyah, 1911, reprint Baghdad: Maktabat al-Muthannā, 1963, p. 267, line 10: *wa-marra yawman ʿalā dār ʿaduwwin lahu*
15 Ibn al-Rūmī, *Dīwān*, vol. 3, p. 996 (#754):

Innī saʾaltu ʾbna abī Ṭāhirin
lim tanbaḥu ʾl-badra idhā mā bahar
Fa-qāla lī aḥsuduhū ḥusnahū
wa annahū ʿālin yafūqu ʾl-bashar
Qultu fa-inna ʾsh-shamsa qad ūtiyat
hādhā wa mā tanbaḥu ghayra ʾl-qamar
Fa-qāla yuʿshī baṣarī ḍawʾuhā
wa laysa ḍawʾu ʾl-badri yuʿshī ʾl-baṣar

16 al-Mīkālī, *al-Muntakhab*, MS, Topkapı Sarayı 8561 A. 2634, fol. 127b = *Kitāb al-Muntakhal*, 2 vols, ed. Y. W. al-Jubūrī, Beirut: Dār al-Gharb al-Islāmī, 2000, vol. 1, p. 495 (#1403). I am grateful to Jamal Elias for having transcribed the *Muntakhab* lines for me from the Topkapı manuscript.
17 Ibn al-Rūmī, *Dīwān*, vol. 3, p. 1068 (#816):

Man kāna min ṭālibī ʾl-anbāʾi yasʾalunī
ʿani ʾl-kilābi limādhā tanbaḥu ʾl-qamarā
Fa laysa yaʿrifu lim yanbaḥnahu aḥadun
illā ʾmruʾun kāna kalban mithlahā ʿuṣurā
Wa-hwa ʾl-mukannī abāhu baʿda mahlakihi
bi-Ṭāhirin wa la-ʿumri ʾllāhi mā ṭahurā
Fa-sāʾilūhu limādhā kāna yanbaḥuhū
fa-inna ṣāḥibakum yūfikumu ʾl-khabarā

18 Ibn al-Rūmī, *Dīwān*, vol. 3, pp. 986–7 (#741):

Faqadtuka yā ʾbna Abī Ṭāhirin
wa uṭʿimtu thuklaka min shāʿiri
Fa-lasta bi-sukhnin wa lā bāridin
wa mā bayna dhayni siwā ʾl-fātiri
Wa anta kadhāka tughaththā ʾn-nufū
-sa taghthiyata ʾl-fātiri ʾl-khāthiri
Tadhabdhaba fannaka bayna ʾl-funū
-ni fa-lā fannun bādin wa lā ḥāḍiri
Raʾaytuka tanbuḥunī sādiran
ka-fiʿlika bi ʾl-qamari ʾl-bāhiri

Wa mā zāla dhālika di'ba 'l-kilā
-bi wa mā dhāka li 'l-badri bi 'd-dā'iri
Wa inna qisayya la-mawtūratun
bi-kulli amīni 'l-quwā hādiri
Wa-inna sihāmī la-mabriyatun
ka-hammika min ʿuddati 'th-thā'iri
Wa-lākin waqāka miʿrātihā
Taḍā'ulu qadrika fī 'l-khāṭiri
Fa-lā takhshā min ashumī qāṣidan
wa-lā ta'manānna mijn al-ʿā'iri

See nn. 4–8 for variant readings. The first 3 lines are also, with slight variation, in Ibn Rashīq, *al-ʿUmdah*, p. 186, and al-Ḥuṣrī, *Jamʿ al-jawāhir*, p. 8.

19 Ibn al-Rūmī, *Dīwān*, vol. 1, p. 103:

Faqadtuka yā 'bna abī Ṭāhirin
Wa uṭmiʿtu thuklāka qabl al-ʿashā'
Fa-lā bardu shiʿrika bardu 'sh-sharābi
Wa lā ḥarru shiʿrika ḥarr aṣ-ṣalā'

20 al-Washshā', *al-Muwashshā, aw al-Ẓarf wa-l-ẓurafā'*, Beirut: Dār Ṣādir, and Dār Bayrūt, 1385/1965, pp. 204–6.
21 al-Washshā', *al-Muwashshā*, p. 206, line 8 and p. 204, line 3.
22 *Fihrist*, p. 164, lines 1, 12.
23 On the narcissus and its virtues, see e.g. al-Ghuzūlī, *Maṭāliʿ al-budūr fī manāzil al-surūr*, Cairo: Maktabat Idārat al-Waṭan, 1299/1882, vol. 1, pp. 99–104.
24 al-Washshā', *al-Muwashshā*, pp. 205–6.
25 al-Suyūṭī, *Ḥusn al-muḥāḍarah fī akhbār Miṣr wa-al-Qāhirah*, Cairo: Maktabah al-Sharafiyyah, 1321/1903, vol. 2, p. 401, lines 14–16 and p. 417, lines 4–6; *cf.* Philip K. Hitti, *History of the Arabs*, 7th edn, London: Macmillan & Co. and New York: St. Martin's Press, 1960, p. 352. (Al-Burāq was the Prophet's mount on his night-journey: see *EAL*, vol. 7, pp. 97, 105.)
26 al-Nawājī, *Ḥalbat al-kumayt fī al-adab wa-al-nawādir al-mutaʿalliqah bi-al-khamriyyāt*, no ed., Cairo: Maktabat Idārat al-Waṭan, 1299/1881, reprint al-Maktabah al-ʿĀlamiyyah, 1938, p. 235, lines 16–17; *cf.* al-Suyūṭī, *Ḥusn al-muḥāḍarah*, vol. 2, p. 402, lines 1–7. Boustany, *Ibn ar-Rūmī*, p. 340, suggests, but without supporting evidence, that it was in support of this particular sentiment that Ibn Abī Ṭāhir composed his work on the debate between the rose and narcissus. Boustany also refers to Ibn Abī Ṭāhir as one of the caliph's "favorites," without evidence.
27 al-Tanasī, *Naẓm al-durr wa-al-ʿiqyān*, ed. Nouri Soudan, Wiesbaden: F. Steiner, 1980, p. 151.
28 Mattock, 'The Arabic Tradition,' p. 157; al-Māridīnī, 'al-Muḥāwarah bayn al-ward wa-al-narjis,' in ʿIzzat al-ʿAṭṭār (ed.), *Munāẓarāt fī al-adab*, Cairo: Lajnat al-Shabībah al-Sūriyyah, 1943, pp. 20–9. See also the *Anwār al-saʿd wa nuwwār al-majd fī al-mufākharah bayn al-narjis wa-al-ward* [Lights of happiness and flowers of glory: The debate between the narcissus and the rose] of Tāj al-dīn ʿAbd al-Bāqī ibn ʿAbd al-Majīd, preserved in al-Nuwayrī, *Nihāyah*, vol. 11, pp. 207–13; and Heinrichs, 'Rose vs Narcissus,' p. 193, n. 29.
29 al-Jāḥiẓ's *Kitāb Mufākharat al-jawārī wa-al-ghilmān* in *Rasā'il al-Jāḥiẓ*, vol. 2, pp. 87–137.
30 Mattock, 'The Arabic Tradition,' pp. 160, 159.
31 Mattock, 'The Arabic Tradition,' p. 156.
32 Heinrichs, 'Rose vs Narcissus,' p. 187; Ibn Ghānim al-Maqdisī (d. 678/1279?), *Kitāb Kashf al-asrār ʿan ḥikam al-ṭuyūr wa-al-azhār. Revelation of the Secrets of the Birds and Flowers,*

ed. Denise Winn, tr. Irene Hoare and Darya Galy, London: Octagon Press, 1980, reprint of the edition of J. H. Garcin de Tassy, Paris: Imprimerie Royale, 1821.

33 Mattock, 'The Arabic Tradition,' p. 157 (emphasis mine).

34 Both are in al-Ḥimyarī, *al-Badīʿ fī waṣf al-rabīʿ*, ed. Henri Pérès, rev. edn, Rabat: Manshūrāt Dār al-Āfāq al-Jadīdah, 1989, pp. 46–9 (response by al-Ḥimyarī, pp. 49–51). On Aḥmad ibn Burd, and for a translation of the debate, see Fernando de la Granja, 'Dos epistolas de Aḥmad ibn Burd al-Aṣgar,' *al-Andalus*, 1960, vol. 25, 383–418. See also Heinrichs, 'Rose vs Narcissus,' pp. 186–93.

The first *surviving* example in the literary debate genre in general, between pen and sword, is also by Aḥmad ibn Burd: see van Gelder, 'Conceit of Pen and Sword.' It is identified as the first *Andalusian* example of its genre, making it part of a tradition. For a recently published debate, see Ibrahim Kh. Geries (ed. and tr.), *A Literary and Gastronomical Conceit. Mufākharat al-Ruzz wa 'l-Ḥabb Rummān: The Boasting Debate Between Rice and Pomegranate Seeds, or al-Maḳāma al-Simāṭiyya (The Tablecloth Maḳāma)*, Wiesbaden: Harrassowitz, 2002.

35 Heinrichs, 'Rose vs Narcissus,' p. 187, and analyzed at pp. 187–93.

36 Heinrichs, 'Rose vs Narcissus,' p. 187. The rose is described by an unnamed flower as the king (*malik*) and one whose effect lasts even when his substance is lost (*in fuqida ʿaynuh lam yufqad atharuh*).

37 al-Ḥimyarī, *Badīʿ*, p. 49, line 8.

38 Boustany, *Ibn ar-Rūmī*, pp. 339 ff.

39 Gregor Schoeler, *Arabische Naturdichtung: die Zahrīyāt, Rabīʿīyāt und Rauḍiyāt von ihren Anfängen bis aṣ-Ṣanaubarī*, Beirut/Wiesbaden: Otto Harrassowitz, 1974, pp. 213–15.

40 Heinrichs, 'Rose vs Narcissus,' p. 184.

41 Heinrichs, 'Rose vs Narcissus,' p. 184 (emphasis mine).

42 See Maḥmūd al-Rabdāwī, *al-Ḥarakah al-naqdiyyah ḥawla madhhab Abī Tammām. I: Fī al-qadīm*, Beirut: Dār al-Fikr, 1967. For the third/ninth century, see especially pp. 97–102 and 219–24. For *badīʿ* and Abū Tammām's poetry, see Stetkevych, *Abū Tammām*, *passim.*

43 *Cf.* Arazi, 'De la voix au calame.'

44 *Irshād*, vol. 3, p. 252, line 7.

45 *Irshād*, vol. 3, p. 252, lines 7–8: *wa yufaḍḍilu al-Buḥturī ʿalā Abī Tammām.*

46 *Murūj*, ¶¶ 2839–40.

47 Stetkevych, *Abū Tammām*, p. 40.

48 al-Ṣūlī, *Akhbār Abī Tammām*, p. 4, lines 2–3 and 6–11. I revise the translation in Stetkevych, *Abū Tammām*, p. 39, but retain her emphasis.

49 On Abū Tammām, see *EAL*, pp. 47–9 and the references cited there, and Margaret Larkin, 'Abu Tammam,' in Michael Cooperson and Shawkat M. Toorawa (eds), *Arabic Literary Culture 500–925*, Detroit: Gale, 2005, in press.

50 On the composition of the *Ḥamāsah*, reportedly compiled by Abū Tammām while snowed in at the home of Abū al-Wafā' in Hamadhān on his way back from seeing ʿAbdallāh ibn Ṭāhir in Khurasān, see Stetkevych, *Abū Tammām*, pp. 282–356.

51 On al-Buḥturī, see *EAL*, pp. 161–2 and the references cited there, and Samer Mahdy Ali, 'al-Buhturi,' in Michael Cooperson and Shawkat M. Toorawa (eds), *Arabic Literary Culture 500–925*, Detroit: Gale, 2005, in press.

52 It was likely at the home of the ʿAlī al-Thughrī (d. 236/850–1) that al-Buḥturī met Abū Tammām (al-Ṣūlī, *Akhbār al-Buḥturī*, p. 63, line 3 to p. 64, line 1 [#12]); *cf.* Saleh Achtor, 'L'Enfance et la jeunesse du poète Buḥturī (206–226/821–840),' *Arabica*, 1954, vol. 1, p. 178.

53 See, for instance, al-Ṣūlī, *Akhbār al-Buḥturī*, p. 119, line 3 (#65): "We were surprised by his speed [of composition] as he was not a master of spontaneity (*laysa bi-ṣāḥib badīh*)," and also the self-characterization in al-Ṣūlī, *Akhbār al-Buḥturī*, p. 91, line 3 (#33) (*wa lam akun ṣāḥib badīh*).

54 al-Badīʿī, *Ṣubḥ al-munabbī fī ḥaythiyyat al-Mutanabbī*, ed. M. Y. ʿArafah, Damascus: Maktabat ʿArafah, 1350/1931, p. 108, line 10. *Cf.* Ibn Rashīq, *al-ʿUmdah*, p. 155, line 11 to p. 156, line 7 for a characterization of Abū Tammām and al-Buḥturī eclipsing other contemporary poets, such as Abū Hiffān and al-Jammāz.

55 Ibn Rashīq, *al-ʿUmdah*, p. 327, lines 5–6.

56 al-Ḥātimī, *al-Risālah al-Mūḍiḥah fī dhikr sariqāt Abī al-Ṭayyib al-Mutanabbī wa-sāqit shiʿrihi*, ed. M. Y. Najm, Beirut: Dār Ṣādir/Dār Bayrūt, 1965, p. 161. Al-Āmidī's *Muwāzanah* is also known as *Kitāb al-Muwāzanah bayn al-Ṭāʾīyayn* (see e.g. *Irshād*, vol. 8, p. 75, line 8).

57 al-Āmidī, *al-Muwāzanah*, vol. 1, pp. 112–33, 276.

58 al-Āmidī, *al-Muwāzanah*, vol. 3, part 2, p. 511, line 6.

59 al-Āmidī, *al-Muwāzanah*, vol. 1, pp. 112–33. The reference by al-Ṣūlī in *Akhbār Abī Tammām*, p. 79, lines 12–13, to a book on the borrowings (*akhdh*) of al-Buḥturī from Abū Tammām by a littérateur (*baʿḍ ahl al-adab*) is possibly to Ibn Abī Ṭāhir's work. The editors of the *Akhbār Abī Tammām* suggest that al-Ṣūlī's might mean Abū al-Ḍiyāʾ Bishr ibn Yaḥyā (see p. 79, n. 4), but this may just as easily be a reference to Ibn Abī Ṭāhir

60 al-Āmidī, *al-Muwāzanah*, vol. 1, p. 112; translation from Stetkevych, *Abū Tammām*, p. 53.

61 al-Marzubānī, *al-Muwashshaḥ*, p. 510, line 3, and p. 511, line 8.

62 al-Marzubānī, *al-Muwashshaḥ*, p. 515, lines 11–12.

63 See Gustav E. von Grunebaum, 'The Concept of Plagiarism in Arabic Theory,' 1944, vol. 3, 234–53; Wolfhart Heinrichs, 'Literary Theory: The Problem of Its Efficiency,' in Gustav E. von Grunebaum (ed.), *Arabic Poetry: Theory and Development*, Wiesbaden: Otto Harrassowitz, 1973, pp. 19–70; Heinrichs, 'An Evaluation of *Sariqa*,' *Quaderni di Studi Arabi*, 1987–88, vol. 5–6, 357–68; Abdelfattah Kilito, *L'auteur et ses doubles: Essai sur la culture arabe classique*, Paris: Editions du Seuil, 1985, pp. 24–40; and al-Rabdāwī, *al-Ḥarakah al-naqdiyyah*.

64 A brief citation is included by al-Āmidī in *al-Muwāzanah*, vol. 3, part 2, p. 511, line 6.

65 al-Rabdāwī, *al-Ḥarakah al-naqdiyyah*, pp. 97–102, groups Ibn Abī Ṭāhir in the 'first wave' of writers to treat plagiarism as a distinct subject, and also identifies him as one of three third/ninth century *kātibs* (sic) to write on the subject, the others being Abū al-Ḍiyāʾ Bishr ibn Yaḥyā (d. ?) and ʿAlī ibn Yaḥyā al-Munajjim (d. 275/888); *cf.* Ahmed Trabulsi, *La critique poétique des arabes jusqu'au Vè siècle de l'Hégire (XIè siècle de J.C.)*, Damascus: Institut français de Damas, 1955, p. 194.

66 ʿAbd al-Qādir al-Baghdādī, *Khizānat al-adab*, 13 vols, ed. ʿA. M. Hārūn, Cairo: Dār al-Kutub, n.d., vol. 3, p. 240, lines 4–6; al-Marzubānī, *al-Muwashshaḥ*, pp. 519–20.

67 al-Ḥātimī, *Ḥilyat al-muḥāḍarah fī ṣināʿat al-shiʿr*, vol. 2, ed. Jaʿfar al-Kitābī, Baghdad: Dār al-Ḥurriyyah li al-Ṭibāʿah/Dār al-Rashīd li al-Nashr, 1979, p. 28.

68 al-Ḥuṣrī, *Zahr al-ādāb*, vol. 1, p. 152, lines 7–8, reports that Ibn Abī Ṭāhir asked Abū Tammām whether he took (*akhadhta*) an idea/motif from another poet, to which Abū Tammām responded in the affirmative, identifying Bashshār ibn Burd.

69 al-Ṣūlī, *Akhbār Abū Tammām*, p. 245, lines 10–11.

70 al-Marzubānī, *al-Muwashshaḥ*, p. 511. Al-Marzubānī mentions another poem in which Ibn Abī Ṭāhir satirizes al-Buḥturī but quotes only the closing line: *Wa qad qatalnāka bi 'l-hijāʾi wa lā-/-kinnaka kalbun qad iltawā dhanabuhu*, "We slew you with satire, but you were a dog with its tail between its legs": see al-Marzubānī, *al-Muwashshaḥ*, p. 537; also in al-Ḥusaynī, *Naḍrat al-ighrīḍ fī nuṣrat al-qarīḍ*, ed. N. ʿA. al-Ḥasan, Damascus: Maṭbūʿāt Majmaʿ al-Lughah al-ʿArabiyyah, 1976, p. 210, where it is cited as an example of *sariqah*. See also al-Ṣūlī, *Akhbār al-Buḥturī*, p. 78 (#22). Al-Rāghib al-Iṣfahānī also records two verses by Ibn Abī Ṭāhir in response to al-Buḥturī's allegations of plagiarism (*Muḥāḍarāt al-udabāʾ*, vol. 1, p. 86):

Ash-shiʿru ẓahru ṭarīqin anta rākibuhū
fa-minhu munshaʿibun aw ghayru munshaʿibī

Wa rubbamā ḍamma bayna ar-rakbi manhajuhū
wa alṣaqa 'ṭ-ṭunuba 'l-ʿālī ilā 'ṭ-ṭunubī

71 *Fihrist*, p. 163, lines 9–13. For the whole passage, see chapter 3 above.
72 *Qaṣā'id*, p. 9 (in the section of his introduction devoted to Ibn Abī Ṭāhir's *formation* and teachers). Huart, Rosenthal, and Ḍayf believe this too.
73 Note the paronomasia between *taṣḥīf* (al-Buḥturī) and *tasaffaḥtu* (Ibn Abī Ṭāhir).
74 al-Ṣūlī, *Akhbār al-Buḥturī*, pp. 131–2 (#83); *cf.* p. 112 (#57).
75 See al-Ṣūlī, *Akhbār Abī Tammām*, p. 173, lines 1–15.
76 See al-Ṣūlī, *Kitāb al-Awrāq: Qism Akhbār al-shuʿarā'*, ed. J. Heyworth-Dunne, London: Luzac and Co., 1934, p. 210, lines 4–11; al-Ṣūlī, *Akhbār Abī Tammām*, pp. 249–58. Al-Tawḥīdī also reports several reports from Abū Tammām on Ibn Abī Ṭāhir's authority, in *al-Baṣā'ir wa-al-dhakhā'ir*, e.g. vol. 9, pp. 215–16 (#21–2), and elsewhere.
77 On Abū al-ʿAynā', who was also one of al-Ṣūlī's teachers, see chapter 7 below.
78 Bonebakker, 'Ibn al-Muʿtazz and *Kitāb al-Badīʿ*', in *CHALABL*, p. 401.
79 al-Ṣūlī, *Akhbār Abī Tammām*, pp. 173–4.
80 Ibn Ḥajar al-ʿAsqalānī, *al-Iṣābah fī tamyīz al-ṣaḥābah*, Calcutta: T. J. M'Arthur Bishop, 1856–88), vol. 1, p. 1198 (correcting 'III, 98' in *GAS*, vol. 1, p. 349, and vol. 2, p. 95).
81 *Irshād*, vol. 7, p. 75, line 7. Yāqūt describes him also as *shāʿir qalīl al-shiʿr*, "a poet of little poetry." In addition to *Kitāb Sariqāt al-Buḥturī min Abī Tammām*, an unfinished *Kitāb al-Sariqāt*, a *Kitāb al-Jawāhir* and a *Kitāb al-Ādāb* are attested. See *GAS*, vol. 2, pp. 64, 532, 562.
82 *Balāghāt al-nisā'*, pp. 53–8.
83 Alī ibn Naṣr, *Encyclopedia of Pleasure by Abul Hasan ʿAli Ibn Nasr al-Katib* [= *Jawāmiʿ al-ladhdhah*], ed. Salah Addin Khawwam, tr. Adnan Jarkas and Salah Addin Khawwam, Toronto: Aleppo Publishers, 1977, pp. 154–69; the translation is Khawwam's.
84 Alī ibn Naṣr, *Encyclopedia of Pleasure*, p. 154.
85 Franz Rosenthal, 'Male and Female: Described and Compared,' in J. W. Wright Jr. and Everett K. Rowson (eds), *Homoeroticism in Classical Arabic Literature*, New York: Columbia Univeristy Press, 1997), p. 28; the translation is Rosenthal's.
86 Rosenthal, 'Male and Female,' p. 29.
87 *Muḥāḍarāt al-udabā'*, vol. 1, p. 76.
88 Goldziher, *Muslim Studies*, vol. 1, p. 96, dates the beginnings of Northern–Southern Arab antagonism to the second half of the first/seventh century. A century later it would compete with the *Shuʿūbiyyah* controversy: "This antagonism, which expressed itself in literature too in increasingly bitter terms, was calculated to rouse the disapproval of the theologians, who saw in its basis an infringement of the principle of equality postulated by Islamic teaching, the more so as the northern Arabs finally went so far as to state that even Jews or foreign *mawālī* were preferable to southern Arabs" (*cf. Aghānī*, vol. 20, pp. 99–100 for Qurayshīs in the second/eighth century who refused to recognize as Arabs Azdīs living in Oman). This is interesting because the rivalry between northern and southern Arabs seems itself to eclipse, or at any rate rival, the tension that develops and is cultivated between the Arabs and the non-Arabs. The major difference between what might be termed a Yemeni *Shuʿūbiyyah* (i.e the Northern–Southern conflict) and the Persian *Shuʿūbiyyah* is that in the former the numbers were small and, theoretically at least, evenly matched, whereas in the latter, the non-Arabs outnumbered the Arabs.

7 THE "BAD BOYS" OF BAGHDAD

1 See Bencheikh, 'Cénacle poétique'; Bencheikh, 'Les secrétaires poètes et animateurs de cénacles aux IIè et IIIè siècles de l'Hégire: contribution à l'analyse d'une production

poétique,' *Journal asiatique*, 1975, vol. 263, 265–315. Also important are the works of Y. A. al-Sāmarrā'ī (see Bibliography).

2 Hilary Kilpatrick, 'Context and the Enhancement of the Meaning of *Akhbār* in the *Kitāb al-Aḡānī*,' *Arabica*, 1991, vol. 38(3), 351–68. See also her *Making the Great Book of Songs: Compilation and the author's craft in Abū l-Faraj al-Iṣbahānī's Kitāb al-aghānī*, London and New York: RoutledgeCurzon, 2002, pp. 89–127.

3 Kilpatrick, 'Context,' p. 352.

4 Kilpatrick, 'Context,' pp. 365–6. Some issues remain to be worked out in Kilpatrick's interesting model. For example, is juxtaposition conscious and deliberate, or fortuitous? This must be explained, as *akhbār* cannot have gravitated toward one another simply because of shared linguistic pointers and markers.

5 See Hilāl Nājī, 'Abū Hiffān: Ḥayātuhu wa-shiʿruhu wa-baqāyā kitābihi *al-Arbaʿah fī akhbār al-shuʿarā*',' *al-Mawrid*, 1399/1979, vol. 9(1), p. 194, for references.

6 Ibn al-Muʿtazz places Ibn Harmah first in his anthology because he marks the end of the era of poets considered Ancient (*qadīm*, pl. *qudamā'*). He quotes al-Aṣmaʿī to the effect that Ibn Harmah is the seal of the poets (*khutima al-shiʿr bi-Ibn Harmah*): Ibn al-Muʿtazz, *Ṭabaqāt al-shuʿarā'*, p. 20, line 4. (Note that one manuscript of the *Ṭabaqāt* begins with Bashshār rather than Ibn Harmah.)

7 I use here the sequence as published in the Farrāj edition of the *Ṭabaqāt al-shuʿarā'*. On the precise number of accounts, taking into account duplication and the manuscripts of al-Irbilī's *Mukhtaṣar Ṭabaqāt al-shuʿarā' li . . . Ibn al-Muʿtazz*, see Ibn al-Muʿtazz, *Ṭabaqāt al-shuʿarā'*, pp. 585–6.

8 Ibn al-Jarrāh, *Kitāb al-Waraqah*, ed. 'A. 'Azzām and 'A. A. Farrāj, Cairo: Dār al-Maʿārif, 1953, pp. 8–9. On Abū al-Fayḍ al-Qiṣāfī, see also Ibn al-Muʿtazz, *Ṭabaqāt al-shuʿarā'*, pp. 304–5.

9 Ibn al-Jarrāh, *Waraqah*, pp. 8–9.

10 Ibn al-Jarrāh, *Waraqah*, pp. 33–4.

11 Ibn al-Jarrāh, *Waraqah*, p. 47–8. The 'proximity' between Abū Hiffān and Ibn Abī Ṭāhir is the most common. Another work in which they are quoted consecutively is Ibn Maʿṣūm, *Anwār al-rabīʿ fī anwār al-badīʿ*, 7 vols, ed. S. H. Shukr, Karbala: Maktabat al-ʿIrfān, 1968–9, reprint 1981, vol. 2, pp. 110–11.

12 Ibn al-Jarrāh, *Waraqah*, p. 56; on al-Sāsī, see p. 56, n. 1.

13 Ibn al-Jarrāḥ, *Waraqah*, pp. 125–6.

14 *Murūj al-dhahab*, ¶¶ 3011–13. The anecdote is given on the authority of Aḥmad ibn al-Ḥārith al-Kharrāz (d. after 257/871), a scholar who heard the recitation of all of the works of his prolific professor, 'Alī ibn Muḥammad al-Madā'inī (d. 228/843): see *Irshād*, vol. 3, p. 5, line 10. Al-Kharrāz was also the transmitter (*rāwiyah*) of al-'Attābī (d. before 220/835).

15 *Irshād*, vol. 1, pp. 151–4 (#10).

16 *Aghānī*, vol. 3, p. 201, line 15 (Ibn Abī Ṭāhir) and vol. 3, p. 202, line 8 (Abū Hiffān).

17 *Fihrist*, p. 3, lines 5–7.

18 *Fihrist*, p. 157, and p. 4, line 7 (the latter omits *udabā'* in certain manuscripts).

19 *Fihrist*, pp. 163, lines 4–6, describing pp. 163, line 7 to p. 168, line 20.

20 *Fihrist*, pp. 164, line 9.

21 I mentioned in chapter 5 above another cluster identified by Ibn al-Nadīm, namely that comprising Ibn al-Muqaffaʿ, Sahl ibn Hārūn, 'Alī ibn Dāwud, al-'Attābī, and Ibn Abī Ṭāhir, in the *Fihrist*'s section on fables and evening storytelling, specifically, "those who composed [*kāna yaʿmalu*] fables and evening stories told through the mouths of animals and other creatures [e.g. humans, *jinn*]" (*Fihrist*, pp. 364, lines 3–5, p. 367, lines 7–10). Here it is not a question of 'proximity' but of outright connection. All were of Persian origin and/or Persophile, and all connected in one way or another with the

translation of works from Persian and/or the composition of works of Persian inspiration or provenance.

22 Jaḥẓah is, incidentally, the only writer other than Ibn Abī Ṭāhir's son credited with a work on the virtues of *Sikbāj* stew: see *Fihrist*, pp. 379, line 2, and p. 164, line 12; *cf.* n. 99 below. See also al-Tawḥīdī, vol. 1 (#762), where Ibn Abī Ṭāhir quotes 'Alī ibn Sulaymān about al-Manṣūr's taste for the food *Mulabbaqah.*

23 al-Tha'ālibī, *al-Tamthīl wa-al-muḥāḍarah*, ed. 'A. M. al-Ḥulw, Cairo: Dār Iḥyā' al-Kutub al-'Arabiyyah, 1381/1961, pp. 91–9. *Cf.* al-Tha'ālibī, *al-I'jāz wa-al-ījāz*, ed. Muḥammad al-Tūnjī, Beirut: Dār al-Nafā'is, 1412/1992, p. 171, where he quotes Ibn Abī Ṭāhir, Abū Hiffān, Manṣūr ibn Bādān, and Abū 'Alī al-Baṣīr all on the same page.

24 al-Khaṭīb al-Baghdādī, *al-Taṭfīl wa-ḥikāyāt al-ṭufayliyyīn wa-akhbāruhum wa-nawādir kalāmihim wa-ash'āruhum*, no ed., Damascus: Maktabat al-Tawfīq, 1346/1927, pp. 56, 73.

25 al-Khaṭīb al-Baghdādī, *al-Taṭfīl*, p. 75.

26 Ibn Bassām, *al-Dhakhīrah fī maḥāsin ahl al-Jazīrah*, 8 parts in 2 vols, ed. Ihsān 'Abbās, Beirut: Dār al-Thaqāfah, 1399/1979, vol. 4(1), p. 293. These represent lines 6 and 7 of a 9–line selection included in al-Ḥuṣrī, *Zahr al-ādāb*, vol. 2, pp. 893–4.

27 See n. 6 in chapter 6 above.

28 al-Marzubānī, *Kitāb Nūr al-qabas al-mukhtaṣar min al-Muqtabas fī akhbār al-nuḥāt wa-al-udabā' wa-al-shu'arā' wa-al-'ulamā'. Die Gelehrtenbiographien des Abū 'Ubaidallāh al-Marzubānī in der Rezension des Ḥāfiẓ al-Yaġmūrī*, ed. Rudolf Sellheim, Wiesbaden: Franz Steiner, 1384/1964, p. 126.

29 al-Nuwayrī, *Nihāyat al-arab fī funūn al-adab*, 33 vols in 27, Cairo: Dār al-Kutub and al-Mu'assasah al-Miṣriyyah al-'Āmmah li-al-Ta'līf wa-al-Tarjamah wa-al-Ṭibā'ah wa-al-Nashr, 1923–85, vol. 10, pp. 97–8, vol. 3, p. 188.

30 al-Nuwayrī, *Nihāyat al-arab*, vol. 10, p. 97. *Cf.* al-Ṣafadī, *Nakt al-ḥimyān*, p. 266.

31 al-Marzubānī, *Kitāb al-Mu'jam fī asmā' al-shu'arā'*, ed. 'A. A. Farrāj, Cairo: Dār Iḥyā' al-Kutub al-'Arabiyyah/Muṣṭafā al-Bābī al-Ḥalabī wa-awlāduh, 1379/1960, p. 398, line 3.

32 *EAL*, p. 546.

33 al-Marzubānī, *Kitāb al-Mu'jam*, p. 185, line 6.

34 al-Jāḥiẓ, *al-Bayān wa-al-tabyīn*, vol. 1, p. 296, line 5.

35 *Irshād*, vol. 15, p. 156, lines 8–9. On 'Alī ibn Sulaymān al-Akhfash al-Ṣaghīr, see *Irshād*, vol. 13, pp. 236–57; and *Fihrist*, p. 91. He was also a friend of Sawwār ibn Abī Shurā'ah (d. after 300/912), a student of Abū al-'Aynā''s, and a satirist of al-Mubarrad, on whom see *Ta'rīkh Baghdād*, vol. 9, p. 212.

36 Ḍayf, *al-Aṣr al-'Abbāsī al-thānī*, p. 415.

37 Bencheikh, 'Cénacle,' p. 46.

38 Bencheikh, 'Cénacle,' p. 51.

39 Bencheikh, 'Cénacle,' p. 46.

40 On poets and their urban environment, see G. E. von Grunebaum, 'Aspects of Arabic Urban Literature mostly in the Ninth and Tenth Centuries,' *Islamic Studies*, 1969, vol. 8, 281–300.

41 See Lassner, *Shaping of 'Abbāsid Rule*, pp. 204–6, references at p. 261, n. 31; and 'al-Ruṣāfah' in *EI2*, vol. 8, pp. 629–30.

42 Samarra was occupied from 221/836 to *c.* 281/894–5. When al-Mutawakkil died, the city, which had flourished under his rule, was abandoned (except by the army). See al-Ya'qūbī, *Kitāb al-Buldān*, pp. 255–68; E. Herzfeld, *Geschichte der Stadt Samarra*, Hamburg: Eckard & Messtorf, 1948; Y. A. al-Sāmarrā'ī, *Sāmarrā' fī adab al-qarn al-thālith al-hijrī*, Baghdad: Maktabat al-Irshād, 1968; and Matthew S. Gordon, *The breaking of a thousand swords: a history of the Turkish military of Samarra, AH 200–275/ 815–889 CE*, Albany: SUNY Press, 2001.

43 I am grateful to Everett Rowson and to Jacob Lassner for their insights about al-ʿAskar.

For an anecdote that places Ibn Abī Ṭāhir in Samarra, see *Irshād*, vol. 3, pp. 95–8, which includes 8 verses in praise of Samarra, the opening lines of which echo Ibn al-Muʿtazz's 18-line 'Dayr ʿAbdūn' poem (see his *Dīwān*, 3 vols, ed. Y. A. al-Sāmarrāʾī, Beirut: ʿĀlam al-Kutub, 1417/1997, vol. 2, pp. 102–6 [#693]):

Saqā Surra-man-rā wa-sukkānahā
wa-dayran li-sawsanihā ʾr-rāhibī
Saḥābun tadaffaqa ʿan raʿdihi ʾṣ-
-ṣafūqi wa-bāriqihi ʾl-wāṣibī
Fa-qad bittu fī dayrihī laylatan
wa-badrun ʿalā ghuṣunin ṣāḥibī
Ghazālun saqāniya ḥattā ʾṣ-ṣabā-
-ḥi ṣafrāʾa ka ʾdh-dhahabi ʾdh-dhāʾibī
ʿAlā ʾl-wardi min ḥumrati ʾl-wajna-
-tayni wa-fī ʾl-āsi min khuḍrati ʾsh-shāribī
Saqānī ʾl-mudāmata mustayqiẓan
wa-nimtu wa-nāma ilā jānibī
Fa-kānat hanātun laka ʾl-waylu min
janāhā ʾlladhī khaṭṭahu kātibī
Fa yā rabbi tub waʿfu ʿan mudhnibin
muqirrin bi-zallatihi tāʾibī

Also in Najar, *Majmaʿ al-Dhākirah*, vol. 5, p. 167.

44 Ibn al-Muʿtazz, *Ṭabaqāt*, pp. 396–416.

45 For references, see Nājī, 'Abū Hiffān,' vol. 9(1), p. 202, who prefers the date of death 257/871 (the 195/810 in *Irshād*, vol. 12, p. 54, lines 5–6, being of course impossible); and Abū Hiffān, *Akhbār Abī Nuwās*, ed. ʿA. A. Farrāj, Cairo: Dār Miṣr, n.d., pp. 7–16. I am grateful to Michael Cooperson for directing me to Nājī's article.

46 See e.g. Ibn al-Muʿtazz, *Ṭabaqāt*, pp. 408–9.

47 Ibn al-Muʿtazz, *Ṭabaqāt al-shuʿarāʾ*, p. 409, line 17.

48 See n. 44 above.

49 For a partial reconstruction of *al-Arbaʿah fī akhbār al-shuʿarāʾ*, see Nājī, 'Abū Hiffān.'

50 E.g. *Taʾrīkh Baghdād*, vol. 9, p. 370, line 3, and al-Suyūṭī, *Bughyah*, vol. 2, p. 31 (#1355).

51 See e.g. *Taʾrīkh Baghdād*, vol. 9, p. 370, line 5.

52 See e.g. *Taʾrīkh Baghdād*, vol. 9, p. 370. Abū Hiffān also figures in thirty-five lines of transmission in the *Kitāb al-Aghānī*, four of which include Ibn Abī Ṭāhir (*Aghānī*, vol. 12, p. 285, line 2; vol. 19, p. 270, line 17, vol. 20, p. 52, line 1; vol. 22, p. 259, line 6). This is not surprising given the large number of transmitters and *udabāʾ* with whom he came into contact. *Cf.* Leon Zolondek, 'An Approach to the Problem of the Sources of the *Kitāb al-Aḡānī*,' *Journal of Near Eastern Studies*, 1960, vol. 19(3), pp. 217–34.

53 al-Tawḥīdī, *al-Baṣāʾir wa-al-dhakhāʾir*, vol. 1 (#59) (discussed in chapter 2 above).

54 al-Qālī, *Dhayl al-Amālī*, vol. 3, p. 96, lines 17–20.

55 *Cf.* the Introduction to Abū Hiffān, *Akhbār Abī Nuwās*, p. 9.

56 See Nājī, 'Abū Hiffān,' vol. 8(3), p. 214.

57 The introduction to Abū Hiffān, *Akhbār Abī Nuwās*, p. 15, quoting al-Waṭwāt, *Ghurar al-khaṣāʾiṣ al-wāḍiḥah wa-ʿurar al-naqāʾiṣ al-fāḍiḥah*, Cairo: al-Maṭbaʿat al-Adabiyyah, 1318/1901. *Cf.* Ibn ʿAsākir, *Taʾrīkh madīnat Dimashq*, ed. Ṣalāh al-dīn al-Munajjid *et al.*, Damascus: Majmaʿah al-Lughah al-ʿArabiyyah, 1952–, vol. 17, p. 430.

58 For one of the many anecdotes pertaining to Abū Hiffān's drinking, see al-Raqīq al-Nadīm, *Quṭb al-surūr*, p. 22, lines 3–9.

59 al-Suyūṭī, *Bughyah*, vol. 2, p. 31, and *Irshād*, vol. 12, pp. 54–5.

60 *Ṭabaqāt al-shuʿarāʾ*, p. 409, lines 5–6 and ff.; al-Khālidīyān, *Kitāb al-Tuḥaf wa-al-hadāyā: Le Livre des Dons et des Cadeaux*, ed. Sāmī al-Dahhān, Cairo: Dār al-Maʿārif, 1956, p. 155. Two verses by Ibn Abī Ṭāhir addressed to Abū al-Ḥasan would also appear to be directed to ʿUbaydallāh ibn Khāqān (and not to ʿAlī ibn Yaḥyā, who has the same patronymic:) see al-Thaʿālibī, *al-Muntaḥal*, ed. A. Abū ʿAlī, Alexandria: al-Maṭbaʿah al-Tijāriyyah, 1319/1901, p. 67; and al-Mīkālī, *al-Muntakhab*, MS Topkapı Sarayı 8561 A. 2634, fol. 69a–69b:

Abā Ḥasanin inna ʾl-khalīfata aṣbaḥat
lanā kaffuhu ghaythan wa-anta saḥābuhā
Fa mā min yadin bayḍāʾa tusdā ilā ʾmriʾin
wa-lā niʿmatin illā ilayka ʾntisābuhā

(amending Thaʿālibī's *muḥābuhā* in line 1).

61 *Irshād*, vol. 4, p. 149, line 10 to p. 150, line 5.

62 *Irshād*, vol. 4, p. 150. The verses read:

Mulūkun thanāhum ka-aḥsābihim
wa-akhlāquhum shibhu ādābihim
Fa-ṭūlu qurūnihimū ajmaʿīn
yazīdu ʿalā ṭūli adhnābihim.

63 *Taʾrīkh Baghdād*, vol. 9, p. 370, line 16 to p. 371, line 1:

Rakibtu ḥamīra al-kirā
li-qillati man yuʿtarā
Li-anna dhawī ʾl-makramā
-ti qad ghuyyibū fī ʾth-tharā

Cf. *Ṭabaqāt al-shuʿarāʾ*, p. 409, lines 3–4. In this version, Abū Hiffān's interlocutor is Ibn Bulbul. For a review of Abū Hiffān's relations with the Thawābah family, see Nājī, 'Abū Hiffān,' vol. 8(3), 194–5. On al-Hadādī, see n. 124 below. Al-Ḥusayn ibn al-Qāsim al-Kawkabī is frequently directly cited by Abū al-Faraj in the *Kitāb al-Aghānī.*

A letter by Ibn Abī Ṭāhir censuring Ibn Thawābah is included by the former in the *Kitāb al-Manthūr wal-manẓūm*: see n. 143 in chapter 4 above.

64 Boustany, *Ibn ar-Rūmī*, pp. 195–6.

65 al-Jāḥiẓ, 'Kitāb al-Ḥijāb,' in *Rasāʾil al-Jāḥiẓ*, vol. 2, pp. 46–7.

66 Nājī, 'Abū Hiffān,' vol. 8(3), p. 195.

67 But the *Book of songs* does include an anecdote (reported through Ibn Abī Ṭāhir) recording the size of a purse Abū Hiffān received from Hārūn al-Rashīd: see *Aghānī*, vol. 19, p. 270, line 17.

68 *Cf.* the remarks of the editor in Abū Hiffān, *Akhbār Abī Nuwās*, p. 16.

69 For references, see Bencheikh, 'Cénacle,' p. 45, n. 88, especially *Irshād*, vol. 18, pp. 286–306.

70 al-Ṣafadī, *Nakt al-himyān*, p. 265, lines 13–14. Al-Ṣafadī adds (lines 14–15) that any of Abū al-ʿAynāʾ's descendants who are blind are therefore verifiably his progeny. On the names Abū al-ʿAynāʾ and Abū ʿAlī al-Baṣīr, *inter alia*, which both describe perception rather than blindness, see August Fischer, 'Arab. *baṣīr* 'scharfsichtig' per antifrasin = 'blind',' *Zeitschrift der Deutschen Morgenländischen Gesselschaft*, 1907, vol. 61, 425–34; and Fedwa Malti-Douglas, 'Pour une rhétorique onomastique: les noms des aveugles chez aṣ-Ṣafadî,' *Cahiers d'onomastique arabe*, 1979, vol. 1, 7–19.

71 al-Ṣafadī, *Nakt al-himyān*, p. 266:

In yaʾkhudhu ʾllāhu min ʿaynayya nūrahumā
fa-fī lisānī wa-samʿī minhumā nūru

Qalbun dhakīyun wa-ʿaqlun ghayru dhī khaṭali
wa-fī famī ʾārimun ka ʾs-sayfi maʾthūru

72 *Irshād*, vol. 18, p. 286, lines 13–16.
73 *Fihrist*, p. 139, line 3. The sources do not identify Abū al-ʿAynāʾ as a teacher of Ibn Abī Ṭāhir *per se*, but he is often directly cited by him, for four *akhbār* in *Balāghāt al-nisāʾ* for instance (pp. 23, 31, 95, 187).
74 *Irshād*, vol. 6, p. 260, lines 9–10.
75 E.g. al-Tawḥīdī, *al-Imtāʿ wa-al-muʾānasah*, vol. 1, p. 58, line 13.
76 al-Tawḥīdī, *al-Imtāʿ wa-al-muʾānasah*, vol. 2, p. 137, lines 6–7, writes that people preferred Abū ʿAlī al-Baṣīr to Abū al-ʿAynāʾ because he was proficient in poetry *and* prose both (*jamaʿa bayn al-faḍīlatayn*). *Cf. Murūj*, ¶ 3020.
77 *Fihrist*, p. 139, line 1, and p. 137, line 2.
78 *Murūj*, ¶ 3020, where al-Masʿūdī notes that he discusses these exchanges in his lost *Kitāb al-Awsaṭ*.
79 On Abū ʿAlī al-Baṣīr, see especially *Ṭabaqāt al-shuʿarāʾ*, pp. 397–8; *Murūj*, ¶¶ 3018–21; al-Ṣafadī, *Nakt al-ḥimyān*, pp. 225–6; and Y. A. al-Sāmarrāʾī, ʻAshʿār Abī ʿAlī al-Baṣīr,ʼ *al-Mawrid*, 1972, vol. 1(3–4), 149–79.
80 al-Marzubānī, *Muʿjam al-shuʿarāʾ*, p. 185.
81 Ibn al-Kāzarūnī, *Mukhtaṣar al-taʾrīkh min awwal al-zamān ilā muntahā al-dawlah al-ʿAbbāsiyyah*, ed. Muṣṭafā Jawād, Baghdad: Mudīriyyat al-Thaqāfah al-ʿĀmmah, 1390/1970, p. 148, line 14, and p. 151, line 8, calls Abū ʿAlī al-Baṣīr a court poet of al-Mutawakkil and al-Muntaṣir respectively.
82 *Murūj*, ¶ 3021:

Idhā mā ʾghtadat ṭullābatu ʾl-ʿilmi mā lahā
min al-ʿilmi illā mā yukhalladu fī ʾl-kutbi
Ghadawtu bi-tashmīrin wa-jiddin ʿalayhim
fa-maḥbaratī samʿī wa-daftaruhā qalbī.

83 al-Marzubānī, *al-Muwashshaḥ*, p. 434, lines 10–17.
84 *Fihrist*, p. 139, line 3.
85 See note 137 in chapter 4 above. On *ʿamila* (literally "to do") and also *ṣanaʿa* (literally, to "make"), see also Schoeler, *Ecrire et transmettre*, p. 118.
86 *Irshād*, vol. 18, p. 300, line 10. On Aḥmad's posts, see Sourdel, *Vizirat ʿabbāside*, vol. 1, pp. 263–5, 287–9.
87 See Sourdel, *Vizirat ʿabbāside*, vol. 1, pp. 287–90.
88 al-Dhahabī, *Siyar aʿlām al-nubalāʾ*, vol. 12, p. 554, and al-Ṣafadī, *al-Wāfī bi-al-wafayāt*, vol. 6, p. 373. As Aḥmad fell out of favor in 248/862, the verse can therefore be dated to shortly before then.
89 *Irshād*, vol. 18, pp. 303–4, records five lines by Abū al-ʿAynāʾ satirizing Aḥmad. Abū al-ʿAynāʾ"s opening hemistich is identical to Ibn Abī Ṭāhir's and his second hemistich uses a similar motif to Ibn Abī Ṭāhir's: "Control your wazīr, he's a real kicker" (*ushkul wazīraka innahu rakkālu*), suggesting a borrowing by one poet from the other.
90 al-Ḥuṣrī, *Zahr al-ādāb*, vol. 2, p. 789, lines 16–17.
91 See item #56 in chapter 4 above.
92 See *EI2*, vol. 3, pp. 879–80.
93 al-Ṣūlī, *Akhbār al-Buḥturī*, pp. 113–14 (#59). For the poem, see al-Buḥturī, *Dīwān*, 2 vols in 1, no ed., Beirut: Dār al-Kutub al-ʿIlmiyyah, 1307/1987, vol. 1, pp. 132–4.
94 *Murūj*, ¶ 2845. *Cf.* al-Ṣūlī, *Akhbār Abī Tammām*, ed. K. M. ʿAsākir *et al.*, Cairo: Maṭbaʿah Lajnat al-Taʾlīf wa-al-Tarjamah wa-al-Nashr, 1356/1937, p. 97, lines 9–10.
95 *Taʾrīkh Baghdād*, p. 170, lines 20–1; *cf.* Bencheikh, ʻCénacle,ʼ p. 45, where he suggests that the twenty years of Abū al-ʿAynāʾ"s life about which the sources are silent were spent in the transmission of Hadith.

96 Abū al-ʿAynāʾ was interested in – or his audience was at any rate receptive to – Persianate stories: see e.g. al-Tawḥīdī, *al-Baṣāʾir wa-al-dhakhāʾir*, vol. 1, pp. 24–5 (#52).
97 See e.g. al-Ṣafadī, *Nakt al-ḥimyān*, p. 268; and al-Marzubānī, *Nūr al-qabas*, p. 323. Al-Shābushtī, *al-Diyārāt*, p. 86, line 9 to p. 87, line 9, reports that Abū al-ʿAynāʾ passed an oral examination on Quranic exegesis, inheritance law, and philology with flying colors. The use of sacred texts by poets and authors of the third/ninth century is discussed briefly in A. M. Zubaidi, 'The impact of the Qurʾān and Ḥadīth on medieval Arabic literature,' in *CHALEUP*, pp. 327–33, 335, 340–1. See also 'Literature and the Qurʾān,' in Jane Dammen McAuliffe (ed.), *Encyclopedia of the Qurʾān*, vol. 3, Leiden, Brill, 2004, pp. 205–21.
98 ʿAlī ibn al-Ḥusayn Ibn Mukarram was the member of a princely family of Oman. For his public exchanges with Abū al-ʿAynāʾ, see e.g. al-Shābushtī, *al-Diyārāt*, pp. 84, 85, 92.
99 al-Raqīq al-Nadīm, *Quṭb al-surūr*, p. 352, lines 1–4.
100 "Do not be arrogant, but come to me" is Q 27:31 (*lā taʿlū ʿalayya wa-ʾtūnī*) and "Go into it [Hell] and do not speak to me" is Q 23:108 (*Wa-ʾkhsaʾū fīhā wa-lā tukallimūni*).
101 al-Ḥuṣrī, *Zahr al-ādāb*, vol. 1, p. 281, lines 11–12.
102 al-Marzubānī, *Muʿjam al-shuʿarāʾ*, p. 403, line 2, describes Abū al-ʿAynāʾ as having written very little poetry (*wa-huwa qalīl al-shiʿr jiddan*) (*cf.* Bencheikh, 'Cénacle,' p. 46). Ibn al-Nadīm mentions a diwan of thirty folios (*Fihrist*, p. 139, line 3); a hundred folios seems to have been a small but respectable amount.
103 al-Marzubānī, *Nūr al-qabas*, p. 323.
104 "*Sajʿu Abī ʾl-ʿAynāʾ min rajʿihi.*" *Cf.* "*Mā huwa illā sajʿun laysa taḥtahu rajʿun*," i.e. "It is nothing but rhyming prose beneath which no profit is to be found" in Lane, p. 1040.
105 E.g. *Murūj*, ¶ 3020.
106 For authors interested in *sariqah*, see al-Rabdāwī, *al-Ḥarakah al-Naqdiyyah*; and *GAS*, vol. 2, p. 64.
107 al-Jurjānī, *al-Wasāṭah bayn al-Mutanabbī wa-khuṣūmihi*, 2nd edn, ed. M. A. Ibrāhīm and ʿA. M. al-Bajāwī, Cairo: Muṣṭafā al-Bābī al-Ḥalabī wa-awlāduh, 1370/1951, p. 221:

Hajawtu ʾbna Abī Ṭāhirin
wa-hwa ʾl-ʿaynu wa ʾr-raʾsu
Wa lawlā sariqātu ʾsh-shiʿri
mā kāna bihi baʾsu
Idhā anshadkum shiʿran
fa-qūlū aḥsana ʾn-nāsu

108 al-Ṣūlī, *Akhbār al-Buḥturī*, pp. 125–6 (#73). On al-Buḥturī's affection for *ghilmān*, see ʿal-Ṣūlī, *Akhbār al-Buḥturī*, pp. 127–8 (#76), especially n. 3, and the numerous verses devoted to them in his *Dīwān*. Al-Jurjānī, *al-Wasāṭah*, p. 222, lines 1–2, likens this third line to one by Abū Tammām: see his *Dīwān*, ed. ʿAzzām, vol. 1, p. 291.
109 Bencheikh, 'Cénacle,' 45–7.
110 Numerous poets composed poems on the occasion of al-Mutawakkil's move to the Jaʿfarī palace. Yāqūt, *al-Buldān*, vol. 1, pp. 87–8, includes *in extenso* the poem by Abū ʿAlī al-Baṣīr (correcting 'al-Baṣrī'), and also a selection from a poem by al-Buḥturī.
111 See Saʿīd ibn Ḥumayd, *Rasāʾil Saʿīd ibn Ḥumayd wa-ashʿāruhu*, ed. Y. A. al-Sāmarrāʾī, Baghdād: Maktabat al-Irshād, 1971, and *EI2*, vol. 8, p. 856.
112 *Fihrist*, p. 137, lines 14–15.
113 See Saʿīd ibn Ḥumayd, *Rasāʾil.*
114 Abū Hilāl al-ʿAskarī, *Dīwān al-maʿānī*, vol. 1, pp. 93–4.
115 *Fihrist*, p. 137, line 17. Eight lines of a poem by Ibn Abī Ṭāhir to Ibn Bulbul are quoted in Abū Hilāl al-ʿAskarī, *Dīwān al-maʿānī*, vol. 1, p. 94:

Abā 'ṣ-Ṣaqri lā zālat min Allāhi niʿmatun
tujaddiduhā 'l-ayyāmu ʿindaka wa 'd-dahrū
Wa lā zālati 'l-aʿyādu tamḍī wa tanqaḍī
wa tabqā lanā ayyāmuka 'l-ghuraru' z-zuhrū
Fa-innaka li 'd-dunyā jamālun wa zīnatun
wa innaka li 'l-aḥrāri dhakhrun huwa 'dh-dhakhrū
Ra'aytu 'l-hadāyā kullahā dūna qadrihī
wa laysa li-shay'in ʿinda miqdārihī qadrū
Fa-lā faḍla illā wa hwa min faḍli jūdihī
wa lā birra illā dūnahū dhālika 'l-birrū
Fa-ahdaytu min ḥalyi 'l-madīḥi jawāhiran
munaṣṣadatan (?) yuzhā bihā 'n-naẓmu wa 'n-nathrū
Madā'iḥa tabqā baʿda mā nuffida 'd-dahru
wa tabhā bihā 'l-ayyāmu mā 'ttaṣala 'l-ʿumrū
Shakartu li-Ismāʿīla ḥusna balā'ihī
wa afḍalu mā tujzā bihi 'n-niʿamu 'sh-shukrū

116 Abū Hilāl al-ʿAskarī, *Dīwān al-maʿānī*, vol. 1, p. 94, line 12 to p. 95, line 11.

117 al-Ḥasan iIbn Makhlad, under-secretary to al-Mutawakkil and vizier to al-Muʿtamid, died in exile in 269/882 after having been dismissed by al-Muwaffaq. *Irshād*, vol. 3, p. 90, citing a lost portion of al-Jahshiyārī's *al-Wuzarā' wa-al-kuttāb* quotes 2 verses by Ibn Abī Ṭāhir to him:

Ammā rajā'u fa-arjā mā amarta bihī
fa kayfa in kunta lam ta'murhu ya'tamirū
Bādir bi-jūdika mahmā kunta muqtadiran
fa-laysa fī kulli ḥālin anta muqtadirū

118 See Sourdel, *Vizirat ʿabbāside*, vol. 1, pp. 315–6, 324–6.

119 See e.g. See Hugh Kennedy, *The Prophet and the Age of the Caliphate*, London: Longman, 1986, p. 188.

120 Ibn Ẓāfir, *Badā'iʿ al-badā'ih*, pp. 69–70 (#63).

121 For other gatherings chez ʿAlī ibn Yaḥyā, see e.g. *Irshād*, vol. 15, p. 159, line 7 to p. 160, line 21, and p. 166, line 13 to p. 167, line 14.

122 *Irshād*, vol. 15, p. 89, lines 1–8, and 15 (emphasis mine).

123 On Abū ʿAbdallāḥ Aḥmad Ibn Abī Fanan, a *kātib* and poet who died between 260/874 and 270/883, see Y. A. al-Sāmarrā'ī, 'Aḥmad ibn Abī Fanan: Ḥayātuhu wa-mā tabaqqā min shiʿrihi,' *Majallat Majmaʿ al-ʿIlmī al-ʿIrāqī*, 1983, vol. 34(4), 131–90; and *GAS*, vol. 2, p. 585. Under the *akhbār* of Abū al-ʿAtāhiyah, Abū al-Faraj (*Aghānī*, vol. 4, p. 107, lines 1–10) records an anecdote recounted to his uncle by Ibn Abī Ṭāhir. Aḥmad ibn Abī Fanan tells him (*qāla lī*. . .) that he was once discussing with Abū al-Fatḥ ibn Khāqān whether Abū Nuwās or Abū al-ʿAtāhiyah was the better poet when al-Ḥusayn ibn al-Ḍaḥḥāk walked in and exclaimed "The mother of the one who prefers Abū Nuwās to Abū al-ʿAtāhiyah is a whore (lit. adulteress)." (Al-) Ḥusayn ibn al-Ḍaḥḥāk, nicknamed the Debauched (al-Khalīʿ) was a poet no doubt known to Ibn Abī Ṭāhir though the sources preserve no explicit mention of direct contact: see *Aghānī*, vol. 7, pp. 143–221; on him, see *GAS*, vol. 2, pp. 518–19.

124 Perhaps the al-Hadādī mentioned in an *isnād* in *Aghānī*, vol. 8, p. 348, line 12.

125 Abū Bakr al-Ḥasan ibn ʿAlī Ibn al-ʿAllāf al-Nahrawānī was a poet and traditionist who died in 318/930 at the age of a hundred. He was close to al-Muʿtaḍid and Ibn al-Muʿtazz. Ibn al-Nadīm (*Fihrist*, p. 194, lines 17–18) writes that he was a prolific poet and that his poetry, collected by his family, together with the accounts of those he eulogized, occupied 400 folios. His most famous piece, an elegy on his cat killed by

neighbors, has been variously interpreted, including as an allegory on the murder of Ibn al-Muʿtazz. See *EI2*, vol. 3, p. 702.

126 Abū Kāmil al-Muhandis is mentioned in an *isnād* in *Aghānī*, vol. 7, p. 185, line 9.

127 Abū al-ʿUbays, his father Abū ʿAbdallāh Aḥmad, and his son Ibrāhīm were well known for their companionship to the caliphs and for their musical talent. Aḥmad is remembered for his exchange of verses with ʿAlī ibn Yaḥyā al-Munajjim. Ibn Abī Ṭāhir's contact with this family is apparent not only from their attendance of the same gatherings, but also from lines of transmission. e.g. the long passage – possibly from a written work of Ibn Abī Ṭāhir – quoted in *Irshād*, vol. 2, pp. 208–16. The Ḥamdūn family is also mentioned in the same broad grouping as Ibn Abī Ṭāhir in the *Fihrist*; on them, see *EI2*, vol. 3, pp. 783–4.

128 *Irshād*, vol. 15, p. 88, lines 12–15.

129 *Irshād*, vol. 15, p. 95, lines 3–4.

130 *Irshād*, vol. 15, p. 96.

131 The lines continue (*Irshād*, vol. 15, p. 96):

When the brimful vessels are poured, we make
believe our own lads are better even than the Arabs.

Idhā suqiya mutraʿa ʾl-kāsāti awhamanā
bi-anna ghilmānanā khayrun min al-ʿarabi

132 Ibn Ẓāfir, *Badāʾiʿ al-badāʾih*, pp. 69–70 (#63), pp. 79–80 (#80), p. 97 (#112), and pp. 222–3 (#256).

133 Ibn Ẓāfir, *Badāʾiʿ al-badāʾih*, pp. 69–70. On Ibn Bulbul, see above; on Aḥmad ibn Abī Fanan, see n. 123 above.

134 Ibn Ẓāfir, *Badāʾiʿ al-badāʾih*, pp. 222–3 (#256); *Irshād*, vol. 15, pp. 166, line 13 to p. 167, line 14.

135 See e.g. al-Thaʿālibī, *al-Kināyah wa-al-taʿrīḍ*, ed. M. B. al-Naʿsānī, Cairo: Maktabat al-Saʿādah, 1326/1908; ed. Usāmah al-Bulayrī. Cairo: Maktabat al-Khānjī, 1997, pp. 48–9.

136 Ibn Ẓāfir, *Badāʾiʿ al-badāʾih*, pp. 79–80 (#80).

137 On ʿAlī, see *Fihrist*, pp. 160–1; *Irshād*, vol. 15, pp. 144–75; and Y. A. al-Sāmarrāʾī, "ʿAlī ibn Yaḥyā al-Munajjim,' *Majallat Majmaʿ al-ʿIlmī al-ʿIrāqī*, 1985, vol. 36(2), 210–61.

138 For them, this mirrored the companionship of their ancestor the minister Faramdhār and Ardashīr: see al-Marzubānī, *Muʿjam al-shuʿarāʾ*, p. 141, lines 15–16. Aḥmad, ʿAlī's grandson, wrote an *Akhbār Banī al-Munajjim wa-nasabuhum fī al-Furs*: see *EI2*, vol. 7, p. 560.

139 See Seeger A. Bonebakker, 'Ibn Abī ʾl-Iṣbaʿ's text of the *al-Badīʿ* of Ibn al-Muʿtazz,' *Israel Oriental Studies*, 1972, vol. 2, pp. 90–1, who points out that the first copyist (in 247/861) of the *Kitāb al-Badīʿ* was ʿAlī ibn Yaḥyā, rather than ʿAlī ibn Hārūn ibn Yaḥyā.

140 *Murūj*, ¶ 3371.

141 Ibn Abī Uṣaybiʿah, *ʿUyūn al-anbāʿ*, p. 272, line 14.

142 al-Baghdādī, *Khizānat al-adab*, 13 vols, ed. ʿA. M. Hārūn, Cairo: Dār al-Kutub, n.d., vol. 5, pp. 255–6, *shāhid* #379.

143 See al-Rabdāwī, *al-Ḥarakah al-naqdiyyah*, p. 96, n. 1.

144 See, for instance, al-Āmidī, *al-Muwāzanah*, vol. 1, p. 127.

ENVOI

1 Even in the 1998 *EAL*, D. S. Richards argues that al-Jāḥiẓ's "writings typify the ʿAbbāsid concept of *adab*" (p. 409).

2 *Taʾrīkh Baghdād*, vol. 3, p. 431, line 20.

3 Makdisi, *Rise of Colleges*, *cf.* Michael Chamberlain, *Knowledge and Social Practice in Medieval Damascus, 1190–1350*, Cambridge: Cambridge University Press, 1995.
4 Charles Pellat, 'Nouvel essai d'inventaire de l'oeuvre ǧāḥiẓienne,' *Arabica*, 1984, vol. 21, 147.
5 Charles Pellat, *The Life and Works of Jāḥiẓ*, tr. D. M. Hawke, London: Routledge & Kegan Paul, 1969, pp. 1, 3, 4–5. This tentative state of affairs is duplicated in Pellat's more recent 'al-Jāḥiẓ,' in *CHALABL*, pp. 78–95.
6 James Montgomery, 'al-Jahiz,' in Michael Cooperson and Shawkat M. Toorawa (eds), *Arabic Literary Culture 500–925*, Detroit: Gale, 2005, in press.
7 Charles Pellat, 'Ǧāḥiẓ à Bagdad et à Samarra,' in *Rivista degli studi orientali*, 1952, vol. 27, 50.
8 Cited in Pellat, *Life and Works*, pp. 7–8 (emphases mine).
9 Pellat, *Life and Works*, p. 7.
10 Pellat, 'Ǧāḥiẓ à Bagdād,' 50.
11 Al-Jāḥiẓ may, like Ibn Abī Ṭāhir, have been a teacher for a short time, but he made more from one dedication than he could from twenty years of teaching.
12 Ibn Abī Ṭāhir does write one book entitled *Kitāb Jamharat Banī Hāshim* [The book of collected (genealogies) of the Banū Hāshim].
13 This is not meant to suggest that al-Jāḥiẓ did not also address such issues. His remarks about plagiarism in 'Kitāb Faṣl bayn al-ʿadāwah wa-al-ḥasad,' quoted in ch. 2 above, are perceptive and important. I am suggesting, rather, that he did not approach these matters as a literary critic per se.
14 The *Kitāb al-Tāj* [Book of the Crown], undoubtedly of Persian inspiration, has been falsely attributed to al-Jāḥiẓ, so too the *Kitāb Tahdhīb al-akhlāq* [On the purification of morals], and the *Kitāb Dalāʾil al-iʿtibār* [The Book of proofs and lessons]. The *Akhlāq al-wuzarāʾ* [Rules of conduct for viziers] is lost but anyway may not have been in the *naṣīḥat al-mulūk* mold. The only two other candidates for ethical writings among al-Jāḥiẓ's works are the *Kitāb al-Ḥijāb* (Book of Chamberlains), al-Jāḥiẓ's authorship of which Pellat has called into question, and the *Risālat al-Maʿād wa-al-maʿāsh fī al-adab wa-tadbīr al-nās wa-muʿāmalātihim* [Letter for this world and the next on manners, conduct, and human relationships].
15 Abū Hilāl al-ʿAskarī, *Kitāb al-Ṣināʿatayn*, p. 425.
16 Ibn Ṭabāṭabā, *ʿIyār al-shiʿr*, p. 75.
17 *Murūj al-dhahab*, ¶ 3025.
18 Al-Marzubānī, *Kitāb al-Muwashshaḥ*, pp. 536–7 (#34).
19 *Taʾrīkh Baghdād*, vol. 4, pp. 211–12, and vol. 10, p. 348; *Irshād*, vol. 3, p. 87.
20 Reynold A. Nicholson, *A Literary History of the Arabs*, Cambridge: Cambridge University Press, 1907, reprint 1966, p. 289.
21 Quoted in Nicholson, *A Literary History*, p. 290.
22 Gaudefroy-Demombynes, *Introduction au «Livre de la poésie et des poètes»*, p. 2 (Ar. pag.).
23 Jesters, bufoons and other comic entertainers seem to have operated with greater leeway, no doubt as a result of the nature of their entertainment.
24 *EAL*, p. 306.
25 Beeston, 'Background Topics,' p. 25.
26 Recounted e.g. of a *warrāq* approached by al-Ṭabarī (Pedersen, *Arabic Book*, p. 50).
27 Al-Jāḥiẓ is well-known for the nights he spent in bookshops. See nn. 42 and 43 in chapter 2 above.
28 E.g. the bookshop of Abū ʿAbdallāh al-Azdī (d. after 230/844), the site of the premier literary salon in his day (*Inbāh*, vol. 2, p. 134, lines 13–15).
29 Pedersen, *Arabic Book*, p. 45.
30 Makdisi, *Rise of Humanism*, p. 232: "Those who wished to distance themselves from the governing power . . . earned their living in professions connected with the production of books or their distribution"; *cf. EI2*, vol. 4, p. 1114.

31 Everett K. Rowson, 'The Philosopher as Littérateur: al-Tawḥīdī and his Predecessors,' *Zeitschrift für Geschichte der arabisch-islamischen Wissenschaften*, 1990, vol. 6, 51–2.
32 Notwithstanding Fatima Mernissi's characterization of Ibn Abī Ṭāhir as "Imam" in *The Forgotten Queens of Islam*, tr. M. J. Lakeland, Minneapolis: University of Minnesota Press, 1993, p. 212, n. 9 (to p. 142).
33 For Ibn Abī Ṭāhir's acquaintaince with Aristotle, see Seeger A. Bonebakker, 'Poets and Critics in the Third Century AH,' in Gustav E. von Grunebaum (ed.), *Logic in Classical Islamic Culture*, Wiesbaden: Otto Harrassowitz, 1970, p. 109.

BIBLIOGRAPHY

Manuscripts and Published Works of Ibn Abī Ṭāhir Ṭayfūr

Ibn Abī Ṭāhir Ṭayfūr, Abū al-Faḍl Aḥmad (d. 280/893), *Kitāb Baghdād*, vol. 6, MS British Museum 1204, Add. 23318, 132 folios, dated 7th/13th *c.* = MS Leiden Or. 5570, 132 folios.

—— *Das Kitâb Baǧdâd von Abu 'l-Faḍl Aḥmad Ibn Abi Ṭāhir Ṭayfūr: Folio 1–26*, ed. Hans Keller, Leipzig: Otto Harrassowitz, 1898.

—— *Sechster Band des Kitâb Baǧdâd von Ahmad Ibn Abî Tâhir Taifûr*, 2 vols, ed. Hans Keller, Leipzig: Otto Harrassowitz, 1908.

—— *Kitāb Baghdād*, ed. Muḥāmmad al-Kawtharī, Cairo: Maktab Nashr al-Thaqāfah al-Islāmiyyah, 1368/1949; repr. *Baghdād fī ta'rīkh al-khilāfat al-'Abbāsiyyah*, Baghdad: Maktabat al-Muthannā, Beirut: Maktabat al-Ma'ārif, 1388/1968; 1972.

—— *al-Manthūr wa-al-manẓūm*, vols 11–12, MS British Museum 1090. Add. 18532, 156 folios, dated 1092/1681.

—— *al-Manthūr wa-al-manẓūm*, vols 11–13, MS Ya'qūb Sarkīs Collection, Al-Ḥikmah University Library, Baghdad, Adab 58, 329 folios, dated tenth/sixteenth century.

—— *[Ikhtiyār] al-Manthūr wa-al-manẓūm*, vols 11–13, MS Medina, private collection = MS Cairo, Dār al-Kutub *adab* 581, 238 folios, dated 1297/1880.

—— *al-Manthūr wa-al-manẓūm: al-Qaṣā'id al-mufradāt al-lattī lā mithla lahā* [= second half of vol. 12], ed. Muḥsin Ghayyāḍ, Beirut and Paris: Turāth 'Uwaydat, 1977.

—— *Balāghāt al-nisā' wa-ṭarā'if kalāmihinna wa-mulaḥ nawādirihinna wa-akhbār dhawāt al-ra'y minhunna wa-ash'āruhunna fī al-Jāhiliyyah wa-al-Islām* [= vol. 11], ed. Aḥmad al-Alfī, Cairo: Press of the Wālidat al-'Abbās al-Awwal School, 1908; repr. Tunis: al-Maktabat al-'Atīqah, 1985; no ed. Beirut: Dār al-Nahḍah al-Ḥadīthah, 1972; ed. Muḥammad Ṭāhir al-Zayn, Kuwait: Maktabat al-Sundus, 1993; ed. 'Abd al-Ḥamīīd Hindawī, Cairo: Dār al-Faḍīlah, 1998; ed. Yūsuf al-Biqā'ī, Beirut: Dār al-Aḥwāl, 1999; ed. Barakāt Yūsuf Habbūd, Sayda: al-Maktabah al-'Aṣriyyah, 2000.

Primary sources

Abū al-Faraj 'Alī ibn al-Ḥusayn al-Iṣbahānī (d. 356/967), *Kitāb al-aghānī*, vols 1–16, Dār al-Kutub, 1345–80/1970–74, 1927–61, vols 17–24, al-Hay'ah al-Miṣriyyah al-'Āmmah li-al-Ta'līf wa-al-Nashr, 1389–94/1970–74. Ed. Ibrāhīm al-Ibyārī, 33 vols., Dār al-Sha'b, 1389–1402/1969–1982.

—— *Maqātil al-Ṭālibiyyīn*, ed. Aḥmad Ṣaqr, Cairo: ʿĪsā al Bābī al-Ḥalabī, Dār Iḥyāʾ al-Kutub al-ʿArabiyyah, 1368/1949.

—— *al-Imāʾ al-shawāʿir*, ed. N. Ḥ. al-Qaysī and Y. A. al-Samarrāʾī, Beirut: Maktabat al-Nahḍah al-ʿArabiyyah, 1404/1984.

Abū Ḥakīmah Rāshid ibn Isḥāq (d. 240/854), *Dīwān Abī Ḥukaymah Rāshid ibn Isḥāq al-Kātib: al-Ayriyyāt*, ed. M. Ḥ. al-ʿArajī, Cologne: Manshūrāt al-Jamal, 1997.

Abū Hiffān al-Mihzamī (d. 257/871), *Akhbār Abī Nuwās*, ed. ʿA. A. Farrāj, Cairo: Dār Miṣr, n.d.

Abū Nuʿaym al-Iṣbahānī, Aḥmad ibn ʿAbdallāh (d. 430/1038), *Ḥilyat al-awliyāʾ wa-ṭabaqāt al-aṣfiyāʾ*, 10 vols in 5, no ed., Cairo: Maktabat al-Khānjī/Maktabat al-Saʿādah, 1351–7/1932–8.

Abū Nuwās (d. *c.* 198/813), *Dīwān*, vols 1–3, ed. Ewald Wagner, vol. 4, ed. Gregor Schoeler, Cairo: Maṭbaʿah Lajnat al-Taʾlīf wa-al-Tarjamah wa-al-Nashr, Wiesbaden: Franz Steiner, 1958–82.

Abū Tammām, Ḥabīb ibn Aws al-Ṭāʾī (d. 231/845), *Dīwān Abī Tammām bi-sharḥ al-Khaṭīb al-Ṭibrīzī*, 4 vols, ed. M. ʿA. ʿAzzām, Cairo: Dār al-Maʿārif, 1957–65.

Abū al-Ṭayyib al-Lughawī al-Ḥalabī, *Marātib al-naḥwiyyīn*, ed. M. A. Ibrāhīm, Cairo: Dār al-Maʿārif, 1375/1955.

Akmal al-Dīn al-Bābartī, Muḥammad ibn Muḥammad (d. 786/1384), *Sharḥ al-Talkhīṣ*, ed. M. M. R. Ṣūfiya, Tripoli: al-Munshaʾat al-ʿĀmmah li-al-Nashr wa-al-Tawzīʿ wa-al-Iʿlān, 1983.

ʿAlī ibn Naṣr al-Kātib (d. 518/1124?), *Encyclopedia of Pleasure by Abul Hasan ʿAli Ibn Nasr al-Katib* [= *Jawāmiʿ al-ladhdhah*], ed. Salah Addin Khawwam, tr. Adnan Jarkas and Salah Addin Khawwam, Toronto: Aleppo Publishers, 1977.

al-Āmidī, Abū al-Qāsim al-Ḥasan ibn Bishr (d. 371/987), *al-Muwāzanah bayna shiʿr Abī Tammām wa-al-Buḥturī*, vols 1–2, 2nd edn, ed. S. A. Ṣaqr, Cairo: Dār al-Maʿārif, 1392/1972; vol. 3 in 2 vols, ed. ʿA. H. Muḥārib, Cairo: Maktabat al-Khānjī, 1410/1990.

—— *al-Muʾtalif wa-al-mukhtalif*, ed. ʿA. A. Farrāj, Cairo: Dār Iḥyāʾ al-Kutub al-ʿArabiyyah, 1381/1961.

[Ibn] al-Anbārī, Abū al-Barakāt (d. 577/1181), *Nuzhat al-alibbāʾ fī ṭabaqāt al-udabāʾ*, ed. Ibrāhīm al-Sāmarrāʾī, Baghdad: Maṭbaʿat al-Maʿārif, 1959; ed. ʿA. ʿĀmir, Stockholm: Almqvist & Wiksell, 1963.

Anonymous, *Jawhar al-anfās fī akhbār banī al-ʿAbbās*, MS Qq-133, Cambridge University Library, dated 1191/1777–8.

Anonymous, *Kārnāmah-ī Ardashīr Papakan*, ed. and tr. D. P. Sanjana, Bombay: Education Society Steam Press, 1896.

Anonymous, *The Subtle Ruse: The Book of Arabic Wisdom and Guile [= Raqāʾiq al-ḥilal fī daqāʾiq al-ḥiyal]*, tr. René R. Khawam, London and The Hague: East-West Publications, 1980. *Raqāʾiq al-hilal wa-daqāʾiq al-ḥiyal: al-Siyāsah wa-al-ḥīlah ʿinda al-ʿArab*, ed. René R. Khawam. London: Dar al Saqi, 1988.

Anonymous, *al-ʿUyūn wa-al-ḥadāʾiq fī aḫbār al-ḥaqāʾiq, chronique anonyme, IV: 256/870–350/961*, 2 vols, ed. Omar Saïdi, Damascus: Institut français de Damas, 1972.

al-ʿAskarī, Abū Aḥmad al-Ḥasan ibn ʿAbdallāh (d. after 382/993), *al-Risāla fī al-tafḍīl bayna balāghatay al-ʿarab wa-al-ʿajam*. In *al-Tuḥfah al-bahiyyah wa-al-ṭurfah al-shahiyyah fīhā sabʿah ʿasharah majmūʿah muntakhabah tashtamil ʿalā adabiyyāt muʿjibah wa-nawādir muṭribah*, no ed., Istanbul: Jawāʾib, 1302/1884–5.

—— *al-Maṣūn fī al-adab*, ed. ʿA. M. Hārūn, Kuwayt: Dāʾirat al-Maṭbūʿāt wa-al-Nashr, 1960.

al-ʿAskarī, Abū Hilāl al-Ḥasan ibn ʿAbdallāh (d. after 395/1005), *al-Ṣināʿatayn al-kitābah wa-al-shiʿr*, ed. ʿA. M. al-Bajāwī and M. A. Ibrāhīm, Cairo: ʿĪsā al-Bābī al-Ḥalabī, 1371/1952.

—— *Dīwān al-maʿānī*, 2 vols, ed. M. ʿAbduh and M. M. al-Shanqīṭī, Cairo: Maktabat al-Qudsī, 1982.

al-Aṣmaʿī, ʿAbd al-Malik ibn Qurayb (d. 213/828), *al-Aṣmaʿiyyāt*, ed. ʿA. Hārūn and A. M. Shākir, Cairo: Dār al-Maʿārif, 1375/1955.

—— *Fuḥūlat al-shuʿarāʾ*, ed. M. ʿA. Khafājī and Ṭ. M. al-Zaynī, Cairo: Maktabat al-Munīriyyah bi-al-Azhar, 1372/1953.

al-Azdī, Abū al-Muṭahhar Muḥammad ibn Aḥmad (d. 5th/11th *c.*), *Ḥikāyat Abī al-Qāsim. Abulkâsim, ein bagdâder Sittenbild*, Heidelberg: C. Winter's Universitätbuchhandlung, 1902.

al-Badīʿī, Yūsuf (d. 1073/1662), *Ṣubḥ al-munabbī fī ḥaythiiyyat al-Mutanabbī*, ed. M. Y. ʿArafah, Damascus: Maktabat ʿArafah, 1350/1931.

al-Baghdādī, ʿAbd al-Qāhir (d. 429/1037), *al-Farq bayna al-firaq*, ed. M. Badr, Cairo: Maktabat al-Maʿārif, 1910. *Moslem Schisms and Sects*, vol. 1, tr. K. Seelye, New York: Columbia University Press, 1920.

al-Baghdādī, ʿAbd al-Qādir ibn ʿUmar (d. 486/1093), *Khizānat al-adab*, 13 vols, ed. ʿA. M. Hārūn, Cairo: Dār al-Kutub, n.d.

—— *al-Taṭfīl wa-ḥikāyāt al-ṭufayliyyīn wa-akhbāruhum wa-nawādir kalāmihim wa-ashʿāruhum*, no ed., Damascus: Maktabat al-Tawfīq, 1346/1927.

al-Bakrī, Abū ʿUbayd ʿAbdallāh ibn ʿAbd al-ʿAzīz (d. 487/1094), *Simṭ al-laʾālī fī sharḥ Amālī al-Qālī*, 3 vols in 2, ed. ʿAbd al-ʿAzīz al-Maymanī, Cairo: Maṭbaʿah Lajnat al-Taʾlīf wa-al-Tarjamah wa-al-Nashr, 1354/1936.

al-Balādhurī, Aḥmad ibn Yaḥyā (d. 279/892), *Futūḥ al-buldān*, ed. M. J. de Goeje, Leiden: E. J. Brill, 1866.

Bar Hebraeus, Abū al-Faraj Yūḥannā Gregorius [= Ibn al-ʿIbrī, Ghirīghūryūs al-Malṭī] (d. 685/1286), *Taʾrīkh mukhtaṣar al-duwal*, ed. Anṭūn Ṣālḥānī, Beirut: Imprimerie Catholique, 1958.

al-Bayhaqī, Ibrāhīm ibn Muḥammad (d. early 4th/10th *c.*), *al-Maḥāsin wa-al-maṣāwī*, ed. M. A. Ibrāhīm, Cairo: Maktabat Naḥḍat Miṣr, n.d., Beirut: Dār Ṣādir and Dār Bayrūt, 1961; repr. Cairo: Dār al-Maʿārif, 1991.

Bernard of Angiers, 'Incipit epistola ad domnum Fulbertum,' in A. Bouillet ed., *Liber miraculorum sancte Fidis*, Paris, Alphonse Picard et Fils, 1897.

al-Bīrūnī, Abū al-Rayḥān Muḥammad ibn Aḥmad (d. after 442/1050), *al-Āthār al-bāqiyah ʿan al-Qurūn al-khāliyah. Chronologie orientalisticher Volker*, ed. C. Eduard Sachau, Leipzig: Brockhaus, 1878; repr. 1923.

al-Buḥturī (d. 284/897), *Dīwān*, 2 vols in 1, no ed., Beirut: Dār al-Kutub al-ʿIlmiyyah, 1307/1987.

al-Ḍabbī, Aḥmad ibn Yaḥyā al-Qurṭubī (d. 599/1202–03), *Bughyat al-multamis fī taʾrīkh rijāl ahl al-Andalus*, Cairo: Dār al-Kātib al-ʿArabī, 1968.

al-Dhahabī, Shams al-Dīn (d. 748/1348), *Taʾrīkh al-Islām wa-wafāyāt mashāhīr al-aʿlām*, vol. 20, ed. ʿUmar ʿAbd al-Salām al-Tadmurī, Cairo: Dār al-Kitāb al-ʿArabī, 1412/1992.

—— *Siyar aʿlām al-nubalāʾ*, 22 vols, ed. Shuʿayb al-Arnaʾūṭ, Ḥusayn al-Asad *et al.*, Beirut: Muʾassasat al-Risālah, 1401–05/1981–85.

—— *al-Mushtabah fī al-rijāl: asmāʾihim wa-ansābihim*, ed. ʿA. M. al-Bajāwī, Cairo: Dār Iḥyāʾ al-Kutub al-ʿArabiyyah, 1962.

—— *Ṭabaqāt al-ḥuffāẓ. Liber classium vivorum*, ed. Ferdinand Wüstenfeld, Göttingen: Vanderhock et Ruprecht, 1833–4.

—— *Tadhkirat al-ḥuffāẓ*, 4 vols, Hyderabad: Maṭbaʿat Dāʾirat al-Maʿārif al-Niẓāmiyyah, 1333–4/1914–15.

Diʿbil ibn ʿAlī al-Khuzāʿī (d. 246/860), *Dīwān*, ed. M. Y. Najm, Beirut: Dār al-Thaqāfah, 1962.

al-Dīnawarī, Abū Ḥanīfah Aḥmad (d. 281/894), *al-Akhbār al-ṭiwāl*, ed. ʿA. ʿĀmir, Cairo: Wizārat al-Thaqāfah wa-al-Irshād al-Qawmī, 1960.

Elias bar Shīnāyā [= Elijah of Nisibis] (d. after 438/1046), *Fragmente syrischer und arabischer Historiker*, ed. Friedrich Baethgen, Leipzig: F. A. Brockhaus, 1884.

al-Fīrūzābādī, Muḥammad ibn Yaʿqūb (d. 817/1414–15), *al-Qāmūs al-muḥīt*, 4 vols, Cairo: al-Ḥusayniyyah al-Miṣriyyah, 1349/1930.

Gardīzī, Abū Saʿīd ʿAbd al-Ḥayy ibn al-Ḍaḥḥāk (d. *c.* mid 5th/11th *c.*), *Zayn al-akhbār*, ed. ʿAbd al-Ḥayy Ḥabībī, Teheran: Dunyā-yi Kitāb, 1363/1984.

al-Ghuzūlī, ʿAlā al-dīn ʿAlī ibn ʿAbdallāh (d. 815/1412), *Maṭāliʿ al-budūr fī manāzil al-surūr*, 2 vols in 1, Cairo: Maktabat Idārat al-Waṭan, 1299/1882.

Ḥājjī Khalīfah, Muṣṭafā ibn ʿAbdallāh [= Kātib Čelebi] (d. 1067/1657), *Kashf al-ẓunūn ʿan asāmī al-kutub wa-al-funūn*, 7 vols, ed. and tr. Gustav Flügel, Leipzig and London: Oriental Translation Fund of Great Britain and Ireland, 1835–58; ed. M. Ş. Yaltkaya and R. B. Kilisli, 2 vols, Istanbul: Maarif Matbaası, 1941–3.

Ḥamzah al-Iṣfahānī, Abū ʿAbd Allāh ibn al-Ḥasan (d. after 350/961), *Taʾrīkh sinī mulūk al-arḍ wa-al-anbiyāʾ*, Beirut: Dār Maktabat al-Ḥayāt, 1961.

al-Ḥātimī, Abū Alī Muḥammad ibn al-Ḥasan (d. 388/998), *al-Risālah al-mūḍiḥah fī dhikr sariqāt Abī al-Ṭayyib al-Mutanabbī wa-sāqit shiʿrihi*, ed. M. Y. Najm, Beirut: Dār Ṣādir/Dār Bayrūt, 1965.

—— *Ḥilyat al-muḥāḍarah fī ṣināʿat al-shiʿr*, vol. 1, ed. Hilāl Nājī, Beirut: Dār Maktabat al-Ḥayāt, 1978., vol. 2, ed. Jaʿfar al-Kitābī, Baghdad: Dār al-Ḥurriyyah/Dār al-Rashīd li-al-Nashr, 1979.

Hilāl al-Ṣābiʾ, Abū al-Ḥusayn ibn al-Muḥassin (d. 448/1055), *Tuḥfat al-umarāʾ fī taʾrīkh al-wuzarāʾ. The Historical Remains of Hilāl al-Sābi, First Part of his Kitab al-Wuzara and Fragment of his History (389–393 AH)*, ed. H. F. Amedroz, Beirut: Catholic Press, 1904.

al-Ḥimyarī, Abū al-Walīd (d. *c.* 440/1048), *al-Badīʿ fī waṣf al-rabīʿ*, ed. Henri Pérès, rev. edn, Rabat: Manshūrāt Dār al-Āfāq al-Jadīdah, 1989.

al-Ḥumaydī, Abū ʿAbd Allāh Muḥammad ibn Abī Naṣr (d. 488/1095), *Jadhwat al-muqtabis fī taʾrīkh ʿulamāʾ al-Andalus*, 2 vols, ed. Ibrāhīm al-Ibyārī, Dār al-Kutub al-Islāmiyyah, Cairo: Dār al-Kitāb al-Miṣrī, Beirut: Dār al-Kitāb al-Lubnānī, n.d.

al-Ḥusaynī, al-Muẓaffar ibn al-Faḍl (d. 656/1244), *Naḍrat al-ighrīḍ fī nuṣrat al-qarīḍ*, ed. N. ʿA. al-Ḥasan, Damascus: Maṭbūʿāt Majmaʿ al-Lughah al-ʿArabiyyah, 1976; repr. Beirut: Dār Ṣādir, 1995.

al-Ḥuṣrī al-Qayrawānī, Abū Isḥāq Ibrāhīm ibn ʿAlī (d. 453/1061), *Zahr al-ādāb wa-thamar al-albāb*, ed. ʿA. M. al-Bajāwī, Cairo: Dār Iḥyāʾ al-Kutub, 1989.

—— *Jamʿ al-jawāhir fī al-mulaḥ wa-al-nawādir* [= *Dhayl Zahr al-ādāb*], ed. ʿA. M. al-Bajāwī, Cairo: Dār Iḥyāʾ al-Kutub al-ʿArabiyyah, 1372/1953.

—— *al-Maṣūn fī sirr al-hawā al-maknūn*, ed. al-Nabawī ʿAbd al-Wāḥid Shaʿlān, Cairo: Dār Iḥyāʾ al-Kutub al-ʿArabiyyah, 1372/1953.

Ibn al-ʿAbbār, Abū ʿAbdallāh Muḥammad (d. 658/1260), *Iʿtāb al-kuttāb*, ed. Ṣāliḥ al-ʿAshtar, Damascus: Majmaʿ al-Lughah al-ʿArabiyyah, 1961.

Ibn ʿAbd al-Barr, Abū ʿUmar Yūsuf ibn ʿAbdallāh (d. 463/1071), *Bahjat al-majālis wa-uns al-mujālis wa-shaḥdh al-dhāhin wa-al-hājis*, 2 vols, ed. M. M. al-Khūlī, Cairo: Dār al-Miṣriyyah li-al-Taʾlīf wa-al-Tarjamah, 1967–70.

Ibn ʿAbd al-Majīd, Tāj al-dīn ʿAbd al-Bāqī (d. 744/1343), ʿAnwār al-saʿd wa-nuwwār al-majd fī al-mufākharah bayn al-narjis wa-al-ward,' in al-Nuwayrī, *Nihāyat al-arab fī funūn al-adab*, vol. 21, Cairo: Dār al-Kutub and al-Muʾassasah al-Miṣriyyah al-ʿĀmmah li-al-Taʾlīf wa-al-Tarjamah wa-al-Ṭibāʿah wa-al-Nashr, 1980, pp. 207–13.

Ibn ʿAbd al-Malik al-Marrākushī, Muḥammad ibn Muḥammad (d. 703/1303), *al-Dhayl wa-al-takmilah li-kitābay al-Mawṣūl wa-al-ṣilah*, 6 vols, ed. Iḥsān ʿAbbās, Beirut: Dār al-Thaqāfah, 1965.

Ibn ʿAbd Rabbihi, Abū ʿUmar Shihāb al-dīn Aḥmad ibn Muḥammad (d. 328/940), *al-ʿIqd al-farīd*, 9 vols, ed. Mufīd Muḥammad Qumayḥah and ʿAbd al-Majīd al-Ṭarḥīnī, Beirut: Dār al-Kutub al-ʿIlmiyyah, 1307/1987.

Ibn Abī ʿAwn (d. 322/934), *The Kitāb al-Tashbīhāt of Ibn Abī ʿAun*, ed. M. ʿA. Khān, London: Messrs Luzac & Co. Ltd/Cambridge University Press, 1950.

Ibn Abī al-Dunyā (d. 281/894), *Makārim al-akhlāq. The Noble Qualities of Character*, ed. J. A. Bellamy, Wiesbaden: Franz Steiner, 1973.

Ibn Abī al-Ḥadīd, ʿIzz al-dīn Abū Ḥāmid (d. 655/1257), *Sharḥ Nahj al-balāghah*, ed. M. A. Ibrāhīm, 20 vols in 11, Cairo: ʿĪsā al-Bābī al-Ḥalabī, 1959–64.

Ibn Abī Hātim, ʿAbd al-Raḥmān ibn Muḥammad (d. 327/938), *al-Jarḥ wa-al-taʿdīl*, 9 vols, no ed., Hyderabad: Maṭbaʿat Majlis Dāʾirat al-Maʿārif al-ʿUthmāniyyah, 1360–73/1942–53.

Ibn Abī Uṣaybiʿah, Abū al-ʿAbbās Aḥmad ibn al-Qāsim (d. 668/1270), *ʿUyūn al-anbāʿ fī ṭabaqat al-aṭibbāʿ*, ed. Nizār Riḍā, Beirut: Dār Maktabat al-Ḥayāt, 1965.

Ibn Abī Yaʿlā, Abū al-Ḥusayn Muḥammad (d. 526/1131), *Ṭabaqāt al-Ḥanābilah*, ed. M. Ḥ. al-Fiqī, Cairo: Maktabat al-Sunnah al-Muḥammadiyyah, 1952.

Ibn ʿAqīl (d. 513/1119), *The Notebooks of Ibn ʿAqīl: Kitāb al-Funūn*, ed. George Makdisi, 2 vols, Beirut: Dar El-Machreq Editeurs, 1970–1.

Ibn ʿAsākir, ʿAlī ibn al-Ḥasan (d. 571/1176), *Taʾrīkh madīnat Dimashq*, ed. Ṣalāh al-dīn al-Munajjid *et al.*, Damascus: Majmaʿah al-Lughah al-ʿArabiyyah, 1952–in progress.

Ibn al-Athīr, ʿIzz ad-dīn (d. 630/1234), *al-Kāmil fī al-taʾrīkh*, ed. C. J. Tornberg, 13 vols, rev. edn, Beirut: Dār Ṣādir/Dār Bayrūt, 1965–7.

Ibn al-Athīr, Ḍiyā al-dīn (d. 637/1239), *al-Lubāb fī tahdhīb al-ansāb*, 3 vols, Beirut: Dār Ṣādir, 1972.

Ibn Bassām al-Shantarīnī, Abū al-Ḥasan ʿAlī Ibn Bassām (d. 542/1147), *al-Dhakhīrah fī maḥāsin ahl al-Jazīrah*, 8 parts in 2 vols, ed. Ihsān ʿAbbās, Beirut: Dār al-Thaqāfah, 1399/1979.

Ibn Dāwūd, Abū Bakr Muḥammad ibn Sulaymān al-Zāhirī (d. 294/907), *al-Zahrah*, 2 vols, ed. Ibrāhīm al-Sāmarrāʾī, al-Zarqāʿ: Maktabat al-Manār, 1406/1985.

Ibn al-Dāyah, Aḥmad ibn Yūsuf (d. 341/951–2), *al-ʿUhūd al-Yunāniyyah*, in ʿUmar al-Mālikī, *al-Falsafah al-siyāsiyyah ʿinda al-ʿArab. La philosophie politique chez les arabes*, Algiers: al-Sharikah al-Waṭaniyyah li-al-Nashr wa-al-Tawzīʿ, 1971.

Ibn Durayd, Abū Bakr (d. 321/933), *Dīwān Shiʿr al-Imām Abī Bakr Ibn Durayd al-Azdī*, ed. M. B. al-ʿAlawī, Cairo: Maṭbaʿah Lajnat al-Taʾlīf wa-al-Tarjamah wa-al-Nashr, 1365/1946.

Ibn Durustawayh (d. 347/958), *Kitāb al-Kuttāb*, ed. Ibrāhīm al-Sāmarrāʾī *et al.*, Kuwait: Muʾassasat Dār al-Kutub al-Thaqāfiyyah, 1397/1977.

Ibn al-Faqīh al-Hamadhānī, Abū Bakr Aḥmad ibn Muḥammad (fl. late 3rd/early 10th *c.*), *Kitāb al-Buldān*, ed. M. J. de Goeje, Leiden: E. J. Brill, 1885

Ibn al-Faraḍī, Ibn al-Walīd ʿAbdallāh Muḥammad ibn Yūsuf (d. 403/1013), *Taʾrīkh ʿulamāʾ al-Andalus*, 2 vols, ed. Ibrāhīm al-Ibyārī, Dār al-Kutub al-Islāmiyyah, Cairo: Dār al-Kitāb al-Miṣrī, Beirut: Dār al-Kitāb al-Lubnānī, 1983.

Ibn Ghānim, ʿIzz al-dīn ʿAbd al-Salām (d. 678/1279?), *Kitāb Kashf al-asrār ʿan ḥikam al-ṭuyūr wa-al-azhār*, ed. J. H. Garcin de Tassy, Paris: Imprimerie Royale, 1821; repr. *Kashf al-asrār ʿan ḥikam al-ṭuyūr wa-al-asrār. Revelation of the Secrets of the Birds and Flowers*, ed. Denise Winn, tr. Irene Hoare and Darya Galy, London: Octagon Press, 1980.

Ibn Ḥabīb al-Baghdādī, Abū Jaʿfar Muḥammad (d. 246/860), *Kitāb al-Muḥabbar*, ed. Ilse Lichtenstader, Hyderabad: Maṭbaʿat Jamʿiyyat Dāʾirat al-Maʿārif al-ʿUthmāniyyah, 1361/1942.

—— *Tahdhīb al-tahdhīb*, 12 vols, Hyderabad: Maṭbaʿat Dāʾirat al-Maʿārif al-Niẓāmiyyah, 1325–37/1907–10; 8 vols, ed. ʿA. M. al-Bajāwī, Cairo: Dār Naḥḍat Miṣr, 1970–2.

—— *al-Iṣābah fī tamyīz al-ṣaḥābah*, 8 vols in 4, Calcutta: T. J. M'Arthur Bishop's Press, 1856–88; repr. Osnäbruck: Biblio Verlag, 1980–1.

Ibn Ḥajar al-ʿAsqalānī, *al-Iṣābah fī tamyīz al-ṣaḥābah*, no ed., Calcutta: T. J. M'Arthur Bishop's Press, 1856–88.

Ibn Ḥayyān al-Qurṭubī, Abū Marwān Ḥayyān ibn Khalaf (d. 469/1076), *al-Muqtabas fī akhbār balad al-Andalus*, ed. ʿA. ʿA. al-Ḥajjī, Beirut: Dār al-Thaqāfah, 1965.

Ibn Ḥazm, Abū Muḥammad ʿAlī ibn Aḥmad (d. 456/1064), *Jamharat ansāb al-ʿarab*, ed. ʿA. M. Hārūn, Cairo: Dār al-Maʿārif, 1971.

Ibn Hibbān al-Bustī (d. 354/965), *Mashāhīr ʿulamāʾ al-amṣār. Die berühmten traditionarier der Islamischen länder*, ed. Manfred Fleischhammer, Cairo: Maṭbaʿah Lajnat al-Taʾlīf wa-al-Tarjamah wa-al-Nashr, 1379/1959.

Ibn Hishām, ʿAbd al-Malik (d. 213/828 or 218/833), *Sīrat rasūl Allāh* [*Das Leben Muhammed's*], 2 vols in 3, ed. Ferdinand Wüstenfeld, Gottingen: Dieterische Universitäts-Buchhandlung, 1858–60.

Ibn al-ʿImād (d. 1090/1679), *Shadharāt al-dhahab fī akhbār man dhahab*, 8 vols, no ed., Cairo: Maktabat al-Qudsī, 1350/1931.

Ibn al-Jarrāḥ, Abū ʿAbdallāh Muḥammad ibn Dāwūd (d. 296/908), *Kitāb al-Waraqah*, ed. ʿA. ʿAzzām and ʿA. A. Farrāj, Cairo: Dār al-Maʿārif, 1953.

Ibn al-Jawzī, Jamāl al-dīn Abū al-Faḍāʾil ʿAbd al-Raḥmān (d. 597/1200, *al-Muntaẓam fī taʾrīkh al-mulūk wa-al-umam*, vols 5–10 [= 257–574/870–1179], ed. Fritz Krenkow, Hyderabad: Maṭbaʿat Dāʾirat al-Maʿārif al-ʿUthmāniyyah, 1357–59/1938–40; 18 vols, ed. Muḥammad ʿAbd al-Qādir al-ʿAṭā *et al.*, Beirut: Dār al-Kutub al-ʿIlmiyyah, 1412/1992.

—— *Akhbār al-ḥamqā wa-al-mughaffalīn*, ed. Kāẓim al-Muẓaffar, Najaf: al-Maktabah al-Ḥaydariyyah, 1966.

—— *Akhbār al-adhkiyāʾ*, ed. M. M. al-Khūlī, Cairo: Maṭābiʿ al-Ahrām al-Tijāriyyah, 1969.

—— *Manāqib Baghdād*, ed. Muḥammad al-Baghdādī, Baghdād: Maṭbaʿat Dar al-Salām, 1392/1972.

—— *Manāqib al-Imām Aḥmad ibn Ḥanbal*, ed. ʿAbdallāh ibn ʿAbd al-Muḥsin al-Turkī and ʿAli Muḥammad ʿUmar, Cairo: Maktabat al-Khānjī, 1979.

Ibn al-Kalbī, Hishām ibn Muḥammad (d. 206/821), *Kitāb al-Aṣnām*, ed. Aḥmad Zakī, Cairo: Dār al-Qawmiyyah li-al-Ṭabāʿah wa-al-Nashr, 1343/1924. *The Book of Idols*, tr. N. A. Faris, Princeton: Princeton University Press, 1952.

Ibn Kathīr, ʿImād al-dīn Ismāʿīl ibn ʿUmar (d. 774/1373), *al-Bidāyah wa-al-nihāyah fī al-taʾrīkh*, 14 vols, no ed., Cairo: Maṭbaʿat al-Saʿādah, 1971.

Ibn al-Kāzarūnī, Ẓahīr al-dīn ʿAlī ibn Muḥammad (d. 697/1298), *Mukhtaṣar al-taʾrīkh min awwal al-zamān ilā muntahā al-dawlah al-ʿAbbāsiyyah*, ed. Muṣṭafā Jawād, Baghdad: Mudīriyyat al-Thaqāfah al-ʿĀmmah, 1390/1970.

Ibn Khaldūn, ʿAbd al-Raḥmān (d. 808/1406), *al-Muqaddimah. Prolégomènes d'Ebn-Khaldoun*, 3 vols, ed. Etienne Quatremère, Beirut: Institut Impériale de France, 1858. *The Muqaddimah, an Inroduction to History*, 3 vols, tr. Franz Rosenthal, 2nd rev. edn, Princeton: Princeton University Press for the Bollingen Foundation, 1967.

Ibn Khallikān, Shams al-dīn (d. 681/1282), *Wafayāt al-aʿyān wa-anbāʾ abnāʾ al-zamān*, 8 vols, ed. Iḥsān ʿAbbās, Beirut: Dār al-Thaqāfah, 1968. *Ibn Khallikan's Biographical Dictionary*, 4 vols, tr. William MacGuckin de Slane, Paris: Oriental Translation Fund of Great Britain and Ireland, 1842–71.

Ibn Makkī al-Ṣiqillī, ʿUmar ibn Khalaf (d. *c.* 501/1107), *Tathqīf al-lisān*, ed. Umberto Rizzitano, Cairo: Centro di studi orientali della Custodia Francescana di Terra Santa, 1956.

Ibn Manẓūr, Muḥammad ibn Mukarram (d. 711/1311), *Lisān al-ʿarab*, 6 vols, ed. ʿA. ʿA. al-Kabīr *et al.*, Cairo: Dār al-Maʿārif, n.d.

—— *Akhbār Abī Nuwās*, ed. M. ʿA. Ibrāhīm, Cairo: Maṭbaʿat al-Iʿtimād, 1924.

Ibn Maʿṣūm, Ṣadr al-dīn ʿAlī (d. after 1107/1705), *Anwār al-rabīʿ fī anwār al-badīʿ*, 7 vols, ed. S. H. Shukr, Karbala: Maktabat al-ʿIrfān, 1968–9; repr. 1981.

Ibn Mughīth al-Ṭūlayṭulī (d. 459/1067), *al-Muqniʿ fī ʿilm al-shurūt*, ed. F. Javier Aguirre Sdaba, Madrid: al-Majlis al-Aʿlā li-al-Abḥāth al-ʿIlmiyyah, Maʾhad al-Taʿāwun maʿa al-ʿĀlam al-ʿArabī, 1994.

Ibn al-Muqaffaʿ (d. after 139/757), *Āthār Ibn al-Muqaffaʿ*, ed. ʿUmar Abū al-Naṣr. Beirut: Maktabat al-Ḥayāt, 1966.

Ibn al-Munajjim, Yaḥyā ibn ʿAlī (d. 300/912), *Kitāb al-nagham*, ed. M. B. al-Atharī, Baghdad: Maktabat al-Rābiṭah, 1369/1950.

Ibn al-Muʿtazz, Abū al-ʿAbbās (d. 296/908), *Ṭabaqāt al-shuʿarāʾ al-muḥdathīn*, 2nd edn, ed. ʿA. A. Farrāj, Cairo: Dār al-Maʿārif, 1968.

—— *Dīwān*, 3 vols, ed. Y. A. al-Sāmarrāʾī, Beirut: ʿĀlam al-Kutub, 1417/1997.

—— *Kitāb al-Badīʿ*, ed. I. J. Kračkovsky, London: S. Austin & Sons/Luzac & Co., 1935.

[Ibn] al-Nadīm, Abū al-Faraj Muḥammad (d. after 385/985), *al-Fihrist li-al-Nadīm*, ed. Riḍā Tajaddod, Teheran: Marvi Offset Printing, 1391/1971. *al-Fihrist li-Ibn al-Nadīm*, ed. Gustav Flügel, Leipzig: F. C. W. Vogel, 1871–72, repr. Beirut: Maktabat al-Ḥayāt, 1966. *The Fihrist of al-Nadīm*, tr. Bayard Dodge, 2 vols, New York: Columbia University Press, 1970.

Ibn Nubātah, Jamāl al-dīn Muḥammad (d. 768/1366), *Sarḥ al-ʿuyūn fī Risālat Ibn Zaydūn*, ed. M. A. Ibrāhīm, Cairo: Dār al-Fikr al-ʿArabī, 1964.

Ibn Qāḍī Shuhbah, Taqī al-dīn Abū Bakr (d. 851/1448), *Ṭabaqāt al-nuḥāt wa-al-lughawiyyīn*, ed. Muḥsin Ghayyāḍ, Najaf: Maktabat al-Nuʿmān, 1973.

Ibn Qays al-Ruqayyāt, ʿUbaydallāh (d. *c.* 80/699), *Dīwān*, ed. M. Y. Najm, Beirut: Dār Ṣādir/Dār Bayrūt, 1958.

Ibn Qayyim al-Jawziyyah (d. 751/1350), *Akhbār al-nisāʾ*, ed. Nizār Riḍā, Beirut: Dār Maktabat al-Ḥayāt, 1979; *Ibn Qayyim al-Ǧauziyya Über die Frauen. Liebeshistorien und Liebeserfahrung aus dem arabischen Mittelalter*, ed. Dieter Bellmann, Munich: Verlag C. H. Beck, 1986.

Ibn Qutaybah, ʿAbdallāh ibn Muslim (d. 276/889), *Adab al-kātib*, ed. M. M. ʿAbd al-Ḥamīd, Cairo: al-Maktabat al-Tijāriyyah, 1355/1936.

—— *al-Maʿārif*, ed. Tharwat ʿUkāshsah, 2nd edn, Cairo: Dār al-Maʿārif, 1969.

—— *al-Shiʿr wa-al-shuʿarāʾ*, ed. A. M. Shākir, Cairo: Dār al-Maʿārif, 1966.

—— *Taʾwīl mukhtalif al-ḥadīth fī radd ʿalā aʿdā ahl al-ḥadīth*, no ed. Baghdad: Dār al-Kitāb al-ʿArabī, n.d.

—— *ʿUyūn al-akhbār*, 4 vols, ed. Yūsuf al-Ṭawīl, Cairo: Maṭbaʿat Dār al-Kutub al-Miṣriyyah, 1925–1930; repr. Cairo: al-Muʾassasah al-Miṣriyyah al-ʿAmmāh li-al-Taʾlīf wa-al-Tarjamah wa-al-Nashr, 1964.

Ibn Rashīq (d. 456/1064), *al-ʿUmdah fī ṣināʿat al-shiʿr wa-naqdihi*, 2 vols, ed. al-Nabawī ʿAbd al-Wāḥid Shaʿlān, Cairo: Maktabat al-Khānjī, 2000.

—— *Qurāḍat al-dhahab fī naqd ashʿār al-ʿArab*, ed. al-Shādhilī Būyaḥya [= Chedly Bouyahia], Tunis: al-Sharikah al-Tūnisiyyah li-al-Tawzīʿ, 1972.

Ibn al-Rūmī, Abū al-Ḥasan ʿAlī ibn al-ʿAbbās (d. *c.* 283/896), *Dīwān*, vol. 3, ed. Ḥusayn Naṣṣār, Cairo: al-Hayʾah al-Miṣriyyah al-ʿĀmmah li-al-Taʾlīf wa-al-Nashr, 1976.

—— *Dīwān*, vol. 2, ed. ʿA. ʿA. Muḥannā, Cairo: Dār wa-Maktabat al-Hilāl, 1991.

Ibn Saʿd (d. 230/845), *Kitāb al-Ṭabaqāt al-kabīr*, 9 vols, ed. Eduard Sachau *et al.*, Leiden: E. J. Brill, 1904–40.

Ibn Saḥnūn, Muḥammad (d. 256/870), *Ādāb al-muʿallimīn*, ed. Maḥmūd ʿAbd al-Mawlā, Algiers: al-Sharikah al-Waṭaniyyah li-al-Nashr wa-al-Tawzīʿ, 1973.

Ibn Saʿīd al-Maghribī, Abū al-Ḥasan ʿAlī (d. 685/1286), *al-Mughrib fī ḥulā al-maghrib*, 2 vols, 2nd edn, ed. Shawqī Ḍayf, Cairo: Dār al-Maʿārif, 1986.

Ibn Shahrashūb, Muḥammad ibn ʿAlī (d. 588/1192), *Maʿālim al-ʿulamāʾ fī fihrist kutub al-Shīʿah wa-asmāʾ al-muṣannifīn minhum qadīman wa-ḥadīthan*, ed. M. al-Kutubī, Najaf: Manshūrāt al-Ḥaydariyyah, 1380/1961.

Ibn al-Shajarī, Hibatallāh ibn ʿAlī (d. 532/1137–8), *al-Ḥamāsah al-Shajariyyah*, 2 vols, ed. ʿAbd al-Muʿīn al-Mulawwaḥī and Asmāʾ al-Ḥimṣī, Damascus: Manshūrāt Wizārat al-Thaqāfah, 1970.

Ibn Ṭabāṭabā, Abū al-Ḥasan Muḥammad (d. 322/934), *Kitāb ʿIyār al-shiʿr*, ed. ʿAbd al-ʿAzīz ibn Nāṣir al-Mānīʿ, Riyadh: Dār al-ʿUlūm li-al-Ṭibāʿah wa-al-Nashr, 1405/1985.

Ibn Ẓāfir al-Azdī, ʿAlī (d. 613/1216), *Badāʾiʿ al-badāʾih*, ed. M. A. Ibrāhīm, Cairo: Maktabat Ānglū-Miṣriyyah, 1970.

Ibn al-Zubayr, Aḥmad ibn ʿAlī al-Qāḍī al-Rashīd [attributed] (d. 526/1167), *Kitāb al-Dhakhāʾir wa-al-tuḥaf*, ed. Muhammad Hamidullah, Kuwait: Maktabat Ḥukūmat al-Kuwayt, 1379/1959. *Book of Gifts and Rarities (Kitāb al-Hadāyā wa-al-Tuḥaf). Selections Compiled in the Fifteenth Century from an Eleventh-Century Manuscript on Gifts and Treasures*, ed. and tr. Ghāda al-Ḥijjāwī al-Qaddūmī, Cambridge, Mass.: Center for Middle Eastern Studies, 1996.

al-Ibshīhī, Bahā al-dīn Muḥammad ibn Aḥmad (d. *c.* 850/1446), *al-Mustaṭraf fī kull fann mustaẓraf*, no ed., Beirut: Manshūrāt Maktabat al-Ḥayāt, 1988.

al-Jāḥiẓ, ʿAmr ibn Baḥr (d. 255/868), *al-Maḥāsin wa-al-aḍdād*, ed. Gerlof van Vloten. Leiden: E. J. Brill, 1898.

—— *al-Ḥayawān*, ed. ʿA. M. Hārūn, 8 vols, Cairo: Muṣṭafā al-Bābī al-Ḥalabī wa-awlāduh, 1356–64/1938–45.

—— *Rasāʾil al-Jāḥiẓ*, 4 vols, ed. ʿA. M. Hārūn, Cairo: Maktabat al-Khānjī, 1384/1964, rev. edn, 1399/1979.

—— ʻKitāb Faṣl mā bayna al-ʿadāwah wa-al-ḥasad,ʼ in ʿA. M. Hārūn (ed.), *Rasāʾil al-Jāḥiẓ*, vol. 1, pp. 333–73.

—— ʻKitāb al-Ḥijāb,ʼ in ʿA. M. Hārūn (ed.), *Rasāʾil al-Jāḥiẓ*, vol. 2, pp. 29–85.

—— ʻal-Muʿallimīn,ʼ in ʿA. M. Hārūn (ed.), *Rasāʾil al-Jāḥiẓ*, vol. 3, pp. 25–51.

—— ʻDhamm akhlāq al-kuttāb,ʼ in ʿA. M. Hārūn (ed.), *Rasāʾil al-Jāḥiẓ*, vol. 2, pp. 183–209.

—— *al-Bukhalāʾ*, ed. Ṭāhā al-Ḥājirī, Cairo: Dār al-Maʿārif, 1967.

—— *al-Bayān wa-al-tabyīn*, 4 vols, ed. ʿA. M. Hārūn, Cairo: Maktabat al-Khānjī, 1968, 2nd edn, 4 vols in 2.

—— *Mufākharat al-jawārī wa-al-ghilmān*, ed. Ch. Pellat, Beirut: Dār al-Makshūf, 1957.

al-Jahshiyārī, Abū ʿAbdallāh Muḥammad ibn ʿAbdūs (d. 331/942), *Kitāb al-wuzarāʾ wa-al-kuttāb*, ed. Muṣṭafā al-Saqqāʿ *et al.*, Cairo: Muṣṭafā al-Bābī al-Ḥalabī wa-awlāduh, 1357/1938; repr. 1980/1401. *Nuṣūṣ ḍāʾiʿah min Kitāb al-Wuzarāʾ wa-al-kuttāb li-Muḥammad ibn ʿAbdūs al-Jahshiyārī*, ed. Mīkhāʾīl ʿAwwād, Beirut: Dār al-Kitāb al-Lubnānī, 1384/1964.

Jamharat rasāʾil al-ʿarab, ed. A. Z. Ṣafwat 4 vols, Cairo: Muṣṭafā al-Bābī al-Ḥalabī wa-awlāduh, 1356/1937.

al-Jumaḥī, Muḥammad ibn Sallām (d. 232/846), *Ṭabaqāt fuḥūl al-shuʿarāʾ*, ed. M. M. Shākir, Cairo: Dār al-Maʿārif, 1952.

al-Jurjānī, ʿAbd al-Qāhir (d. 471/1079), *Dalāʾil al-iʿjāz fī ʿilm al-maʿānī*, ed. Rashīd Riḍā, Cairo: Maktabat al-Khānjī, 1366/1946.

al-Jurjānī, al-Qāḍī ʿAlī ibn ʿAbd al-ʿAzīz (d. 392/1002), *al-Wasāṭah bayn al-Mutanabbī wa-khuṣūmihi*, 2nd edn, ed. M. A. Ibrāhīm and ʿA. M. al-Bajāwī, Cairo: Muṣṭafā al-Bābī al-Ḥalabī wa-awlāduh, 1370/1951.

Kārnāmah-ī Ardashīr, see Anonymous.

al-Khālidīyān, Abū Bakr Muḥammad (d. 380/990) and Abū ʿUthmān Saʿīd (d. 391/1001), *Kitāb al-Tuḥaf wa-al-hadāyā: Le Livre des Dons et des Cadeaux*, ed. Sāmī al-Dahhān, Cairo: Dār el Maʿārif, 1956.

—— *al-Ashbāh wa-al-naẓāʾir min ashʿār al-mutaqaddimīn wa-al-jāhiliyyah wa-al-mukhaḍramīn*, 2 vols, ed. Muḥāmmad Yūsuf, Cairo: Dār al-Maʿārif, 1958–65.

Khalīfah ibn Khayyāṭ al-ʿUṣfurī (d. 240/854), *al-Taʾrīkh*, ed. A. Ḍ. al-ʿUmarī, Najaf: Maktabat al-Adab, 1967.

al-Khassāf, Aḥmad ibn ʿUmar (d. 261/874), *Adab al-qāḍī*, ed. Farhat Ziadeh, Cairo: American University in Cairo Press, 1978.

al-Khaṭīb al-Baghdādī, Abū Bakr Aḥmad ibn ʿAlī (d. 463/1071), *Taʾrīkh Baghdād*, 14 vols, no ed., Cairo: Dār al-Saʿādah, 1349/1931.

—— *al-Taṭfīl wa-ḥikāyāt al-ṭufayliyyīn wa-akhbārihim wa-nawādir kalāmihim wa-ashʿārihim*, no ed., Damascus: Maktabat al-Tawfīq, 1346/1927, pp. 56, 73.

al-Khwārizmī, Abū ʿAbdallāh Muḥammad ibn Aḥmad (d. early 5th/11th *c.*), *Kitāb Mafātīḥ al-ʿulūm*, ed. Gerlof van Vloten, Leiden: E. J. Brill, 1895.

Kurd, M., see *Rasāʾil al-bulaghāʾ*.

Lisān al-dīn Ibn al-Khaṭīb, Abū ʿAbdallāh Muḥammad ibn ʿAbdallāh (d. 776/1374), *al-Siḥr wa-al-shiʿr. Poesía árabe clásica: antología titulada 'Libro de la magía y de la poesía'*, tr. J. M. Continente Ferrer, Madrid: Instituto Hispano-Arabe de Cultura, 1981.

al-Maʿarrī, Abū al-ʿAlāʾ (d. 449/1058), *Risālat al-Ghufrān*, ed. Bint al-Shāṭiʾ, Cairo: Dār al-Maʿārif, 1950.

al-Maqqarī, Aḥmad ibn Muḥammad (d. 1021/1612), *Nafḥ al-ṭīb min ghuṣn al-Andalus al-raṭīb wa-dhikr wazīrihā Lisān al-dīn Ibn al-Khaṭīb. Analectes sur l'histoire et la littérature des arabes d'Espagne par al-Makkari*, ed. Reinhart Dozy *et al.*, 2 vols, Leiden: E. J. Brill, 1855, 1861; repr. Amsterdam: Oriental Press, 1967.

al-Maqrīzī, Aḥmad ibn ʿAlī (d. 845/1442), *al-Mawāʿiẓ wa-al-iʿtibār fī dhikr al-khiṭaṭ wa-al-āthār*, 5 vols, Cairo: Institut français d'archéologie orientale, 1911–32.

al-Māridīnī, Abū al-Ḥasan ʿAlī ibn Muḥammad (d. late 9th/15th *c.*), 'al-Muḥāwarah bayn al-ward wa-al-narjis,' in ʿIzzat al-ʿAṭṭār (ed.), *Munāẓarāt fī al-adab*, Cairo: Lajnat al-Shabībah al-Sūriyyah, 1943, pp. 20–9.

al-Marzubānī, Abū ʿUbaydallāh Muḥammad (d. 384/994), *al-Muwashshaḥ fī maʾākhidh al-ʿulamāʾ ʿalā al-shuʿarāʾ*, ed. ʿA. M. al-Bajāwī, Cairo: Dār Nahḍah, 1965. *Min al-ḍāʾiʿ min*

Muʿjam al-shuʿarāʾ li-al-Marzubānī, ed. Ibrāhīm al-Sāmarrāʾī. Beirut: Muʾassasat al-Risālah, 1404/1984.

—— *Kitāb al-Muʿjam fī asmāʾ al-shuʿarāʾ*, ed. ʿA. A. Farrāj, Cairo: Dār Iḥyāʾ al-Kutub al-ʿArabiyyah/Muṣṭafā al-Bābī al-Ḥalabī wa-awlāduh, 1379/1960.

—— *Kitāb Nūr al-qabas al-mukhtaṣar min al-Muqtabas fī akhbār al-nuḥāt wa-al-udabāʾ wa-al-shuʿarāʾ wa-al-ʿulamāʾ. Die Gelehrtenbiographien des Abū ʿUbaidallāh al-Marzubānī in der Rezension des Ḥāfiẓ al-Yaġmūrī*, ed. Rudolf Sellheim, Wiesbaden: Franz Steiner, 1384/1964.

al-Marzūqī, Aḥmad ibn Muḥammad (d. 421/1030), *Sharḥ Dīwān al-ḥāmasah*, ed. Aḥmad Amīn and ʿA. M. Hārūn. Cairo: Lajnat al-Taʾlīf wa-al-Tarjamah wa-al-Nashr, 1371–2/1951–2.

al-Masʿūdī, ʿAlī ibn al-Ḥusayn (d. 345/946), *Murūj al-dhahab wa-maʿādin al-jawhar*, rev. edn, 8 vols, ed. Ch. Pellat, Beirut: al-Jāmiʿah al-Lubnāniyyah, 1966–79. *Les prairies d'or*, 9 vols, ed. and tr. C. Barbier de Meynard and Pavet de Courteilles, Paris: Imprimerie Nationale, 1861–77.

—— *al-Tanbīh wa-al-ishrāf*, ed. M. J. de Goeje, Leiden: E. J. Brill, 1894; ed. ʿA. I. al-Ṣāwī, Cairo: Dār al-Ṣāwī li-al-Ṭabʿ wa-al-Nashr wa-al-Taʾlīf, 1357/1938.

al-Masʿūdī, ʿAlī Nūr al-dīn (fl. 616/1219), *al-Mukhtār min Quṭb al-surūr fī awṣāf al-anbidhah wa-al-khumūr*, ed. ʿAbd al-Ḥafīẓ Manṣūr, Tunis: Nashr Muʾassasah ʿAbd al-Karīm ibn ʿAbdallāh, 1976.

al-Maydānī, Abū al-Faḍl Aḥmad ibn Muḥammad (d. 518/1124), *Majmaʿ al-amthāl*, 2nd edn, ed. M. M. ʿAbd al-Ḥamīd, Cairo: al-Maktabah al-Tijāriyyah al-Kubrā, 1959.

al-Mīkālī, Abū al-Faḍl ʿUbaydallāh (d. 436/1044–5), *al-Muntakhab al-Mīkālī*, MS Topkapı Sarayı 8561 A. 2634. 611 Ḥ

—— *Kitāb al-Muntakhal*, 2 vols, ed. Yahyā Wahīb al-Jubūrī, Beirut: Dār al-Gharb al-Islāmī, 2000.

Miskawayh, Abū ʿAlī Aḥmad ibn Muḥammad (d. *c.* 421/1030), *al-Ḥikmah al-khālidah* [= *Jāvīdān-i khirad*], ed. ʿAbd al-Raḥmān Badawī, Cairo: Maktabat al-Nahḍah al-Miṣriyyah, 1952.

al-Mubarrad, Muḥammad ibn Yazīd (d. 285/898), *al-Kāmil*, 4 vols, ed. M. A. al-Dālī, Beirut: Muʾassasat al-Risālah, 1406/1986.

al-Mufaḍḍal al-Ḍabbī (d. *c.* 164/780–81), *al-Mufaḍḍalīyāt*, ed. A. M. Shākir and ʿA. M. Hārūn, Cairo: Dār al-Maʿārif, 1941.

Muḥammad ibn Sayf al-dīn Aydamur (d. late 7th/13th *c.*), *al-Durr al-farīd wa-bayt al-qaṣīd*, MS Fatih 3761, Süleymaniye; MS Ayasofya 3864, Süleymaniye, dated 694/1294–5.

al-Muḥibbī, Muḥammad Amīn ibn Faḍlallāh (d. 1111/1699), *Janī al-jannatayn fī tamyīz nawʿay al-muthanniyayn*, Damascus: Maktabat al-Qudsī wa-al-Badīr, 1348/1929.

al-Mutanabbī, Abū al-Ṭayyib (d. 354/955), *Dīwān Abī al-Ṭayyib al-Mutanabbī*, ed. ʿAbd al-Wahhāb ʿAzzām, Cairo: Lajnat al-Taʾlīf wa-al-Tarjamah wa-al-Nashr, 1944.

al-Muzanī, Ismāʿīl ibn Yaḥyā (d. 264/878), *Sharḥ al-Sunnah*, ed. Jamāl ʿAzzūn. Medina: Maktabat al-Ghurabāʾ al-Athariyyah, 1995/1415.

al-Nawājī, Shams al-dīn Muḥammad ibn Ḥasan (d. 859/1455), *Ḥalbat al-kumayt fī al-adab wa-al-nawādir al-mutaʿalliqah bi-al-khamriyyāt*, no ed., Cairo: Maktabat Idārat al-Waṭan, 1299/1881; repr. al-Maktabat al-ʿĀlamiyyah, 1938.

al-Nuwayrī, Shihāb ad-dīn Aḥmad ibn ʿAbd al-Wahhāb (d. 733/1332), *Nihāyat al-arab fī funūn al-adab*, 33 vols in 27, Cairo: Dār al-Kutub and al-Muʾassasah al-Miṣriyyah al-ʿĀmmah li-al-Taʾlīf wa-al-Tarjamah wa-al-Ṭibāʿah wa-al-Nashr, 1923–85.

al-Qālī, Abū ʿAlī Ismāʿīl ibn al-Qāsim (d. 356/967), *al-Amālī* [including *Dhayl al-Amālī*] 4 vols in 2, 3rd edn, ed. I. Y. Ibn Diyāb, Cairo: Maktabat al-Saʿādah, 1373/1953.

al-Qalqashandī, Abū al-ʿAbbās Aḥmad (d. 821/1418), *Ṣubḥ al-aʿshā fī ṣināʿat al-inshā'*, 14 vols, Cairo: Dār al-Kutub al-Khidiwiyyah, 1913–20; repr. Cairo: Wizārat al-Thaqāfah wa-al-Irshād al-Qawmī, 1963.

(Ibn) al-Qifṭī, Jamāl al-dīn ʿAlī ibn Yūsuf (d. 646/1248), *Kitāb ikhbār al-ʿulamā'* [= *Ta'rīkh al-ḥukamā'*], ed. Julius Lippert, Leipzig: Theodor Weicher, 1903.

—— *Inbāh al-ruwāt ʿalā anbāh al-nuḥāt*, 3 vols, ed. M. A. Ibrāhīm, Cairo: Dār al-Kutub, 1369–71/1950–5.

—— *al-Muḥammadūn min al-shuʿarā'*, ed. Ḥasan Muʿammirī, Riyadh: Dār al-Yamāmah li-al-Baḥth wa-al-Tawzīʿ wa-al-Nashr, 1970.

al-Rāghib al-Iṣfahānī, Abū al-Qāsim Ḥusayn ibn Muḥammad (d. early 5th/11th *c.*), *Muḥāḍarāt al-udabā' wa-muḥāwarāt al-shuʿarā' wa-al-bulaghā'*, 4 vols in 2, no ed., Beirut: Manshūrāt Maktabat al-Ḥayāt, 1961.

al-Raqīq al-Nadīm, Abū Isḥāq Ibrāhīm (d. 417/1026), *Quṭb al-surūr fī awṣāf al-khumūr*, ed. Aḥmad al-Jundī, Damascus: Maṭbūʿāt Majmaʿ al-Lughat al-ʿArabiyyah, 1969.

Rasā'il al-bulaghā', 4th edn, ed. Muḥammad Kurd ʿAlī, Cairo, Maṭbaʿat Lajnat al-Ta'līf wa-al-Tarjamah wa-al-Nashr, 1374/1954.

al-Ṣafadī, Ṣalāh al-dīn Khalīl ibn Aybak (d. 764/1362), *al-Wāfī bi-al-wafayāt. Das Biographische Lexikon des Ṣalāḥaddīn Ḫalīl ibn Aibak Aṣ-Ṣafadī*, 29 vols, ed. Helmut Ritter *et al.*, Deutsche Morgenländische Gesellschaft, Leipzig: F. A. Brockhaus, Istanbul and Wiesbaden: Franz Steiner, Istanbul: Staatsdruckerei, 1931–99.

—— *Nakt al-himyān fī nukat al-ʿumyān*, ed. Aḥmad Zaki, Cairo: Maṭbaʿat al-Jamāliyyah, 1911, repr. Baghdad: Maktabat al-Muthannā, 1963.

Saʿīd ibn Ḥumayd (d. after 257/871), *Rasā'il Saʿīd ibn Ḥumayd wa-ashʿāruhu*, ed. Y. A. al-Sāmarrā'ī, Baghdād: Maktabat al-Irshād, 1971.

al-Sakhāwī, Shams al-dīn Muḥammad ibn ʿAbd al-Raḥmān (d. 902/1497), *al-Iʿlān bi-al-tawbīkh li-man dhamma ahl al-ta'rīkh*, ed. Franz Rosenthal, Baghdad: Maktabat al-ʿĀnī, 1382/1963.

al-Samʿānī, ʿAbd al-Karīm ibn Muḥammad. (d. 562/1166), *Kitāb al-ansāb*, 13 vols, ed. ʿAbd al-Muʿīd Khān, Hyderabad: Dā'irat al-Maʿārif al-ʿUthmāniyyah, 1382–1402/1962–82.

—— *Adab al-imlā' wa-al-mustamlī. Die Methodik des Diktatkollegs*, ed. Max Weisweiler, Leiden: E. J. Brill, 1952.

al-Sarrāj, Abū Muḥammad Jaʿfar ibn Aḥmad (d. 500/1106), *Maṣāriʿ al-ʿushshāq*, 2 vols, no ed., Beirut: Dār Ṣādir, n.d.

al-Shābushtī, Abū al-Ḥasan ʿAlī ibn Muḥammad (d. *c.* 388/998), *al-Diyārāt*, 2nd edn, ed. Kūrkīs ʿAwwād. Baghdād: Maktabat al-Muthannā, 1386/1966.

al-Shāfiʿī, Muḥammad ibn Idrīs (d. 204/819), *al-Risālah*, ed. A. M. Shākir, Beirut: Dār al-Kutub al-ʿIlmiyyah, n.d.

al-Shahrastānī Muhammad ibn ʿAbd al-Karīm (d. 548/1153), *al-Milal wa-al-niḥal*, 2 vols. in 1, 2nd edn, ed. Muḥammad ibn Fatḥallāh Badrān, Cairo: Maktabat Anglū-Miṣriyyah, 1956.

al-Sharīf al-Murtaḍā, ʿAlī ibn al-Ḥusayn (d. 436/1044), *Amālī al-Murtaḍā: Ghurar al-fawā'id wa-durar al-qalā'id*, ed. M. A. Ibrāhīm, Cairo: Muṣṭafā al-Bābī al-Ḥalabī wa-awlāduh, 1954.

al-Shaybānī, Ibrāhīm ibn Muḥammad (d. 298/911), *al-Risālat al-ʿadhrā' li-Ibrāhīm Ibn al-Mudabbir* [misattributed], ed. Zakī Mubārak, Cairo: Maktabat Dār al-Kutub, 1350/1931.

al-Shimshāṭī, Abū al-Ḥasan ʿAlī ibn Muḥammad (d. 377/987), *al-Anwār wa-maḥāsin al-ashʿār*, vol. 2, ed. S. M. Yūsuf and ʿA. A. Farrāj, Kuwait: Wizārat al-Aʿlām, 1399/1978.

al-Ṣūlī, Abū Bakr Muḥammad ibn Yaḥyā (d. 335/946), *Kitāb al-Awrāq: Qism Akhbār al-shuʿarāʾ*, ed. J. Heyworth-Dunne, London: Luzac and Co., 1934.
—— *Akhbār al-Rāḍī wa-al-Muttaqī aw Taʾrīkh al-dawlah al-ʿAbbāsiyyah min sanat 322 ilā sanat 333 Hijriyyah, min Kitāb al-Awrāq*, ed. J. Heyworth-Dunne. London: Luzac and Co., 1935.
—— *Ashʿār awlād al-khulafāʾ wa-akhbāruhum min Kitāb al-Awrāq*, ed. J. Heyworth-Dunne, London: Luzac and Co., 1936.
—— *Akhbār Abī Tammām*, ed. K. M. ʿAsākir *et al.*, Cairo: Maṭbaʿah Lajnat al-Taʾlīf wa-al-Tarjamah wa-al-Nashr, 1356/1937.
—— *Akhbār al-Buḥturī*, ed. Ṣāliḥ al-Ashtar, Damascus: Maktabat al-Majmaʿah al-ʿIlmī al-ʿArabī, 1378/1958.
—— *Mā lam yunshar min "Awrāq" al-Ṣūlī*, ed. Hilāl Nājī, Beirut: ʿĀlam al-Kutub, 1420/2000.
al-Suyūṭī, Jalāl al-dīn Abū al-Faḍl ʿAbd al-Raḥmān ibn Abī Bakr (d. 911/1505), *Lubb al-lubāb*, ed. Ṣāliḥ al-Ashtar, Damascus: Maktabat al-Majmaʿah al-ʿIlmī al-ʿArabī, 1378/1958.
—— *Bughyat al-wuʿāt fī ṭabaqāt al-lughawiyyīn wa-al-nuḥāt*, 2 vols, ed. M. A. Ibrāhīm, Cairo: Muṣṭafā al-Bābī al-Ḥalabī wa-awlāduh, 1384/1964–5.
—— *Ḥusn al-muḥāḍarah fī akhbār Miṣr wa-al-Qāhirah*, 2 vols, ed. M. A. Ibrāhīm, Cairo: Maktabah al-Sharafiyyah 1321/1903.
al-Ṭabarī, Abū Jaʿfar Muḥammad ibn Jarīr (d. 310/923), *Taʾrīkh al-rusul wa-al-mulūk*, 15 vols, ed. M. J. de Goeje *et al.*, Leiden: E. J. Brill, 1879–1901. *The History of al-Ṭabarī*, gen. ed. Ehsan Yar-Shater, Albany: SUNY Press, 1985–98: *Volume 35: The Crisis of the ʿAbbāsid Caliphate*, tr. George Saliba, 1985; *Volume 38: The Return of the Caliphate to Baghdad*, tr. Franz Rosenthal, 1985; *Volume 32: The Reunification of the ʿAbbāsid Caliphate*, tr. C. E. Bosworth, 1987; *Volume 1: General Introduction and From the Creation to the Flood*, tr. Franz Rosenthal, 1989; *Volume 34: Incipient Decline*, tr. Joel L. Kraemer, 1989; *Volume 37: ʿAbbāsid Recovery*, tr. P. M. Fields, 1989; *Volume 31: The War between Brothers*, tr. Michael Fishbein, 1992.
al-Ṭālaqānī, Abū al-Ḥasan (fl. 5th/11th *c.*), *Risālat al-amthāl al-Baghdādiyyah allatī tajrī bayn al-ʿāmmah*, ed. Louis Massignon, Cairo: Maktabat al-Raʿamsīs, n.d.
al-Tanasī, Muḥammad ibn ʿAbdallāh (d. 899/1494), *Naẓm al-durr wa-al-ʿiqyān, al-qism al-rābiʿ: Fī mahāsin al-kalām. Westarabische Tropik: Naẓm IV des Tanasī*, ed. Nouri Soudan, Wiesbaden: F. Steiner, 1980.
al-Tanūkhī, Abū ʿAlī al-Muḥassin ibn ʿAlī (d. 384/994), *al-Mustajād min faʿalāt al-ajwād*, ed. M. Kurd ʿAlī, Damascus: Maṭbūʿāt al-Majmaʿ al-ʿIlmī al-ʿArabī, 1365/1946.
—— *Nishwār al-muḥāḍarah wa-akhbār al-mudhākarah*, 8 vols, ed. ʿAbbūd al-Shaljī, Beirut: Dār Ṣādir, 1391–3/1971–3.
—— *al-Faraj baʿd al-shiddah*, 5 vols, ed. ʿAbbūd al-Shāljī, Beirut: Dār Ṣādir, 1398/1978.
al-Tawḥīdī, Abū Ḥayyān (d. after 400/1009), *al-Imtāʿ wa-al-muʾānasah*, 3 vols, ed. Aḥmad Amīn and Aḥmad al-Zayn. Cairo: Maṭbaʿah Lajnat al-Taʾlīf wa-al-Tarjamah wa-al-Nashr, 1939–44.
—— *Akhlāq al-wazīrayn*, Damascus: Maṭbūʿāt al-Majmaʿ al-ʿIlmī al-ʿArabī, 1965.
—— *al-Baṣāʾir wa-al-dhakhāʾir*, 4 vols, ed. Ibrāhīm al-Kīlānī, Damascus: Maktabat Aṭlas, 1964; 9 vols in 6, ed. Wadād al-Qāḍī, Beirut: Dār Ṣādir, 1988.
al-Thaʿālibī, ʿAbd al-Malik ibn Muḥammad (d. 429/1038), *Bard al-akbād fī al-aʿdād*, in *Khams rasāʾil*, no ed., Constantine: Maktabat al-Jawāʾib, 1301/1884, pp. 101–42.
—— *al-Muntaḥal*, ed. A. Abū ʿAlī. Alexandria: al-Maṭbaʿah al-Tijāriyyah, 1319/1901.

—— *al-Kināyah wa-al-taʿrīḍ*, ed. M. B. al-Naʿsānī, Cairo: Maktabat al-Saʿādah, 1326/1908; ed. Usāmah al-Bulayrī. Cairo: Maktabat al-Khānjī, 1997.

—— *Laṭāʾif al-maʿārif*, ed. Ibrāhīm al-Ibyārī and Ḥ. K. al-Ṣayrafī. Cairo: Muṣṭafā al-Bābī al-Ḥalabī wa-awlāduh, 1960.

—— *al-Tamthīl wa-al-muḥāḍarah*, ed. ʿA. M. al-Ḥulw, Cairo: Dār Iḥyāʾ al-Kutub al-ʿArabiyyah, 1381/1961.

—— *Khāṣṣ al-khāss*, no ed., Beirut: Manshūrāt Dār Maktabat al-Ḥayāt, 1966.

—— *al-Iʿjāz wa-al-ījāz*, ed. Muḥammad al-Tūnjī, Beirut: Dār al-Nafāʾis, 1412/1992.

—— *Thimār al-qulūb fī al-muḍāf wa-al-mansūb*, 2 vols, ed. Ibrāhīm Ṣāliḥ, Cairo: Dār al-Bashāʾir, 1414/1994.

Thaʿlab, Abū al-ʿAbbās Aḥmad ibn Yaḥya (d. 291/904), *Majālis Thaʿlab*, ed. ʿA. M. Hārūn, Cairo: Dār al-Maʿārif, 1960.

al-ʿUbaydī, ʿUbaydallāh ibn ʿAbd al-Majīd (fl. 8th/14th *c.*), *Sharḥ al-maḍnūn bihi ʿalā ghayr ahlih*, ed. I. B. Yahūdā, Cairo: Maktabat al-Saʿādah, 1913–15.

al-ʿUkbarī, Abū al-Baqāʾ ʿAbdallāh ibn al-Ḥusayn (d. 616/1219), *Sharḥ al-tibyān*, 2 vols, no ed., Cairo: al-Maṭbaʿah al-ʿĀmirah al-Sharafiyyah, 1308/1890.

Usāmah ibn Munqidh (d. 584/1188), *al-Badīʿ fī naqd al-shiʿr*, ed. A. A. Badawī *et al.*, Egypt: Wizārat al-Thaqāfah, n.d.

al-Warrāq, Maḥmūd ibn Ḥasan (d. 225/840), *Dīwān*, ed. ʿA. R. al-ʿUbaydī, Baghdad: Maktabat Dār al-Baṣrī, 1969.

al-Washshāʾ, Abū al-Tayyib Muḥammad ibn Isḥāq (d. 325/937), *al-Muwashshā, aw al-Ẓarf wa-al-ẓurafāʾ*, no ed., Beirut: Dār Ṣādir and Dār Bayrūt, 1385/1965.

al-Waṭwāṭ, Abū Isḥāq Muḥāmmad ibn Ibrāhīm ibn Yaḥyā (d. 719/1318), *Ghurar al-khaṣāʾiṣ al-wāḍiḥah wa-ʿurar al-naqāʾiṣ al-fāḍiḥah*, Cairo: al-Maṭbaʿat al-Adabiyyah, 1318/1901.

al-Yaghmūrī, Yūsuf ibn Aḥmad (d. 673/1274): see al-Marzubānī, *Kitāb Nūr al-Qabas*

al-Yaʿqūbī, Aḥmad ibn Abī Yaʿqūb (d. 284/897), *al-Taʾrīkh*, 2 vols, ed. M. Th. Houtsma, Leiden: E. J. Brill, 1883; repr. 1969; no ed., Beirut: Dār Bayrūt and Dār al-Ṣādir, 1369/1960.

—— *Kitāb al-Buldān*, ed. M. J. de Goeje, Leiden: E. J. Brill, 1892.

Yāqūt al-Ḥamawī, Abū ʿAbdallāh Yaʿqūb ibn ʿAbdallāh (d. 626/1229), *Muʿjam al-buldān. Jacut's geographisches Wörterbuch*, 6 vols, ed. Ferdinand Wüstenfeld, Leipzig: F. A. Brockhaus, 1866–73.

—— *Irshād al-arīb fī maʿrifat al-adīb*: *Dictionary of Learned Men*, 7 vols, ed. D. S. Margoliouth, London: Luzac & Co., 1907–1931; *Muʿjam al-udabāʾ*, 20 vols in 10, ed. A. F. Rifāʿī, Cairo: Maṭbūʿāt Dār al-Maʾmūn, 1936–8, repr. Cairo: Dār al-Fikr, 1400/1980; *Muʿjam al-udabāʾ*, 6 vols, ed. Ihsān ʿAbbās, Beirut: Dār al-Kutub al-ʿIlmiyyah, 1411/1991.

al-Zajjājī (d. 337/949), ʿAbd al-Raḥmān ibn Isḥāq, *Majālis al-ʿulamāʾ*, ed. ʿA. M. Hārūn, Cairo: Maktabat al-Khānjī, Riyadh: Dār al-Rifāʿī, 1403/1983.

—— *Amālī al-Zajjājī*, ed. ʿA. M. Hārūn, 2nd edn, Beirut: Dār al-Jīl, 1407/1987.

al-Zamakhsharī, Abū al-Qāsim Maḥmūd ibn ʿUmar (d. 538/1144), *al-Kashshāf ʿan ḥaqāʾiq al-tanzīl wa-ʿuyūn al-aqāwīl wa-wujūh al-taʾwīl*, 4 vols, no ed., Beirut: Dār al-Maʿrifah, n.d.

al-Zubaydī al-Andalusī, Abū Bakr Muḥammad (d. 379/989–90), *Ṭabaqāt al-naḥwiyyīn wa-al-lughawiyyīn*, ed. M. A. Ibrāhīm, Cairo: Dār al-Maʿārif, 1973.

Secondary literature

ʿAbbās, Iḥsān, *Taʾrīkh al-naqd al-adabī ʿinda al-ʿArab*, Beirut: Dār al-Amānah, 1971.

—— *'Abd al-Ḥamīd ibn Yaḥyā al-Kātib wa-mā tabaqqā min rasā'ilihi wa-rasā'il Sālim Abī 'l-'Alā'*, Amman: Dār al-Shurūq, 1988.

Abbott, Nabia, 'Arabic Paleography,' *Ars Islamica*, 1941, vol. 8(1–2), 65–104.

—— *Studies in Arabic Literary Papyri*, 3 vols, Chicago: Oriental Institute/University of Chicago Press, 1957–67.

'Abdel-Meguid, 'Abdel-'Aziz, 'A Survey of the Terms Used in Arabic for "Narrative" and "Story",' *Islamic Quarterly*, 1954, vol. 1, 195–204.

Abu Deeb, Kamal, *Al-Jurjānī's Theory of Poetic Imagery*, Warminster: Aris and Phillips, 1979.

—— 'Literary Criticism,' in *CHALABL*, pp. 339–87.

Achtor, Saleh [= Ṣāliḥ al-Ashtar], 'Buḥturī, un poète arabe du IIIè siècle de l'hégire,' dissertation, University of Paris, 1953.

—— 'L'Enfance et la jeunesse du poète Buḥturī (206–226/821–840),' *Arabica*, 1954, vol. 1, 166–86.

Āghā Buzurg al-Ṭihrānī, M. M., *Dharī'ah ilā taṣānīf al-Shī'ah*, vol. 4, Najaf: Maṭba'at al-Gharrā, 1360/1941.

Ahmed, Munir-ud-din, *Muslim Education and the Scholars' Social Status up to the 5th century Muslim Era (11th century Christian Era) in the light of Ta'rīkh Baghdād*, Zürich: Verlag 'Der Islam,' 1968.

Ahsan, M. M., *Social Life Under the Abbasids, 170–289 AH, 786–902 AD*, London and New York/Beirut: Longman/Librairie du Liban, 1979.

Ali Samer Mahdy, 'al-Buhturi,' in Michael Cooperson and Shawkat M. Toorawa (eds), *Arabic Literary Culture 500–925*, Detroit: Gale, 2005, in press.

Allen, Roger, *The Arabic Literary Heritage*, Cambridge: Cambridge University Press, 1998.

Amar, Emile, 'Prolégomènes à l'étude des historiens arabes par Khalîl ibn Aibak As-Safadî publiés et traduits d'après les manuscrits de Paris et de Vienne,' *Journal asiatique* 10è série, 17 (1911), 5–48, 251–308, 465–532, 18 (1912), 243–97.

Amedroz, H. F., review of *Kitāb Baghdād*, ed. Keller in *Journal of the Royal Asiatic Society*, 1908, 855–64.

Arazi, Albert, 'De la voix au calame et la naissance du classicisme en poésie,' *Arabica*, 1997, vol. 44(3), 377–406.

Arazi, Albert and 'Ami El'ad, '«L'Épître à l'Armée». Al-Ma'mūn et la seconde Da'wa,' part 1, *Studia Islamica*, 1987, vol. 66, 2–770; part 2, 1988, vol. 67, 29–74.

Arberry, A. J., 'New Material on the *Kitāb al-Fihrist* of Ibn al-Nadīm,' *Islamic Research Association Miscellany*, 1948, vol. 1, 35–45.

Arjomand, Said Amir, ''Abd Allah Ibn al-Muqaffa' and the 'Abbasid Revolution,' *Iranian Studies*, 1994, vol. 27(1–4), 9–36.

Ashtiany, Julia *et al.* (eds), *'Abbāsid Belles-Lettres*, The Cambridge History of Arabic Literature (*CHALABL*), Cambridge: Cambridge University Press, 1990.

Ashtor, Eliyahu, *Histoire des prix et des salaires dans l'orient médiéval*, Paris: S.E.V.P.E.N., 1969.

'Athamina, Khalil, 'Al-Qaṣaṣ: its emergence, religious origin and its socio-political impact on early Muslim society,' *Studia Islamica*, 1992, vol. 76, 53–74.

—— '"Al-Nabiyy al-Umiyy": An Inquiry into the Meaning of a Qur'anic Verse,' *Der Islam*, 1992, vol. 69(1), 61–80.

'Awwād, Kūrkīs, *Khazā'in al-kutub al-qadīmah fī al-'Irāq*, Baghdad: Maktabat al-Ma'ārif, 1948.

—— *Fihrist makhṭūṭāt Khizānat Ya'qūb Sarkīs al-muhdā'ah ilā Jāmi'at al-Ḥikmah bi-Baghdād*, Baghdad: Maktabat al-'Ānī, 1385/1966.

Ayalon, David, 'Concerning Population Estimates in the Countries of Medieval Islam,' *Journal of the Economic and Social History of the Orient*, 1985, vol. 28, 1–9.
al-Aʿẓamī, M. M., *Studies in Early Hadith Literature*, Beirut: al-Maktab al-Islāmī, 1968.
Āzarnūsh, Āzartāsh, 'Ebn Abī Ṭāher Ṭayfūr,' in K. M. Bujnūrdī (ed.), *Dāʿirat al-maʿārif-i buzurg-i Islāmī*, Teheran: Markaz Dāʿirat al-maʿārif-i buzurg-i Islāmī, 1367/1988, vol. 2, pp. 672–76.
Balty-Guesdon, M. G. 'Le Bayt al-Hikma de Baghdad,' *Arabica*, 1992, vol. 34(2), 131–50.
Barthold, W. W. 'Die persische Šuʿūbija und die moderne Wiesenschaft,' *Zeitschrift für Assyriologie*, 1912, vol. 26, 249–66.
Basset, René, 'Deux manuscrits d'une version arabe inédite du receuil des Sept vizirs,' *Journal asiatique*, 1903, 10ème série, vol. 2, 43–83.
Bäuml, F. H., 'Varieties and Consequences of Medieval Literacy and Illiteracy,' *Speculum*, 1980, vol. 55(2), 237–65.
Beeston, A. F. L. *et al.* (eds), *Arabic Literature to the End of the Umayyad Period*, The Cambridge History of Arabic Literature (*CHALEUP*), Cambridge: Cambridge University Press, 1983.
—— 'Background Topics,' in *CHALEUP*, pp. 1–26.
Belcher, Stephen, 'The Diffusion of the Book of Sindbād,' *Fabula*, 1987, vol. 28(1), 34–57.
Bencheikh, Jamal Eddine, 'Les secrétaires poètes et animateurs de cénacles aux IIè et IIIè siècles de l'Hégire: contribution à l'analyse d'une production poétique,' *Journal asiatique*, 1975, vol. 263, 265–315.
—— 'Le cénacle poétique du calife al-Mutawakkil (m. 247): contribution à l'analyse des instances de légitimation socio-littéraires,' *Bulletin d'études orientales*, 1977, vol. 29, 33–52.
—— *Poétique arabe: essai sur les voies d'une création*, Paris: Editions Anthropos, 1975; with a new preface, Paris: Gallimard, 1989.
Bergé, Marc, 'Abū Ḥayyān al-Tawḥīdī,' In *CHALABL*, pp. 112–24.
Bernards, Monique, *Changing Traditions: Al-Mubarrad's Refutation of Sībawayh and the Subsequent Reception of the Kitāb*. Leiden: Brill, 1997.
Biberstein-Kazimirski, Albert de, *Dictionnaire arabe-français*, 2 vols, Beirut: Librairie du Liban, 1975.
Bishop, Terence A. M. (ed.), *Scriptores Regis; facsimiles to identify and illustrate the hands of royal scribes in original charters of Henry I, Stephen, and Henry II*, Oxford: Clarendon Press, 1961.
Blachère, Régis, *Histoire de la littérature arabe des origines à la fin du XVe siècle de J.-C.* I–III. Paris: Adrien Maisonneuve, 1952–66.
Blois, François de, *Burzōy's voyage to India and the origin of the book of Kalīlah wa Dimnah*, London: Royal Asiatic Society, 1990.
Bloom, Jonathan, *Paper before Print: the history and impact of paper in the Islamic world*, New Haven, Yale University Press, 2001.
Bonebakker, Seeger A., 'Reflections on the *Kitāb al-Badīʿ* of Ibn al-Muʿtazz,' in *Atti del terzo Congresso di studi arabi e islamici*, Naples: Istituto universitario orientale, 1967, pp. 191–209.
—— 'Poets and Critics in the Third Century AH,' in G. E. von Grunebaum, *Logic in Classical Islamic Culture*, Wiesbaden: Otto Harrassowitz, 1970, pp. 85–111.
—— 'Ibn Abī 'l-Iṣbaʿ's text of the *al-Badīʿ* of Ibn al-Muʿtazz,' *Israel Oriental Studies*, 1972, vol. 2, 85–97.
—— *Materials for the history of Arabic rhetoric: from the Ḥilyat al-Muḥāḍara of Ḥātimī (Mss 2934 and 590 of the Qarawiyyīn Mosque in Fez)*, Napoli: Istituto orientale, 1975.
—— '*Adab* and the Concept of *Belles-lettres*,' in *CHALABL*, pp. 16–30.

—— "Ibn al-Muʿtazz and *Kitāb al-Badīʿ*,' in *CHALABL*, pp. 388–411.

—— 'Ancient Arabic Poetry and Plagiarism: A Terminological Labyrinth,' *Quaderni di Studi Arabi*, 1997, vol. 15, 65–92.

Bosworth, C. E., 'The Ṭāhirids and Ṣaffārids,' in R. N. Frye (ed.), *Cambridge History of Iran*, vol. 4, *The Period from the Arab invasion to the Seljuqs*, Cambridge: Cambridge University Press, 1968, pp. 90–135.

—— 'The Ṭāhirids and Arabic Culture,' *Journal of Semitic Studies*, 1969, vol. 14, 45–79.

—— 'The Ṭāhirids and Persian Literature,' *Iran*, 1969, vol. 7, 103–6.

—— 'An early Arabic mirror for princes: Ṭāhir Dhū 'l-Yamīnain's epistle to his son 'Abdallāh (206/821),' *Journal of Near Eastern Studies*, 1970, vol. 24, 25–41.

—— 'The Heritage of Rulership in Early Islamic Iran and the Search for Dynastic Connections with the Past,' *Iranian Studies*, 1978, vol. 11, 7–34.

—— 'The Persian Impact on Arabic Literature,' in *CHALEUP*, pp. 483–96.

—— 'Ebn Abī Ṭāher Ṭayfūr,' in *Encyclopaedia Iranica*, vol. 5, ed. Ehsan Yar-Shater *et al*, Costa Mesa: Mazda, 1996, vol. 5, pp. 663–4.

Boustany, Said, *Ibn ar-Rūmī. Sa vie et son oeuvre*, Beirut: Publications de l'Université Libanaise, 1967.

Bouwsma, W. J., *A Usable Past: Essays in European Cultural History*, Berkeley: University of California Press, 1990.

Boyce, Mary, 'Middle Persian Literature,' in Ilya Gershevitch *et al.* (eds), *Handbuch der Orientalistik*, vol. 4, *Iranistik*, 2(1): *Litteratur*, Leiden: E. J. Brill, 1968, pp. 31–66.

Brock, Sebastian, 'The Dispute Poem: From Sumer to Syriac,' *Bayn al-Nahrayn*, 1979, vol. 7(28), pp. 417–26.

Brockelmann, Carl, *Geschichte der arabischen Litteratur*, 2 vols, Leiden: E. J. Brill, 1937–42, rev. edn, 2 vols, 3 supplements, Leiden: E. J. Brill, 1943–9.

Brünner, Helmut, *Altägyptische Erziehung*, Wiesbaden: Otto Harrassowitz, 1956, pp. 101–2.

Bulliet, Richard W., 'The Age Structure of Medieval Islamic Education,' *Studia Islamica*, 1983, vol. 57, 105–17.

Busse, Héribert, 'Das Hofbudget des Chalifen al-Muʿtaḍid billah,' *Der Islam*, 1967, vol. 43, 11–36.

Calder, Norman, *Studies in Early Muslim Jurisprudence*, Oxford: Oxford University Press, 1993.

Carter, Michael G., 'The *Kātib* in Fact and Fiction,' *Abr Nahrain*, 1977, vol. 11, 42–55.

Cejpek, Jan, 'Iranian Folk-Literature,' in Jan Rypka *et al.* (eds), *History of Iranian Literature* (*HIL*) , Dordrecht: D. Reidel Publishing Company, 1968, pp. 607–710.

Cerquiglini, Bernard, *Eloge de la variante: histoire critique de la philologie*, Paris: Seuil, 1989.

Chamberlain, Michael, *Knowledge and Social Practice in Medieval Damascus, 1190–1350*, Cambridge: Cambridge University Press, 1995.

Christensen, Arthur, *Les gestes des rois dans les traditions de l'Iran antique*, Paris: Librairie orientaliste Paul Geuthner, 1936.

—— *L'Iran sous les Sassanides*, Copenhagen: Levin and Munksgaard, 1944.

Clanchy, M. T., *From Memory to Written Record: England 1066–1307*, 2nd edn, Cambridge, Mass.: Blackwell 2nd ed, 1993.

Cook, Michael, *Early Muslim dogma: A source-critical study*, Cambridge: Cambridge University Press, 1981.

—— 'The Opponents of the Writing of Tradition in Early Islam,' *Arabica*, 1997, vol. 44(4), 437–530.

Cooperson, Michael, *Classical Arabic Biography: The Heirs of the Prophets in the Age of Al-Ma'mūn*, Cambridge: Cambridge University Press, 2000.

Crone, Patricia, *Slaves on Horses: the Evolution of the Islamic Polity*, Cambridge: Cambridge University Press, 1980.

Crosby, E. W., '*Akhbār al-Yaman wa-Ashʿāruhā wa-Ansābuhā*: The History, Poetry and Genealogy of the Yemen of ʿAbīd b. Sharya al-Jurhumī,' dissertation, Yale University, 1985.

Ḍayf, Shawqī, *al-ʿAṣr al-ʿAbbāsī al-awwal*, Cairo: Dār al-Maʿārif, 1966.

—— *al-ʿAṣr al-ʿAbbāsī al-thānī*, Cairo: Dār al-Maʿārif, 1973.

Dawood, A., 'A comparative study of Arabic and Persian Mirrors for Princes from the 2nd to the 6th century AH,' dissertation, University of London, 1965.

Dictionary of the Middle Ages, 8 vols, ed. J. R. Strayer *et al.* (eds), New York: Scribner, 1982–9.

Dijk, J. J. A. van, *La sagesse suméro-accadienne*, Leiden: E. J. Brill, 1953.

Dodge (tr.): see Ibn al-Nadīm, *al-Fihrist*

Donner, Fred McGraw, *The early Islamic conquests*, Princeton, Princeton University Press, 1981.

Dozy, Reinhart, *Supplément aux dictionnaires arabes*, 2 vols, Paris: G.-P. Maisonneuve et Larose, 1967.

Driver, G. R. (ed), *Aramaic Documents of the Fifth Century BC*, rev. edn, Oxford: Clarendon Press, 1957.

Drory, Rina, 'Three Attempts to Legitimize Fiction in Classical Arabic Literature,' *Jerusalem Studies in Arabic and Islam*, 18 (1994), 146–64.

—— 'The Abbasid Construction of the Jahiliyya: Cultural Authority in the Making,' *Studia Islamica*, 1996, vol. 83(1), 33–49.

Duby, Georges, *Rural Economy and Country Life in the Medieval West*, tr. Cynthia Postan, Columbia: University of South Carolina Press, 1968.

Dunlop, D. M., *Arab Civilization to AD 1500*, London/Beirut: Longman/Librairie du Liban, 1971.

Duri, A. A.,*The rise of historical writing among the Arabs*, ed. and tr. Lawrence I. Conrad, Princeton: Princeton University Press, 1983.

Eche, Youssef [= Yūsuf al-ʿIshsh] *Les Bibliothèques arabes publiques et sémi-publiques en Mésopotamie, en Syrie et en Egypte au Moyen Age*, Damascus: Institut français de Damas, 1967.

Edmonson, Munro, *Lore: An Introduction to the Science of Folklore and Literature*, New York: Holt, Rinehart & Winston, 1971.

Eid, Hadi (ed. and tr.), *Lettre du calife Hârûn Al-Rasîd à l'empereur Constantin VI*, Paris: Cariscript, 1992.

El Tayib, Abdulla, 'Pre-Islamic Poetry,' in *CHALEUP*, pp. 27–113.

Elʿad, Amikam, 'Characteristics of the Development of the ʿAbbāsid Army (Especially Ahl Khurāsān and Al-Abnāʾ Units) with Emphasis on the Reign of al-Amīn and al-Maʾmūn,' dissertation, The Hebrew University of Jerusalem, 1986.

Encyclopaedia of Arabic Literature, ed. Julie Scott Meisami and Paul Starkey, London and New York: Routledge, 1998.

Encyclopaedia of Islam, 4 vols, ed. M. Th. Houtsma *et al.*, Leiden: E. J. Brill, 1913–38. *Dāʾirat al-maʿārif al-islāmiyyah*, 13 vols, ed. M. Th. Houtsma, Cairo: Dār al-Shaʿb, 1969.

Encyclopaedia of Islam, 2nd edn, 11 volumes, ed. H. A. R. Gibb *et al.*, Leiden: Brill, 1954–2003.

Encyclopaedia Iranica, 12 vols–in progress, ed. Ehsan Yar-Shater, London, Boston: Routledge & Kegan Paul, 1982–present.

Ess, Josef van, *Frühe mu'tazilitische Häresiographie, zwei Werke des Nāshi' al-Akbar (gest. 293 H)*, Beirut/Wiesbaden: Franz Steiner, 1971.

—— *Theologie und Gesellschaft im 2. und 3. Jahrhundert Hidschra. Eine Geschichte des religiösen Denkens im frühen Islam*, 6 vols, Berlin and New York: de Gruyter, 1991–7.

Fiey, J. M., *Chrétiens syriaques sous les Abbasides surtout à Baghdad (749–1258)*, Louvain: Secrétariat du Corpus Scriptorum Christianorum Orientalium, 1980.

Fischer, August, 'Arab. *baṣīr* 'scharfsichtig' per antifrasin = 'blind',' *Zeitschrift der Deutschen Morgenländischen Gesselschaft*, 1907, vol. 61, 425–34.

Fischer, August and Erich Bräunlich, *Schawāhid-Indices. Indices der Reimwörter und der Dichter der in den arabischen Schawāhid-kommentaren und in verwandten Werken erläuteren Belegverse*, Leipzig: Otto Harrassowitz, 1945.

Fischer, Michael M. J. and Mehdi Abedi, *Debating Muslims: Cultural Dialogues in Postmodernity and Tradition*, Madison: University of Wisconsin Press, 1990.

Fleischhammer, Manfred, 'Hinweise auf schriftliche Quellen im Kitāb al-Aġānī,' *Wiener Zeitschrift für die Kunde des Morgenlandes*, 1979, vol. 28(1), 53–62.

Fournier, Paul, 'Etudes sur les fausses décrétales,' *Revue d'histoire européenne*, 1906, vol. 7, 33–51.

Frye, Richard N. (ed.), *The Cambridge History of Iran*, vol. 4: *The Period from the Arab Invasion to the Seljuqs*, Cambridge: Cambridge University Press, 1975.

Gamal, Adel S., 'The Organizational Principles in Ibn Sallām's *Ṭabaqāt Fuḥūl al-Shu'arā'*. A Reconsideration,' in J. R. Smart (ed.), *Tradition and Modernity in Arabic Language and Literature*, Richmond: Curzon Press, 1996, pp. 186–209.

Garsoïan, Nina, 'Byzantium and the Sasanians,' in Ehsan Yar-Shater (ed.), *The Cambridge History of Iran*, vol. 3(1): *The Seleucid, Parthian and Sasanian Periods*, Cambridge: Cambridge University Press, 1983, pp. 568–92.

Gaudefroy-Demombynes, Maurice (ed. and tr.), *Introduction au "Livre de la poésie et des poètes" d'Ibn Qotaïba*, Paris: Les Belles Lettres, 1947.

Gelder, G. J. H. van, 'The Conceit of Pen and Sword: on an Arabic Literary Debate,' *Journal of Semitic Studies*, 1987, vol. 32(2), 329–60.

—— 'Arabic Debates of Jest and Earnest,' in G. J. Reinink and H. L. J. Vanstiphout (eds), *Dispute Poems and Dialogues in the Ancient and Mediaeval Near East: Forms and Types of Literary Debates in Semitic and Related Literatures*, Leuven: Departement Oriëntalistiek/Uitgeverij Peeters, 1991, pp. 199–212.

Geries, Ibrahim Kh. *Un genre littéraire arabe: al-Maḥâsin wa-l-masâwî*, Paris: G.-P. Maisonneuve et Larose, 1977.

—— (ed. and tr.), *A Literary and Gastronomical Conceit. Mufākharat al-Ruzz wa 'l-Ḥabb Rummān: The Boasting Debate Between Rice and Pomegranate Seeds, Or al-Makāma al-Simāṭiyya (The Tablecloth Makāma)*, Wiesbaden: Harrassowitz, 2002.

Ghazi, M. F., 'La littérature d'imagination en arabe du IIè/VIIè au Vè/XIè siècles,' *Arabica*, 1957, vol. 4(2), 164–76.

—— 'Un groupe social: 'Les Raffinés' (Ẓurafā'),' *Studia Islamica*, 1959, vol. 11, 39–71.

Gibb, H. A. R., 'The Social Significance of the Shu'ūbiyya,' in Stanford J. Shaw and William R. Polk (eds), *Studies on the Civilization of Islam*, Boston: Beacon Press, 1962, pp. 62–73.

Goldziher, Ignaz, *Die Richtungen der islamischen Koranauslegung*, Leiden: E. J. Brill, 1921.

—— *Muhammadenische studien*, 2 vols, Halle: Max Niemayer, 1888–90. *Muslim Studies*, vol. 1, ed. S. M. Stern, tr. C. R. Barber and S. M. Stern, London: George Allen & Unwin Ltd, 1967.

Goodblatt, David M., *Rabbinic Instruction in Sasanian Babylonia*, Leiden: E. J. Brill, 1975.

Goody, Jack and Ian Watt, 'The Consequences of Literacy,' in Jack Goody (ed.), *Literacy in Traditional Societies*, Cambridge: Cambridge University Press, 1968, pp. 27–68.

Gordon, Matthew S., *The breaking of a thousand swords: a history of the Turkish military of Samarra, AH 200–275/815–889 CE*, Albany: SUNY Press, 2001.

Graham, William M., *Beyond the Written Word: Oral aspects of scripture in the history of religion*, Cambridge: Cambridge University Press, 1987.

de la Granja, Fernando, 'Dos epistolas de Aḥmad ibn Burd al-Aṣgar,' *al-Andalus*, 1960, vol. 25, 383–418.

Grignaschi, Mario, 'Les "Rasā'il 'Arisṭāṭālīsa 'ilā-l-Iskandar" de Sālim Abū-l-'Alā' et l'activité culturelle à l'époque omayyade,' *Bulletin d'études orientales*, 1967, vol. 19, 8–83.

Grohmann, Adolf and Raif Georges Khoury, *Chrestomathie de papyrologie arabe: documents relatifs à la vie privée, sociale et administrative dans les premiers siècles islamiques*, Leiden: E. J. Brill, 1993.

Gruber, E. A., *Verdienst und Rang, die Faḍā'il als literarisches und gesellschaftliches Problem im Islam*, Freiburg: Schwarz, 1975.

Gruendler, Beatrice, *Medieval Arabic Praise Poetry: Ibn al-Rūmī and the patron's redemption*, London and New York: RoutledgeCurzon, 2003.

Grunebaum, Gustav E. von, 'The Concept of Plagiarism in Arabic Theory,' *Journal of Near Eastern Studies*, 1944, vol. 3, 234–53.

—— *Medieval Islam*, Chicago: University of Chicago Press, 2nd edn, 1953.

—— 'Zum Lob der Stadt in der arabischen Prosa,' In von Grunebaum, *Kritik und Dichtkunst*, Wiesbaden: Otto Harrassowitz, 1955, pp. 80–6.

—— 'Aspects of Arabic Urban Literature mostly in the Ninth and Tenth Centuries,' *Islamic Studies*, 1969, vol. 8, 281–300.

—— *Themes in Medieval Arabic Literature*, ed. D. S. Wilson, London: Variorum Reprints, 1981.

Guest, Rhuvon, *Life and Works of Ibn Er Rûmî*, London: Luzac & Co., 1944.

Günther, Sebastian, *Quellenuntersuchungen zu den «Maqātil al-Ṭālibiyyīn» des Abū 'l-Farağ al-Iṣfahānī (gest. 356/967). Ein beitrag zur Problematik der mündlichen und schriftlichen Überlieferung im Islam des Mittelalters*, Hildesheim/New York: Georg Olms Verlag, 1991.

—— 'Maqātil Literature in Medieval Islam,' *Journal of Arabic Literature*, 1994, vol. 25(3), 192–212.

Gutas, Dimitri, *Greek Wisdom Literature in Arabic Translation: A Study of the Graeco-Arabic Gnomologia*, New Haven: American Oriental Society, 1975.

—— *Greek thought, Arabic culture: the Graeco-Arabic translation movement in Baghdad and early 'Abbāsid society (2nd–4th/8th–10th centuries)*, London & New York: Routledge, 1998.

Haddārah, M. M. *Mushkilat al-sariqāt fī al-naqd al-'arabī: dirāsah tahlilīyyah muqāranah*, 2nd edn, Beirut: al-Maktab al-Islāmī, 1975.

Hafsi, Ibrahim, 'Recherches sur le genre "Ṭabaqāt" dans la littérature arabe,' *Arabica*, 1976, vol. 23(3), 227–65; 1977, vol. 24(1), 1–41; vol. 24(2), 150–86.

al-Ḥakīmī, Ḥ. 'A. 'A., *'Kitāb al-muntaẓam' li-Ibn al-Jawzī: Dirāsah fī manhajihi wa-mawāridihi wa-ahammīyatihi*, Beirut: 'Ālam al-Kutub, 1405/1985.

Halm, Heinz, *Shiism*, trans. Michael Bonner, Edinburgh: Edinburgh University Press, 1991.

Hamidullah, Muḥammad, *Majmū'at al-wathā'iq al-siyāsiyyah li-al-'ahd al-nabawī wa-al-khilāfah al-rāshidah*, 4th edn, Beirut: Dār al-Nafā'is, 1983.

Hammer-Purgstall, J. von., 'Über die Menschenklasse welche von den Arabern Schoubijje genannt wird,' *Sitzungsberichte der Kais. Akademie der Wissenschaften in Wien, Philosophische-historische Klasse*, 1848, vol. 1, 330–87.

Hamori, Andras, *On the art of medieval Arabic Literature*, Princeton: Princeton University Press, 1974.

Havelock, Eric A., *Preface to Plato*, Cambridge, Mass., The Belknap Press, 1963.

—— *Origins of Western Literacy*, Toronto: Ontario Institute for Studies in Education, 1976.

—— *The Literate Revolution in Greece and Its Cultural Consequences*, Princeton: Princeton University Press, 1982.

Heinrichs, Wolfhart, *Arabische Dichtung und griechische Poetik*, Beirut and Wiesbaden: Franz Steiner Verlag for the Orient-Institute der Deutsche Morgenländische Gesellschaft, 1969.

—— 'Literary Theory: The Problem of Its Efficiency,' in Gustav E. von Grunebaum (ed.), *Arabic Poetry: Theory and Development*, Wiesbaden: Otto Harrassowitz, 1973, pp. 19–70.

—— 'Authority in Arabic Poetry,' in George Makdisi *et al.* (eds), *La notion d'autorité au Moyen Age: Islam, Byzance, Occident*, Paris: Presses Universitaires de France, 1982, pp. 263–72.

—— 'Poetik, Rhetorik, Literaturkritik, Metrik und Reimlehre,' in Helmut Gätje (ed.), *Grundriss der Arabischen philologie, Band II: Literaturwissenschaft*, Wiesbaden: Otto Harrassowitz, 1987, pp. 177–207.

—— 'An Evaluation of *Sariqa*,' *Quaderni di Studi Arabi*, 1987–88, vols 5–6, 357–68.

—— 'Rose versus Narcissus. Observations on an Arabic Literary Debate,' in G. J. Reinink and H. L. J. Vanstiphout (eds), *Dispute Poems and Dialogues in the Ancient and Mediaeval Near East: Forms and Types of Literary Debates in Semitic and Related Literatures*, Leuven: Departement Oriëntalistiek/Uitgeverij Peeters, 1991, pp. 179–98.

Herzfeld, E., *Geschichte der Stadt Samarra*, Hamburg: Eckard & Messtorf, 1948.

Hirschfeld, H. 'A Volume of essays by Al Jāḥiẓ,' in T. W. Arnold and R. A. Nicholson (eds), *A Volume of Oriental Studies presented to Edward G. Browne*, Cambridge: Cambridge University Press, 1922, pp. 200–9.

Hitti, Philip K., *History of the Arabs*, 7th edn, London: Macmillan & Co. and New York: St. Martin's Press, 1960.

Horovitz, Josef, 'Alter und Ursprung des Isnad,' *Der Islam*, 1918, vol. 8, 39–76.

Huart, Clément, review of *Kitāb Baghdād*, ed. Keller, in *Journal asiatique*, 10ème série, 1909, vol. 13, 533–55.

—— 'Ibn Abī Ṭāhir,' in *EI*, vol. 2, p. 357.

Humbert, Geneviève, *Les voies de la transmission du* Kitāb *de Sībawayhi*, Leiden: E. J. Brill, 1995.

—— 'Le *Kitāb* de Sībawayhi et l'autonomie de l'écrit,' *Arabica* 1997, vol. 44(4), 553–67.

Inostrantsev, K., *Persidskaia literaturnaia traditsiia v pervye vieka Islama*, St. Petersburg: Zapiski Imperial Academy, 1909.

'Izz al-Dīn, Ḥ., *al-Kalimāt wa-al-ashyā': Dirāsah fī jamāliyyāt al-qaṣīdah al-jāhiliyyah*, Cairo: Dār al-Fikr al-'Arabī, 1988.

al-Jābī, Bassām 'Abd al-Wahhāb (ed.), *Mu'jam al-a'lām*, Limassol: Al-Jaffān wa-al-Jābī, 1988.

Jamil, M. F. 'Islamic wirāqah, "stationery," during the early Middle Ages,' dissertation, University of Michigan, 1985.

Jeffery, Arthur, *The Foreign Vocabulary of the Quran*, Baroda: Oriental Institute, 1938.

Johansen, Baber, 'Formes de langage et de fonction publiques: Stéréotypes, témoins et offices dans la preuve par l'écrit en droit musulman,' *Arabica*, 1997, vol. 44(3), pp. 333–76.

Jones, Alan, 'The Qur'ān-II,' in *CHALEUP*, pp. 228–45.

Jones, M. B. J., 'The *Maghāzī* literature,' in *CHALEUP*, pp. 344–51.

Justi, Ferdinand, *Iranisches Namenbuch*, Marburg: N. G. Elwert'sche Verlagsbuchhandlung, 1895.

Juynboll, G. H. A., *The authenticity of the tradition literature*, Leiden: E. J. Brill, 1969.

——*Muslim Tradition: Studies in chronology, provenance and authorship of early ḥadīth*, Cambridge: Cambridge University Press, 1983.

Kanazi, G. J., *Studies in the Kitāb aṣ-Ṣināʿatayn of Abū Hilāl al-ʿAskarī*, Leiden: E. J. Brill, 1989.

Karabacek, Josef von, 'Das arabische Papier. Eine historisch-antiquarische Untersuchung,' *Nationalbibliothek, Mitteilungen aus der Sammlung der Papyrus Erzherzog Rainer*, 1887, vols 2–3, 87–178.

Karp, L. A. 'Sahl. b. Hārūn [d. 215/830]: The Man and his Contribution to *Adab*,' dissertation, Harvard University, 1992.

Kennedy, Hugh, *The Early Abbasid Caliphate: A Political History*, London: Croom Helm, 1981.

—— *The Prophet and the Age of the Caliphate*, London: Longman, 1986.

—— 'From Oral Tradition to Written Record in Arabic Genealogy,' *Arabica*, 1997, vol. 44(4), 531–44.

Khalidi, Tarif, *Islamic Historiography. The Histories of Masʿūdī*, Albany: SUNY Press, 1975.

al-Khāqānī, ʿAlī, *Shuʿarāʾ Baghdād min taʾsīsihā ḥatta al-yawm*, 2 vols, Baghdad: Maṭbaʿat Asad, 1382/1962.

Khoury, Raif Georges, 'Pour une nouvelle compréhension de la transmission des textes dans les trois premiers siècles islamiques,' *Arabica*, 1987, vol. 34(2), 181–96.

Kilito, Abdelfattah, *L'auteur et ses doubles: essai sur la culture arabe classique*, Paris: Editions du Seuil, 1985. *The Author and his Doubles*, tr. Michael Cooperson, Syracuse, Syracuse University Press, 2001.

Kilpatrick, Hilary, 'Context and the Enhancement of the Meaning of *Akhbār* in the *Kitāb al-Aghānī*,' *Arabica*, 1991, vol. 38(3), 351–68.

—— 'Criteria of Classification in the "*Ṭabaqāt fuḥūl al-shuʿarāʾ*" of Muḥammad b. Sallām al-Jumaḥī (d. 232/846),' in Rudolph Peters (ed.), *Proceedings of the Ninth Congress of the Union Européenne des arabisants et islamisants*, Leiden: E. J. Brill, 1981, pp. 141–52.

—— *Making the Great Book of Songs: Compilation and the author's craft in Abū l-Faraj al-Iṣbahānī's Kitāb al-Aghānī*, London and New York: RoutledgeCurzon, 2002.

Kimber, R. A., 'Ibn Abī Ṭāhir Tayfūr,' in *EAL*, pp. 306–7.

Kister, M. J., 'The Seven Golden Odes,' *Rivista degli studi orientali*, 1969, vol. 44, 27–36.

—— 'The Sīrah literature,' in *CHALEUP*, pp. 352–67.

Kračkovsky, I. J., *Izbrannje sočinenija*, vol. 6, Moscow-Leningrad: Akademiya Nauk, 1955.

Kraemer, Joel L., *Humanism in the Renaissance of Islam: The Cultural Revival during the Buyid Age*, Leiden: E. J. Brill, 1986.

Kremer, Alfred von, *Culturgeschichte des Orients unter den Chalifen*, 2 vols, Vienna: W. Braumüller, 1875–77; repr. Aalen: Scientia Verlag, 1966.

Lane, E. W., *Arabic-English Lexicon*, 8 vols, London and Edinburgh: Williams and Norgate, 1863–93; repr. 2 vols, Cambridge: The Islamic Texts Society, 1984.

Larkin, Margaret, 'Abu Tammam,' in Michael Cooperson and Shawkat M. Toorawa (eds), *Arabic Literary Culture 500–925*, Detroit: Gale, 2005, in press.

Lassner, Jacob, *The Topography of Baghdad in the Early Middle Ages*, Detroit: Wayne State University Press, 1970.

—— *Islamic Revolution and Historical Memory: An Inquiry into the Art of ʿAbbāsid Apologetics*, New Haven: American Oriental Society, 1986.

—— *The Shaping of ʿAbbāsid Rule*, Princeton: Princeton University Press, 1980.

Latham, J. D., 'Ibn al-Muqaffaʿ and early ʿAbbasid prose,' in *CHALABL*, pp. 48–77.

—— 'The beginnings of Arabic prose literature: the epistolary genre,' in *CHALEUP*, pp. 162–72.

Lecomte, Gérard, *Ibn Qutayba (mort en 276/889): L'homme, son oeuvre, ses idées*, Damascus: Institut français de Damas, 1965.

—— 'Muḥammad b. al-Ǧahm al-Barmakī, gouverneur philosophe, jugé par Ibn Qutayba,' *Arabica*, 1958, vol. 5, 263–71.

Leder, Stefan, 'Authorship and Transmission in Unauthored Literature: The *akhbār* attributed to al-Haytham b. ʿAdī,' *Oriens*, 1988, vol. 31, 67–81.

—— 'Prosa-Dichtung in der aḫbār-Überlieferung. Narrative Analyse einer Satire,' *Der Islam*, 1987, vol. 64, 6–41.

—— 'The Literary Uses of the *Khabar*,' in A. Cameron and Lawrence I. Conrad (eds), *The Byzantine and Early Islamic Near East I: Problems in the Literary Source Material*, Princeton: The Darwin Press, 1992, pp. 277–315.

—— (ed.), *Story-telling in the framework of non-fictional Arabic literature*, Wiesbaden: Harrassowitz, 1998.

Le Strange, Guy, *The Lands of the Eastern Caliphate*, Cambridge: Cambridge University Press, 1905.

—— *Baghdad during the Abbasid Caliphate*, Oxford: The Clarendon Press, 1900.

Lindsay, James E., 'Prophetic Parallels in Abu ʿAbd Allah al-Shiʿi's Mission to the Kutama Berbers, 893–910,' *International Journal of Middle East Studies*, 1992, vol. 24(1), pp. 39–56.

Lord, Albert, *The Singer of Tales*, Cambridge: Harvard University Press, 1960.

Lowry, Joseph E. 'The Legal-Theoretical Content of the *Risāla* of Muḥammad b. Idrīs al-Shāfiʿī,' dissertation, University of Pennsylvania, 1999.

Lyall, Charles James, *Some Aspects of Ancient Arabic Poetry as Illustrated by a Little-Known Anthology*, London, H. Milford, Oxford University Press for the British Academy, 1918.

—— *The Mufaḍḍaliyāt: An Anthology of Ancient Arabian Odes, II, translation and notes*, Oxford, Clarendon Press, 1918, pp. xvii–xviii.

McAullife, Jane Dammen, (ed.), *Encyclopedia of the Qur'an*, 5 vols, Leiden: E. J. Brill, 2001–in progress.

Macdonald, Duncan B., 'The Earlier History of the Arabian Nights,' *Journal of the Royal Asiatic Society*, 1924, 353–97.

Madelung, Wilferd, 'The Hāshimiyyāt of al-Kumayt and Hāshimī Shiʿism,' *Studia Islamica*, 1989, vol. 70, 5–26.

—— *Religious Trends in Early Islamic Iran*, Albany: SUNY Press for the Persian Heritage Foundation, 1988.

Madigan, Daniel A. *The Quran's Self-Image*, Princeton and Oxford: Princeton University Press, 2001.

Makdisi, George, *The Rise of Humanism in Classical Islam and the Christian West, with special reference to scholasticism*, Edinburgh: Edinburgh University Press, 1990.

—— *The Rise of Colleges: Institutions of Learning in Islam and the West*, Edinburgh: Edinburgh University Press, 1981.

Malti-Douglas, Fedwa, *Woman's Body, Woman's Word: Gender and Discourse in Arabo-Islamic writing*, Princeton: Princeton University Press, 1991.

—— *Structures of Avarice: The Bukhalā' in Medieval Arabic Literature,* Leiden: E. J. Brill, 1985.

—— 'Dreams, the Blind and the Semiotics of the Biographical Notice,' *Studia Islamica,* 1980, vol. 51, 137–62.

—— 'Pour une rhétorique onomastique: les noms des aveugles chez aṣ-Ṣafadî,' *Cahiers d'onomastique arabe,* 1979, vol. 1, 7–19.

Marrou, Henri-Irénée, *A History of Education in Antiquity,* tr. G. Lamb, New York: Sheed & Ward, 1956.

Massé, Henri, 'Du genre littéraire 'Débat' en arabe et en persan,' *Cahiers de civilisation médiévale,* 1961. vol. 4, 137–47.

Mattock, J. N., 'The Arabic Tradition: Origins and Developments,' in G. J. Reinink and H. L. J. Vanstiphout (eds), *Dispute Poems and Dialogues in the Ancient and Mediaeval Near East: Forms and Types of Literary Debates in Semitic and Related Literatures,* Leuven: Departement Oriëntalistiek/Uitgeverij Peeters, 1991, 153–63.

Meisami, Julie S., *Medieval Persian Court Poetry,* Princeton: Princeton University Press, 1987.

—— 'An Anatomy of Misogyny?' *Edebiyât,* 1995, new series, vols 5–6, 303–15.

Melchert, Christopher, 'The Adversaries of Aḥmad Ibn Ḥanbal,' *Arabica,* 1997, vol. 44(2), 234–53.

—— 'Religious Policies of the Caliphs from al-Mutawakkil to al-Muqtadir, AH 232–295/ AD 847–908,' *Islamic Law and Society,* 1996, vol. 3, 316–42.

Menasce, J. -P. de, 'Zoroastrian Literature after the Muslim Conquest,' in R. N. Frye (ed.), *Cambridge History of Iran,* vol. 4, *The Period from the Arab invasion to the Seljuqs,* Cambridge: Cambridge University Press, 1968, pp. 543–65.

Mez, Adam, *Die Renaissance des Islâms,* Heidelberg: C. Winter, 1922. *The Renaissance of Islam,* tr. D. S. Margoliouth and S. Khuda-Bakhsh, London: Luzac & Co., 1937.

Mittwoch, Eugen, 'Die literarische Tätigkeit Ḥamza al-Iṣbahānīs,' *Mitteillungen des Seminars für Orientalische Sprachen,* 1909, vol. 12, 109–69.

Monroe, James, 'Oral Composition in Pre-Islamic Poetry,' *Journal of Arabic Literature,* 1972, vol. 3, 1–53.

Montgomery, James E., 'Of Models and Amanuenses: The Remarks on the *Qasida* in Ibn Qutayba's *Kitab al-Shi'r wa'l-Shu'ara',*' in Robert Hoyland and Philip Kennedy (eds), *Islamic Reflections, Arabic Musings: Studies in Honour of Professor Alan Jones,* Cambridge: Gibb Memorial Trust, 2004), pp. 1–47.

—— 'Sundry Observations on the Fate of Poetry in the Early Islamic Period,' in J. R. Smart (ed.), *Tradition and Modernity in Arabic Language and Literature,* Richmond: Curzon, 1996, pp. 49–60.

—— 'al-Jahiz,' in Michael Cooperson and Shawkat M. Toorawa (eds), *Arabic Literary Culture 500–925,* Detroit: Gale, 2005, in press.

Moreh, Shmuel, *Live Theatre and Dramatic Literature in the Medieval Arab World,* New York: New York University Press, 1992.

Morony, Michael G., *Iraq After the Muslim Conquest,* Princeton: Princeton University Press, 1984.

Mottahedeh, Roy P., 'The Shuʿūbīyah Controversy and the Social History of Early Islamic Iran,' *International Journal of Middle East Studies,* 1976, vol. 7, 161–82.

—— *Loyalty and Leadership in Early Islamic Society,* Princeton: Princeton University Press, 1980.

Muḥammadī, Muḥammad, *al-Tarjamah wa-al-naql ʿan al-Fārisiyyah fī al-qurūn al-Islāmiyyah al-ūlā,* 2 vols, Beirut: Manshūrāt Qism al-Lughah al-Fārisiyyah wa-Ādābihā fī al-Jāmiʿat al-Lubnāniyyah, 1964.

al-Munajjid, Salāḥ al-dīn, *Dirāsah fī ta'rīkh al-khaṭṭ al-ʿarabī mundhu bidāyatihi ilā nihāyat al-ʿaṣr al-umawī*, Beirut: Dār al-Kitāb al-Jadīd, 1972.

Najar, Brahim, *La mémoire rassemblée. Poètes arabes «mineurs» des IIe/VIIIe et IIIe/IXe siècles*, Clermont-Ferrand: La Française d'Edition et d'Imprimerie, 1987.

—— [= Ibrāhīm al-Najjār], *Majmaʿ al-Dhākirah, aw Shuʿarāʾ ʿAbbāsiyyūn mansīyūn. Recherches sur le corpus des poètes «mineurs» du 1er siècle du califat abbasside*, 5 vols, Tunis: Manshūrāt Kullīyat al-Ādāb wa-al-ʿUlūm al-Insāniyyah, 1987–90.

Nājī, Hilāl, 'Abū Hiffān: Ḥayātuhu wa-shiʿruhu wa-baqāyā kitābihi *al-Arbaʿah fī akhbār al-shuʿarāʾ*,' *al-Mawrid*, 1399/1979, vol. 8(3), 191–250 and 1400/1980, vol. 9(1), 187–206.

al-Najjār, A. M. *al-ʿAttābī: adīb Taghlib fī al-ʿaṣr al-ʿAbbāsī*, Cairo: Dār al-Fikr al-ʿArabī, 1975.

Nallino, C.-A., *Sens pris par le mot adab aux divers siècles. Divisions possibles de l'histoire de la littérature arabe*, tr. Charles Pellat, Paris: G. P. Maisonneuve, 1950.

Nelson, Kristina, *The Art of Reciting the Qur'an*, Austin: University of Texas Press, 1985.

Nichols, Stephen G., 'Introduction: Philology in a Manuscript Culture,' *Speculum*, 1990, vol. 61(1), 1–11.

Nicholson, Reynold A., *A Literary History of the Arabs*, Cambridge: Cambridge University Press, 1907.

Norris, H. T., '*Shuʿūbiyyah* in Arabic Literature,' in *CHALABL*, pp. 31–47.

—— 'Fables and Legends,' in *CHALABL*, pp. 136–45.

Noth, Albrecht (with the collaboration of Lawrence I. Conrad), *The Early Arabic Historical Tradition: A Source-Critical Study*, 2nd edn, tr. Michael Bonner, Princeton: The Darwin Press, 1994.

Omar, Farouk [= Fārūq ʿUmar], *al-Khilāfah al-ʿAbbāsiyyah fī ʿaṣr al-fawḍā al-ʿaskariyyah: 247–334/861–946*, 2nd edn, Baghdad: Maktabat al-Muthannā, 1977.

—— *ʿAbbāsiyāt, studies in the history of the early ʿAbbāsids*, Baghdad: Dār al-Ḥurriyyah, 1976.

Ong, Walter J., *Orality and Literacy: The Technologizing of the Word*, London: Methuen, 1982.

Osman, Ghada, 'Oral vs. Written transmission: The case of Ṭabarī and Ibn Saʿs,' *Arabica*, 2001, vol. 48(1), 66–79.

Parry, Milman, *L'Epithète traditionelle dans Homère*, Paris: Société Editrice Les Belles Lettres, 1928.

Pedersen, Johannes, *The Arabic Book*, tr. Geoffrey French, Princeton: Princeton University Press, 1984.

—— 'The Islamic preacher: *wāʿiẓ, mudhakkir, qāṣṣ*,' in Samuel Löwinger and Joseph Somogyi (eds), *Ignace Goldziher Memorial Volume*, Budapest: Globus Nyomdai Müintézet, 1948, pp. 226–51.

Pellat, Charles, *Le milieu basrien et la formation de Ǧāḥiẓ*, Paris: Adrien Maisonneuve, 1953.

—— *The Life and Works of Jāḥiẓ*, tr. D. M. Hawke, London: Routledge & Kegan Paul, 1969.

—— *Ibn al-Muqaffaʿ, mort vers 140/757 "Conseilleur du calife"*, Paris: G.-P. Maisonneuve et Larose, 1976.

—— 'Ǧāḥiẓ à Bagdad et à Samarra,' in *Rivista degli studi orientali*, 1952, vol. 27, 47–57.

—— 'Nouvel essai d'inventaire de l'oeuvre ǧāḥiẓienne,' *Arabica*, 1984, vol. 21, 147–80.

Perry, B. E., 'The Origins of the Book of Sindbād,' *Fabula*, 1960, vol. 3, 1–94.

Petersen, E. L., *ʿAlī and Muʿāwiya in Early Arabic Tradition: Studies on the Genesis and Growth of Islamic Historical Writing until the End of the Ninth Century*, Copenhagen: Munksgaard, 1964.

Pinto, O., 'Al-Fatḥ b. Khāqān, favorito di al-Mutawakkil,' *Rivista degli studi orientali*, 1931, vol. 13, 133–49.

Pritchett, Frances W., *The Romance Tradition in Urdu: Adventures from the Dastan of Amir Hamzah*, New York: Columbia University Press, 1991.

al-Qāḍī, Wadād, 'Early Islamic State Letters: The Question of Authenticity,' in Averil Cameron and Lawrence I. Conrad, *The Byzantine and Early Islamic Near East I: Problems in the Literary Source Material*, Princeton: The Darwin Press, 1992, pp. 215–75.

al-Rabdāwī, Maḥmūd, *al-Ḥarakah al-naqdiyyah ḥawla madhhab Abī Tammām. I: Fī al-qadīm*, Beirut: Dār al-Fikr, 1967.

Rāghib, Yūsuf, 'Lettres Arabes, I,' *Annales Islamologiques*, 1978, vol. 14, 15–35.

—— 'Lettres nouvelles de Qurra b. Sharīk,' *Journal of Near Eastern Studies: Arabic and Islamic Studies in Honor of Nabia Abbott*, 1981, vol. 40(3), 173–87.

—— 'La parole, le geste et l'écrit dans l'acte de vente,' in *Arabica*, 1997, vol. 44(3), 407–422.

Reinink G. J. and H. L. J. Vanstiphout (eds), *Dispute Poems and Dialogues in the Ancient and Mediaeval Near East: Forms and Types of Literary Debates in Semitic and Related Literatures*, Leuven: Departement Oriëntalistiek/Uitgeverij Peeters, 1991.

Reynolds, Dwight F. (ed.), *Interpreting the Self: Autobiography in the Arabic Literary Tradition*, Berkeley and London: University of California Press, 2001.

Richter, Gustav, *Studien zur geschichte der Älterer arabischen Fürstenspiegel*, Leipzig: J. C. Hinrichs, 1932.

Ritter, Hellmut, 'Philologika I,' *Der Islam*, 1928, vol. 17, 15–23.

Roberts, Nancy J., 'Voice and Gender in Classical Arabic *Adab*: Three Passages from Aḥmad Ṭayfūr's "Instances of the Eloquence of Women",' *al-'Arabiyya*, 1992, vol. 25, 51–72.

Rosenthal, Franz, 'Male and Female: Described and Compared,' in J. W. Wright Jr. and Everett K. Rowson (eds), *Homoeroticism in Classical Arabic Literature*, New York: Columbia University Press, 1997, pp. 25–31.

—— 'From Arabic Books and Manuscripts XVI: As-Sarakhsī [?] on the Appropriate Behavior for Kings,' *Journal of the American Oriental Society*, 1995, vol. 115(1), 105–10.

—— *Knowledge Triumphant*, Leiden: E. J. Brill, 1970.

—— *A History of Muslim Historiography*, 2nd edn, Leiden: E. J. Brill, 1968.

—— 'Ibn Abī Ṭāhir Ṭayfūr,' in *EI2*, vol. 3, 692–3.

—— *Humor in Early Islam*, Philadelphia: University of Pennsylvania Press, 1956.

—— *The Technique and Approach of Muslim Scholarship*, Analecta Orientalia 24. Rome: Pontificum Institutum Biblicum, 1947.

—— *Aḥmad b. aṭ-Ṭayyib al-Sarakhsī*, New Haven: American Oriental Society, 1943.

Rosenthal (tr.): see Ibn Khaldūn, *al-Muqaddimah*

Ross, E. Denison, 'Ibn Muqaffa' and the Burzoē Legend,' *Journal of the Royal Asiatic Society*, 1926, 503–5.

Rotter, Gerhard, 'Zur Überlieferung einiger historischer werke Madā'inīs in Ṭabaris Annalen,' *Oriens*, 1974, vols 23–4, 101–33.

Rouse, Richard H. and Mary A. Rouse, '*Statim invenire*: Schools, Preachers, and new Attitudes to the Page,' in Robert Benson and Giles Constable, with Catherine D. Lanham (eds), *Renaissance and Renewal in the Twelfth Century*, Cambridge: Harvard University Press, 1982, pp. 201–25.

Rowson, Everett K., 'The Philosopher as Littérateur: al-Tawḥīdī and his Predecessors,' *Zeitschrift für Geschichte der arabisch-islamischen Wissenschaften*, 1990, vol. 6, 50–92.

Rubin, Zeev 'The Reforms of Khusro Anūshirwān,' in Averil Cameron and Lawrence I. Conrad (eds), *The Byzantine and Early Islamic Near East: Papers of the First Workshop on Late Antiquity and Early Islam*, Princeton: The Darwin Press, 1995, pp. 227–97.

Rypka, Jan, History of Persian Literature up to the beginning of the 20th Century,' in J. Rypka *et al.* (eds), *History of Iranian Literature*, Dordrecht: D. Reidel Publishing Company, 1968, pp. 69–352.

Sabari, Simha, *Mouvements populaires à Bagdad à l'époque ʿabbasside, IXe–XIe siècles*, Paris: Librairie d'Amérique et d'Orient Adrien Maisonneuve, 1981.

Sabra, A. I., 'The Appropriation and Subsequent Naturalization of Greek Science in Medieval Islam: A Preliminary Statement,' *History of Science*, 1987, vol. 25, 1–21.

Sadan, Joseph 'Kings and Craftsmen: A Pattern of Contrasts; On the History of a Medieval Arabic Humoristic Form. Part 1,' *Studia Islamica*, 1982, vol. 56, 5–49.

al-Sāmarrāʾī, Y. A., *Sāmarrāʾ fī adab al-qarn al-thālith al-ḥijrī*, Baghdad: Maktabat al-Irshād, 1968.

—— *Rasāʾil Saʿīd ibn Ḥumayd wa-ashʿāruhu*, Baghdad: Maktabat al-Irshād, 1971.

—— 'Ashʿār Abī ʿAlī al-Baṣīr,' *al-Mawrid*, 1972, vol. 1(3–4), 149–79.

—— 'Aḥmad ibn Abī Fanan: Ḥayātuhu wa-mā tabaqqā min shiʿrihi,' *Majallat Majmaʿ al-ʿIlmī al-ʿIrāqī*, 1983, vol. 34(4), 131–90.

—— ''Alī ibn Yaḥyā al-Munajjim,' *Majallat Majmaʿ al-ʿIlmī al-ʿIrāqī*, 1985, vol. 36(2), 210–61.

Sbath, Paul, ed. and tr., *Choix de livres qui se trouvaient dans les bibliothèques d'Alep (au XIIIe siècle)*, Cairo: Institut d'Egypte, 1946.

Schoeler, Gregor, *Arabische Naturdichtung: die Zahrīyāt, Rabīʿīyāt und Rauḍiyāṭ von ihren Anfängen bis aṣ-Ṣanaubarī*, Beirut and Wiesbaden: Otto Harrassowitz, 1974.

—— 'Verfasser und Titel des dem Ǧāḥiẓ zugeschrieben sog. *Kitāb at-Tāǧ*,' *Zeitschrift der Deutschen Morgenländischen Gesselschaft*, 1980, vol. 130, 217–25.

—— 'Bashshār b. Burd, Abū 'l-ʿAtāhiyah, Abū Nuwās,' in *CHALABL*, pp. 275–99.

—— 'Die Frage der schriftlichen oder mündlichen Überlieferung der Wissenschaften im frühen Islam,' *Der Islam*, 1985, vol. 62, 201–30.

—— 'Wieteres zur Frage der schriftlichen oder mündlichen Überlieferung der Wissenschaften im frühen Islam,' *Der Islam*, 1989, vol. 66, 38–67.

—— 'Mündliche Thora und Ḥadīṯ. Überlieferung, Schreibverbot, Redaktion,' *Der Islam*, 1989, vol. 66, 213–51.

—— 'Schreiben und Veröffentlichen. Zu Verwendung und Funktion der Schrift in der ersten islamischen Jahrhunderten,' *Der Islam*, 1992, vol. 69, 1–43.

—— 'Writing and Publishing. On the Use and Function of Writing in the First Centuries of Islam,' *Arabica*, 1997, vol. 44(3), 423–35.

—— Ecrire et transmettre dans les débuts de l'Islam, Paris: Presses universitaires de France, 2002.

Sellheim, Rudolf, 'Abū ʿAlī al-Qālī. Zum Problem mündlicher und schriftlicher Überlieferung am Beispiel von Sprichwörtersammlungen,' in Hans R. Roemer and Albrecht Noth (eds), *Studien zur Geschichte und Kultur des Vorderen Orients. Festschrift für Bertold Spuler zum siebzigsten Geburtstag*, Leiden: E. J. Brill, 1981, pp. 362–74.

—— *Die klassisch-arabischen Sprichwörtersammlungen: inbesondere die des Abū ʿUbaid*, Gravenhage: Mouton, 1954.

Sergeant, R. B., 'Early Arabic Prose,' in *CHALEUP*, pp. 114–53.

Sezgin, Fuat, *Geschichte des arabischen Schrifttums*, 12 vols to date, Leiden: E. J. Brill, 1967–in progress.

Shalaq, ʿAlī, *Marāḥil taṭawwur al-nathr al-ʿarabī fī namādhijih*, 2 vols, Beirut: Dār al-ʿIlm li-al-Malāyīn, 1991.

Sharon, Moshe, *Black Banners from the East*, 2 vols, Jerusalem: Magnes Press and Leiden: E. J. Brill, 1983, 1990.

Shoshan, Boaz, 'High Culture and Popular Culture in Medieval Islam,' *Studia Islamica*, 1991, vol. 73, 67–108.

Sibai, M. M., *Mosque Libraries, an historical study*, London and New York: Mansell, 1987.

Ṣiddīqī, M. Z., *Ḥadīth Literature. Its Origin, Development and Special Features*, rev. edn, Cambridge: The Islamic Texts Society, 1993.

Silvestre, Hubert, 'Le problème des faux au Moyen Age,' *Le Moyen Age*, 1960, vol. 66, 351–70.

de Slane (tr.): see Ibn Khallikān, *Wafayāt*

Smith, W. R., *Kinship and Marriage in early Arabia*, Cambridge: Cambridge University Press, 1885.

Sourdel, Dominique, *Le vizirat ʿabbāside de 749 à 936 (132 à 324 de l'Hégire)*, 2 vols, Damascus: Institut français de Damas, 1959–60.

—— 'Le "Livre des secrétaires de ʿAbdallāh al-Baghdādī",' *Bulletin d'études orientales*, 1952–4, vol. 14, 128–52.

Sourdel-Thomine, Janine, 'Les origines de l'écriture arabe à propos d'une hypothèse récente,' *Revue des études islamiques*, 1963, vol. 31, 151–7.

—— 'Aspects de l'écriture arabe et de son développement,' *Revue des études islamiques*, 1980, vol. 48(1), 9–23.

Sprenger, Aloys, 'On the origin and progress of writing down of historical facts among the Muslims,' *Journal of the Asiatic Society of Bengal*, 1856, vol. 25, 303–29, 375–81.

—— *Das Leben und die Lehre des Mohammed*, 2nd edn, vol. 3, Berlin: Nicolai, 1869.

Sprengling, Martin, 'From Persian to Arabic,' *American Journal of Semitic Languages and Literatures*, 1939–40, vols 56–7, 175–224, 325–36.

Stetkevych, Jaroslav, *Muḥammad and the Golden Bough*, Bloomington: Indiana University Press, 1997.

Stetkevych, Suzanne P., *Abū Tammām and the Poetics of the ʿAbbāsid Age*, Leiden: E. J. Brill, 1991.

Stewart, Devin J., *Islamic Legal Orthodoxy: Twelver Responses to the Sunni Legal System*, Salt Lake City: Utah University Press, 1998.

Stock, Brian, *The Implications of Literacy: Models of Interpretation in the Eleventh and Twelfth Centuries*, Princeton: Princeton University Press, 1982.

Sublet, Jacqueline, 'Nom écrit, nom dit: Les personnages du théâtre d'ombres d'Ibn Dāniyāl,' *Arabica*, 1997, vol. 44(4), 545–52.

Tafassoli, Aḥmad, *Tārīkh-i adabiyat-i Irān pīsh az Islām*, Teheran: Sokhan, 1997.

Talas, Muḥammad Asʿad, *L'enseignement chez les arabes. La Madrasa Nizamiyya et son histoire*, Paris: Librairie Orientaliste Paul Geuthner, 1939.

Toorawa, Shawkat M., 'Ibn Abī Ṭāhir Ṭayfūr (d. 280/893): Merchant of the Written Word,' dissertation, University of Pennsylvania, 1998.

—— 'Notes Toward a Biography of Ibn Abi Tahir Tayfur (d. 893).' *University of Mauritius Research Journal: Social Studies & Humanities*, 1998, vol. 1, 121–40.

—— 'Ibn Abi Tahir vs. al-Jahiz.' In *ʿAbbasid Studies. Occasional Papers of the School of ʿAbbasid Studies. Cambridge, 6–10 July 2002*, ed. James Montgomery, Leuven: Peeters, 2004, pp. 247–61.

—— 'Ibn Abī Ṭāhir Ṭayfūr' in *Arabic Literary Culture 500–925*, ed. Michael Cooperson and Shawkat M. Toorawa, Detroit: Gale, 2005, in press.

—— 'Defining *adab* by (re)defining the *adīb*: Ibn Abī Ṭāhir Ṭayfūr and Writerly Culture.' In *Defining Fiction and Adab in Medieval Arabic Literature*, ed. Philip Kennedy, Wiesbaden: Harrassowitz, 2005, forthcoming.

Toorn, Karel van der, 'The Ancient Near Eastern Literary Dialogue as a Vehicle of Critical Reflection,' in G. J. Reinink and H. L. J. Vanstiphout (eds), *Dispute Poems and Dialogues in the Ancient and Mediaeval Near East: Forms and Types of Literary Debates in Semitic and Related Literatures*, Leuven: Departement Oriëntalistiek/Uitgeverij Peeters, 1991, pp. 59–76.

Trabulsi, Ahmed, *La critique poétique des arabes jusqu'au Vè siècle de l'Hégire (XIè siècle de J.C.)*, Damascus: Institut français de Damas, 1955.

Wagner, Ewald, 'Die arabische Rangstreitdichtung und ihre Einordnung in die allgemeine Literaturgeschichte,' *Akademie der Wissenschaften und der Literatur in Mainz. Abhandlungen der geistes- und sozial-wissenschaftlichen Klasse*, 1962, vol. 8, 437–76.

Wakin, Jeanette, *The Function of Documents in Islamic Law. The Chapters on Sales from Ṭahāwī's Kitāb al-Shurūṭ al-Kabīr*, Albany: SUNY Press, 1972.

Weisweiler, Max, 'Das Amt des Mustamlī in der arabischen Wissenschaft,' *Oriens*, 1951, vol. 4, 27–57.

Werkmeister, Walter, *Quellenuntersuchungen zum Kitāb al-ʿIqd al-farīd des Andalusiers b. ʿAbdrabbih (246/860–328/940): Ein Beitrag zur arabischen Literaturgeschichte*, Berlin: Klaus Schwarz Verlag, 1983.

Ullmann, Manfred *et al.* (eds), *Wörterbuch der klassischen arabischen Sprache*, Wiesbaden: Otto Harrasowitz, 1970–in progress.

Wüstenfeld, Ferdinand, *Die Geschichtschreiber der Araber und ihre Werke.* Göttingen: Dieterichsche verlagbuchhandlung, 1882.

Yājī, A. M., 'Sahl Ibn Hārūn. Edition des fragments avec traduction précédée d'une introduction sur cet auteur et ses oeuvres,' dissertation, Université de Paris, 1956.

Zakeri, Mohsen, *Sāsānid Soldiers in Early Muslim Society: The origins of ʿAyyārān and Futuwwa*, Wiesbaden: Otto Harrassowitz, 1995.

Zambaur, E. M. von, *Manuel de généalogie et de chronologie pour l'histoire de l'Islam*, Hanover: H. Lafaire, 1927.

al-Zayyāt, Ḥ., 'Ṣuḥuf al-kitābah wa-ṣināʿat al-waraq fī al-Islām,' *al-Mashriq*, 1954, 1–30, 158–88, 625–43.

Zolondek, Leon, 'An Approach to the Problem of the Sources of the *Kitāb al-Aġānī*,' *Journal of Near Eastern Studies*, 1960, vol. 19(3), 217–34.

—— *Diʿbil b. ʿAlī: The life and writings of an early ʿAbbāsid Poet*, Louisville: University of Kentucky Press, 1961.

Zubaidi, A. M., 'The impact of the Qur'ān and Ḥadīth on medieval Arabic literature,' in *CHALEUP*, pp. 322–43.

Zwettler, Michael, *The Oral Tradition of Classical Arabic Poetry: Its Character and Implications*, Columbus: Ohio State University Press, 1978.

INDEX

Note: Kitāb is abbreviated to *K.* and ignored alphabetically, and 'ibn' in medial position is abbreviated to 'b.'

'Abd al-Ḥamīd al-Kātib (d. 132/750) 8, 116
'Abbās b. Nāṣiḥ al-Thaqafī (d. *c.* 238/852) 55
al-'Abbās b. al-Aḥnaf (d. after 193/808) 87
'Abīd/'Ubayd b. Sharyah (*fl.* late 2nd/8th) 62
abnā' 55, 73
Abū 'Abdallāh (d. 255/869) 75
Abū al-'Aynā' (d. 282/896) 53, 58, 72, 89, 108, 112–17; and Abū 'Alī al-Baṣīr 113–14, 117; and Abū Hiffān 105; and al-Buḥturī 116; his work on al-Jarjarā'ī (d. 265/879) 114–15; and Ibn Abī Ṭāhir 105, 114; and Ibn Mukarram 115–16; and al-Mutawakkil 114, 117; and patronage 112; and the Quran 115; Shiism of 72; on blindness 112–13, 117
Abū al-Faraj (d. 356/967) 3, 16, 26, 72–3, 75, 102, 103
Abū al-Ṭarīf 118
Abū 'Ubaydah (d. after 209/824–5) 85
Abū al-'Ubays b. Ḥamdūn (*fl.* 3rd/9th c.) 118, 177n127
Abū 'Alī al-Baṣīr (d. *c.* 251/865) 60, 108, 109, 118; and Abū al-'Aynā' 113–14; and patronage 113; Shiism of 74; on oral/aural transmission 113; views on Abū Nuwās 113
Abū Bakr b. Shādhān (d. 376/986) 23
Abū Ḍiyā' al-Naṣībī (*fl.* 3rd/9th c.) 98–9
Abū Fir'awn al-Sāsī (d. early 3rd/9th c.) 105
Abū Ḥakīmah (d. 240/854) 36, 37
Abū Hiffān (d. 257/871) 29, 58, 61, 108, 110–12; and Abū al-'Aynā' 105; and Abū Tammām 97; and bibliophiles 25; and al-Buḥturī 112; and donkeys 111–12; and Ibn Abī Ṭāhir 29–31, 104, 107; and al-Jāḥiẓ 110–11; and *kātib*s 61–2; and patronage 111, 112; and 'Ubaydallāh b. Yaḥyā b. Khāqān (d. 263/877) 111; indigence of 29, 111; on Alī b. Yaḥyā 112; on Ibn Abī Ṭāhir's literary thefts 116; on Tha'lab 61; on the Banū Thawābah 111–12; personality of 111
Abū Tammām (d. 231/845 or 232/846) 4, 13, 61, 72, 88, 93–9, 121; and al-Buḥturī 45, 93–9; and Ibn Abī Ṭāhir 44–59
Abu Tammām/al-Buḥturī question 45, 93–101; al-Ṣūlī on 94; al-Mas'ūdī on 94
adab 1, 5, 12, 132n31; conceptions of 1, 125
advice literature 14, 46, 78–9, 80–1; of Ibn Abī Ṭāhir 78–9
afsāna 48
Aḥmad b. Ḥanbal (d. 241/855) 9
Aḥmad b. Burd al-Aṣghar (d. 445/1053–4) 93
akhbār (sing. *khabar*) 1, 24, 44, 80; Hilary Kilpatrick on 102–3; 'proximity' 102–8, in *al-Dhakhīrah fī maḥāsin ahl al-Jazīrah* 108, in the *Fihrist* 105–7, in *Irshād al-arīb* 105, in *K. Murūj al-dhahab* 105, in *K. Nihāyat al-arab* 108, in *K. Nūr al-qabas* 108, in *K. Ṭabaqāt al-shu'arā' al-muḥdathīn* 104, in *K. al-Tamthīl wa-al-muḥāḍarah*

107, in *K. al-Tatfīl* 107–8, in *K. al-Waraqah* 104–5; variance in 29–31
al-Akhfash al-Ṣaghīr (d. 315/927) 109, 113
Alexander the Great 49, 82
ʿAlī b. Dāwūd (*fl.* 3rd/9th c.) 47, 49, 80
ʿAlī b. Yaḥyā b. al-Munajjim (d. 275/888–9) 14, 75, 88, 109, 118, 120–1; and Ibn Abī Ṭāhir 120–1; as patron 121, 124; Ibn al-Muʿtazz on 120; library of 120, 124
ʿAllān al-Warrāq (*fl.* 3rd/9th c.) 57
al-Āmidī (d. 371/987) 95–6; on Ibn Abī Ṭāhir 96
ambivalence toward texts and textuality 20–6
ʿāmmah 10–11, 91
anthology 4, 5, 7, 17, 44, 124, 139n88
antiquarians 31
Anūshirwān (r. 531–79 CE) 78, 80
Arabic 8; and literacy 9–11; and social mobility 10; and women 12; as a mother tongue 13; mistakes in 10; of the Bedouin 10; use 12; rise of writing in 7–9; scripts of 8–9, 134n10
Arabization 7
Arabs and non-Arabs 100–1
ʿArīb (d. 277/890) 115
Aristotle 52, 179n33
al-Arzānī (d. 415/1024) 19
asāṭīr al-awwalīn 80
aṣḥāb al-maṣāḥif 57
aṣḥāb al-kutub 58
al-ʿAskar 109
al-ʿAskarī, Abū Aḥmad (d. 382/993) 85
al-ʿAskarī, Abū Hilāl (d. after 395/1005) 40–1, 84
al-Aṣmaʿī (d. *c.* 216/831) 45, 72, 110, 113
asmār (sing. *samar*) 79–82
al-ʿAttābī (d. 208/823 or 220/835) 28, 47, 76–7, 80; and Persian language 76; Ibn Abī Ṭāhir's book on 76
authors 26–9; anonymous 28, 29; imitating 27–8; intentionally misattributing 27–8
autodidacticism 15, 124, 128–9
ayyām al-ʿArab 37, 80

Bāb al-Shām 56, 98
badīʿ 93
al-Baghdādī, ʿAbd al-Qāhir (d. 429/1037) 42
Balāghāt al-nisāʾ 12, 99
Barmakids 76, 81, 82
Bayt al-Ḥikmah 14, 28, 57, 81
bibliophiles 23, 25; Abū Hiffān on 25
Bookmen's Market 14–15, 55–7; fire in 151n49
books 1, 13–15, 19, 20, 124, 129; and book-places 13–15; as material objects 15, 25; banned 20; circulation of 32–3; Ibn Durayd on 4; importance of 18–19; lovers of 23, 25; 'print run' 32–3; reliance on 20–1, 24–5
booksellers 14, 58
bookshops 15, 57, 124; family run 152n60
al-Buḥturī (d. 284/897) 61, 72, 88, 93–9, 116–7; and Abū al-ʿAynāʾ 116–7; and Abū Tammām 93–9; and Ibn Abī Ṭāhir 40, 88–9, 97–8; *sariqah* of 116–7; and the Muʿtazilites 72; preference of al-Battī (d. 406/1015) for 94
al-Bukhārī (d. 256/870) 9
al-Bushtī (d. 348/959) 21
Buzurgmihr 78, 81–2

centers of learning 2–312, 12–15, 5
chanceries 60
chancery schools 13
codification of poetry 15–17
contest 99–101
copyists 19, 26–7, 32, 47, 57, 59, 139n88; as indigent 58, 59; as unscrupulous 26–7, 47, 58
cost of living in Baghdad 54–5

debate and disputation literature 87–101
Demons of al-ʿAskar: *see Shayāṭīn al-ʿAskar*
al-Dhahabī (d. 748/1348) 39
Diʿbil (d. 246/860) 61, 88, 121
donkeys 42, 111–12, 114
al-Dīnawarī (d. before 290/902–3) 79
doctrine 71–2, 73–5, 85

educational system 13; age of students in 52; curriculum of 32; in chancery schools 13; in mosques 13; preparatory 13
eloquents (*bulaghāʾ*) 59–65

fables: *see asmār, khurāfāt,* storytellers
faḍāʾil genre 84–5
al-Faṣīḥ 19
al-Fatḥ b. Khāqān (d. 247/861) 14, 25, 120, 125; library of 14, 120
al-Fayruzān (*fl.* 3rd/9th c.) 57
al-Fihrist 33–4

forgery 18, 26–9; and the *dīwān al-khātam* 142n51

genealogy 84, 95
Greek 11–12; as administrative language 7

al-Hadādī (*fl.* 3rd/9th c.) 118
Hadith 9, 17, 24, 115
Ḥammād al-Rāwīyah (d. after 163/780) 15–17
Ḥammād b. Isḥāq (*fl.* early 3rd/9th c.) 26–7
Ḥamzah al-Iṣfahānī (d. 350/961) 85
al-Ḥarīrī (d. 350/961) 80
Hārūn al-Rashīd (d. 193/809) 14, 81, 82
al-Ḥasan b. Sahl (d. 236/850) 81
al-Ḥātimī (d. 388/998) 95
Hazār afsāna 48, 49
ḥikāyāt 80
al-Ḥīrah 80
Ḥunayn b. Isḥāq (d. 264/877) 32, 1105, 21
hypomnēma and *syngramma* 2

Ibn ʿAbd Rabbihi (d. 328/940) 18
Ibn Abī Duʾād (d. 240/854) 125
Ibn Abī Fanan (d. between 260/874 and 270/883) 107, 118, 120, 176n123
Ibn Abī Kāmil (*fl.* 3rd/9th c.) 118
Ibn Abī Ṭāhir, Abū al-Faḍl Aḥmad (d. 280/893); and Abū ʿAbdallāh al-Ḥasanī (d. 255/869) 75; and Abū al-ʿAynāʾ 105, 114; and Abū Ḥakīmah 36, 37; and Abū Hiffān 29–31, 104, 107, 110; and Abū Tammām 37, 44–59; and ʿAlī b. Yaḥyā 120–1; and anthologies 4, 17, 44, 64–70, 124; and attribution 43; and books 20–1; and bookshops 55–6; and al-Buḥturī 40, 88–9, 97–8, 291–4; and contest 99–100; and Ibn Abī Fanan 120; and Ibn al-Muʿtazz 33, 36, 37–8; and Ibn Qutaybah 38–9, 61; and Ibn al-Rūmī 88, 89–90; and Ismāʿīl b. Bulbul 117–8, 120; and al-Jāḥiẓ 124–7; and Khurasan 73, 75, 100; and al-Kisrawī 119–20; and patronage 43, 62, 123, 125–6, 128–9; and Persia 72–3, 75–82, 100; and Persian stories 79–82; and Persian language 77; and ruse 29; and Saʿīd b. Ḥumayd 46, 85, 117–8; and *sariqah* (plagiarism/literary theft) 95–9, 116, 117–8; and the 'Shayāṭīn al-ʿAskar' 104, 107, 108–22; and the Shuʿūbiyyah 82–6; and storytelling 46–50, 80–2; and al-Ṣūlī 22, 98; and al-Ṭabarī 5, 133n33; and al-Tammār 120; and textuality 20–1; and translation 80; as *adīb* of new type 2–4, 6, 60–3, 100–1, 123–9; as author 61–70; as bookman 56–60; as *kātib* 60–2; as poet 35–43; as prose stylist (*balīgh*) 59; as storyteller/fabulist 46–50; as transmitter/narrator (*rāwī*) 39, 43–6, 123–4; as teacher 51–6; as *warrāq* (bookman) 56–60; biographers of 60; birth of 3; clustered: by Shawqī Ḍayf 109; in the *Fihrist* 47, 106–7; by Ibn al-Muʿtazz in *K. Ṭabaqāt al-shuʿarāʾ al-muḥdathīn* 104, 109–10; by al-Thaʿalibī in *K. al-Tamthīl wa-al-muḥāḍarah* 107; by Said Boustany with authors of both prose and poetry 6; by Ibn Durayd with authors of peerless works 5; by al-Shaybānī with 'kuttāb' 61; by al-Marzubānī with the 'Shayāṭīn al-ʿAskar' 108, 119, 120; by Ibn al-Nadīm with storytellers 47; death and burial of 3; full name of 72–3; Ibn al-Muʿtazz on 33, 35–8; Ibn al-Nadīm on storytelling of 46–7, 50; Ibn al-Rūmī's satires of 89–90; in Basra 140n26; in the *Ṭabaqāt al-shuʿarāʾ al-muḥdathīn* 35–8; in the *Akhbār Abī Tammām* 44, 94, 98–9; indigence of 29, 62; individualism of 121–2, 123–9; on the Abū Tammām/al-Buḥturī question 96–9; on the literary thefts of Saʿīd b. Ḥumayd 117; on the 'Muʿallaqāt' 5; on the Ṭāhirids 46, 76; Persian origin of 72–3; poetry about Abū al-ʿAynāʾs prose 116; about Abū Tammām and al-Buḥturī 95; about al-Buḥturī 97, 168n70; about contest 100; about dogs 89; about donkeys 42; about the family of Muḥammad 74; about al-Jarjarāʾī 114, 121; about al-Kisrawī 42, 119; about the moon 89; about al-Mubarrad 100; about his penis 36; about Yaḥyā b. ʿUmar 74; anthologized 40; attributed to Abū Tammām 36; catalog of surviving verses 146n28; uncollected in a *dīwān* 40; using *taṭrīz* 40–1; poetry of 36; ʿAbd al-Qāhir al-Baghdādī on 42; Abū Ḥakīmah on 36; Abū Hilāl al-ʿAskarī on 40–1; Abū Tammām on

37; al-Āmidī on 96; al-Buḥturī on 39–40; al-Dhahabī on 39; Ibn Ṭabāṭabā on 41–2; al-Khaṭīb al-Baghdādī on 39; al-Marzubānī on 39; al-Masʿūdī on 39; al-Mīkālī on 60; al-Sakhāwī on 39; Yāqūt on 39; views of Western scholars on 5; of non-Western scholars on 5–6, 35; Shiism of 73–5; views on Abū al-ʿAynā'’s prose 116; works 62–70; confusion about 154n105; characterization of 62–3, 77; chronology of 154n107; Persian models for 77–8; titles of 63–70
Ibn al-ʿAllāf 118, 176n125
Ibn al-Bawwāb (d. *c.* 413/1022) 8
Ibn Dallān/Dīlān (?) 46
Ibn Dāwūd (d. 297/910) 5
Ibn Durayd (d. 321/933)4, 57, 74, 85; on books 4
Ibn Ghānim al-Maqdisī (d. 678/1279?) 92
Ibn Harmah al-Qurashī (d. *c.* 176/792) 24, 170n6
Ibn al-Jahm (*fl.* 3rd/9th c.) 61
Ibn Lankak (d. *c.* 360/970) 55, 88
Ibn al-Marzubān (d. 309/921) 84, 163n120
Ibn al-Mudabbir (d. 279/893) 115
Ibn Mukarram (*fl.* 3rd/9th c.) 108; and Abū al-ʿAynā' 115–16
Ibn al-Muqaffaʿ (d. *c.* 142/759) 1, 14, 28, 32, 47, 49, 79, 80–1
Ibn Muqlah (d. 328/940) 8
Ibn al-Muʿtazz (d. 296/908) 35–8; and Ibn al-Rūmī 88; and roses 88; on ʿAlī b. Yaḥyā 120; on Ibn Abī Ṭāhir 33, 36–7, 38
Ibn al-Nadīm (d. between 380/990–1 and 388/998) on anonymous works 29; taxonomy of his *Fihrist* 33–4; listing of Ibn Abī Ṭāhir's works 62; on storytelling 47–50
Ibn Qutaybah (d. 276/889) 1, 3, 84, 85, 100, 127–8; and administratve manuals 8; and Ibn Abī Ṭāhir 38–9, 61
Ibn al-Rūmī (d. 283/896) 6, 74–5, 88; al-Maʿarrī on 75; and Ibn Abī Ṭāhir 88; and the narcissus 88; and patronage 112; and Shiism 74–5
Ibn Saʿdān (*fl.* mid 3rd/9th c.) 53, 105
Ibn Saḥnūn (d. 256/870) 52
Ibn Sallām al-Jumaḥī (d. *c.* 232/847) 35
Ibn Shahrashūb (d. 588/1192) 72
Ibn al-Sikkīt (d. *c.* 243/867) 54
Ibn Ṭabāṭabā (d. 322/934) 41–2
Ibn Thawābah (d. 277/890) 88, 111–12
Ibn Ẓāfir (d. 613/1216) 120
Ibn al-Zayyāt (d. 233/847) 125, 126
Ibrāhīm b. al-ʿAbbās al-Ṣūlī (d. 243/857) 60
Ibrāhīm b. al-Mudabbir (d. 279/892–3) 88, 114–17; on al-Buḥturī 115
ijāzah 18–19
ikhtiyār (selection/choice) 17, 44
illiteracy 10
indices 134n12
Ismāʿīl b. Bulbul (d. 278/892) 88, 112, 117–18, 120; and ʿAlī b. Yaḥyā b. al-Munajjim 118
Ismāʿīl b. Isḥāq (d. 282/895) 25

Jaʿfar b. [Muḥammad b.] Ḥamdān (d. 323/935) 51
Jāhiliyyah 11, 84
al-Jāḥiẓ (d. 255/868) 1, 3, 25, 57, 61, 87, 92, 109; and Arabness 126; and authorship 27–8; and Ibn Abī Ṭāhir 124–7; and Muʿtazilites 125–6; and patronage 71; and textuality 21; on *ʿāmmah* 10; on Abū Hiffān 110–11; uncertainties about 124–5
al-Jahshiyārī (d. 331/942) 49–50
al-Jarjarā'ī (d. 265/879)114, 115

Kalīlah wa-Dimnah 80, 81
kātib (pl. *kuttāb*) 8, 60–1, 83–4; and administrative manuals 8; and Shuʿūbīyah 82–4; in the meaning of author 60–70; Michael Carter on 61;
al-Khansā' (d. after 23/644) 12
khāṣṣ(ah)/ʿāmm(ah) 53–4, 91
al-Khubza'aruzzī (d. 327/938) 137n50
khurāfāt (sing. *khurāfah*) 46–9
Khurasan 73, 75–6
al-Kisrawī, ʿAlī b. Mahdī (d. between 283/896 and 289/902) 118; Ibn Abī Ṭāhir and 119–20
K. al-Aghānī 3, 26, 73, 103; Ibn Abī Ṭāhir in 3
K. Akhbār Abī al-ʿAynā' 113–14
K. Akhbār Abī Tammām 44, 98
K. al-Bayān wa-al-tabyīn 10, 127
K. Baghdād 3, 63, 67, 76, 79, 82, 100
K. Faḍl al-kilāb ʿalā kathīr mimman labisa al-thiyāb 84

K. Faḍl al-ʿArab ʿalā al-ʿAjam 67, 85–6, 100
K. al-Hudhaliyyah wa-al-Makhzūmī 33, 81
K. Khwadāy-Nāmag 79, 80
K. al-Manthūr wa-al-manẓūm 4, 8, 13, 19, 20, 62, 67
K. al-Mu'allifīn 4, 67, 144n128
K. Mufākharat al-ward wa-al-narjis 87–8, 90
K. Qalaq al-mushtāq 4
K. Sariqāt [. . .] 4, 37, 44, 45, 95–7
K. Ṭabaqāt al-shuʿarāʾ al-muḥdathīn 35–8, 88
K. Tarbiyat Hurmuz b. Kisrā Anūshirwān 14, 63, 78–9
K. al-Zahrah 5, 40
kuttāb (pl. katātīb) 13, 52–3, 54

laḥn al-ʿāmmah 10
letters 60; in *K. al-Manthūr wa-al-manẓūm* 4, 8; preserved in the sources; 134n15
libraries 13–14, 120
literacy 1, 130n4; and Arabic language 9–11; and refinement 9–10
literary heritage 15–17
literary networks of Baghdad 102–10, 118–22

al-Maʿarrī (d. 449/1058) 75
al-Madāʾinī (d. 228/868) 3, 32
al-Mādarāʾī (d. 303/915) 22
al-Mahdī (169/785) 15–16
majlis, majālis (literary gatherings) 55, 118–22; *chez* Ibn al-Mudabbir 116–7; *chez* al-Kisrawī 119–20; *chez* ʿAlī b. Yaḥyā 118, 120
maktab 52
al-Ma'mūn (d. 218/833) 14, 125; and the Muʿtazilites 125; biography of 82
Manāqib al-Turk 125–6
al-Māridīnī (*fl.* 9th/15th c.) 92–3
Marw al-Rūdh 72, 78
al-Marzubānī (d. 384/994) 43, 96, 108
al-Masʿūdī (d. 345/946) 62, 74, 78, 113; Imāmī Shiism of 74; on Abū Tammām/al-Buḥturī question 94
memorization 9, 18, 21, 23, 24, 41, 53
al-Mīkālī (d. 436/1044) 4, 60, 89
'mirrors for princes': *see* advice literature
modern(ist) poets 35; Kamal Abu Deeb on 37
mu'addib (tutor) 51–3
'al-Muʿallaqāt' 5, 13, 53
muʿallim 52
Muʿāwiyah (d. 60/680) 7
al-Mubarrad (d. 285/898) 3, 61, 132n22
al-Mufaḍḍal al-Ḍabbī (d. *c.* 163/780) 15–17
al-Mufaḍḍaliyyāt 17
mufākharah 87, 92; *see also* precedence
Muḥammad (d. 11/632) 11, 74; biography 9, 17, 80, 138n85; emulation of 138n85; illiteracy (*ummiyyah*) of 11; on flowers 91
Muḥammad b. Faḍl al-Kātib (*fl.* mid 3rd/9th c.) 108
muḥdath/qadīm 126
mujūn 29, 109, 121–2
munāẓarah 92, 167n34; *see also* contest
al-Muʿtaḍid (d. 289/902) 20
Muʿtazilites 125–6
al-Mutawakkil (d. 247/861) 91, 120; and Abū al-ʿAynāʾ 72, 114, 117; and roses 91; and Shiism 72; assassination of 126

al-Naḍr b. al-Ḥārith (d. *c.* 2/624) 80
narcissus 87–8, 91–3
al-Nawājī (d. 859/1455) 91
Nawrūz 117
northern vs southern Arabs 169n88

oral formulae 18, 22, 138n79
oral testimony 18
oral/aural scholarly contact 18–19, 21–6, 124, 139n1; and Sībawayhi 19
orality 11; and literacy 12–13, 136n32; and textuality 11–12

paper 56–9; affordability of 59; introduction of 56, 124; production of 56
patrons 14, 125–6
patronage 42–3, 62, 71–2, 77, 125–6, 128
Persian culture 75–6, 92
Persian language 76–7; and Ṭāhirids 77
Persian literature 76–82, 84
plagiarism/literary theft: *see sariqah*
Plato 11
poetry 127–8; canon 42; codification of 15–17
poets 42; 'majors' vs 'minors' 42, 128
popular literature 33
preachers 13, 79–80
precedence 87–8, 90, 92–3
pre-Islamic myths 161n78
'proximity': *see akhbār*

qiṣaṣ al-anbiyāʾ 79
quṣṣāṣ 79–80; *see also* preachers, storytellers
Quran 1, 2, 11, 17, 52, 80, 82, 84, 138n79; as an oral entity 11, 136n32, 136n42; *qirāʾāt* (variant readings) 139n86; reciters 23

al-Rāghib al-Iṣfahānī (d. early 5th/11th c.) 40–1
al-Raqīq al-Nadīm (d. 417/1026) 29–30
rāwī 17, 43–6
readership 1, 31–4
rose vs narcissus 87–93
roses 91–2
al-Ruṣāfah 13, 109
Rustam and Isfandiyār 80

ṣaḥafī 22–3
al-Ṣāḥib b. ʿAbbād 48, 113
Sahl b. Hārūn (d. 215/830) 33, 47, 49, 80, 81–2; al-Jāḥiẓ on 81; and Shuʿūbiyyah 81
Saʿīd b. Ḥumayd (d. 252/866) 46, 61, 75, 84–5, 117–8; and ʿArīb 115; Ibn Abī Ṭāhir on plagiarism/literary theft of 117; plagiarism/literary theft of Ibn Abī Ṭāhir 118
al-Sakhāwī (d. 902/1497) 39
Sālim (*fl.* 2nd/8th c.) 14, 32
Salm 28
samar (pl. *asmār*) 48–50; and Alexander 49; and al-Jahshiyārī 49–50
Samarra 72, 109, 112, 113
al-Sarakhsī (d. 286/899) 99–100
sariqah 24, 26, 45, 95–7, 116–7, 147n61; of Saʿīd b. Ḥumayd 46; Wolfhart Heinrichs on 45–6; vs borrowing 46
Sasanian administration 7
Sasanian culture 78, 83, 84, 91
Sawwār b. Abī Shurāʿah (*fl.* early 4th/10th) 97
Sayf al-dawlah (d. 335/967) 127
al-Ṣaymarī, Abū al-ʿAnbas (d. 275/888) 85
scribal hands 8
'Shayāṭīn al-ʿAskar' 108–21; Jamal Eddine Bencheikh on 109; Shawqī Ḍayf on 109; gatherings of 108–9, 118–20; members of 118–9
al-Shaybānī, Ibrāhīm b. Muḥammad (d. 298/911) 61
Shiism 53–4, 71–2, 73–5, 93, 151n49; in contest between rose and narcissus 93; 'of poets' 75
Shuʿūbiyyah 82–6, 87, 100; as a literary movement 83; rejoinders to 85
shurūṭ (document drafting) literature 8
Sībawayhi (d. *c.* 177/793) 10, 19, 32; and al-Kisāʾī (d. 189/805) 10; transmission of *al-Kitāb* 19
sikbāj stew 84, 115
siyar al-mulūk 82
Spain 61
storytellers and storytelling 46–50, 79–82
study circles 13
al-Ṣūlī, Muḥammad b. Yaḥyā (d. *c.* 335/946) 14, 72, 74, 113, 124; and the Abū Tammām/al-Buḥturī question 98; and reliance on books 22–4; library of 14, 23–4; *sariqah* of 24; views on Ibn Abī Ṭāhir 22, 98
sūq al-warrāqīn: *see* Bookmen's Market
syngramma and *hypomnēma* 2

ṭabaqāt works 19
al-Ṭabarī (d. 314/923) 5, 20, 77, 78, 79
Ṭāhirids 46, 76, 77
al-Tammār, Yaʿqūb (*fl.* 3rd/9th c.) 108, 120
al-Tanasī (d. 899/1494) 223
al-Tanūkhī (d. 384/994) 87
Ṭāq al-Ḥarrānī 57
al-Tawḥīdī (d. after 400/1009) 29, 30–1, 59
Ṭayfūr 72–3
teachers 52–4; salary of 54–5
"textual communities" 25
textual precedents 11
textuality 11–13; ambivalence toward 20–6; variance and 29–31
Thaʿlab (d. 290/904) 53, 61
translation 14, 80
transmission; errors in 22, 24; of knowledge 9; oral 9, 31

ʿUbaydallāh b. Aḥmad Ibn Abī Ṭāhir (d. 313/925) 57, 84, 106; *Taʾrīkh* of 120, 156n133
ʿUyūn al-akhbār 5

variants 29–31

warrāq (pl. *warrāqūn*): *see* copyists
al-Washshāʾ (d. 325/937) 53, 91
wijādah 24
writerly culture 1; shift to 1, 7–15, 17, 27, 123–4, 128–9; A. F. L. Beeston on 2;

Jonathan Bloom on 2, 9; Sebastian Günther on 3; Gregor Schoeler on 2
writerly exchanges 69, 84, 85, 88–90, 97, 113, 114, 115–16, 117–20, 136n33; *K. Murāsalāt al-ikhwān wa-muḥāwarāt al-khillān* 119
writing 48–63; ambivalence about 33, 48–63; in early Arabia 7; works on 132n24
Yaḥyā b. ʿUmar (d. 250/864) 74; elegy on 74–5
Yāqūt (d. 626/1229) 62; listing of Ibn Abī Ṭāhir's works 62
Yazdajird 76
al-Yazīdī, al-Faḍl (d. 278/891) 62

ẓarf 9–10, 29, 91, 156n136
Zoroastrian culture 78

An environmentally friendly book printed and bound in England by www.printondemand-worldwide.com

PEFC Certified

This product is from sustainably managed forests and controlled sources

www.pefc.org

PEFC/16-33-415

MIX

Paper from responsible sources

FSC® C004959

www.fsc.org

This book is made entirely of sustainable materials; FSC paper for the cover and PEFC paper for the text pages.

#0382 - 091214 - C0 - 234/156/14 - PB